MEDIA AND CRIMINAL JUSTICE

THE CSI EFFECT

Dennis J. Stevens, PhD
University of North Carolina–Charlotte
and
Belmont Abbey College

JONES AND BARTLETT PUBLISHERS
Sudbury, Massachusetts
BOSTON   TORONTO   LONDON   SINGAPORE

World Headquarters
Jones and Bartlett Publishers
40 Tall Pine Drive
Sudbury, MA 01776
978-443-5000
info@jbpub.com
www.jbpub.com

Jones and Bartlett Publishers
Canada
6339 Ormindale Way
Mississauga, Ontario L5V 1J2
Canada

Jones and Bartlett Publishers
International
Barb House, Barb Mews
London W6 7PA
United Kingdom

Jones and Bartlett's books and products are available through most bookstores and online booksellers. To contact Jones and Bartlett Publishers directly, call 800-832-0034, fax 978-443-8000, or visit our website, www.jbpub.com.

Substantial discounts on bulk quantities of Jones and Bartlett's publications are available to corporations, professional associations, and other qualified organizations. For details and specific discount information, contact the special sales department at Jones and Bartlett via the above contact information or send an email to specialsales@jbpub.com.

Production Credits
Publisher, Higher Education: Cathleen Sether
Acquisitions Editor: Sean Connelly
Associate Editor: Megan R. Turner
Production Manager: Julie Champagne Bolduc
Production Assistant: Jessica Steele Newfell
Associate Marketing Manager: Jessica Cormier
Manufacturing Buyer: Amy Bacus
Composition: Glyph International
Cover Design: Kristin E. Parker
Cover Image: © Simon Wild/Alamy Images
Printing and Binding: Malloy, Inc.
Cover Printing: Malloy, Inc.

Library of Congress Cataloging-in-Publication Data
Stevens, Dennis J.
  Media and criminal justice : the CSI effect / Dennis J. Stevens.
    p. cm.
  Includes bibliographical references and index.
  ISBN 978-0-7637-5531-7 (alk. paper)
  1. Mass media and criminal justice—United States.   2. Mass media and criminal justice.   3. Criminal justice, Administration of—United States. 4. Mass media—Influence. I. Title.
  P96.C742U67 2010
  345.73'05—dc22
                        2009036519

6048
Printed in the United States of America
13 12 11 10 09   10 9 8 7 6 5 4 3 2 1

This book is dedicated to Primo Levi, writer, chemist, and Auschwitz survivor; a person whom this author has never met, yet his presence through his words inspired the conclusion of this book: "Monsters exist, but they are too few in number to be truly dangerous. More dangerous are the common man, the functionaries ready to believe and to act without asking questions."

Brief Contents

Contents

10 Methods and Findings 311

11 Recommendations to Reduce Wrongful Convictions and Eliminate Capital Punishment 331

Foreword

In *Media and Criminal Justice: The CSI Effect*, accomplished author Dennis J. Stevens once again works his magic as a writer and a researcher, and gives us a book that stimulates thought about the justice system. Stevens is the author of almost one hundred scholarly articles and a number of books that are "must reads" for those who truly want to understand the American criminal justice system. In this book, he confronts the gross injustice of wrongful convictions and capital punishment, and squarely identifies overzealous prosecutors as the crux of the recent spate of exonerations on which the American media has fed.

Many excellent prosecutors are relentless in their pursuit of convictions, and justice is often served through their actions. Sometimes, however, charges may be improperly brought and convictions pursued even after those who represent the public in criminal prosecutions learn of significant exculpatory evidence. In 2007, for example, North Carolina prosecutor Michael Nifong was disbarred following an ethics review by the Disciplinary Hearing Commission of the North Carolina State Bar Association. The Commission established that Nifong persisted in a well-publicized rape prosecution of three Duke University lacrosse team members, even after the veracity of the supposed "victim" had been destroyed by elaborate media exposés. Nifong's reluctance to drop charges against the men—even once their innocence was established—wreaked havoc with their lives and cost each of them a great deal of personal anguish. Their families were forced to bear the huge financial burden of hiring defense teams to refute the prosecutor's apparently malicious allegations. In reaching the decision to revoke Nifong's license to practice law, the disciplinary commission cited prosecutorial misconduct and called Nifong's actions "a politically motivated act that he inexplicably allowed to fester for months after it was clear the defendants were innocent."

Texas prosecutor Craig Watkins stands in stark contrast to Nifong. In 2008, the *Wall Street Journal* called Watkins "the only prosecutor in America who is making his name getting people out of prison." Watkins is the district attorney in Dallas County, Texas. He became the first African-American district attorney in Texas history following his election in 2006, and has since been using DNA evidence to examine more than 400 guilty verdicts obtained by his predecessors. Watkins created a Conviction Integrity Unit in his office in 2007, and within a year the unit was able to win exonerations for six men who had been wrongfully convicted of crimes ranging from rape and murder to robbery.

Not everyone agrees that Watkins is doing a good job. "I think he's doing a grave disservice in trying to create this image that the criminal justice system is fatally flawed, and that only people like Craig Watkins can save it," said Joshua Marquis, a member of the board of the National District Attorneys Association.

What makes his story all the more interesting is that Watkins follows a long line of "get tough on crime" prosecutors who occupied the district attorney's office in Dallas County since the early 1950s. One of them, the legendary Henry Wade, served as district attorney from 1951 to 1986 and successfully prosecuted Jack Ruby for the murder of Lee Harvey Oswald. Wade gained national notoriety for never losing a case that he personally prosecuted and for winning capital convictions almost every time he asked juries to return them.

Prosecutors like Henry Wade are, of course, *supposed* to seek convictions. The adversarial system through which justice is achieved in this country depends on vigorous representation by both sides in a criminal case. But we must never forget that the ultimate goal of any criminal proceeding is *justice*—for the accused as well as for victims and the aggrieved.

The line that separates prosecutors like Watkins and Nifong is not due to a lack of vigor, education, or preparation, but to a difference in fundamental vision about the nature of justice itself. The goal of justice is furthered by many institutionalized practices, including discovery (by which important items of evidence are shared by the prosecution and defense), *habeas corpus* (the fundamental right to appeal unfair convictions), and by common and statutory laws, which allow for defenses to criminal liability based on justifications and necessity. But it is brought down to the personal level and made relevant by the individual actions of justice system representatives.

Media and Criminal Justice: The CSI Effect will help all of us to think more clearly about the nature of justice, the costs it exacts, and our personal roles in achieving it. To paraphrase Martin Luther King, "The arc of the moral universe is long, but it tends to swing toward justice." I believe that *Media and Criminal Justice: The CSI Effect* will enhance the moral universe in which we live and move us closer to the ever elusive goal of justice.

Frank Schmalleger, PhD
Distinguished Professor Emeritus
The University of North Carolina at Pembroke

Preface

Is America caught up in events that are as ambiguous as they are deadly? Americans in 15 states were so outraged by their chances of becoming victims of violent crime that they prompted legislators to sanction the use of deadly force when confronted by a gangster or a neighbor. Advocates call these "stand your ground laws" and opponents call them "shoot first laws." In Clearwater, Florida, a man was gunned down by his neighbor after a shouting match over the trash, and a Port Richey, Florida prostitute fired a weapon point-blank at her 72-year-old client who wouldn't return her favors.

The law forbids arrest, detention, prosecution, and civil suit of persons covered by the law. The greatest injustice a democratic legal system can perpetrate against its population is to punish an individual for a crime he or she has never committed. The *ne plus ultra* (highest point) of injustice in a democratic nation is the wrongful conviction and execution of its constituents.

Media and Criminal Justice: The CSI Effect examines the relationship between the popular media—motion pictures, popular television dramas, and news reports—and the weakening of fundamental rights, leading to high points of injustice. The popular media has made incredible contributions to the criminal justice community, the American people, and democracy, but it also provides its own version of the world of crime, which heightens the fear of victimization. This phenomenon will be referred to as the *CSI Effect*, which changes real-world expectations of crime and crime control by affecting the decisions of witnesses, victims, jurors, and justice professionals. One central idea is that criminal justice practices among its ranks of professionals (police, corrections officers, prosecutors, and judges) have changed to keep pace with the social images defined, glorified, and justified by the popular media through the *CSI Effect*.

The *CSI Effect* is a product of the popular media's ability to encourage aggressive "reactive" justice initiatives, glorify vigilantism, and provide fictitious accounts of crime and control of crime. It will be argued that the *CSI Effect* sets the criminal justice apparatus toward unlawful intrusion into the private lives of the American population in the name of justice. For example, the popular media depicts a "good" police strategy as an aggressive response, as opposed to preventive initiatives and quality-of-life arrests, regardless of the guilt of the person or seriousness of the violation. Finally, it alters accounts of crime and crime control, which include the fictitious notion that every crime is reported, every violator is detected, apprehended, and arrested, and every suspect is judiciously convicted and imprisoned. The implication arising from this perspective is that the American judicial process is flawless. The popular media's portrait of a criminally violent offender and the criminal justice practices associated with detection, apprehension, and conviction share few similarities with official statistics, policy, and experiences among justice practitioners. As a result, official misconduct is tolerated, wrongful convictions continue, and capital punishment allegedly serves a higher purpose.

Media and Criminal Justice: The CSI Effect helps identify the primary strategies and players within the justice system. It argues that at the core of the wrongful conviction phenomenon and the death penalty are prosecutors, because they alone possess the authority to initially charge (or indict) a suspect or to release a suspect regardless of guilt. *Media and Criminal Justice: The CSI Effect* goes beyond the standard paradigm of transferring knowledge, as it depicts the realities of the media, wrongful convictions, and the death penalty. It links justice practices and scholarly research to real-world experiences, issues, careers, systems, and procedures, helping readers become informed about these issues.

To better understand the attitudes of prosecutors, 444 prosecutors from across the country were surveyed about their jobs and their ideas about justice. Some will disagree with the recommendations provided, which include community prosecution and prevention, changes in law school admission policies and curriculum, limiting prosecutor discretion, and ending capital punishment as a sanction.

■ The Flow of This Book

Chapter 1 explains the *CSI Effect* and describes the popular media and its contributions to American society. Chapter 2 characterizes the motion picture industry, popular television dramas, news reports, and comic books. Chapters 3, 4, and 5 focus on the wars fueled through the *CSI Effect* which include: the wars on crime, junkies, sex offenders, poverty, terrorists, and immigrants. Chapter 6 describes crime scene investigations, forensic science, and junk science. Chapter 7 explains prosecutorial activities at the federal, state, and local levels. Chapter 8 examines wrongful convictions and its primary causes. Chapter 9 addresses the death penalty, and Chapter 10 explains the research design used to test the perimeters of the theory of this work, outlines the characteristics of the 444 prosecutors tested, and provides the results from participants in this study. Finally, Chapter 11 offers recommendations that will reduce wrongful convictions and end capital punishment as a sanction. Should readers have any questions, comments, or contributions to share, feel free to contact the author at dennisj.stevens@hotmail.com.

Acknowledgments

As with most publications, numerous contributors supported this project, although the opinions offered belong to the author. This author wishes to acknowledge the efforts of the graduate assistants who made his job easier through their research and survey contributions: Kimberly E. Cox (PhD candidate, University of Vienna); Lacey Cochran Stewart (Makenzy's mom); Linda Moss; Jennifer Taylor and Bessey Hutchinson (both PhD candidates, University of Southern Mississippi); Sergeant Luke Thompson (Gulfport Police Department, Mississippi); and Sergeant Dan Steel (Biloxi Police Department, Mississippi, on leave at law school). Also, assistant researchers at Sacred Heart University, Fairfield, Connecticut, should be acknowledged, including Sara Dastoli, Sarah M. Olschan, and Theresa M. Raytar.

Frank Schmalleger, my colleague, mentor, and friend, wrote an amazing foreword, in addition to his other contributions, including the inspiration to continue this work. Also, appreciation goes to my colleagues, readers of early chapters, and attendees of presentations on the early theoretical concepts at Sacred Heart University: Professor Matt Semel (a former New York City public defender); Dr. Patrick Morris (a former police sergeant in Norwalk, Connecticut); and Dr. Jim McCabe (a former New York City police detective and commander). I also thank Mark A. Stevens, my son, who provided some theoretical perspectives in several chapters because of his extraordinary analytical capacity and experiences in the criminal justice community. My loving daughter Alyssa P. Stevens unselfishly lent an ear and provided encouragement and inspiration to complete this work.

Additionally, there are 444 prosecutors across the United States to thank for their contributions and many letters that accompanied their completed surveys, which were included where appropriate throughout this work.

Others who aided in the development of this work include the very hard-working and bright personnel at Jones and Bartlett, including Cathleen Sether, Jeremy Spiegel, Julie Bolduc, Megan Turner, and Jessica Cormier. Thanks also go to Vastavikta Sharma at Glyph International and Jeanne Hansen.

Finally, acknowledgment goes to the reviewers of this work:

Michael L. Arter
Penn State Altoona

Michael Costelloe
Northern Arizona University

Paul C. Leccese
Old Dominion University

Charles A. Loftus
Arizona State University

Kirk Miller
Northern Illinois University

Nicole Romeiser
University of Maryland

About the Author

Dennis J. Stevens received a PhD from Loyola University of Chicago in 1991. Currently, he teaches as an adjunct professor in the Department of Sociology at the University of North Carolina, Charlotte, and Belmont Abbey College. He worked for the University of Southern Mississippi as director of its criminal justice PhD program, and also taught at the University of Massachusetts, Boston, and Salem State College. As a criminal justice–sociology department director in North Carolina, he created and implemented a criminal justice lock-step curriculum, enrolling hundreds of students at five locations. In addition to teaching traditional students, he has taught and counseled law enforcement and correctional personnel at law academies such as the North Carolina Justice Academy, and felons at maximum-security penitentiaries.

Dr. Stevens has published several books and almost 100 scholarly and popular literature articles on policing, corrections, and criminally violent sexual predators. He has also been retained by private agencies to develop use of force protocols; by state legislators to examine recidivism rates and the flow of drugs into prisons; by federal agencies to study corruption among narcotics officers; and by the US military and foreign governments to aid in related research.

As a volunteer, Dr. Stevens has guided many sexually abused children and their families through church-affiliated programs in New York, North Carolina, and South Carolina, and has led group crisis sessions among various police and correctional agencies, such as for officers of the New Orleans Police Department after Hurricane Katrina.

The Media and the *CSI Effect*

Any intelligent fool can make things bigger, more complex, and more violent. It takes a touch of genius—and a lot of courage—to move in the opposite direction.

Albert Einstein

▶ ▶ **CHAPTER OBJECTIVES**

- Articulate criminal justice practices that led to the development of this book
- Enhance the reader's knowledge about the influence of the popular media upon the criminal justice process
- Comprehend the media's relationship with criminal justice
- Describe the extent of the media's influence on social perspectives
- Provide a definition of the *CSI Effect*

■ Introduction

America is caught up in events that are as ambiguous as they are deadly, from policing foreign cities, to violence in American churches, to the hard experiences of unemployment and house foreclosures. Yet implicit to American lifestyles are the fundamental rights of a democratic nation as its population experiences an economic collapse with new political leaders in the first decade of a new millennium.[1] In this new day, at the core of American political ideals is the *rule of law* (i.e., the US Constitution), and a wrongful conviction—convicting a person of a crime he or she never committed—violates fundamental prerogatives of liberty, and it follows that executing an innocent person is inexcusable. What's examined in this work are the factors that weaken democratic principles by targeting individuals through wars on crime, junkies, sex offenders, poverty, and immigrants, which are, in part, defined and encouraged by the popular media: motion pictures, popular television dramas, news reports, and newspapers.[2-4] During the 60th Emmy Awards telecast in the fall of 2008, Oprah Winfrey helps guide this work: "Nothing connects us quite like television."[5] However, at the heart of this work is an assumption that the popular media, through a conceptual framework referred to as the *CSI Effect* (discussed later in this chapter), helps to further wrongful convictions and capital punishment with the aid of American prosecutors.

■ Prosecutor Work Ethic

> At the heart of the wrongful conviction phenomenon and the continuation of executions are prosecutors who alone possess the authority to initially charge (or indict) a suspect; if they don't act, little, if anything, happens toward obtaining justice.[6]

Most criminal justice professionals exemplify professional practice and perform their judicial obligations as treasured components of a great nation. However, a few practitioners, including prosecutors who are derelict in their behavior, are responsible for the majority of wrongful convictions, the release of guilty suspects, and the prolonged use of capital punishment. If a prosecutor declines to indict a suspect in a capital case (for more details, see Chapter 9), could the prosecutor's action produce a decline in unlawful executions, too?

The evidence in this book, which includes data from 444 prosecutors, supports the idea that the *CSI Effect* is an untenable product of the popular media because it encourages the criminal justice apparatus toward unlawful intrusion into the already difficult private lives of the American population, and furthers wrongful convictions while stabilizing capital punishment as a plausible sanction.

■ Public Safety Versus Liberty

An obvious scenario is that the American criminal justice community works hard to provide public safety, on one hand, and to safeguard *liberty* (the right of the public to choose) or freedom, on the other. Justice is the spirit of freedom, that unyielding principle of democracy as orchestrated through courtrooms, where it has been shaped by the rules of evidence, hearsay, visible accusers, and cross-examination and has been established through trial and error over centuries. It isn't perfect, but it can be tinkered with, adjusted, and the problems that step outside the rule of law can be condemned and changed to match their expectations. However, the adversarial process across the planet is under attack because at times it is both compelling and chaotic. Everyone, whether they are guilty or innocent, is entitled to a fair trial. Peter L. Berger clarifies that the first wisdom of those who study societal issues is that it is harder than expected to make the obvious apparent because "things are not what they seem . . . social reality turns out to have many layers of meaning. The discovery of each new layer, changes the perception of the whole."[7(p23)] It should come as no surprise that implicit in Berger's perspective is the realization of the quantitative and qualitative hurdles that must be reached to achieve the learning objectives of this book.

■ Learning Objectives of This Work

The power to prosecute is an enormous responsibility and it is the least protected governmental intrusion upon private lives, advances C. Ronald Huff.[8] Decisions to prosecute are centered more on what the popular media proclaims is real, such as crime and how to control crime.[9] The power of the media is incredibly huge, and it has many opportunities to promote an appropriate image, but as Albert Einstein revealed, it takes a touch of genius and a lot of courage. However, the evidence in this work will show that the popular media glorifies corrupt supercop behavior through television dramas that emphasize vigilante and unlawful behavior in the name of justice, which also provides prosecutors with a playing field to do as they wish. Unsupervised prosecutorial discretion and consistent presentations of the media's version of reality opens the door to official violence, including wrongful convictions and executions.

What can be gained from this work is a better understanding of the primary elements of the problems, which will hasten policy makers toward a method of supervision and recommendations toward compliance (see Chapter 11). An appeal is extended to the new political administration to bring the change promised to a system that is weighed heavily upon by so many (see the chapters on the wars on crime, junkies, sex offenders, poverty, and immigrants) and has disrupted or ended their lives through disgrace, frustration, and sometimes execution whereby current reform is meaningless. The aim of this work is to reduce wrongful convictions and eliminate capital punishment as a legal sanction. First, some experiences that led to this book should be shared.

■ Practices That Led to the Development of This Book

The curiosity to examine the relationship among prosecutors, wrongful convictions, and executions arose from a study of patrol officers at the Boston Police Department who were associated with sexual assault and domestic 911 emergency calls.[10] The lessons learned from that study were that the typical police officer does not work in a vacuum when delivering police services, particularly at a crime scene. This thought is consistent with Maria Haberfeld and Lior Gideon, who argue that the mission of the police to serve the "public is always subjected to the ultimate vision of the current governing body,"[11(p11)] which is also the body that creates and passes laws and policy.

Police officers as first responders limit their official activities at crime scenes to their job descriptions, which amount to securing the crime scene and nothing more. Their motives for limited activities were interpreted from data that reveal a lack of professional training and a lack of professional supervision (more specifically, their supervisors employed intimidation methods to control them). The thinking was that the *chain of custody* (defined in Chapter 6) linked to evidence from sexual assault crime scenes must flow from detectives to prosecutors (it was strongly suggested by supervisors that first responders contaminated evidence as though they were "bulls in a china shop"). What experienced patrol officers thought after 10 years (on average) of securing crime scenes was irrelevant, and their written reports about the conditions of the crime scene, witnesses, victims, and other factors were scrutinized by intimidating supervisors who suggested that officers described accounts that matched the expectations of their job description (not what they saw). Patrol officers were often surprised by the suspects who were eventually indicted and by those who were immediately released. An abundance of scientific studies are consistent with the findings that prosecutors legally possess the discretion to release or charge or indict a suspect for sexual assault or rape regardless of the quality of evidence and police reports.[12-15] When prosecutors indict suspects for more serious crimes than an arrest report states, the Center for Public Integrity argues that prosecutors then ask reporting officers to *stand up* (lie or support untruthful scenarios).[16]

Another motivator for writing this book emerged after a peer review of a monograph about the death penalty.[17] That work reveals that the final decision to charge an individual arrested in a capital crime, regardless of the evidence, depended on prosecutorial discretion. I took that to mean that a prosecutor has the authority and power to charge or not to charge a suspect with a capital case; less often than expected, a prosecutor's decision is rarely subjected to overview, a thought consistent with the literature.[18] It was an easy stone's toss from these two perspectives (Boston's first responders and prosecutorial capital case indictments) to conduct a study consisting of 444 prosecutors. The results were so illuminating that it requires a book to explain the results. The core of this new information is consistent with a study conducted by the Center for Public Integrity that reveals that since 1970, individual judges and appellate court panels cited prosecutorial misconduct as a "factor when dismissing charges, reversing convictions, or reducing sentences in more than 2,000 cases."[19] In thousands more cases, judges labeled prosecutorial behavior inappropriate but upheld convictions using a doctrine called *harmless error*. The center found that a few prosecutors were responsible for the most misconduct.

> Most wrongful convictions are avoided through the meticulous efforts and work ethics of justice practitioners, which includes police investigators and prosecutors.

■ Three Assumptions

Three assumptions contribute to this work.

Enlightened Awareness

In part, this work utilizes the insight from a prominent criminologist who referred to news making criminology as a "call for action" among those who study crime and punishment. His point is an attempt to move the public toward an "enlightened self-awareness about crime, justice, and society."[20] Therefore, the centerpiece of this work is to enhance reader awareness of the consequences of the *CSI Effect* and its influence upon aggressive reactive police strategies, *vigilantism* (self-appointed doer of justice),[21] and fictitious accounts of crime, all leading to wrongful convictions and executions.

Prosecutor Power

Prosecutors are the most powerful single individuals in American government because if the prosecutor does not act, judges and juries are helpless; reports from police officers and analyses from forensic crime laboratories are meaningless toward a criminal conviction without a prosecutor's effort.[22] Additionally, in most jurisdictions at least 95 percent of all cases that come to the prosecutor's attention never reach a jury, suggesting that the only trial those defendants received took place in the office of a prosecutor.[23]

Prosecutorial Deviance

Why would an individual with little or no criminal history commit an extraordinary act such as to initiate and promote a wrongful conviction, especially one that leads to a defendant's execution?[24–26] It's a troubling thought, but almost anyone, given the right situational influences, can abandon moral scruples and cooperate in violence and oppression—even murder (see this book's Dedication).[27,28] Among strong influences for some members of the criminal justice community is the *CSI Effect*.

■ Public Behavior and Researchers

Walter Lippmann argued that a half century ago Americans spent most of their time earning a living, and when they were home, they pursued idle pleasures more than they examined constitutional issues and policy.[29,30] Study after study, at that time, reported that the American public had little knowledge of public policy. In the final analysis, this view implies that the public lacks a working understanding of criminal justice behavior.[31,32] Recently, Phillip E. Converse argued that most Americans are minimally consistent and minimally stable and have a minimal level of conceptualization when it comes to the formation of their opinions.[33,34]

Researchers Mislead Readers

Although most researchers, including Lippmann and Converse, do their best to measure what their participants actually know about criminal justice policy and practices, some researchers continue to mislead readers as a result of "the ambiguous way in which survey questions are worded and the way in which poll results are reported and interpreted in the mass media," argues George F. Bishop.[35(pxv)] Another prominent researcher, David Weisburd, provides evidence that many well-funded academic researchers tend to develop misconceptions about criminal justice policy and practices, especially when those researchers are studying the attitudes of personnel, clients, or customers involved with the funding agency.[36] As a consequence, many researchers published their work for one another or supported their own academic interests or the interests of the funding agency. Weisburd suggests that these inefficiencies, which are identified in many justice studies and public opinion perspectives, are more often closely linked to the researcher's naïveté or lack of practical experience than to a flaw of the criminal justice program, practice, or perspective. These thoughts are consistent with Randal G. Shelden's argument that history has been largely written by the privileged—those in power or the power brokers (see the following sections regarding the history of crime and punishment).[37,38] What will be described in the pages ahead is that the popular media adds its biases and versions to circumstance, too. Nonetheless, many flawed studies supported by biased historical accounts are reinforced through the *CSI Effect* and are employed to develop criminal justice policy only to end in disappointment, imprisonment, and sometimes an execution, a trend that continues as of the writing of this work.

■ Who Controls the Popular Media?

Some argue that the popular media provides programming demanded by the public, but others say that the media sets the form, shape, and context of its programming under the influence of the power brokers or elitist socioeconomic class (the superrich). Page and Shapiro advance that in some situations, elitist thoughts and priorities shape public opinion, specifically through such avenues as news commentaries.[39] Elitist control is so strong that elitists' ideas can manipulate or mislead the public into a policy preference. In the last two decades, media studies have moved beyond claims of minimal effects by demonstrating how various characteristics of news stories—point of view (framing), connection to political offices (priming), emotional content, or causal implications—change public opinion.[40] For example, now that the national elections of 2008 are history, the repetitious commentary by news reporters about the candidates, the electoral process, and the outcome of those elections continues to ring in the ears of their audiences. It almost seemed as if the reporters were running for office.

Conversely, it is clear that public opinion and knowledge about justice policy are largely an independent force that often influences elitist ideals, rather than vice versa.[41] One study documents that the American people are individually consistent, stable, and hold practical knowledge (sometimes through personal experiences and the experiences of others that are articulated in group meetings and as a result of training and educational processes).[42,43] As Nancy E. Marion and Willard M. Oliver argue, when an individual has a strong philosophy, a concrete belief system, or possesses knowledge about a topic, he or she can make sound decisions, not necessarily right or wrong decisions, but decisions that are consistent with his or her own belief system.[44] This thought implies that belief systems play a major role in the decision-making process of an individual, regardless of whether he or she has experience or applicable knowledge about a given topic, such as criminal investigations or forensic science. Individuals take information they already have, simplify the complexity of an issue, and derive a steadfast conclusion.[45] For example, police investigation dramas that depict forensic analysis are woven into viewers' thoughts despite the viewers' lack of actual working knowledge of forensic analysis; to take issue with some of the public's perspectives about the reliability of forensic science practices is seen to be similar to taking issue with their patriotism.[46,47] In essence, these thoughts are the building blocks of the *CSI Effect*. Nonetheless, in 1991 Shanto Iyengar asked who is responsible for the inadequacies and failures depicted by the popular media, historians, and misguided researchers.[48,49]

> It is argued by prominent scholars that anyone who "studies crime and justice shares a sense of frustration about the way the media depictions dominate the common viewpoint on crime and criminal justice, often in a way that distorts reality."[50(pxiii)]

A distorted perspective about eliminating crime prevails among many Americans, and their conclusion is often associated with the relationship between the pervasiveness of crime and the potency of the criminal justice system—more cops, less crime. This perspective seeks criminal justice to deter crime, a thought that is inconsistent with a Gallup Poll that asked participants the best approach to lowering crime in the United States.[51] Sixty-one percent of the participants reported that crime should be dealt with through social and economic programs, such as education and job training, and 31 percent said that more resources should be provided to enhance the criminal justice system. For some of us this finding contradicts the latest police television dramas. What many of us know about crime and its history can often be traced to motion pictures, popular television dramas, and news reports.

■ History of Crime

One perspective about the history of crime, advises prominent criminologists, historians, and philosophers, is that mankind has attempted to control criminal behavior since recorded history without much success; victimization is present in our families, easily observable on our streets, and exists in our churches and temples despite modern technology and a professional police presence.[52–54] Over 100 years ago, Emile Durkheim advised that crime is really a natural kind of social activity, "an integral part of all healthy societies."[55(p67)] Marcus Felson added that "crime feeds off the physical form of local life, whether in a village, town, city, suburb, or university campus. That form is organized by how people and things move about in everyday life."[56(p75)] For some criminals, crime is a way of life; for others, it is the result of unfortunate circumstances or a personal pathology, offers Frank Schmalleger.[57] If poverty, unemployment, and early childhood experiences were the primary sources of crime, then providing respectable jobs, decent incomes, and therapy would help resolve some of the crime; however, chronic offenders mock conventional opportunities and see little advantage in outreach programs. Before leaving this thought, if college instructors were surveyed, they would probably report that most criminal justice majors initially believe that crime can be eliminated[58]; one plausible reason for student hesitance is associated with the *CSI Effect* and its illusion of stopping crime through the employment of cold hard force, including police brutality and prosecutor misconduct. Yet the reality is that the most advantageous alternative to crime is to control it, and mankind has been attempting to control crime throughout its known history through punishment.[59]

■ Punishment: Confinement and Executions

What is known about law and morality or right from wrong is that they are neither naturally bestowed nor are they consistent across historic time. What is consistent (even up to the present day) is that the natural law prevails; a law of the strongest dominates the entire history and presence of mankind on this planet.[60] Death was the preferred method of administrating justice, and those who held a monopoly of power administered it[61,62] (see Chapter 9 for more details on capital punishment). Public execution precedes Western civilization as the basic form of punishment and continues to be the primary form of punishment or threat of punishment employed by many governments, yet its use has declined in modern England, Canada, and most Western European nations.[63] For example, in ancient Rome and during much of the Middle Ages in Europe and England, death and torture were expected forms of punishment (i.e., in the early Roman Empire, Christians, political activists, and soldiers of conquered nations were condemned) and were very popular forms of entertainment. Public executions also notified the public that the state held power over life and death and to defy the state had consequences. The public gathered at the event, cheered, joked with one another, and played with their children while an execution or torture was in progress.[64] Some might ask if violent events continue to hold entertainment value.

Nonetheless, confinement or jails were holding places for criminals who would eventually be executed or tortured in a public exhibition or used as forced labor. Later in Western historic accounts, the Germanic Law Codes of Anglo-Saxon England record the use of prisons for thieves and witches, but the most common form of punishment in England and Western Europe was mutilation, death, exile, or compensation.[65] In the violent century following the Norman conquest of England in 1066, the Crown imposed centralized authority through laws and administration, which eventually led to the development of the Tower of London as the first royal prison; its residents included the Crown's enemies and prisoners of war. A few centuries later, the tower and other jails warehoused debtors and those who interfered with the Crown, including perjurers, frauds, and those who misinformed the courts. By 1520, there were 180 imprisonable offenses in English Common Law, including vagrancy, breaking the peace, infamy, illegal bearing of arms, and morals.[66] In royal prisons the types of accommodations varied from foul to comfortable; wealthy prisoners could pay their way out or up to a higher floor at the Tower of London. When one gate of the tower burned, a new gate was built, the Newgate Tower.[67] The compensation jailers received from those confined and from public executions was a way to raise funds and pay staff members. Sometimes tens of thousands of spectators would jam the street outside Newgate Tower to catch the last gasps of a condemned felon.[68] In 1807, for example, an estimated 40,000 people gathered to watch murderess Elizabeth Godfrey be hanged, and a resulting stampede claimed the lives of 100 people.

In the 1600s and 1700s, England and other Western European nations transported thousands of criminals to isolated islands and distant lands. England and Ireland transported thousands of felons to their Australian penal colonies. Prisoners who committed further felonies there were transported to Norfolk Island, some 1,000 miles off the east coast of Australia, and were met with severe punishment. The warden, Captain Alexander Maconochie, described Norfolk Island as a "living hell."[69(p197)] There was little need for Captain Maconochie to describe to Parliament the vicious floggings, the cruelty of a lack of facilities, the heavy manacles, and the line of savage dogs patrolling the shores because those were typical accounts of most jailers during that time.[70]

A thumbnail historic account of prisons can aid in a better understanding of the justice system's response to violators, which includes a "prosecuting attitude" that leads to punitive (retaliatory or just deserts) action.[71(pp28–31)] In part, the thinking goes that the government or the Crown seized people in a ritual of public torture and execution for the benefit of public entertainment and a display of power. Because most prisoners met this fate, the conditions in most facilities were dreadful. Some facilities were actually closed mines, sewer systems (as were jails in ancient Rome),[72] and caves and tunnels (such as Old New-Gate Prison and Copper Mine in East Granby, Connecticut in 1707). Sometimes facilities were raised towers, such as Newgate Tower in London and Newgate Prison in Manhattan. Men, women, and children were confined with the seriously mentally ill and psychopaths; little, if any, supervision or methods of protection were used; disease was pervasive; human waste was everywhere, furthering dysentery; and every known vicious act was visited upon those populations by other prisoners, personnel, and those who were free. Even in early American penal history, inmates were considered to be property of the state, and as such the rules of humanity did not apply.

To better understand the evolution of prisons as punishment, consider that 18th century Pennsylvanians murdered and assaulted one another, surpassing most of their English and American contemporaries. Research shows that Pennsylvanians victimized their family members, neighbors, enemies, and rivals regardless of whether they were wealthy or poor. Pennsylvania was renowned as the "best poor man's country on earth" and memorialized as the "Peaceable Kingdom."[73] From these beginnings and with their knowledge of imprisonment in the Old World (Western Europe and England), the Quakers in Pennsylvania, in particular, were appalled at the violence among Pennsylvanians and the treatment of prisoners, the conditions of those facilities, and issues of forced labor. The Quakers promoted isolationism as an alternative to the death penalty, torture, and foulness of confinement strategies, and they helped develop the Pennsylvania Prison System, which eventually promoted the acceptance of punishment with a desire to rehabilitate in terms of humane confinement.[74]

Prisoner Rights in the 21st Century

Although prisoners in American facilities hold diminished or limited constitutional rights (see *Wolff v. McDonnel*, 1974),[75] they are protected by the Constitution's prohibition of cruel and unusual punishment, as found in the Eighth Amendment, and can pursue 42 U.S.C.A. § 1983 (1871; recodified 1979) federal litigation against correctional systems and correctional officers.[76] This protection requires that prisoners be afforded a minimum standard of care and protection. Criminal justice personnel, including volunteers and contract vendors, must (1) defuse danger where it exists and (2) provide services without compromising individual constitutional guarantees, especially due process.[77] In the final analysis, the responsibility of criminal justice personnel, in general, is public safety, and a way to accomplish this aim is to reduce the risk of danger. Reducing risk means just that: in volatile encounters, nothing can be done to escalate danger, and personnel must work toward its reduction.[78,79] That said, it is evident that corrections in modern day America is far different than Newgate Tower, but it is also different from the way it is portrayed on popular television dramas, such as *Law & Order: Special Victims Unit* episodes.

Popular Media's Perspective of Prisons

Television dramas produce their own version of reality in American prisons. For example, in *Law & Order: Special Victims Unit*, Season 9, Episode 15, "Undercover," Detective Olivia Benson (Mariska Hargitay) goes undercover at Sealview, a women's prison in New York (Bedford Hills is the women's facility in New York), to investigate a murder and a rape. Upon her arrival at the prison, Benson submits to a full body and cavity search conducted by a lecherous-acting male "guard" (the correct term is "correctional officer") who comments, while feeling Benson's thighs, "someone has been working out."

"Pervert," Benson screams and pushes the guard against the wall. Detective Fin Tutuola (Ice-T) is also undercover as a guard and is observing the intake process.

Tutuola jumps between the guard and Benson. He waves his baton in the air, and before striking Benson, he leans toward her and whispers in her ear, "Scream like it hurts." He strikes her and yells, "Never attack an officer! Got that, bitch?"[80] Tutuola's supervisor says, "This isn't Rikers," but adds with a smile, "Not bad for your first day on the job."[81]

The New York State Department of Correctional Services (NYS DOCS) tolerates little unprofessional correctional personnel performance.[82] NYS DOCS correctional personnel, similar to corrections personnel across the country, are trained in *defensible conduct* (conduct that is not capable of a public defense against charges of impropriety)[83] and are aware of litigation potentials, their responsibilities, and their dedication to the correctional community, which depends on professional performance. Intake is monitored and recorded but rarely performed by unqualified personnel; female prisoners are processed by female correctional intake officers.

That said, the implication is that aggressive physical abuse and lewd comments are correctional benchmarks of prized personnel and expected behavior of personnel in state penitentiaries. Sometime after Benson's search, she is led from the common areas of the prison by Captain Lowell Harris (Johnny Messner), also referred to as a guard; Harris apparently exposes himself to Benson before attempting to rape her. Tutuola saves the day. In court, Benson comments that Harris almost killed her, to which the defense lawyer advises that "the law gives Officer Harris every right to strike an inmate to force compliance."

Scholarly Literature, Media, and Criminal Justice

Studies show that the popular media shapes social views of the *criminal justice community* (law enforcement that includes prosecutors, courts, and corrections) in several ways,[84] such as:

- A dramatic device for representing the sociopolitical context in which events take place and how this context influences events
- A comparator that sets a moral benchmark and provides a mark of accuracy or authenticity
- A prism that exposes a perspective at odds with official descriptions

Largely, the popular media sets in motion inappropriate and immoral responses toward targeted populations (see Chapters 3–5) and discourages support for a reformist agenda.

Other justice realities that are altered by the popular media and how those deceptions change real-world expectations and ultimately the behavior of criminal justice practitioners, especially prosecutors, is one focus of this book.

■ The Media's Relationship with Criminal Justice

It is curious that the media possesses so much power over who gets arrested, charged, or indicted and who gets convicted, as well as what kind of treatment a person should expect when he or she is in the grips of a police officer or correctional personnel. It is common knowledge that the media can also compel consumer purchases, such as which automobile to drive, what style of clothing to wear and where to buy it, and which pharmaceutical product to use for long-lasting sexuality or clear vision.[85] It could be argued that the media socially constructs (stereotypes) the framework of the appearance (physical features) and history (childhood experiences) of an offender, what crimes the alleged offender is capable of committing, how these crimes were committed, and tells cops, prosecutors, judges, and jurors what to do about it.[86–88] Think of it this way: The media can describe motive, opportunity, appearance, and an historical account of an individual who allegedly committed a crime and then justify the behavior of criminal justice personnel in response to the person whom the media had defined as corrupt and immoral.

> The evidence reveals that justice accountability does not depend upon whether an individual committed a crime or not, but how the media portrays the individual in relationship to the crime.[89]

The popular media plays an important role in understanding criminal justice in five ways:

- It is a dramatic device for representing the sociopolitical and economic context in which most events take place and how this context influences events.[90]
- The popular media is a comparator that sets the moral benchmark and provides a mark of accuracy or authenticity (of the good guys and the bad guys).[91]
- The popular media exposes a perspective of criminal justice that is at odds with official descriptions and supports assumptions of punishment and vigilante roles; at the other extreme, the media offers appropriate agendas of rehabilitation and prevention.[92]
- The popular media socially constructs and defines which real-world experiences and issues are significant and which experiences are irrelevant.[93]
- The popular media socially constructs and describes gender, race, and ethnicity, which includes the femininity of women and characteristics of an incompetent person and how those roles characterize the behaviors of being an aggressor, victim, or being ineligible for justice sanctions, including trial.[94–96]

■ What Viewers See and Hear

Why viewers believe what they see and hear from the popular media is another matter. One answer is that people largely retain only 10 percent of the information they read, 20 percent of the information they hear, and 50 percent of the information they see and hear, suggesting that motion pictures and television have a clear advantage over other forms of communication, such as books.[97] Quality presentations can appear to be more truthful than lower quality presentations. Quality presentations that provide untruths don't require an apology or a retraction.

> The greater the quality of the message, the more it is accepted as truth (regardless of the integrity of the message).[98]

For example, in a drug trafficking case in New Orleans, a half million dollars in cash was confiscated from a drug courier by the police. The crime lab wanted to conduct a visual analysis of the bills to determine their age, insisting that this analysis would enhance the case against the drug peddlers. A New Orleans officer said that the lab technician saw a process on *CSI: Miami* and took the cash to test it to determine its age. The lab technician was referring to Episode 92 ("Free Fall") in which a lengthy optical analysis helped establish that the $100 bills were at least 16 years old. If *CSI: Miami*'s lab expert, Calleigh Duquesne (Emily Procter), wanted to know the age of the bills, she could have looked at the series date (and possibly the letter engraved on the bill that indicates a minor revision), which gets updated with any design change or appointment of a new secretary of the treasury of the United States and has been printed on the front of all US paper currency since 1869.[99] In an attempt to be consistent with the quality of the presentation, producers of the media might want to consider an enhancement of the integrity levels of their subject matter, too.

■ The Media Shapes Social Perspectives

The importance of the media is that it shapes social perspectives, or public opinion, and official policy despite the fact that it is a prominent form of portrayal, particularly of criminal justice practices and policy.[100–102] For example, in one scene of *Law & Order*, Episode 266, "DRI-102," Assistant District Attorney (ADA) Serena Southerlyn (Elisabeth Rohm) is learning to protect herself from a dangerous defendant by a New York City police trainer. The officer informs her to protect her face and neck against a knife thrust with her hands, and the Kevlar (highly advanced body armor) "will protect the rest of you."[103] This is not entirely true; Kevlar protects best against blows such as punches or bullets. It can protect against commercially manufactured knives or ice picks, but it will only slow, rather than completely stop, a thrust.[104]

■ Media and Politics

Government propaganda has employed a variety of techniques to influence public opinion in the past century, but largely it has avoided the truth.[105] Televised episodes concerning police investigations and forensic science failures of both local and federal agencies continue to plague Americans at home, in politics, and abroad. For example, Brandon Mayfield, a Portland, Oregon lawyer, was arrested and held for two weeks in Madrid in 2004 after a terrorist attack on the train system. The FBI insisted it had found forensic trace evidence, including fingerprints, on several crucial pieces of evidence. However, the Spanish authorities disagreed with American technology and FBI political interests, and they released Mayfield without charge. Mayfield, a Muslim, filed suit saying he was singled out because of his faith.[106]

Since 9/11 the federal approach to the arrest and prosecution of terrorists appears to be racially motivated and couched in a war on immigrants, as described in Chapter 5. Some argue that the intelligence communities of other countries and many American political watchdog groups hold strong reservations about the FBI's forensic technology, which is wrapped in a political agenda of sorts.[107] Clarifying this issue is the testimony of a legislative counsel for the American Civil Liberties Union (ACLU): "The 9/11 Commission report exhaustively details significant failures of the intelligence agencies, including the Federal Bureau of Investigation (FBI) and the Central Intelligence Agency (CIA), and proposes major structural changes to address those failures. The failure to 'connect the dots' to prevent the terrorist attacks of 9/11 must rank among the worst intelligence failures in American history."[108]

Nonetheless, the Western world, including high-ranking government officials, is under the impression that prime time dramas mirror reality. For example, in early 2007 the then Prime Minister of the United Kingdom, Tony Blair, found himself involved in a racist bullying row involving Shilpa Shetty, resulting from the prime time show *Celebrity Big Brother*. Actually, a racist account could have been easily fabricated by the media to enhance ratings. In France, the state is demanding the scrubbing of gritty vulgar words and brand name identification from films and television series. News reporters manufacture their own slant on crime, and this finding is not limited to the United States. For example, in informing the public about murder in America, news reporters emphasize personal traits of an offender, but Turkish news reporters accentuate social and situational causes of murder.[109] It's politics as usual, but the media provides its own cutting-edge reality centered on the fantasies of politicians who understand little about the rule of law and accept the media's rationale for criminal justice corruption as amplified through television (detailed later in this chapter).

■ Media and Terrorism

Following the theme of socially constructed events by the media, one wonders in what way the media shapes international terrorism. Simon Cottle examined television news programming in six countries—Australia, the United Kingdom, the United States, India, Singapore, and South Africa—over a two-week period in 2004.[110] His sample consisted of 27 television channels, four international satellite providers, 56 different news programs, and 560 broadcast news programs. In almost 10,000 broadcast news items, there were 1,662 terror-related news items (17 percent). During the period studied, terrorist activities were not imminent, and it could be said that the media played a role in enhancing the fear of terrorism among listeners.

■ Media and the Fear of Crime

The fear of crime can mean different things to different people, imply Wesley Skogan and Michael G. Maxfield.[111] Intrinsic to most definitions is the fear of victimization, yet the consequences come down to similar behavioral changes, often in a negative way. By increasing fear, these manifestations of disorder are presumed to weaken the informal community controls that prevent crime.[112] Police departments often try to reduce the public's fear of crime through police community relations efforts and by minimizing the amount of reported crime. The police have frequently acted on the assumption that concerted efforts to solve crime and arrest criminals would reduce unwarranted fears. Some fear-reduction strategies have been tried over the years, but they were never rigorously tested.[113]

Dread of Becoming a Victim

A survey of over 3,000 participants conducted by the College of Criminology and Criminal Justice at Florida State University[114] found that most participants are fearful of the following:

- Being murdered
- Being sexually assaulted
- Being robbed or mugged
- Having their home broken into when they are home
- Having their home broken into when they are out
- Having their car stolen

Cities with a greater population density reported higher levels of fear, and ethnicity also plays a role; Latinos are the most fearful, blacks are less fearful than Latinos, and both Latinos and blacks are more fearful than whites. The randomness of violence beyond high-crime areas makes people anxious, argues Robert Blendon, an expert who tracks public opinion surveys for Harvard University's School of Public Health.[115,116] Those incidents send a symbolic message to people that crime is out of control. Extreme examples include 9/11, the massacre of 33 students at the Virginia Tech campus, and the five gunned-down students at Northern Illinois University in early February 2008. Some students felt at risk and took precautions, and others wondered where to find a safe place in their world. Their daily behavior was distinctively different. If fearful people flee from hard-working, middle-class cities and seek safety in the countryside, these fears can result in urban decay. Yet the media continues its proliferation of crime coverage, enhancing a fear of crime among its audiences. Other studies show that college students are susceptible to suggestion from the media when formulating opinions about criminal justice policy (and life, relationships, and fun).[117] For example, a study about attitudes toward gun control among college students used both ideological (attribution styles) and instrumental (fear of crime) perspectives and then tested whether viewing the film *Bowling for Columbine* influenced their attitudes. Participants in the experimental group reported significantly more support for gun control policies. Another study posits that the more crime-related television people watch, the more fearful they become, and they increasingly support punitive action and stricter punishment that could include capital punishment.[118]

■ Media Distortion and Advertisers

The popular media includes advertisers who have distorted truths in health and beauty products, home and entertainment amenities, and even muscle building and weight loss products, reveals documentary news reporters at ABC.[119] Although other reporters have also discovered these fabrications and misrepresentations, the influence of earlier distortions lingers and shapes both the expectations and perceptions of many individuals.

■ Media, Integrity, and What Criminal Justice Is Supposed to Be

Simon Cottle argues that we live in promotional times when *spin doctors* employed by government, organizations, celebrities, and pressure groups mirror the rise of an increasingly media-aware and a *mediatized* society—a society where both commercial interests and cultural identities compete for media space and strategically mobilize forms of communicative power. The established media, as Cottle explains, mediatizes shapes and facilitates and conditions the "communication of conflicts."[120(p21),121] From Gregg Barak's perspective,[122] the media is so powerful that it attempts to dictate what the criminal justice community is supposed to be, what the legal processes are, and what practices performed by the criminal justice players (practitioners, victims, offenders, judges, and juries) are appropriate and ethical.[123] In a search for appropriateness and integrity in popular media dramas, the following examples are fairly typical:

- In *Law & Order: Criminal Intent*'s Episode 86, "No Exit," ADA Carver (Courtney B. Vance) tells the grand jury that "if you see a bleeding man, it is your responsibility to help him."[124] Unless New York state law has a vastly different law than what is taught throughout American Bar Association certified law schools, only one-half of this statement is accurate.[125] A bystander has no legal responsibility to aid an injured person. The only person who has an obligation to assist an injured person is the individual who actually caused the injury and those who are mandated to do so, such as police officers and other specific public personnel. If such an obligation described by ADA Carver existed, there would be no need for the numerous good-samaritan laws in this country to protect bystanders who aid injured persons from future litigation.

- In *CSI*'s Episode 81, "Butterfield," after Gil Grissom (William Petersen) and Catherine Willows (Marg Helgenberger) found traces of blood and bleach in the bathroom drains, Sara Sidle (Jorja Fox) edged through the home's crawl space to check the plumbing traps. She spotted a reddish liquid, probably blood, water, and bleach, gathered under a drainage pipe. She crawled to it and looked straight up into the pipes without protective goggles.[126]
- In *CSI: Miami*'s Episode 148, "Wrecking Crew," which aired November 2, 2008, lab tech Ryan Wolfe (Jonathan Togo) snaked a public toilet with a device that provided an image of the pipe's contents.[127] Leaning onto the clean, white commode while on his knees, he wore gloves and a white shirt but no protective eye gear. His female assistant wore a white medical-type gown, and quietly, with an admiring grin, looked on to the man's work. Later Ryan somehow (without tools) unbolted an S-shaped pipe below the toilet's flange. He then appeared to be in a basement of sorts and stood atop a platform, where he shoved a clawlike device into the pipe he had freed and retrieved a shell casing, which helped close the case. The lab technicians searched the public toilet days after the crime occurred when they decided the gunman tossed a single shell casing into the toilet. They were right!

■ The *CSI Effect*

The popular media has made incredible contributions (see Chapter 2 for details), but it also provides its own version of crime and the criminal justice process, which heightens the fear of victimization and changes real-world expectations about crime and how to control it. This phenomenon is referred to as the *CSI Effect*. The popularity of the media's portrayal of crime science investigations (CSI, not to be confused with the media's link solely to forensic science; see Chapter 6 for details) and crime itself are profound, affecting police officers, prosecutors, defense attorneys, judges and jurors, forensic scientists, victim service providers, medical personnel, witnesses, and victims' families, explains the National Institute of Justice (NIJ).[128] The NIJ should also include counselors and correctional personnel in prisons and jails, probation and parole agencies, private providers of justice services, justice trainers, policy makers, and families and friends of offenders.[129] Although the entertainment value of the popular media is worth experiencing, it justifies laziness and corruption among justice personnel, including prosecutors, says Richard Willing.[130]

> The ultimate illusion produced through the *CSI Effect* is an unrealistic expectation that every crime scene will yield plentiful evidence that can be analyzed through a foolproof forensic science technique and will be presented as such in the courtroom.[131]

The *CSI Effect* is a consequence of the popular media's skill to accomplish the following:

- Encourage aggressive, reactive criminal justice strategies
- Glorify vigilantism[132] among justice practitioners and members of the public
- Promote fictitious accounts of crime, crime control, and its process

The popular media depicts a good police strategy as an aggressive, reactive response (for example, a person commits a crime and the police respond, as opposed to preventive initiatives and quality-of-life arrests), regardless of the guilt of the person or seriousness of the violation. Examples include justice reactive responses to the wars on crime, junkies, sex offenders, poverty, and immigrants (see Chapters 3–5), which include zero-tolerance strategies, sex offender registers, and critical special weapons and tactics (SWAT) and tact deployments, to name a few. Results from aggressive justice initiatives include wrongful convictions and continuation of the death penalty as a plausible criminal sanction. The notion of aggressive, reactive police strategies seems abstract, thus a concrete example might help: Ninety minutes after the Boston Red Sox won the World Series at Yankee Stadium, an estimated 80,000 jubilant and mostly young college students converged on Fenway Park in Boston.[133] Victoria Snelgrove was one of those college students, but she wouldn't be going home for the Thanksgiving break. She was killed by a police projectile that was fired into the crowd. It injured many people but slammed into Victoria's eyes. Police attempted to disperse revelers because they were afraid the crowd would spin out of control. Had authorities prepared (prevention and proactive policing) for the event instead of reacting to it, Victoria Snelgrove would have marched at her graduation with her classmates.

The *CSI Effect* depicts a good person as an individual who acts as an enforcer, judge, juror, and executioner at the same time, or what can be called a vigilante (i.e., Dirty Harry, Detective Elliot Stabler). The media is an enabler of the supercop mentality (see Chapters 3–5 for details). It opens the door to almost every element that contributes to a wrongful conviction (see Chapter 8) and pro-death-penalty attitudes (see Chapter 9). For example, the 2007 to 2008 television drama offered by FOX entitled *K-Ville* (perhaps the "K" is for Katrina) poorly represented the New Orleans Police Department's response after Hurricane Katrina. Similar to *CSI, Law & Order*, and their spinoffs, *K-Ville* dodges much of the racial politics of policing by having the criminals represented by white, wealthy corporate leaders or middle-class professionals while the police are racially (and gender) diverse. Police brutality is seen as necessary and as an honorable method to fight crime, which is a consistent theme among most movies and television dramas since *Dirty Harry* (1971). *K-Ville*'s central character, similar to other media detective shows, is concerned that he breaks the law when apprehending suspects, but he reports that New Orleans is too lawless for him to perform his job and maintain the law at the same time. Although *K-Ville* never made it out of its first season, other television programs are consistent with these thoughts. For example, in *The Shield*, Vic Mackey (Michael Chiklis) is in charge of a crime gang unit. He enforces the law, but he and his unit work outside the law because the streets in Los Angeles are corrupt. Mackey strikes deals with drug traders, harasses gang members, and shot another a police officer in the face point blank because the officer threatened to expose Mackey's unit as corrupt.

Popular television shows and the movie industry promote supercop vigilantes, such as Clint Eastwood in *Dirty Harry* (1971); Charles Bronson in *Death Wish* (1974); Mel Gibson in *Lethal Weapon* (1987); Bruce Willis in *Die Hard* (1988) and *Live Free or Die Hard* (2007); Jackie Chan and Chris Tucker in *Rush Hour 2* (2001); Matt Damon and Leonardo DiCaprio in *The Departed* (2006); Edward Norton and Colin Farrell in *Pride and Glory* (2008), and Liam Neeson in *Taken* (2009). Although a few of these films are dated, local television stations often rerun these films and others (i.e., *Batman, Spider-Man*, and *Iron Man*). While the author was working on this chapter, one television station televised a *Death Wish* marathon featuring all five sequels (1974–1994), back to back; and another television station competitively offered the *Dirty Harry* collection *(Dirty Harry/Magnum Force/The Enforcer/Sudden Impact/The Dead Pool)*. One problem, among others, is that none of these performances typically describe an American police detective regardless of his or her rank.[134] The other side of vigilantism is compliance and often tolerance of police authority among the American population. This thought is challenged by policy makers, but one reason community policing efforts can fail is that only a few of the residents are represented at community meetings, and many others are fearful of the police and their motives (for more detail, see Chapter 4).[135]

Finally, consequences of the *CSI Effect*'s fictitious accounts of crime and criminal investigations raise real-world expectations about crime and crime control. For example, every crime is reported; every violator is detected, apprehended, and arrested; and every defendant who is lawless is legally convicted (see Chapter 8) and imprisoned, and some receive a death sentence (see Chapter 9).[136,137] Another example of fictitious accounts have led the way in the justice arena to deliver more forensic evidence because the popular media emphasizes that every criminal case can be solved through the employment of high-tech forensic science as seen on prime time drama crime shows such as *CSI, Criminal Minds*, and *Law & Order*.[138] Yet in reality, forensic science is limited because of a lack of funding, personnel (including human error), and standards (see Chapter 8).[139] The *CSI Effect* depicts glamour, certainty, self-discipline, objectivity, and truth and justice, all rolled into one, and in doing so it effortlessly accommodates much-heralded successes, argues David Wilson.[140,141] What you need to know right now is that generally the *CSI Effect* promises that the judicial process is flawless. Its downside promotes the criminal justice apparatus toward unrealistic and unlawful intrusion into the private lives of the American population, which gives rise to wrongful convictions, and it reassures that capital punishment serves a purpose.[142]

■ Summary

Prosecutors' work ethics suggest that at the heart of the wrongful conviction phenomenon and the continuation of executions are prosecutors who alone possess the authority to initially indict a suspect. If prosecutors don't act, little, if anything, happens toward justice. What can be gained from this work is a better understanding of the primary elements of the problems that will hasten policy makers toward a method of supervision and recommendations toward compliance.

The assumptions that underlie this book are associated with an enlightened awareness, prosecutor power, and prosecutor deviance. However, some researchers continue to mislead readers; also, some well-funded academic researchers tend to develop misconceptions about criminal justice policy and practices. These inefficiencies, which are identified in many justice studies, are more often linked to the researcher's naïveté or lack of practical experience than to a flaw of the criminal justice program, practice, or perspective. These thoughts are consistent with the idea that history has been largely written by the privileged, therefore the media provides many flawed studies that are supported by biased historic accounts and are used to develop criminal justice policy only to end in disappointment, imprisonment, and sometimes an execution.

Although crime is an integral part of all healthy societies, mankind has attempted to control criminal behavior throughout recorded history without much success. What is known about law and morality or right from wrong is that they are neither naturally bestowed nor are they consistent across historic time. What is consistent is that natural law prevails; the law of the strongest dominates the entire history and presence of mankind on this planet.

The popular media sets in motion inappropriate and immoral responses toward targeted populations and discourages support for a reformist agenda. The evidence reveals that justice accountability does not depend upon whether an individual committed a crime or not, but how the media portrays the individual in relationship to the crime.

The media is important to understanding criminal justice because it is a dramatic device for representing the sociopolitical and economic context in which most events take place and how this context influences events; it is a comparator that sets the moral benchmark and provides a mark of accuracy or authenticity. It exposes a perspective that is at odds with official descriptions and supports assumptions of punishment and vigilante roles; at the other extreme, it offers appropriate agendas of rehabilitation and prevention, and it socially constructs and defines which real-world experiences and issues are significant and which experiences are irrelevant.

The popular media also provides its own version of crime and the criminal justice process, which heightens the fear of victimization and changes real-world expectations about crime and how to control it. This phenomenon is referred to as the *CSI Effect*. The ultimate illusion produced through the *CSI Effect* is an unrealistic expectation that every crime scene will yield plentiful evidence that can be analyzed through a foolproof forensic science technique and will be presented as such in the courtroom. The *CSI Effect* is a consequence of the popular media's skill in encouraging aggressive, reactive criminal justice strategies; to glorify vigilantism among justice practitioners and members of the public; and to promote fictitious accounts of crime, crime control, and its process. The *CSI Effect* promises that the judicial process is flawless. Its downside promotes the criminal justice apparatus toward unrealistic and unlawful intrusion into the private lives of the American population, which gives rise to wrongful convictions and reassures that capital punishment serves a purpose.

■ References

1. Cory, P. (2005, October). *Keynote speech by the Honorable Peter deCarteret Cory at the conference.* Paper presented at Unlocking Innocence: An International Conference on Avoiding Wrongful Convictions, Winnipeg, Manitoba, Canada.

2. Shelton, D. E. (2008). *The "CSI Effect:" Does it really exist?* Washington, DC: National Institute of Justice. Retrieved May 25, 2008, from http://www.ncjrs.gov/pdffiles1/nij/221501.pdf

3. Stevens, D. J. (2008). Forensic science, prosecutors, and wrongful convictions. *Howard Journal of Criminal Justice, 47*(1), 31–51.

4. Stevens, D. J. (2009). CSI Effect, prosecutors, and wrongful convictions. *Criminal Law Bulletin, 45*(4), 47–53.

5. Collins, S. (2008, September 22). These Emmy Awards are not a popularity contest. *Los Angeles Times.* http://www.latimes.com/entertainment/news/la-et-emmy22-2008sep22,0,6618115.story

6. Krug, P. (2001, Autumn). Prosecutorial discretion and its limits. *The American Journal of Comparative Law, 50*, 643–664.

7. Berger, P. L. (1963). *Invitation to sociology: A humanistic perspective.* Garden City, NY: Anchor Books.

8. Huff, C. R. (2002). Wrongful conviction and public policy: The American Society of Criminology 2001 presidential address. *Criminology An Interdisciplinary Journal, 40*(1), 1–18.

9. Gordon, S. C., & Huber, G. A. (2002). Citizen oversight and the electoral incentives of criminal prosecutors. *American Journal of Political Science, 46*(2), 334–351.

10. Stevens, D. J. (2006). Training and management impact sexual assault conviction rates in Boston. *Police Journal, 79*(2), 125–154.

11. Haberfeld, M., & Gideon, L. (2008). *Policing is hard on democracy, or democracy is hard on policing?* Upper Saddle River, NJ: Pearson.

12. Konradi, A. (1997, Winter). Too little, too late: Prosecutors' pre-court preparation of rape survivors. *Law and Social Inquiry, 22*(1), 1–54.

13. Frohmann, L. (1991, May). Discrediting victims' allegations of sexual assault: Prosecutorial accounts of case rejections. *Social Problems, 38*(2), 213–226.

14. Krug, "Prosecutorial Discretion."

15. Spohn, C., Beichner, D., & Davis-Frenzel, E. (2001). Prosecutorial justification for sexual assault case rejection: The gateway to justice. *Social Problems, 48*(2), 206–235.

16. Center for Public Integrity. (2003). *Harmful error: Investigating America's local prosecutors.* Washington, DC.

17. Paternoster, R., Brame, R., & Bacon, S. (2008). *The death penalty: America's experience with capital punishment.* New York: Oxford Press.

18. Krug, "Prosecutorial Discretion."

19. Center for Public Integrity, *Harmful Error.*

20. Barak, G. (2007). Notes from news-making criminology: Reflections on the media, intellectuals, and crime. *Justice Quarterly, 5*(4), 565–587. Retrieved September 5, 2007, from http://www.greggbarak.com/custom4_2.html

21. *Merriam-Webster online dictionary.* Retrieved November 13, 2008, from http://www.merriam-webster.com/dictionary/vigilantism

22. Marion, N. E., & Oliver, W. M. (2006). *The public police of crime and criminal justice.* Upper Saddle River, NJ: Prentice Hall.

23. Center for Public Integrity, *Harmful Error,* ii.

24. This thought represents a question I have raised throughout my academic career. Stevens, D. J. (1999). Interviews with women convicted of murder: Battered women syndrome revisited. *International Review of Victimology, 6*, 117–135.

25. Stevens, D. J. (1994). The depth of imprisonment and prisonization: Levels of security and prisoners' anticipation of future violence. *The Howard Journal of Criminal Justice, 33*(2), 137–157.

26. Stevens, D. J. (1992). Research note: The death sentence and inmate attitudes. *Crime & Delinquency, 38*(2), 272–279.

27. Zimbardo, P. (2007). *The Lucifer Effect: Understanding how good people turn to evil.* New York: Random House.

28. Katz, F. E. (1993). *Ordinary people and extraordinary evil.* Albany: State University of New York Press.

29. Lippmann, W. (1993). *The phantom public.* New York: Transaction.

30. Lippmann, W. (2008). *Public opinion.* New York: BiblioLife.

31. Campbell, A., Converse, P. E., Miller, W. E., & Stokes, D. E. (1960). *The American voter.* New York: John Wiley & Sons.

32. Converse, P. E. (1964). The nature of belief systems in mass publics. In D. E. Apter (Ed.), *Ideology and discontent.* New York: Free Press.

33. Converse, "Nature of Belief Systems."

34. Marion & Oliver, *Public Police of Crime.*

35. Bishop, G. F. (2006). *The illusion of public opinion: Fact and artifact in American public opinion polls.* New York: Roman and Littlefield.

36. Weisburd, D. (2002, November). *Hot spots policing experiments and criminal justice research: Lessons from the field.* Paper presented for the Campbell Collaboration/Rockefeller Foundation meeting, Bellagio, Italy.

37. Shelden, R. G. (2008). *Controlling the dangerous classes: A critical introduction to the history of criminal justice* (2nd ed.). Boston: Allyn & Bacon.

38. National Immigration Forum. Retrieved August 17, 2008, from http://www.immigration-forum.org/

39. Page, B. I., & Shapiro, R. Y. (1992). *The rational public: Fifty years of trends in Americans' policy preferences.* Chicago: University of Chicago Press.

40. Popkin, S., & Kabashima, I. (2007). Introduction: Changing media, changing politics. *The Japanese Journal of Political Science, 8,* 1–6.

41. Marion & Oliver, *Public Police of Crime.*

42. Nie, N. H., Verba, S., & Petrocik, J. R. (1966). *The responsible electorate: Rationality in presidential voting, 1936–1960.* Cambridge, MA: Harvard University Press.

43. Smith, E. R. A. N. (1989). *The unchanging American voter.* Berkeley: University of California Press.

44. Marion & Oliver, *Public Police of Crime.*

45. Carmines, E. G., & Kuklinski, J. H. (1990). Incentives, opportunities, and the logic of public opinion in American political representation. In J. A. Ferejohn & J. H. Kuklinski (Eds.), *Information and democratic processes.* Urbana: University of Illinois Press.

46. Roane, K. R., & Morrison, D. (2005, April 14). The CSI Effect. *US News and World Report.* Retrieved January 13, 2008, from www.usnews.com

47. Layton, J. (2006). *How crime scene investigation works.* Retrieved January 13, 2008, from http://science.howstuffworks.com/csi.htm. Much of her information was provided by Joe Clayton, a laboratory agent and primary scene responder for the Colorado Bureau of Investigation.

48. Iyengar, S. (1991). *Is anyone responsible? How television frames political issues.* Chicago: University of Chicago Press.

49. Iyengar, S. (1990). Shortcuts to political knowledge: The role of selective attention and accessibility. In J. A. Ferejohn & J. H. Kuklinski (Eds.), *Information and democratic process.* Urbana: University of Illinois Press.

50. Surette, R. (2007). *Media, crime, and criminal justice: Images, realities, and policies* (3rd ed.). Belmont, CA: Thompson Higher Education.

51. US Department of Justice. (2006). *Sourcebook of criminal justice statistics online. Table 2.28.* Albany, NY: Office of Justice Programs. Retrieved November 13, 2008, from http://www.albany.edu/sourcebook/pdf/t2282006.pdf

52. Erikson, K. T. (1966). *Wayward puritans.* New York: John Wiley.

53. Hickey, H. W. (1997). *Serial murderers and their victims* (2nd ed.). Belmont, CA: Wadsworth Thomson.

54. Straus, M. A., Gelles, R. J., & Steinmetz, S. K. (1980). *Behind closed doors: Violence in the American family.* New York: Anchor Books.

55. Durkheim, E. (1958). *The rules of sociological method* (S. A. Solovay & J. H. Mueller, Trans.). Glencoe, IL: Free Press. Also cited in Erikson, K. T., *Wayward Puritans.*

56. Felson, M. (1998). *Crime & everyday life* (2nd ed.). Thousand Oaks, CA: Pine Forge Press.

57. Schmalleger, F. (2000). World of the career criminal. In D. J. Stevens (Ed.), *Corrections perspective.* Madison, WI: Coursewise.

58. Bell, J. G., Clow, K. A., & Ricciardelli, R. (2008, March). Causes of wrongful conviction: Looking at student knowledge. *Journal of Criminal Justice Education, 19,* 75–95. Although this research did not specifically hit on crime as a perspective as old as mankind, it does say that "criminal justice majors were not more knowledgeable in the areas of police and lawyer behavior." One implication of the researchers' conclusion is that criminal justice majors hold less knowledge than expected about the function of policing in present and past societies; many may be under the spell of the popular media, which suggests that violent offenders would cease to exist if offenders were dealt with in a violent manner, including execution, by authorities.

59. Samenow, S. E. (1998). *Before it's too late.* New York: Times Books. One perspective is prevention, starting at a young age, by parents and institutions, including the criminal justice community.

60. Drapkin, I. (1989). *Crime and punishment in the ancient world.* Washington, DC: Lexington.

61. Stevens, D. J. (2005). The history of prisons: Continental Europe and England. *The encyclopedia of criminology.* New York: Routledge/Taylor & Francis.

62. Marx, K. (1978). The eighteenth Brumaire of Louis Bonaparte. In R. C. Tucker (Trans.), *The Marx-Engles reader.* New York: Norton. (Original work published 1852)

63. Morris, N., & Rothman, D. J. (1997). *The Oxford history of the prison: The practice of punishment in Western society.* New York: Oxford University Press.

64. Stevens, "The History of Prisons."

65. Peters, E. M. (1998). Prison before the prison: The ancient and medieval worlds. In N. Morris & D. J. Rothman (Eds.), *The Oxford history of the prison.* New York: Oxford University Press.

66. Peters, "Prison Before the Prison."

67. For example, at the Newgate Tower prison in England, being confined on a higher floor of the tower translated to a better quality lifestyle despite being jailed. Getting to those higher floors cost money. Those without funds lived in the lower sections of the tower. Morris & Rothman, *Oxford History of the Prison.*

68. Grovier, K. (2008). The Gaol: The story of Newgate, London's most notorious prison. London: Hodder Murray.

69. Morris, N. (2002). *Maconochie's gentlemen: The story of Norfolk Island and the roots of modern prison reform.* New York: Oxford University Press. Captain Alexander Maconochie is known as a strong reformer of the British prison system, in particular, and his accomplishments influenced early release systems, including probation and parole options through his innovation of the mark system, which provided hope for prisoners to build credit toward release.

70. Morris, *Maconochie's Gentlemen.*

71. Foucault, M. (1995). *Discipline and punishment: The birth of the prison.* New York: Vintage Books.

72. Morris & Rothman, *Oxford History of the Prison.*

73. Marietta, J. D., & Rowe, G. S. (2008). College Park: University of Pennsylvania.

74. Morris & Rothman, *Oxford History of the Prison.*

75. The US Supreme Court said in Wolff v. McDonnel (1974) that although prisoners' constitutional rights were diminished upon conviction, and although jails and prisons can and must curtail rights to maintain discipline and control for the security and protection of all, not all rights are given up at the prison gate.

76. Cornell Law School. (2008). *Prisoner's rights.* Retrieved October 8, 2008, from http://topics. law.cornell.edu/wex/prisoners_rights

77. Logan, C. H. (1993). *Criminal justice performance measures for prisons.* Bureau of Justice Assistance. Center for program evaluation. Retrieved June 8, 2009 from http://www.ojp. usdoj.gov/bjs/pub/pdf/pmcjs.pdf

78. Smith, M. E. (2001, June). *What future for "public safety" and "restorative justice" in community corrections?* (NCJ 187773). Washington, DC: National Institute of Justice. Retrieved November 22, 2008, from http://www.ncjrs.org/txtfiles1/nij/187773.txt

79. Kurki, L. (1999). *Incorporating restorative and community justice into American sentencing and corrections. Research in brief-sentencing and corrections: Issues for the 21st century* (NCJ 175723). Washington, DC: US Department of Justice, National Institute of Justice/Corrections Program Office. Retrieved January 11, 2005, from http://www.ncjrs.org/pdffiles1/nij/175723.pdf

80. NYS DOCS personnel (and most enforcement personnel) do not whisper in the ear of an inmate before a strike with an impact weapon, such as baton, because reaction time and distance are critical. In the circumstance of this encounter, the officer would be trained to deliver one solid strike to the opponent's knee, which would end the encounter. A strike elsewhere in this situation would provide a serious disadvantage inside the optimum striking range and reaction distance. The first tactical response (although this situation did not necessarily call for one) is pepper spray. Information provided by tact trainer who wishes to remain anonymous at NYS DOCS Albany Training Academy, Albany, New York. (*Note:* This information is also consistent with a first strike trainer's information at North Carolina Justice Academy, Salemburg, North Carolina.)

81. Rikers is a New York City facility, and Sealview as portrayed in this episode (although Sealview Prison does not exist in NY) is a state facility. Exchanging personnel from city to state systems is not a likely prospect: different employer, different training, different unions.

82. New York State Department of Correctional Services. (n.d.). *Rules and regulations–corrections.* Retrieved November 22, 2008, from http://www.dos.state.ny.us/info/nycrr.htm

83. Cooper, T. L. (2008). *Handbook of administrative ethics* (2nd ed.). New York: CRC.

84. Bennett, J. (2006). The good, the bad and the ugly: The media in prison films. *Journal of Criminal Justice, 45*(2), 97–115.

85. When *Law & Order* began airing in reruns on TNT, new digital technology was used to insert product placements (paid appearances of name-brand products) into the show. The easiest to spot is Coca-Cola; any time you see a Coke can sitting on a desk, it has been added digitally. (*Source:* TV.com)

86. Iyengar, *Is Anyone Responsible?*

87. Wilson, D. (2006, September 14). Crime lab investigation. *The Guardian.* Retrieved January 14, 2008, from http://www.guardian.co.uk/commentisfree/story/0,1871923,00.html

88. Wilson, D. (2008). *Centre for Criminal Justice Police and Research.* Retrieved January 15, 2008, from http://www.lhds.bcu.ac.uk/criminaljustice/

89. McMullen, J. L., & McClung, M. (2006). The media, the politics of truth, and the coverage of corporate violence: The Westray disaster and the public inquiry. *Critical Criminology: An International Journal, 14*(1), 67–86.

90. Bennett, "The Good, the Bad and the Ugly."

91. Chermak, S., McGarrell, E., & Gruenewald, J. (2006). Media coverage of police misconduct and attitudes toward police. *An International Journal of Police Strategies and Management, 29*(2), 261–281.

92. Phillips, N. D., & Strobl, S. (2006). Cultural criminology and kryptonite: Apocalyptic and retributive constructions of crime and justice in comic books. *Crime, Media, Culture, 2*(3), 304–331.

93. Beckett, K., & Sasson, T. (2000). *The politics of injustice.* Thousand Oaks, CA: Pine Forge Press.

94. Cavender, G., Bond-Maupin, L., & Jurik, N. C. (1999, October). The construction of gender in reality crime TV. *Gender and Society, 13*(5), 643–663.

95. Estep, R. (1982). Women's roles in crime as depicted by television and newspapers. *The Journal of Popular Culture,16*(3), 151–156. This reference suggests that this thought is hardly new.

96. This reference provides a discussion of incompetence and mental illness roles produced by the media. Montgomery, J., & Brooks, M. H. (2005). Use of a television crime-drama series to promote legal understanding in mentally ill, incompetent defendants: A pilot study. *Journal of Forensic Sciences, 50*(2), 465–469.

97. Tierney, P. R. (2003). *The competitive advantages of rich media.* Retrieved November 4, 2008, from http://www.econtentmag.com/downloads/WhitePapers/jun03/tierney.htm

98. Upshaw, L. B. (2007). *Truth: New rules for marketing in a skeptical world.* New York: American Management Association.

99. TV.Com. (2007). *CSI Miami.* Retrieved August 22, 2007, from http://www.tv.com/csi-miami/show/8460/summary.html

100. Barak, G. (2007). Mediatizing *Law & Order*: Applying Cottle's architecture of communicative frames to the social construction of crime and justice. *Crime Media Culture, 3*(1), 101–109.

101. Bracken, C. C. (2006). Perceived source credibility of local television news: The impact of television form and presence. *Journal of Broadcasting & Electronic Media, 50*(4), 723–741.

102. Robbers, M. L. (2005). The media and public perceptions of criminal policy issues: An analysis of *Bowling for Columbine* and gun control. *Journal of Criminal Justice and Popular Culture, 12*(2), 77–95.

103. TV.Com. (2007). *Law & Order.* Retrieved August 22, 2007, from http://www.tv.com/law-and-order/show/180/trivia.html?season=12&tag=season_dropdown;dropdown;11

104. DuPont Advanced Fiber Systems. (2007). *DuPont Kevlar MTP for knife-stab protection.* Retrieved August 22, 2007, from http://www2.dupont.com/Kevlar/en_US/assets/downloads/K16975KevlarMTP.pdf

105. Stevens. "CSI Effect, prosecutors, and wrongful convictions."

106. FBI apologizes to lawyer held in Madrid bombings: Man feels he was singled out because he's Muslim. (2006). *MSNBC*. Retrieved July 27, 2007, from http://www.msnbc.msn.com/id/5053007/

107. Miller, A. J. (2007). *An open letter to the FBI*. Retrieved September 15, 2007, from http://www.iww.org/projects/gdc/openlet.shtml

108. American Civil Liberties Union. (2004, August 4). ACLU Testimony of Timothy H. Edgar, legislative counsel, at a hearing on "9/11 Commission recommendations: Counterterrorism analysis and collection-the requirement for imagination and creativity" before the House Permanent Select Committee on Intelligence. Retrieved September 15, 2007, from http://www.aclu.org/natsec/emergpowers/14499leg20040804.html

109. Dayioglu, M. (2007, June). *Media representations of murder: A comparison of American and Turkish news reports*. Paper presented at the annual conference of the Turkish Institute for Police Studies, Istanbul, Turkey.

110. Cottle, S. (2006). Mediatizing the global war on terror: Television's public eye. In A. P. Kavoori & T. Fraley (Eds.), *Media, terrorism, and theory: A reader*. Lanham, MD: Rowman and Littlefield.

111. Skogan, W., & Maxfield, M. G. (1981). *Coping with crime*. Beverly Hills, CA: Sage.

112. Beckett & Sasson, *The Politics of Injustice*.

113. Police Foundation. (n.d.). *Police strategies to reduce citizen fear of crime*. Retrieved July 6, 2004, from http://www.policefoundation.org/docs/citizenfear.html

114. College of Criminology and Criminal Justice, Florida State University. (n.d.). *Fear of crime & related perceptions: A statewide survey of Florida. 1997*. Retrieved July 8, 2008, from http://www.criminology.fsu.edu/TA/fear/sld003.htm

115. Blendon, R. Harvard science. Retrieved June 8, 2009 from http://www.harvardscience.harvard.edu/directory/researchers/robert-j-blendon

116. Stevens, D. J. (2003). *Community policing in the 21st century*. Boston: Allyn Bacon.

117. Robbers, "Media and Public Perceptions."

118. Callanan, V. J. (Ed.). (2005). *Feeding the fear of crime: Crime-related media and support for three strikes*. New York: LFB Scholarly.

119. Our bodies, myths, lies and straight talk. (2006, June 16). *ABC News. 20/20*. Retrieved June 17, 2006, from http://abcnews.go.com/

120. Cottle, "Mediatizing the Global War on Terror."

121. Cottle, S. (2003). *News, public relations, and power*. Los Angeles: Sage.

122. Barak, "Mediatizing Law & Order."

123. One obvious cure might be that the standards of all entry personnel into the criminal justice community must possess a competitive education from an accredited institution of higher learning, solid experiences, and strong indicators of integrity that include both adult and juvenile drug-free and crime-free backgrounds.

124. TV.Com. (2007). *Law & Order: Criminal Intent*. Retrieved August 22, 2007, from http://www.tv.com/law-and-order-criminal-intent/show/1381/summary.html

125. TV.Com, *Law & Order: Criminal Intent*.

126. TV.Com. (2007). *CSI Las Vegas*. Retrieved May 30, 2008, from http://www.tv.com/csi/show/19/episode_guide.html

127. Personal observation of the episode by the author. November 2, 2008.

128. US Department of Justice. (2006). *National Institute of Justice annual report, 2005*. Washington, DC: Author. Retrieved May 24, 2008, from http://www.ncjrs.gov/pdffiles1/nij/213267.pdf

129. Hooper, R. (2008). *Television shows scramble forensic evidence*. Retrieved May 24, 2008, from http://www.newscientist.com/channel/opinion/mg18725163. 800-television-shows-scramble-forensic-evidence.html

130. Willing, R. (2004, August 5). CSI Effect has juries wanting more evidence. *USA Today*. Retrieved September 12, 2008, from http://www.usatoday.com/news/nation/2004-08-05-csi-effect_x.htm

131. Holmgren, J. A., & Pringle, H. M. (n.d.). The CSI Effect and the Canadian jury. *Gazette Magazine, 62*(20). Retrieved June 8, 2009, from http://www.rcmp-grc.gc.ca/gazette/archiv/vol69n2-eng.pdf

132. *Merriam-Webster,* http://www.merriam-webster.com/dictionary/vigilantism.

133. Farragher, T., & Abel, D. (2004, October 22). Postgame police projectile kills an Emerson student: O'Toole accepts responsibility but condemns acts of punks. *Boston Globe*. Retrieved November 12, 2008, from http://www.boston.com/sports/baseball/redsox/articles/2004/10/22/postgame_police_projectile_kills_an_emerson_student/

134. Flaherty, J. (2007, September 27). *K-Ville makes police brutality acceptable*. Retrieved May 31, 2008, from http://mostlywater.org/k_ville_makes_police_brutality_acceptable

135. Walker, S., & Katz, C. M. (2008). *The police in America: An introduction* (6th ed.). New York: McGraw Hill.

136. Escobar, E. J. (2001). Race, police, and the making of a political identity: Mexican Americans and the Los Angeles Police Department, 1900–1945. *The American Historical Review, 106*(2), 578–579.

137. Skogan, W. G., Steiner, L., DuBois, J., Gudell, J. E., & Fagan, A. (2002). *Community policing and the new immigrants: Latinos in Chicago*. Washington, DC: US Department of Justice, National Institute of Justice. Retrieved August 17, 2008, from http://www.ncjrs.gov/pdffiles1/nij/189908.pdf

138. Stevens, "Forensic Science, Prosecutor Discretion."

139. Briody, M. (2004). The effect of DNA evidence on homicide cases in court. *Australian and New Zealand Journal of Criminology, 37*(2), 231–252.

140. Wilson, "Crime Lab Investigation."

141. Wilson, "Centre for Criminal Justice."

142. Boese, A. (2004). *Hippo eats dwarf: A field guide to hoaxes and other B.S.* New York: Basic Books.

Motion Pictures, Popular Television Dramas, and News Reports

CHAPTER

2

I felt a certain amount of embarrassment about doing it [covering the trial] on a regular basis. Every time we did O.J., the ratings went up 10 percent.

Ted Koppel

▶ ▶ CHAPTER OBJECTIVES

- Provide a better understanding of the movie industry, popular television performances, news reports, and comic books
- Provide a description of the impact of the popular media on crime and the criminal justice process through the *CSI Effect*
- Provide information about what people watch on television and how they are affected by infotainment
- Share a characterization about journalism and pack journalism
- Provide a better understanding of the popular media among the American people and politics

■ Introduction

Chapter 1 presents the idea that the impact of the popular media through the *CSI Effect* changes real-world expectations of crime and crime control.

The American criminal justice system has entered a new period of crime control in which the behavior of policy makers, criminal justice practitioners, and the general population is increasingly shaped by technology. The mass media are a key part of that technology. Motion pictures, popular television dramas, news reports, comic books, and other means of popular communication are called mass media because they reach out and profoundly influence policy makers, criminal justice practitioners, and the masses. This chapter is dedicated to characterizing the fundamentals of the popular media and how these communicational devices relate to crime and crime control.

The chapter begins with a brief overview of the income-producing capabilities of the movie industry, and it provides an historic account of the motion picture industry and describes the movie industry's fascination with crime. The chapter compares the expenses of a family of four at the movies versus other forms of entertainment. Movie ratings are highlighted, and the top-grossing films of 2008 are featured. The most popular television dramas that are broadcast during a week are discussed, as are their audience numbers. The relationship between *infotainment*, politics, and the criminal justice community is described. The chapter also provides a description of what has become common practice among reporters: *pack journalism*, which is defined as a collection of behavior and conditions by which substantial groups of reporters from diverse and typically large media outlets collaborate in the same physical surroundings to cover the same story. Detailed in this chapter are the advantages of the popular media, which include promoting competency and justice efficiency in aiding in arrests, and the liberation of females and children across the globe.

■ Motion Pictures

Estimated highlights of the Motion Picture Association of America for 2008 are as follows:[1]

- $9.8 billon in domestic box office sales
- $28 billon in worldwide box office sales
- $106 million to make and market a major film ($66 million in negative costs and $34.5 million in marketing costs in 2007)
- 610 films released
- 1.4 billon tickets sold
- $31 million spent on advertising (11 percent newspapers, 35 percent television in 2007)

The movie industry's goal is cash flow and profit. Two strong explanations for its success are that moviegoers are satisfied and it's inexpensive entertainment. Most theaters have excellent access for commuters, seating is reasonably close to the screen, and parking is free; on the other hand, prime events, such as professional sporting events, are usually held in hard-to-get-to stadiums that are crowded with aggressive audiences, waiting lines for restrooms, security checks, exiting traffic jams, and police officers. Unless tickets have been purchased from the event facility's box office (if available), $10 to $35 is added to each ticket purchased through a ticket concession of some type, such as Ticketmaster. The overall costs of going to a movie are reasonable compared to stadium events; although movies might not be as memorable as stadium events (see Table 2-1). The average admission for other events varies: Football games are around $64 each, if you can get tickets; basketball games are $55 each, if you can get tickets; theme parks are $50, but you have to travel; NASCAR events are $118, and again you have to travel; and World

TABLE 2-1 COMPARATIVE ADMISSION: INDIVIDUAL AND FAMILY OF FOUR

Event	Cost per person (low to high, each)	Cost for family of four (least expensive ticket price)
Football game (NFL) (Indianapolis Colts, 2007)	$64–$1,200	$256 + parking + snacks
Basketball game (NBA) (Los Angeles Lakers, 2008)	$55–$1,400	$220 + parking + snacks
Theme park (Six Flags Over Georgia, Atlanta)	$50, kids $29	$158 + parking + snacks
Baseball game (MLB) (Boston Red Sox, 2008)	$25–$600	$100 + parking + snacks
Theater (Broadway Across America) (*Monty Python's Spamalot*, San Antonio, Texas, matinee)	$110–$268	$440 + parking + snacks
NASCAR (Daytona 500) (February 2008)	$118–$1,465	$472 + parking + snacks
WWE (Boston, Massachusetts, 2008)	$50–$803	$400 + parking + snacks
Movie	$10, kids $5	$30 + snacks

Source: Developed by the author (admission prices checked online at random on January 14, 2008).[2]

Wrestling Entertainment (WWE) events are $50, if you want to sit high above the action where you need binoculars to observe the smackdowns. Overall, the purchase price of snacks is huge. For instance, at a Boston Red Sox game (May, 2009), domestic beer was $7.50 and a hot dog was $5.50 (condiments consist of mustard and ketchup only). However, admission for a motion picture is around $10 for adults, $8 for students and seniors, and $5 for kids ($7.18 average ticket cost in 2008); and snacks are available and sometimes pricey, but you can sneak in a candy bar or two and a canned soft drink and not be subjected to the standard searches conducted at stadium events. Parking at stadium events is an added expense that can range from $15 to $59 per event, but parking at a movie theater is generally free, and it doesn't take forever to get home afterwards. Also, theaters run on schedule, whereby other event schedules are determined by numerous factors, including the weather which can be a serious issue if the event has a no-refund policy. It comes down to price, stress, and predictability.

History of Motion Pictures

Motion pictures blossomed in the 1920s, expanding on the foundations of film from earlier years.[3] Most American film productions at the start of the decade occurred in or near Hollywood, although some films were still being made in New Jersey and in Astoria on Long Island (Paramount). By the mid-1920s, motion pictures were big business (with a capital investment totaling over $2 billion), with some theaters offering double features. By the end of the decade, there were 20 Hollywood studios, and the demand for films was greater than ever. The greatest output of feature films occurred in the 1920s and 1930s, averaging about 800 film releases in a year, compared to 610 films in 2008.

Motion Picture Industry Today

America has an estimated 40,000 theaters, a third more than a decade ago.[4] The movie industry and theater operations are changing rapidly through digital equipment and competition. In an attempt to help monitor what is presented in the theaters, the movie industry rates the content of their films. For example, the film rating committee uses the following ratings:

- A G-rated motion picture contains nothing in theme, language, nudity, sex, violence, or other matters that would offend parents whose younger children view the motion picture. No nudity, sex scenes, or drug use are shown; violence is minimal.
- A PG-rated motion picture is suitable for children, but it has a more mature theme than some G-rated motion pictures. There may be some profanity, some depictions of violence that are not intense, or brief nudity. There is no drug use content in a PG-rated motion picture.
- A PG-13 rating is a sterner warning to parents to determine whether their children younger than age 13 years should view the motion picture because some material might not be suitable for them. PG-13 films may go beyond the PG rating in theme, violence, nudity, sensuality, language, adult activities, or other elements.
- An R-rated motion picture contains adult material—adult themes, adult activity, hard language, intense or persistent violence, sexually-oriented nudity, or drug abuse. Children younger than age 17 are not allowed to attend R-rated motion pictures unless accompanied by a parent or adult guardian.
- An NC-17-rated motion picture is one that most parents would consider patently too adult for their children aged 17 and younger. It does not mean that the film is obscene or pornographic.

In 2008, six of the top 10 grossing films were PG-13 rated, two were PG rated, and two were G rated, suggesting that viewers make decisions about which movies to see based on the rating. Those top 10 films are as follows (amounts are rounded millions)[5]:

1. *The Dark Knight*, $531, PG-13
2. *Iron Man*, $318, PG-13
3. *Indiana Jones & the Kingdom of the Crystal Skull*, $317, PG-13
4. *Hancock*, $228, PG-13
5. *Wall-E*, $224, G
6. *Kung-Fu Panda*, $215, PG
7. *Madagascar: Escape 2 Africa*, $177, PG
8. *Twilight*, $177, PG-13
9. *Quantum of Solace*, $167, PG-13
10. *Dr. Seuss' Horton Hears a Who*, $155, G

Movies and Crime

How many films display crime, violence, vigilantism, or lawlessness to portray the goals and stereotypes of criminals that could have influenced wrongful convictions? Largely, good versus evil [i.e., *The Dark Knight* and *Iron Man*], or morally appropriate versus inappropriate [*Twilight* and *Dr. Seuss' Horton Hears a Who*], are central themes of most films, depending on your point of view, but what is valued and rewarded relates to grossing or income rather than content. PG-rated movies produce a large flow of income as evidenced by the above data. There are few, if any, controls on what the motion picture industry does or how they do it. For example, a study at the Harvard School of Public Health suggests that movie ratings have grown more lenient over the past decade, and the evidence shows that movies have more violent and sexually explicit content and continue to be rated PG-13.[6] At times, ratings are "confusing and murky descriptions of movie content," says Sharon Waxman. Although a small percentage of all crimes known to the police involved sexual homicide or murder, almost 30 percent of all movie themes involved those topics, and the most-watched movies (and television performances) capitalize on murder and sexual assault, suggesting that these crimes are a daily routine.[7]

Motion pictures (similar to television) do more than capitalize on crime; they promote the cultural embeddedness of the emotional and sensual parameters that constitute the foreground of criminal activity. For example, an analysis of the film *Chicago* exposes the social circulation of important cultural motifs that help make sense of why certain kinds of emotional and sensual features might be attended to in the accounts of the commission of crimes by offenders.[8] Motion pictures and the media rewrite cultural history and justify the activity of the characters within the script. In *Chicago*, one way to interpret the cultural nuances of the day was to kill and tell. The implication is that killers of that era, at least female killers, would volunteer their guilt. In contrast, motion pictures set in the same era about Al Capone and the Mafia demonstrate a strict silence about mob murders.

The 1970s brought radical criticisms of police into mainstream America with films like *Serpico*, *Chinatown*, and *Policewomen*, which exposed police corruption and brutality. However, the 1970s ultimately led to new heroes. In *Death Wish*, Paul Kersey (Charles Bronson), a New York City architect, becomes a one-man vigilante squad after his wife is murdered by street thugs. He randomly stalks and kills would-be muggers on the streets after dark. *Dirty Harry* (Clint Eastwood) was a San Francisco detective who became a vigilante; he was brutal and violent, yet sympathetic. Movie viewers accepted Kersey and Dirty Harry because there was too much press about crime, and it was necessary to maintain the public perception that vigilantes, even among police officers, were necessary.[9]

This justification was developed in Hollywood then perfected years later by the Bush administration, which made the explicit argument that "we need cops (and soldiers and federal agents) to break the rules," as implied in Bruce Willis's *Die Hard* (1988) and *Live Free or Die Hard* (2007).[10] In fact, from this perspective, the rules that include the US Constitution are problematic and un-American. There are good people and there are criminals, and we don't need to worry about how the bad guys are treated. The job of keeping America safe is necessarily dirty, and the police need to break the rules to keep Americans safe, goes the reasoning.

■ Television

Television impacts the decisions made by policy makers and criminal justice practitioners and shapes public opinion. Television programmers face similar questions as politicians: Do Americans want to confront their problems or escape them? asked James Poniewozik in a summer 2009 *Time* article.[11]

However, programmers are often confused about what to program; therefore they program their version of reality which includes how individuals should behave, how individuals should misbehave, and what to do about it when they do. One political analyst explains the popular media's version of reality this way:

> The struggle over who gets what, when, and how is largely carried out in the mass media. Media power is concentrated in the leading television news networks (ABC, CBS, NBC, CNN), national newspapers (*Washington Post, New York Times, Wall St. Journal*), and newsmagazines (*Newsweek, Time, U.S. News & World Report*). Television is the first true mass communication medium because it is in virtually every home. .... Today the Internet is assuming the proportions of mass media, partly under the auspices of existing media as in the case of www.cnn.com or www.newsweek .com.[12(p321)]

What People Watch on Television

The following list shows the top 10 broadcast television programs compiled by Nielsen Media Research for the week of June 1–June 7, 2009[13]:

Top 10 Broadcast TV Rankings: June 1–June 7, 2009

Rank	Program Name	Network	Audience (millions)
1	*NBA FINALS ON ABC—GM 2(S)*	ABC	14,061
2	*NBA FINALS ON ABC—GM 1(S)*	ABC	13,042
3	*LAW AND ORDER: SVU*	NBC	11,562
4	*NCIS*	CBS	11,256
5	*MENTALIST, THE—TUESDAY*	CBS	10,875
6	*TWO AND A HALF MEN*	CBS	10,095
7	*NBC NEWS: OBAMA WH HOUSE*	NBC	9,169
8	*NBC NEWS: OBAMA WH HOUSE*	NBC	9,039
9	*60 MINUTES*	CBS	8,890
10	*LAW AND ORDER*	NBC	8,866

Of the top 10 Broadcast television performances during the week of June 1, 2009, five of those performances featured crime. Also, of the top 10 Cable television performances during the same week, the top performances included *Burn Notice, NCIS,* and *Law & Order* (3 crime dramas). And Nielsen Television (TV) Ratings for Primetime: Season-to-Date for the 2008–2009 Season Through 06/07/09 report nine of those programs related to crime.

Top 20 Primetime Network Series: 2008-2009 Season Through July 12, 2009

Rank	Program Name	Network	Audience (millions)	Episodes
1	*AMERICAN IDOL—WEDNESDAY*	FOX	16,542	19
2	*AMERICAN IDOL—TUESDAY*	FOX	15,823	17
3	*DANCING WITH THE STARS*	ABC	14,334	21
4	*DANCING W/STARS RESULTS*	ABC	11,930	17
5	*NBC SUNDAY NIGHT FOOTBALL*	NBC	11,804	16
6	*CSI*	CBS	11,700	30
7	*NCIS*	CBS	11,692	34
8	*MENTALIST, THE*	CBS	11,351	30
9	*DESPERATE HOUSEWIVES*	ABC	10,021	25
10	*60 MINUTES*	CBS	9,880	34
11	*CRIMINAL MINDS*	CBS	9,765	30
11	*GREY'S ANATOMY—THU 9PM*	ABC	9,690	30
11	*TWO AND A HALF MEN*	CBS	9,777	35

(continued)

Rank	Program Name	Network	Audience (millions)	Episodes
14	*CSI: MIAMI*	CBS	9,621	34
15	*CSI: NY*	CBS	9,115	29
16	*WITHOUT A TRACE*	CBS	8,897	28
17	*SURVIVOR: GABON*	CBS	8,728	11
18	*ELEVENTH HOUR*	CBS	8,321	21
19	*BACHELOR, THE*	ABC	8,222	9
20	*COLD CASE*	CBS	8,126	26

Source: Nielsen Media Research retrieved June 11, 2009, from http://tvlistings.zap2it.com/ratings/season.html

Finally, regarding the week of May 18–24, 2009, the top ten syndicated television performances included *Law & Order: SVU* and *CSI: NY*.

Television and Its Fascination with Crime

Television has long been fascinated with crime.[14] It is difficult to separate television news reports (discussed later in this chapter) from television dramas, yet to better understand television's impact on the American criminal justice system, it is helpful to do so. Popular television dramas have included crime as a prominent feature over the past several decades, report numerous experts.[15] Historically, prime-time television has devoted at least one-third of its time to crime, without counting news reports. Crime and law enforcement programs have virtually littered television programming for the past four decades and have included such diverse programs as *The Avengers; The Mod Squad; Kojak; Baretta; Hawaii Five-O; The Rockford Files; Dragnet; Starsky and Hutch; Columbo; Hill Street Blues; Magnum, P.I.; Cagney & Lacey; Simon & Simon; Miami Vice; T.J. Hooker; In the Heat of the Night; Murder, She Wrote; L.A. Law; The Commish; NYPD Blue; Walker, Texas Ranger; The X Files; Homicide; Law & Order; The Practice; Nash Bridges; JAG; Judging Amy; The Fugitive; The District; Level 9; The Job; Without a Trace;* and *Cold Case.*

Since the 1950s and 1960s, television dramas such as *Dragnet* and *Adam 12* have characterized the police as professionals walking a thin blue line of heroes who protect the good guys from the bad guys. The new generation of cops on film and TV—later refined and popularized by stars from Dennis Franz in *NYPD Blue* to Christopher Meloni in *Law & Order: Special Victims Unit* who portray troubled, violent, flawed, but ultimately sympathetic heroes—break the rules, but the rules are the problem. These cops torture people based on a hunch, and they are always right. The person they torture is always the guilty party, and the violent detectives always get information from torturing these individuals that they would not have gotten otherwise.

The addition of several new criminal-justice-type dramas to recent broadcast seasons, such as all the variations of *CSI* and *Law & Order*, enhance the public's fascination with crime. The question about both motion pictures and popular television dramas relates to validating the context of the presentations, which will never be successfully challenged because of the popularity of certain presentations and the income they produce. Then, too, one source suggests that American audiences tolerate the media's arrogance and lack of integrity because the media provides an entertainment value of great importance. Secretly, many viewers might like to beat up a sex offender, but those sex offenders might violently respond. One study shows that television producers pretty much do whatever they wish because of a lack of public outrage or legal sanctions.[16] Finally, although it would appear to be difficult to discover an accurate measure, one estimate is that American children and adolescents spend 22 to 28 hours per week viewing television, more than any other activity except sleeping. By the age of 70 years they will have spent 7 to 10 years of their lives watching TV, advises the Kaiser Family Foundation. Also, the total average time of television viewing per household from 2005 to 2006 was eight hours and 14 minutes per day.[17] As the dismal economy forced people to hunker down at home in the fall of 2008, Nielsen reported that the average person tuned in to 151 hours of TV per month.[18] Also, one source suggests that it takes an estimated 400 hours to develop a 30-minute segment of a popular television drama.

Television and Criminal Justice

In the world of criminal justice, offenders and victims are routinely processed, but those processes have been challenged in the 21st century through television dramas because criminal justice practice must deal with the delusional *CSI Effect* and unprofessional practices of police officers, prosecutors, and jailers.[19,20] In the 20th century, the media developed its full capacity for influencing the public in Europe and North America, but in the 21st century, television performances are one of the main means to inform as well as to manipulate the public.

Television Infotainment and Politics

Infotainment employed by the media includes television's focus on the "deception" of crime and the criminal justice processes, experts argue.[21] Infotainment relates to the deception of celebrity crimes, suggesting that those crimes are individual issues (Paris Hilton, Lindsay Lohan, Hugh Grant), the deception of corporate celebrities who are in trouble (often short-term fraud events), and the deception of long-term concealment of fraud that illustrates incompetence on the part of business and governmental regulatory authorities. In this regard, for instance, the billions of dollars of federal stimulus money provided to corporations ranging from AT&T to Dell to FedEx to Tyson Foods have little media attention, yet the corporate mismanagement of equally giant corporations, such as AIG and General Motors, take center stage. Infotainment suggests that the global economic downturn is emphasized by the media and ignores the continued accumulated power that has been derived during the economic downturn by drug, oil, and communication cartels. There are many corporate and individual winners in a global economic downturn, yet the popular media decides what is news or entertainment and what isn't.

Then, too, television executives decide which realities are high profile and merit attention.[22] For example, Princess Diana died within days (August 31, 1997) of a real hero in comparison—Mother Teresa (September 5, 1997), a Nobel Peace Prize recipient. Yet one estimate shows that over a 10-year period (1997 to 2007), 124 American prime-time television programs featured Princess Diana, compared to 12 programs that featured Mother Teresa, and an estimated 197 articles featured Princess Diana, compared to 47 articles about Mother Teresa.[23] Ironically, the People's Princess, as Diana is called, was buried holding a set of rosary beads given to her by Mother Teresa weeks before. To better explain this perspective, noted columnist Erma Bombeck suggested not to "confuse fame with success. Madonna is one, Helen Keller is the other."

Said another way, Barb Neff from Santa Monica, California, expresses her thoughts that "members of the media never grasp that they are not representative of the country as a whole."

Nonetheless, infotainment has been successfully employed as a deception of reality in the United States, and in the United Kingdom. For example, the East German police program *Polizeiruf 110*, which was broadcast from 1971 to 2005, showed how the state used the entertainment media to promote particular perspectives about crime, police, society, and the state.[24] The name "*Polizeiruf 110*" means "police call 110," which is the number to be called for emergency police service (such as 999 in the United Kingdom and 911 in the United States). The name not only made every child memorize this number but also demonstrated that all crime was dealt with by the ordinary, or rank and file, police officer rather than special departments, such as crime–gang units. In the United Kingdom, the long-running program *The Bill*, a televised version of police work, contains a more soaplike emphasis on ongoing hidden agenda story lines, and *Prime Suspect* police dramas attempt to tackle hard-hitting social issues, including racism, child abuse, and homophobia. In the United States, *CSI* prime-time dramas employ forensic technology that has yet to be fully operational (or budgeted) in routine police investigations. It is implied that forensic science is the benchmark of good policing when, in fact, most officers (62 percent) across the nation are patrol officers assigned to traffic and provide police service to 911 calls, reports the Bureau of Justice Statistics.[25]

Infotainment comes in many forms. The media thinks that their position takes priority over public safety—that is, the media has demonstrated its position on entertainment versus public safety. For example, Nester DeJesus shot a Tampa police officer with a semiautomatic weapon, took a hostage, and hid in a downtown building. During negotiations with Sergeant John Bennett, DeJesus continually asked about the condition of Officer Lois Marrero, the officer he had shot, but she died as a result of the earlier gunfight. Negotiations broke down when DeJesus learned the truth from a television news report. Bennett thought the truth would put DeJesus in a more dangerous frame of mind. "Once they know someone is dead," Bennett said, "it's easier to kill again."[26]

■ News Reports

News stories are designed to entertain, as demonstrated by the news organizations' priority to dominate their presentations with crime reports that are featured as action news, suggests Gilliam and Iyengar.[27] The prevalence of this type of reporting has led to a crime narrative, or script, regarding certain truths about crime. News reporters and media management can easily distort and adversely affect police activities both on the set and in the streets, even to a point of reinforcing wars on crime and junkies (see Chapter 3), wars on sex offenders and poverty (see Chapter 4), and the war on immigrants (see Chapter 5).

What Is Journalism?

There are many experts who can address this question in a reasonable manner; however, two perspectives that greatly characterize journalism are those of Tony Harcup, who argued that the basic task of journalism lies in the effort to create publicness (i.e., to override barriers of social communication),[28] and Karen Sanders, who argued that journalism exists just to tell the truth.[29] The realities of criminal justice practitioners' experiences can be distorted, sometimes unintentionally and sometimes through error or intention by news reporters. Are news reports truthful? Richard Salent, former president of CBS News, said, "Our job is to give people not what they want, but what we decide they ought to have," and Rubin Frank, former president of NBC News, said, "News is what someone wants to suppress. Everything else is advertising."[30] Consistent with these thoughts are the resignations of reporters and editors from national newspapers, such as Patricia Smith (a Pulitzer Prize finalist) of the *Boston Globe* and her editor, Stephen Glass, in a separate allegation of plagiarism.[31] Additionally, Dan Rather resigned from CBS because he misrepresented the facts. Then, too, Jayson Blair of the *New York Times* resigned after being caught fictionalizing some of his best stories and reporting interviews with people he had never met.[32]

Regardless, news reporters continue to deceive the public and boldly tell their audience what criminal justice is and how it works. For example, when Dr. Gary Bell, a Seattle-based forensic odontologist (an expert who compares bite marks), conducted a workshop in New York City, the *New York Post* and the *New York Times* published stories about the workshop, referring to it as a study (empirical evidence). The *New York Post* article reported that "Examiners in one [bite mark] study falsely identified an innocent person as the biter 63 percent of the time."[33] According to Bell, it was careless and improper for any statistical inferences regarding error rate or reliability to have been drawn from the data, which must have been provided to media representatives, much to his surprise.[34] A source suggested that even the use of the *New York Post*'s title, "Clueless Crime Labs" and the phrase "falsely identified an innocent person" in the *New York Times* story were misrepresentations and untruths when describing the results of the so-called study.[35] Bell added that the workshop had nothing to do with innocence, which would remain a legal issue, and one concern was that if potential jurors saw those articles, how would the articles impact the jurors' future decisions? These facts are telling and reveal that many news agencies make efforts to regulate themselves, but news agencies continue to deceive the public in many ways; for example, consider the common practice of pack journalism.

Pack Journalism

A common practice among reporters who are covering an event is pack journalism, which can be defined as "a collection of behavior and conditions by which substantial groups of reporters from diverse and typically large media outlets collaborate in the same physical surroundings to cover the same story," states Gerald-Mark Breen and Jonathan Matusitz.[36] Pack reporters cite or draw from the same available information simultaneously, generally with the same intention and the same "pack-like instincts,"[37(p137)] and they execute the same gathering and reporting methods.[38] Reporters flock like a cluster of birds, where each journalist observes carefully what the other journalists are writing, doing, and highlighting. The journalists often travel from mega-event to mega-event, lodge together in a closely linked group of hotels overlooking the streets, and congregate outside of courthouses, other government buildings, or at an accident scene. Typically, their primary goal is to obtain comments from the important sources and individuals.[39,40] Modern reporting, as evidenced by the national elections of 2008, is integrated into traditional political journalism,[41] which produces agenda setting whereby some observers have argued that it produces flawed and highly manipulated news.[42–44] Breen and Matusitz report that:

> Pack journalists, or those who implement the practice, are at fault, because they perpetuate questionable issues of journalistic laziness, short-term and long-term misguidance and paranoia to readers and viewers (due to sensationalizations and the redundant reporting styles), an increased invasion of privacy into celebrities and citizens who become the focus of news events, a reduction of independence in news reporting, the potential hazard of lost credibility in the content of news reported by packs, and economic and fiscal mismanagement.

Pack reporting can result in a loss of independent reporting and can be explained by a type of groupthink, offered Irving Janis.[45] A group mentality can yield news coverage in a one-sided manner; it has also nearly eradicated the credibility of the news through the employment of deceptive and excessive expression.[46,47] One expert observed that it is "easier to file the same story as their colleagues. They can share the research, the cab fare, the information, and the work—and in some cases the ignorance."[48] Peter McWilliams clarifies that "the news media are, for the most part, the bringers of bad news . . . and it's not entirely the media's fault; bad news gets higher ratings and sells more papers than good news."[49]

News reporters and their editors influence public opinion. They deny their power, "claiming they only mirror society; but the 'myth of the mirror' is that the media do play key roles in setting the American political agenda by determining what news is to be covered, how much, and in what context."[50(p321)]

■ Comic Books

Comic book protagonists restore public order by returning the community to a constructed, nostalgic ideal, or status quo—the way things used to be.[51] The implied message delivered in comic books is one of vigilantism, in which "moral justice trumps legitimate criminal procedure," argue Nickie D. Phillips and Stacie Strobl.[52] Based on a content analysis of 20 contemporary best-selling comic books, themes of organized crime, often involving complex transnational networks, are more prevalent than street crimes. However, the response to crime remains focused on vigilante methods and on the restoration of traditional lifestyles.

■ Power of the Media

Nancy Marion says that "it is obvious that the media's impact on criminal justice and public opinion can be enormous."[53(p111)] Marion describes several powers of the media that can affect the criminal justice policy process[54(pp290–297)]:

- Influencing public opinion: People form an opinion about justice policy based on what they see about crime in the media.
- Influencing and shaping public and political agendas: The media can select the issues they wish to draw attention to.
- Whistle-blowing: The media oversees the actions of individuals, including politicians, and reporters can investigate these actions to determine if any wrongdoing has taken place.
- Causing crime: The media can influence the behavior of individuals when they show violent acts that can be copied by others, and children are more likely to be violent or aggressive after watching violent television programs.[55] Conversely, it would seem that child viewers could emulate other children's achievements.
- Influencing trials: Trial by media implies that the media can provide extensive coverage of a situation or a person's relationship before a case comes to trial and ultimately impact juries and judges, such as O.J. Simpson and the impeachment trial of President William Clinton.[56]
- Deterring future criminal behavior: Information about the plight of other criminals can deter potential criminals from committing crimes.
- Helping fight crime: Public service announcements about issues such as the dangers associated with drug abuse and intoxicated drivers and programs such as McGruff the Crime Dog can alleviate some criminal activities.

■ Advantages of the Popular Media

The advantages of the popular media include its entertainment value, its growth of corporate America by advertising and displaying products and services, and its lifestyle choices among audiences. The media also provides other advantages as discussed in the following sections:

Promotes Competency

A pilot study of incompetent defendants who participated in a program that used videotaped segments of the television crime drama *Law & Order*, among other techniques, was employed to promote their competency to stand trial. The study showed marked improvements in the areas of understanding, reasoning, and appreciation.[57] Another study explored the utility of newspaper articles as an alternative data source to learn about litigation against the police and government agencies. Data were obtained from a content analysis of articles published in the *Los Angeles Times*, the *New York Times*, and the *Chicago Sun-Times* from 1993 to 2003.[58] Newspaper articles can be accessed electronically, and data collection techniques are relatively inexpensive and quick. Because most newspapers are archived, they can provide an historic perspective for lawsuits; equally important, they can provide general information linked to real estate purchases and issues, employment, and health issues. When purchasing a home or relocating, newspaper archives and the Internet are available to help individuals make informed decisions.

Promotes Justice Efficiency

The media pushes the justice community to become more efficient; for example, in *CSI: Miami*, Episode 84, "The Score," a zNose is used in the drama, demonstrating its incredible potential as a new electric sensor device employed by the US Department of Homeland Security and local police departments (who have also learned of this new product) to detect and analyze vapors and identify trace particles.[59]

Positive Health Messages

Popular TV shows and movies receive PRISM Awards for scientific accuracy in showing tobacco, alcohol, and drug abuse. Entertainment industry leaders and more than 50 entertainment programs were recognized at the Second Annual PRISM Awards ceremony in Hollywood for their outstanding efforts to accurately depict the science of drug, alcohol, and tobacco abuse and addiction. "HHS Secretary, Donna Shalala, said, 'We need to stand up and applaud when the power of television and film is used to help deliver positive health messages. The entertainment industry can help educate all Americans, and especially younger people, about the good choices they can make for their health, and the real-life consequences of bad choices.'"[60]

Problem-Solving Advantages

A study shows that certain viewers may be particularly influenced by fictional media portrayals and can learn and understand the content at a deeper level, thereby enhancing their own problem-solving efforts in real-life situations.[61]

Helps with Arrests

Television crime dramas can help people to recognize suspicious behavior and report it to the police. The following is such an example:

> The local newspaper, *The Free Lance-Star*, reported the discovery of a body in a dumpster outside a motel. The following day, the paper reported the arrest of the murderer, thanks in part to the quick action of one of the motel residents. While police were securing the crime scene, one of the by-standers was approached by a man who asked her what was going on. When she told him about the body, he ran across the street and jumped onto a waiting van. She later told a reporter that she had "watched enough *Law & Order* episodes to know suspicious behavior when she sees it." She got out her camera-phone and started taking photographs of the man and the license plate on the van. The police downloaded the photos, tracked down the van, and had the killer in custody 39 hours after the discovery of the body.[62]

Holds Government Accountable

The media's role in the policy evaluation stage is the "most important when they force government to be held accountable for its action," say Marion and Oliver.[63] For example, the media exposed the possibility that Mike Nifong, a North Carolina prosecutor, withheld evidence and mishandled a rape case against three Duke University lacrosse players, resulting in his disbarment, disgrace, and ultimate bankruptcy. It was implied by the media that Nifong pressed the rape case to boost his reelection chances in a contested Democratic primary.[64] Another example can be typified by the chief justice of the supreme court in West Virginia, who vacationed on the French Riviera with the CEO of Massey Energy, which had millions of dollars' worth of appeals before the West Virginia court. Thanks to an ABC News investigation, photos of the judge and CEO surfaced showing them on vacation together in France and Monaco.[65]

Furthers Western Democratic Ideals and Literacy

The media furthers Western democratic ideals, including capitalism and individuality, argues Kuldip R. Rampal.[66] The demise of totalitarianism in the former Soviet Union and its Eastern European satellite states in the early 1990s provided added opportunities for liberal democratic systems and market economies in economically and politically closed societies. Rampal advises that those opportunities provided media liberalization and media globalization. Marshall McLuhan's projected global village is increasingly a reality, made possible by the communication revolution—satellite and cable television, multinational media conglomerates, such as those of Rupert Murdoch and Time Warner Communications, and, increasingly, the Internet.[67]

Trade Liberalization and Economic Growth

Largely through American media, opportunities are provided around the globe for people to become consumers of media entertainment, which can result in a rise of literacy levels in Asian, African, and former Soviet countries. In this context, the media includes entertainment software. For example, Crandall and Sidak reported that in 2004 revenues for entertainment software products and directly-related accessories were $10.5 billion. In 2004, US sales of entertainment software reached $8.2 billion; total world sales reached $25.4 billion (in addition to the previously discussed movie worldwide totals).[68] One implication of this perspective is that the American media industry has continued to participate in the expansion of democracy and economic liberalization since the 1990s. One obvious concern is that global media corporations "transmit their Western images and commercial values directly into the brains of 75 percent of the world's population. The globalization of media imagery is surely the most effective means ever for cloning cultures to make them compatible with the Western corporate vision."[69] Specifically, cultural imperialism or cultural dependency occurs with the Western countries' influence through the media and technology on the language, values, and attitudes (including religion), ways of organizing public life, styles of politics, forms of education and professional training, clothing styles, and many other cultural habits that include health and positive environments.

Provides Attention to Crime and Guides Legislation

The media's participation in reporting and investigating sexual assault and domestic violence can ultimately aid in specific legislation to protect children, such as Megan's Law and mandatory arrest policies. For example, in New York, the Family Protection and Domestic Violence Intervention Act of 1994, similar to legislation in other states, was enacted to enhance the protection of victims through the arrest and prosecution of domestic violence offenders. Nationally, the movement toward mandatory arrest policies for domestic violence was a response to centuries of arrest avoidance practices.[70]

Aids in Liberation of Females and Children

Of equal interest, the influence of the American media and its cultural presentation of American ideals circle the planet, which includes, if not equality, the seeds of liberation for women and children. Efforts are also under way to deal with the smuggling of children and women to benefit sexual exploitation, perhaps in part through the contributions of the media. Many nations are attempting to pass laws and enforcement policies in an effort to deal with family violence and human trafficking and, in part, require the media's support to aid them in this endeavor. For example, it is clear that violence against women is being given a higher priority, with increasing numbers of police authorities establishing special units to protect women and deal with human trafficking in the United States as well as other countries, from the Scandinavian Peninsula to South Africa to Bangladesh. For example, the Scandinavian countries (which include Denmark, Finland, Iceland, Norway, and Sweden) and Bangladesh are debating new laws to protect women,[71,72] and South Africa is well on its way to creating specialized human trafficking legislation that will protect women and children. It is a signatory to the United Nations Protocol to Prevent, Suppress, and Punish Trafficking in Persons, Especially Women and Children, and the South African Law Reform Commission is currently investigating the issues.[73]

Some Tentative Thoughts About the Popular Media

The popular media shapes public opinion and ultimately behavior[74,75]; in some respects the popular media and the criminal justice community operate in concert with each other by the media reporting on criminal justice policy (regardless of the quality of the policy) and practices, and criminal justice policy shaping what the media reports on (regardless of the accuracy of the reports).[76] Therefore, policy and practices are inseparable from the interests, goals, and expectations of the American public. Although it seems reasonable that the popular media defines their version of crime and what to do about it, maybe Americans relate to those versions when it serves a purpose to do so because there are other powerful social institutions that help shape behavior.[77] A person who gets assaulted at a park, for example, because a suspect observed a movie jammed with violence, appears to represent an avoidance of the consequences of the suspect's action rather than a primary factor leading to the crime—it's an excuse. "Excuses are socially approved vocabularies for mitigating or relieving responsibility when conduct is questioned," argues Stanford M. Lyman and Marvin B. Scott.[78] The popular media provides a way out of personal accountability, which may be one reason crime had declined in recent years. Nonetheless, intrinsic to this thought (which includes employing the media as a scapegoat) is the give and take among policy, media, politics, and public opinion, resulting in the media's descriptions of crime and justice, the acceptance (and in some cases tolerance) of the criminal justice community and the public, and a way out of the consequences of our actions. The advantages of the popular media are its entertainment value to its audiences, its opportunities for corporate growth, and its choices that can enhance lifestyles and relationships. As you wander through the pages of the following chapters and examine the thoughts, studies, and anecdotes, the following thought should remain predominant:

> The media can provide more choices (and often better choices than its audience experiences), but final decisions about behavior, for most of us, are conscious decisions made by the individual.[78]

■ Summary

This chapter discussed the motion picture industry, popular television dramas, news reports, and comic books. It explained some of the historic accounts about motion pictures and reported the top-grossing films in terms of millions of dollars. What people watch on television was discussed along with the media's fascination with crime and crime control. Television infotainment and its impact on politics were presented. News reports, journalism, and pack journalism were characterized.

It was suggested that the media can affect criminal justice policy by shaping public opinion. People form an opinion about justice policy based on what they see about crime in the media; the media can select the issues they wish to draw attention to; and the media can act as a whistle-blower, particularly overseeing the actions of individuals, including politicians, and reporters can investigate these people to determine if any wrongdoing has taken place. Conversely, the media can also enhance crime by influencing the behavior of individuals when they perform violent acts that can be emulated by others, particularly children; the media can influence trials, or trial by media, which implies that the media can provide extensive coverage of a situation or a person's relationship before a case comes to trial; the media can help deter future criminal behavior through information about the plight of other criminals; and finally the media helps fight crime through public service announcements about issues such as the dangers associated with drug abuse and intoxicated drivers.

The advantages of the popular media worldwide include the promotion of competency and justice efficiency, and it can represent a positive health message. It can also aid in problem-solving strategies and the arrest process, help keep American government accountable, further Western democratic ideals and literacy, and provide attention to crime and guide meaningful legislation. Finally, the media aids in trade liberalization and economic growth, and it can aid in the liberation of females and children across the globe. The popular media shapes public opinion and ultimately behavior; in addition, official policy and practices are inseparable from the interests, goals, and expectations of the American public.

Overall, the media provides more choices, and sometimes better choices, than its audience experiences, but it was emphasized that the final decision about committing a crime has more to do with individual choice rather than what is seen in the media.

References

1. Motion Picture Association of America. (2008). Retrieved June 9, 2009 from http://www. mpaa.org/2008%20MPAA%20Theatrical%20Market%20Statistics.pdf

2. For example, in October 2008, my daughter (Alyssa P. Stevens) and I attended a Bruins hockey game in Boston. The costs were as follows: tickets, $245 each, second row, off center, near the glass; beers, $7; candy, $5; hot dogs, $5; cab to the hotel, $20; hotel $250 per night. (Night with my daughter–priceless!)

3. Dirks, T. (2006). *Film history of the 1920s*. Retrieved July 25, 2007, from http://www.filmsite. org/20sintro.html

4. "Digital Technology Is Changing Cinema." Economist.com. (2007, July 14). *The final frontier*. Retrieved June 9, 2009, from http://www.economist.com/business/displaystory.cfm?story_ id=9495437

5. Motion Picture Association of America, http://www.mpaa.org.

6. Waxman, S. (2004, July 14). Television study finds film ratings are growing more lenient. *New York Times*. Retrieved July 27, 2007, from http://select.nytimes.com/gst/abstract.html? res=F50A15F9345F0C778DDDAE0894DC404482&n=Top%2fReference%2fTimes%20Topi cs%2fOrganizations%2fM%2fMotion%20Picture%20Association%20of%20America

7. Beckett, K., & Sasson, T. (2000). *The politics of injustice*. Thousand Oaks, CA: Pine Forge Press.

8. O'Brien, M., Tzanelli, R., & Yar, M. (2005). Kill-n-tell (& all that jazz): The seductions of crime in Chicago. *Crime, Media, Culture, 1*(3), 243–261.

9. Flaherty, J. (2007, September 14). *K-Ville* makes police brutality acceptable. *Znet*. Retrieved September 31, 2007, from http://www.zmag.org

10. Flaherty, "*K-Ville* Makes Police Brutality."

11. Poniewozik, J. (2009, June 1). Change the channel. With their new schedules, TV networks try to figure out how to deliver good times in hard times. *Time, 173*(21), 22.

12. Dye, T. R. (2007). *Politics in America, basic edition* (7th ed.). Upper Saddle River, NJ: Prentice Hall.

13. Nielsen. (n.d.). *Top TV ratings*. Week of June 1, 2009. Retrieved June 11, 2009, from http:// blog.nielsen.com/nielsenwire/tag/law-and-order/

14. Soulliere, D. M. (2002). Prime-time murder: Presentations of murder on popular television justice programs. *Journal of Criminal Justice and Popular Culture, 10*(1), 12–38.

15. Soulliere, "Prime-Time Murder."

16. Bracken, C. C. (2006). Perceived source credibility of local television news: The impact of television form and presence. *Journal of Broadcasting & Electronic Media, 50*(4), 723–741.

17. Kaufman, R. (2007). *Kill your television*. Retrieved June 10, 2009 from http://www. turnoffyourtv.com/".

18. Nielsen Wire. Americans watching more TV than ever. Retrieved June 10, 2009, from http:// blog.nielsen.com/nielsenwire/tag/tv-viewership/

19. Rauxloh, R. (2005). Goodies and baddies: The presentation of German police and criminals in East and West television drama. *German Law Journal, 6*(6). Retrieved June 10, 2009, from http://www.germanlawjournal.com/article.php?id=607.

20. Wilson, D. (2006, September 14). Crime lab investigation. *The Guardian*. Retrieved January 14, 2008, from http://www.guardian.co.uk/commentisfree/story/0,1871923,00.html

21. Levi, M. (2006). The media construction of financial white-collar crimes. *British Journal of Criminology, 46*(6), 1037–1057.

22. Chancer, L. S. (2005). *High-profile crimes: When legal cases become social causes.* Chicago: University of Chicago Press.

23. A review by the author of *TV Guide* during that period in the 12 largest American cities and a review of the *New York Times, Los Angeles Times, Chicago Tribune, Houston Chronicle, Washington Post, San Francisco Chronicle, Atlanta Journal, Boston Globe, Cincinnati Enquirer, Miami Herald,* and others, also over a 10-year period (1997 to 2007).

24. Rauxloh, "Goodies and Baddies."

25. Bureau of Justice Statistics. (n.d.). *Local police departments, 2003* (NCJ 210118). Washington, DC: US Department of Justice. Retrieved January 8, 2008, from http://www.ojp.usdoj.gov/bjs/abstract/lpd03.htm

26. Herdy, A., & Deggans, E. (2001, July 15). Police, TV media see shooting differently. *St. Petersburg Times*. Retrieved June 11, 2006, from http://www.sptimes.com/News/071501/TampaBay/Police_TV_media_see_.shtml

27. Gilliam, F. D., Jr., & Iyengar, S. (2000). Prime suspects: The influence of local television news on the viewing public. *American Journal of Political Science, 44*(3), 560–573.

28. Harcup, T. (2004). *Journalism: Principles and practice.* London: Sage.

29. Sanders, K. (2003). *Ethics and journalism.* London: Sage.

30. The Press Room. (n.d.). *Media distortions.* Retrieved June 14, 2006, from http://www.whatreallyhappened.com/RANCHO/LIE/lie.html

31. Coverup at the *Boston Globe* (nd). Retrieved June 10, 2009, from http://www.transparencynow.com/globe3.htm

32. Mostert, M. (2005, February 25). *Weeding out reporters who lie.* Retrieved May 22, 2008, from http://www.renewamerica.us/columns/mostert/050225

33. Hamilton, B., & Cohen, S. (2008, September 21). Clueless and crime labs: Pros slam *CSI* as junk. *New York Post.* Retrieved October 16, 2008, from http://www.nypost.com/seven/09212008/news/nationalnews/clueless_crime_labs_130091.htm

34. Crime Lab Report. (2008, October 15). Crime labs under police unresolved issues. *Crime Lab Report, 2*(10). Retrieved October 20, 2008, from http://www.crimelabreport.com:80/library/monthly_report/10-2008.htm

35. Santos, F. (2007, January 28). Evidence from bite marks, it turns out, is not so elementary. *New York Times.* Retrieved October 16, 2008, from http://www.nytimes.com/2007/01/28/weekinreview/28santos.html?_r=2&oref=slogin&oref=slogin

36. Breen, G. M., & Matusitz, J. (2008). Communicating the negative aspects of pack journalism to media reporting. *Global Media Journal, 7*(12). Retrieved May 22, 2008, from http://lass.calumet.purdue.edu/cca/gmj/sp08/gmj-sp08-breen-matusitz.htm

37. McNair, B. (2000). *Journalism and democracy: An evaluation of the political public sphere.* New York: Routledge.

38. Sanders, *Ethics and Journalism.*

39. Frank, R. (2003). These crowded circumstances: When pack journalists bash pack journalism. *Journalism, 4*(4), 441–458.

40. Glascock, J. (2004). The Jasper dragging death: Crisis communication and the community newspaper. *Communication Studies, 55*(1), 29–47.

41. Rosenstiel, T. (2005). Political polling and the new media culture. *Public Opinion Quarterly, 69*(5), 698–715.

42. Frank, "These Crowded Circumstances."

43. Broder, D. S. (2000). *Behind the front page.* New York: Simon & Schuster.

44. Sanders, *Ethics and Journalism.*

45. Janis, I. L. (1972). *Victims of groupthink: A psychological study of foreign policy decisions and fiascos.* Boston: Houghton Mifflin.

46. Frank, "These Crowded Circumstances."

47. Stoddard, A. B. (2005). The new pack journalism. *Congressional Quarterly, 63*(11), 1–11.

48. Ben-David, L. (2000). *Why are they saying all those terrible things about Israel?* New York: Routledge.

49. Thinkexist.com. *Peter McWilliams quotes.* Retrieved June 12, 2009, from http://thinkers.net/forum/showthread.php?t=3584

50. Dye, *Politics in America.*

51. Phillips, N. D., & Strobl, S. (2006). Cultural criminology and kryptonite: Apocalyptic and retributive constructions of crime and justice in comic books. *Crime, Media, Culture, 2*(3), 304–331.

52. Phillips & Strobl, "Cultural Criminology and Kryptonite."

53. Marion, N. E. (1995). *A primer in the politics of criminal justice.* New York: Harrow and Heston.

54. Marion, N. E., & Oliver, W. M. (2008). *The public policy of crime and criminal justice.* Upper Saddle River, NJ: Pearson.

55. Parenti, M. (1992). *Make-believe media: The politics of entertainment.* Belmont, CA: Wadsworth.

56. Linder, D. O. (2009). *Famous trials.* Retrieved June 10, 2009, from http://www.law.umkc.edu/faculty/projects/ftrials/ftrials.htm

57. Montgomery, J., & Brooks, M. H. (2005). Use of a television crime-drama series to promote legal understanding in mentally ill, incompetent defendants: A pilot study. *Journal of Forensic Sciences, 50*(2), 465–469.

58. Archbold, C. A. (2006). Newspaper accounts of lawsuits involving the police: An alternative data source. *Journal of Crime & Justice, 29*(2), 1–23.

59. TV.Com. (2007). *CSI: Miami.* Retrieved August 22, 2007, from http://www.tv.com/csi-miami/show/8460/summary.html

60. National Institutes of Health. (1998, May 5). *Popular TV shows and movies receive Prism Awards for scientific accuracy in showing tobacco, alcohol, and drug abuse entertainment.* Retrieved July 27, 2007, from http://www.nih.gov/news/pr/may98/nida-05.htm

61. Calvert, S. L., Strouse, G. A., & Murray, K. J. (2006). Empathy for adolescents' role model selection and learning of DVD content. *Journal of Applied Developmental Psychology, 27*(5), 444–455.

62. Internet Movie Database. (2007). *Law & Order*. Retrieved October 8, 2007, from http://www. imdb.com/title/tt0098844/

63. Marion & Oliver, *Public Policy of Crime*.

64. McCarty, D., & Feeley, J. (2008, January 15). Nifong, Duke lacrosse prosecutor, files bankruptcy (Update 3). *Bloomberg*. Retrieved May 11, 2008, from http://www.bloomberg.com/apps/ news?pid=20601079&refer=home&sid=aCZsc7aJFP5k

65. Sauer, M. (2008, May 14). W. Va. chief justice had vacationed with CEO seeking overturn of $70 million judgment. *ABC News*. Retrieved May 15, 2008, from http://abcnews.go.com/ Blotter/story?id=4852923&page=1

66. Rampal, K. R. (2005). Cultural imperialism or economic necessity?: The Hollywood factor in the reshaping of the Asian film industry. *Global Media Journal, 4*(6). Retrieved May 22, 2008, from http://lass.calumet.purdue.edu/cca/gmj/sp05/gmj-sp05-rampal.htm

67. McLuhan, M., & Powers, B. (1988). *The global village: Transformations in world life and media in the 21st century*. London: Oxford University Press.

68. Crandall, R. W., & Sidak, J. G. (2006). *Video games: Serious business for America's economy*. Retrieved May 23, 2008, from http://search.ssrn.com/sol3/papers.cfm?abstract_id=969728

69. Merrill, J. C. (2005). Professionalization: Fusion of media freedom and responsibility. *Global Media Journal, 4*(6). Retrieved May 23, 2008, from http://lass.calumet.purdue.edu/cca/gmj/ sp05/gmj-sp05-merrill.htm

70. New York State's Response to Domestic Violence. (2006). *Systems and services making a difference*. New York: State of New York. Retrieved June 10, 2009, from http://www.opdv.state.ny.us/ whatisdv/about_dv/nyresponse/nysdv.pdf

71. Lindstrom, P. (2004). Violence against women in Scandinavia: A description and evaluation of two new laws aiming to protect women. *Journal of Scandinavian Studies in Criminology and Crime Prevention, 5*(2), 220–235.

72. Naved, R. T., & Persson, L. A. (2005). Factors associated with spousal physical violence against women in Bangladesh. *Studies in Family Planning, 36*(4), 289–300.

73. Pithey, B. (2004). Do new crimes need new laws? Legal provisions available for prosecuting human trafficking. *SA Crime Quarterly, 9*, 7–10.

74. Woods, J. (2005). The common enemy rationale: An attempt to apply concepts of cognitive consistency to the portrayals of the United States in the foreign press. *Global Media Journal, 4*(7). Retrieved May 22, 2008, from http://lass.calumet.purdue.edu/cca/gmj/fa05/gmj-fa05-woods.htm

75. Converse, P. E. (1990). Popular representation of information. In J. A. Ferejohn & J. H. Kuklinski (Eds.), *Information and democratic process*. Urbana: University of Illinois Press.

76. Iyengar, S., & McGrady, J. (2007). *Media politics: A citizen's guide*. New York: W. W. Norton.

77. Asimow, M., & Mader, S. (2004). *Law and popular culture: A course book*. New York: Peter Lang.

78. Lyman, S. M., & Scott, M. B. (1989). *A sociology of the absurd* (2nd ed.). Dix Hills, NY: General Hall.

79. Gottfredson, M. R., & Hirschi, T. (1990). *A general theory of crime*. Stanford, CA: Stanford University.

Wars on Crime and Junkies

CHAPTER 3

Be careful when you fight the monsters, lest you become one; and if you gaze for long into an abyss, the abyss gazes also into you.

Friedrich Nietzsche

▶ ▶ CHAPTER OBJECTIVES

- Describe the war on crime and the media's version of crime
- Characterize the social interactionist perspective and its application
- Identify civil liability litigation against police departments and the litigation strategy of police departments against gangs
- Characterize the war on junkies and the media's version of drug addiction
- Identify the consequences of the wars on crime and junkies upon criminal justice strategies

■ Introduction

The previous chapters characterized the media's incredible efforts to contribute to better lifestyle choices among Americans, but through the *CSI Effect*, realities become blurred and expectations about crime and law enforcement change in unexpected ways.

Most of us do pretty well separating fantasy from reality, yet the wise Friedrich Nietzsche suggests that if the criminal justice community is not cautious when delivering services, the consequences can be devastating. It will be argued in this chapter that attractive criminal justice strategies characterized by the popular media often depict reactive (as opposed to proactive and preventive) criminal justice initiatives during the wars on crime and junkies, the wars on sex offenders and poverty (Chapter 4), and the war on immigrants (Chapter 5), which enhance wrongful convictions and validate violent behavior, including the death penalty. That is, the popular media plays an ultimate role in the performance of the justice community (i.e., state and local police, prosecutors, courts, and corrections) by favoring, for example, aggressive reactive justice tactics that can border on unconstitutional intrusions; vigilantism by officers and the public, which furthers constitutional violations; and fictitious accounts of crime, crime control, and the criminal justice process. The war on crime and the war on junkies have political and social implications that alter public safety outcomes to include greater public disrespect for enforcement and more civil litigation, fewer rights for targeted groups, and larger prison populations, which can easily impact wrongful conviction rates.

■ Separation of Powers Doctrine

Before getting started it needs to be said that the creation of laws in a democratic system is not necessarily a criminal justice community prerogative; laws (and often policy) that are enforced by local and federal law enforcement personnel are a product of legislators and elected municipal and local officials, sometimes with the aid of oversight committees and appointees, as opposed to decisions made by the chief of police, director of the FBI, or an individual patrol officer or special agent, implies the International Association of Chiefs of Police.[1] More to the point, one definition of government can be defined as "the organized use of force to ensure social order."[2] American democracy has been organized and legislated through three distinct branches of government that are articulated in the separation of powers doctrine, which include the following[3]:

- Executive branch (law enforcing)
- Legislative branch (law making)
- Judiciary branch (interpreting laws)

This division of authority confirms a check and balance system that was intentionally designed to reduce the risk that a single branch can act independently and abuse its power. The Separation of Powers Doctrine was adopted by the framers of the US Constitution to ensure protection of fundamental liberties as concluded in *Gregory v. Ashcroft* (501 U.S., 452, 458, 1991).[4] Imagine the chaos of a patrol officer and a prosecutor (prosecutors are part of the executive branch and are therefore law enforcers) creating laws as they routinely perform their jobs, or US senators conducting common felony arrests and interrogations (for more details, see Chapters 7 and 8).

Nonetheless, a consensus exists among public administrators and police executives that many police officers and prosecutors (see Chapter 7) apply their own individual codes or personal agendas on the job.[5,6] They develop and respond to their own laws. The complexities of the organizational structure, shifts in societal norms, strong presence of union stewardships, and emphasis on individual rights have made the control of deviant and illegal practices by police officers and prosecutors a perplexing task, argues Richard F. Groeneveld[7] (see Chapter 8 for details on prosecutor misconduct). The control of police officers can become a greater task when officers are indoctrinated with a war on crime and a war on junkies; those wars can take precedence over the rule of law (i.e., the US Constitution; no one is above the law),[8] and officers can engage in reactive measures, including vigilantism. That is:

- Officers who are engaged in a war (enemy versus us; or good versus evil) employ unconstitutional aggressive behavior.
- Officers' misconduct becomes a greater measure of a good cop than the rule of law; unconstitutional behavior justifies the means.
- Others in authority turn a blind eye to police misconduct.

Jon B. Gould and Stephen D. Mastrofski recently studied police officers in a major urban metropolis who were engaged in a war on crime and junkies; it was learned that the most powerful predictor affecting the probability of unconstitutional behavior by the officers was when they explicitly searched for drugs (see more details later in this chapter and in the section on judicial blindness in Chapter 11).[9] An assumption that can arise from that study is that when officers believe they are engaged in a war of sorts, it is more likely that constitutional violations will become pervasive. Wesley G. Skogan concludes that this pattern suggests that the wars on crime and junkies contribute to a higher rate of illegal searches by the police, leading to an increase in wrongful convictions.[10] Nietzsche's thoughts at the beginning of this chapter seem to be cautioning officers about looking into the abyss because, indeed, it looks back.

Additionally, the popular media performances (as evidenced by motion pictures, television dramas, and news reports described in Chapter 2) include strategies whereby a person (most often a police officer) characterizes vigilante (see Chapter 2) behavior fueled by retaliatory issues toward offenders and innocent persons alike; vigilante behavior can be motivated by the idea of an eye for an eye, or *lex talionis* (see Chapter 9 for more detail).[11] The basic tenant of American democratic policing demands that the criminal justice community is accountable to the rule of law and the community,[12–14] and the criminal justice community must respect the rights and guarantee the security of their constituents—due process (equality) must prevail. However, recall the initial question asked in the Preface: Why would an individual with little or no criminal history commit an extraordinary act such as to initiate and promote a wrongful conviction, especially if the process can lead to a defendant's execution? In part, a war on crime (along with the wars on junkies, sex offenders, poverty, and immigrants; see Chapters 4–5) can help develop the circumstances that can change the behavior among some justice professionals.

Central to this work is the implication that wrongful convictions (and release of guilty suspects) are enhanced, in part, because of the battered and misguided "pursuit of devils—drug dealers, child molesters, environmental polluters, white-collar criminals, and terrorists—all of whom must be rounded up at all cost,"[15] or a war on crime.

■ War on Crime

The war on crime, generated by American presidents and reinforced by the popular media (or the other way around, depending on which side of the doggy's tail you're observing), is probably one of the most illogical notions about crime next to the wars on junkies, sexual offenders, poverty, and immigrants.[16,17] For over 50 years, the United States has waged a war on crime and pushed local police departments into an adoption of a *crime fighter model* in response to President Lyndon Johnson's declaration of a war on crime in 1965. One result of a crime fighter model is a greater reliance on reactive aggressive police strategies. In part, those strategies can include the development and deployment of tactical units and frequent employment of zero tolerance, which can give rise to civil liability lawsuits against officers and police agencies. Aggressive strategies tend to promote public disrespect, leading to more deviance. The question is not if aggressive reactive police policies control crime more efficiently than other initiatives, but does the war on crime (and other wars described in Chapters 4–5) promote retaliatory police conduct more often than proactive, preventive, or community relations initiatives? It also provides fewer opportunities for proactive approaches (i.e., quality-of-life arrests and community policing) that can coexist with reactive strategies. To be clear, professional researchers and justice practitioners acknowledge that *probable cause* (explained later in this chapter) arrests are necessary to control crime and to bring a police agency closer to its public safety mission.[18,19]

> The war on crime, through the contribution of the media and federal generosity (i.e., financial support, training, and equipment), is the most expensive war waged in American history, producing few, if any, gains.[20–22]

Before moving on, two contradictory perspectives require attention:

- Crime is down, spirited in part by:
  - Due process rebellion (by constituents through litigation)
  - Professional police commanders pursuing proactive and preventive initiatives through evidence-based policing (explained later)
  - Enhanced individual values, including personal accountability, among members of the general public (more later)
- Fear of crime is up, in part by:
  - Political leaders who scare the public into believing that the American people are at war with crime
  - Reinforcement by the popular media through the *CSI Effect*

To suggest that crime is down as a result of the war on crime does not fit the statistics; at the peak of the war, violent crime was at all-time highs. For example, the media blasted presidential ideals and efficiently complicated the issues of the war on crime. There were over 2.7 million cover stories in American newspapers describing the war on crime from 1982 to 1995.[23] Also, in a study of *Newsweek* cover stories from 1946 to 1995, one researcher showed that "crime and justice in the news media consistently demonstrates that the media help to construct, rather than simply represent, the interconnected social realities of crime and justice."[24]

President Ronald Reagan addressed the nation on September 11, 1982: "We must make America safe again, especially for women and the elderly who face so many moments of fear. You have every right to be concerned. We live in the midst of a crime epidemic that took the lives of more than 22,000 people last year and has touched nearly one third of American households, costing them about $8.8 billion per year."[25] The American public accepted the continuation of the war on crime, and one answer was to step up police reactive initiatives, particularly among inner-city residents who primarily were financially less well off than other residents (see Chapter 4 for details on the war on poverty). It was supposed to be a quick war.

A generation later, the war on crime is fought in the residential streets of mega-metropolises, such as Chicago and Los Angeles, and in rural cities, such as Renton, Washington and Alexandria, Ohio, between dangerously armed thugs and local police, some of whom have been trained at the Federal Law Enforcement Training Center (FLETC) in Glynco, Georgia or at one of its satellite training campuses across the country (for more information visit FLETC's website at http://www.fletc.gov/). Reacting to crime is one result of the war on crime politics and media contributions, but prudent police officials and some policy makers also turned reactive policing inside out and deployed proactive police strategies with an aim toward prevention.[26] Nonetheless, it appears that the media favors reactive aggressive police responses, including tactical units, more often than other strategies.

Tactical Units

Police tactical units are one result of the war on crime. Traditionally, police prioritize their strategies through a *paramilitary model* (a chain of command or a hierarchal bureaucratic structure where orders come down the chain of command and reports go up the chain of command).[27] At first glance, a police paramilitary model can give rise to a police renaissance through the art of war and through strategies such as special weapons and tactics (SWAT) or a critical tact unit; in another sense, their deployment is consistent with American television dramas' rationale of what policing should be.[28] One reality is that 90 percent of the routine among police officers has more to do with a social worker model than a warrior model associated with a *critical incident*.[29,30] Conceptually, a critical incident can refer to the apprehension of emotionally disturbed offenders, organized domestic terrorists, hostage takers, barricaded subjects, riot control, high-risk warrant service, or sniper incidents.[31] One way to deal with critical incidents is through tact units. With proper equipment, including communication, tact units can control critical incidents and reduce the amount of risk for both the public and the officers.

Officers Assaulted and Killed but Neglected by Popular Media

The media often neglects to emphasize that police officers and federal law enforcement officers are often at risk; for example, the FBI reported that:

- While performing their duties in 2007, 59,201 police officers were assaulted (the rate of assaults was 11.4 per 100 sworn officers).
- Of all officers who were assaulted in 2007, the largest percentage (32 percent) were responding to disturbance calls (family quarrels, bar fights, etc.).
- In 2007, 1,650 federal law enforcement officers were assaulted.
- During 2007, 57 police officers were feloniously killed in the line of duty.[32]

By circumstance, 16 of these deaths occurred as a result of ambush situations; 16 died during arrest situations; 11 were killed while handling traffic pursuits or stops; 6 died responding to disturbance calls; 3 died while investigating suspicious persons or circumstances; 3 died during tactical situations; 1 died while conducting investigative activities; and 1 died while handling and transporting prisoners. In addition to the officers who were feloniously killed, 83 officers were accidentally killed while performing their duties. Also, a few police officers routinely conduct felony arrests, engage in gun fights, or utilize violence when confronting violators.[33] For that reason, patrol officers (68 percent of all local police officers are assigned to traffic and service call duties[34]) are not as prepared to effectively respond to critical incidents as SWAT units.[35]

SWAT

SWAT was developed by Commander Daryl Gates of the Los Angeles Police Department in 1967. Commander Gates referred to special weapons and tactics, or SWAT, as a police unit designed to respond to local critical incidents. SWAT was conceived as an urban counterinsurgency bulwark. Its aim is to aggressively respond to any altercation with the same technical know-how and weapons systems employed in military battles, which can translate to tactically controlling a serious incident without injury or death thereby enhancing public safety mandates. A description of tactical unit models can be characterized as local police providing traditional police services through a ready response deployment of tactically equipped and trained officers to volatile situations that are beyond the capabilities of normally equipped and trained department personnel.[36]

Nationwide, SWAT or tact units have metastasized from emergency response teams into a standard part of everyday policing.[37,38] In 1982, 59 percent of police departments that responded to a study had an active paramilitary police unit.[39]

Fifteen years later, nearly 90 percent of those same agencies had an active para-military unit; and the number of paramilitary police callouts quadrupled between 1980 and 1995.[40,41]

Tactical Unit Deployment

When tact teams are called, the members gear up together, are briefed, and an active shooter(s) is designated.[42] This is the officer who will employ deadly force when ordered to do so (justifiable homicide is explained later). Extreme events, such as the following, are tragic altercations that justify the use of tact units:

- Columbine
- Virginia Tech[43]
- Northern Illinois University
- Terrorist attacks[44]
- North Hollywood bank robbery

For example, on February 28, 1997, at Bank of America, SWAT and patrol officers were confronted by two heavily armed robbers. The shootout resulted in the wounding of 11 people (nine police officers and two civilians) and the deaths of both bank robbers. The large number of injuries made this one of the bloodiest single cases of violent crime in the 1990s and one of the most significant bank robberies in America. A Web site search provided 37,000 hits, YouTube had 29 videos about the robbery that had been viewed by over 1 million viewers each, the movie industry developed two movies about the incident, and popular television police dramas developed eight different reenactments of the robbery. Months after the incident, news reporters continued to talk about the event, but there were few media presentations about proactive police strategies (prevention or more efficient methods toward public safety) or strategies to harden the target, a perspective that can work well with efficient enforcement techniques (i.e., promote and guide technology, strategies, and environmental changes to make robbery a difficult task).

Similar to the development of many police tactical units across the country, the Memphis Police Department (MPD) learned that a well-trained and well-equipped unit is necessary to accomplish the mission of public safety. For example, 28 years ago the MPD tact unit rescued three doctors and a nurse who were held hostage during a 32-hour siege at a local hospital.[45] A year later, a 30-hour police siege included seven men who held a Memphis police officer hostage.[46] Although Officer Robert Hester was beaten to death, his fellow officers heard his cries for help as they surrounded the house. Officers had flashlights taped to the barrels of their guns and few methods to communicate with one another. A police report concluded there was little that could have been done differently, but it also concluded that the police had overestimated the ability of MPD's tact unit and the efficiency of their equipment.

Deadly Force

Tact officers are trained in the philosophy of time versus opportunity when handling hostage–rescue situations.[47] Tact members can employ aggressive action and deadly force when directed by a tact commander, consistent with departmental guidelines and laws.[48] Regular training maintains both the expertise and the cohesion of the group, which in turn enhances the confidence and pride of the unit. Tact units are developed to protect public safety before, during, and after critical incidents through appropriate training and regimentation.

Justifiable Homicide

The killing of a felon by police is justified when it is done to prevent imminent death or serious bodily injury to the officer or another person.[49] Police and tact units justifiably kill, on average, nearly 400 felons each year. Some say that justifiable homicide reports are underreported, likewise it is difficult to ascertain with any accuracy how many of those justifiable homicides were the result of tact units.[50] The taking of a person's life, in general, can be considered justifiable homicide if the act is committed in self-defense, during the defense of others, while trying to prevent a serious crime, and in the line of duty.[51]

The *CSI Effect* has kicked up the fear of crime, and legislators in 15 southern states added a new twist to justifiable homicide known by advocates as *stand your ground laws* and by opponents as *shoot first laws* (discussed in the Preface). Police engage in disparate gunfights on the wicked streets of Boston and in the crowded alleyways of Los Angeles, and although it is unintended, innocent civilians are killed. In Clearwater, Florida a man was gunned down by his neighbor after a shouting match over the trash, and a Port Richey, Florida prostitute fired a weapon point-blank at her 72-year-old client who wouldn't return her favors. The law in 15 states says that any person who is attacked (or perceives to be in imminent danger) in a public place "does not have a duty to retreat if he or she reasonably believes that such force is necessary to prevent imminent death or great bodily harm."[52] The law forbids arrest, detention, prosecution, and civil suit of persons covered by the law. What has changed since you read your last criminal justice book are the choices of the American people, but what can never change are the fundamental rights of every democratic citizen.[53] Do these laws seem to support a self-appointed doer of justice or what can be called a vigilante?

Realities of Police Use of Force

Some police officers consider the tact unit accolades as a huge motive to pursue a career in policing, and some police veterans look forward to the excitement of a violent altercation with criminals, especially if a tactical approach is deployed.[54,55] Judged on the criminally violent behavior of some criminals and the training associated with warfare among officers, it is easy to accept the idea that some officers look upon violence as an expectation and part of their job description. However, in a national study of traditional use of force, officers use less force than expected, particularly compared to what the media shows. That is[56]:

- An estimated 19 percent (44 million) of US residents aged 16 years or older had face-to-face contact with a police officer in 2005.
- About 9 of 10 people who had contact with police thought that the police acted properly.
- An estimated 2 percent of people who had contact with police said they experienced a threat or use of force by officers against them.

One way to interpret these findings is to say that a traditional police officer employs or threatens to use force only as a last resort, if at all. On the other hand, experienced police officers easily relate to the implication that "active cops or the cops who make the most collars (arrests) and get the most action on the street, often have records marked by troubling signposts of brutality, productive arrest and citation records, and medals for heroism."[57] These are *tells* of officers who typically engage in misconduct.

Typical Tact Unit

A typical tactical unit can be illustrated by the Memphis Police Department (MPD). The MPD's tact unit is described as an elite unit, specially trained to respond to various emergency situations.[58] MPD's tact unit is responsible for handling barricade situations, hostage rescues, counterterrorism, and high-risk felony apprehensions. Although the unit is not subject to regular calls for service like other police units, this unit responded to 63 radio calls, initiated 14,482 specials, made 124 arrests, issued 454 tickets, and handled 15 barricade–hostage situations in 2006. The unit also participated in 12 VIP security details, 34 community outreach programs, and 14 gun seizures during that year.

An Example of Tact Deployment

Concluding a year's war on crime, or what can be called *Operation Community Shield*, US Immigration and Customs Enforcement (ICE) agents teamed up with local police agencies and arrested over 2,400 gang members from 239 gangs residing in 23 states.[59] Those arrested included members of Mara Salvatrucha (MS-13), Surenos, 18th Street Gang, Latin Kings, Bloods, Crips, Armenian Power, Street Thug Criminals, Brown Pride, Asian Dragon Family, Avenue Assassins, Spanish Gangster Disciples, Big Time Killers, and Hermanos Pistoleros Latinos. Roughly 922 of those arrested were from the seriously violent street gang MS-13. For federal and local police agencies to a find a legal yet appropriate balance between enforcement and civil rights is probably one of the largest challenges in this century.

Media's Version of Tact Deployment

Operation Community Shield served the community, police, and potential victims well, but apparently the media can change things, too.[60] Heavy consumers of crime-related media, after the media adds its magic (fantasy), are more fearful of crime, more likely to believe that crime is increasing, more likely to rate crimes seriously, more likely to believe that the world is just, less likely to support rehabilitation, and much more likely to support stricter sanctions, including capital punishment.[61] This provides evidence that is consistent with George Gerbner's cultivation hypothesis of a mean world perspective. Gerbner suggests that the television set has become a principle member of the family and the family member who tells the stories. McQuail and Windahl reveal that cultivation theory presents television not as a window on or a reflection of the world, but a world in itself.[62]

That said, it is not difficult to accept the appropriateness of a paramilitary police model in a democratic nation as terrorists (and the altercations previously mentioned) engage in horrendous crimes against unarmed civilians—on the subways in London, on the trains in Madrid, Spain, and at the World Trade Center in New York City.[63]

Critics of Tact Units

Despite the paramilitary advantage during hostage situations, at-risk warrant encounters, hazardous police–criminal altercations, and the notion that officers must provide public safety, due process can be ignored when tact units replace typical models of policing, a product of the war on crime.[64,65] The most common use of tact teams is to serve narcotics warrants, usually with forced unannounced entry (no-knock warrants) into homes because of the clear and present danger linked to those assignments,[66] and the frequency of their deployment is more often than you might anticipate. The media may glorify tact units with action performances of SWAT engaged in combat, yet sometimes innocent bystanders are confronted and there are errors in targeted locations.[67]

Also, community members, especially those in disadvantaged neighborhoods (more details later), who witnessed tact units engaged in battle, reported that they held feelings of defenselessness and suspicion of police power, and their fear of becoming a victim of a violent crime at the hands of the police and criminals increases.[68,69] In jurisdictions where tact unit operations are active (because, in part, of critical incident frequencies), the population can be more fearful of the police than they are of criminals because the police are organized and use legalized violence (one perspective is that the NYPD has almost 38,000 gang members dressed in blue).[70] Nonetheless, the idea of 38,000 officers in NYC is meritorious if you need to call 911.

Some might argue that military training, expectations, and mandates that help breed young men or women into outstanding warriors can produce a dangerous dissent for street cops and can fuel violence among violence-prone persons. From what we thought were friendly, dedicated local police, the media launched political acceptance of a federally funded, military-trained, asset-forfeiture-empowered, multijurisdictional task force that specializes, some say, in home invasion and forceful action against a targeted American population that is suspected of smoking marijuana, being a suspect as a sports bookmaker, or being an immigrant.[71] For example, Fairfax, Virginia police declared that the killing of Salvatore J. Culosi, aged 37 years, was an accident; a SWAT officer unintentionally fired his weapon.[72] The Commonwealth of Virginia's attorney Robert F. Horan, Jr. says that when a person fires a gun without malice and as a result someone is unintentionally killed, that person has not committed a crime. Also, a police spokesperson said that the use of SWAT teams by Fairfax police was appropriate for apprehending bookmakers.[73]

Disadvantaged Neighborhoods and Tact Deployment

Constituents in disadvantaged neighborhoods often view police tactical units as abusive and hypocritical, and neighborhood members are resentful of the war on crime rhetoric because it targets their communities more than affluent communities, argues Peter Cassidy.[74] These residents say they are unfairly targeted, victimized by police, and see police intrusion as an "occupational army."[75] Some of these individuals also experience great pressures to comply with the social values and norms of the community, which basically hold the position that police are the bad guys. News reports focus hard on beating the enemy in the streets. This derogatory opinion seems to originate from, and also helps perpetuate, the continual state of conflict between the members of these communities and the police.[76] However, whether police tactical units represent an occupational army or not, for many law abiding individuals who enjoy carefree lifestyles, it is often police officers who voluntarily place themselves at-risk to protect those lifestyles from victimization. The truth of the matter is that in America there are many selfish individuals who feel that they can do whatever they want to whomever they please.

Police Response to Suspects: Arrests[77]

In 2006 the FBI estimated that 14,400,000 arrests were conducted by local police officers across the country, which is equivalent to approximately 4,832.5 arrests per 100,000 inhabitants.[78] Criminologists, psychologists, and researchers seek to find explanations to promote an arrest, aside from the crime itself, and seek contributing factors other than *probable cause* (a reasonable belief, based on facts and circumstances, that a person is committing, has committed, or is about to commit a crime).[79] For example, in the 1970s a series of studies examined the importance of the constituent's role in establishing a positive basis for police–constituent relations. These studies and others that followed have illustrated how a person's demeanor is a powerful predictor of subsequent police action. Reisig, McCluskey, and Mastrofski report that throughout 1996 and 1997 they were successful in predicting those factors.[80] By using the *social interactionist theory* (described later) as conceptual guidance, their study focused on a single aspect of constituent demeanor: disrespect.

Social Interactionist Theory

One way to explain the social interactionist theory is to say that people act toward things and events based on the meaning those things and events have for that individual, and meanings are derived from social exchanges and modified through individual interpretation, which can include situational factors, such as body language and the presence of a third party. This theory can explain a suspect's disrespect for the police; for example, when an individual believes that he or she has been harmed (as a result of a tact unit in the community), the individual assumes that the police put him or her, an innocent person, at risk. This individual ignores the original reason for police intrusion, such as a hostage situation or an armed robbery that turned violent. The innocent person feels justified in forming a grievance or even seeking litigation against the police. These feelings, the theory implies, can be enhanced if an individual feels a need to protect his or her social identity if he or she feels humiliated or helpless because of the encounter with the tact unit. Imagine arriving home from a day's work or a long day at school to be greeted by a garrison of heavily armed, battle-dressed police officers shouting commands. It is easy to see how feelings of humiliation, helplessness, and fear can materialize.

The third-party factor also explains disrespect by suggesting that an audience helps intensify the social exchange, particularly when an individual identifies with the audience. Urban sociologists refer to this phenomenon as *showing nerve* to maintain one's social image.[81] Social interactionist theory can explain why some individuals behave disrespectfully toward the police in an attempt to relieve, for example, the humiliation or helplessness experienced as a result of police tactical intrusion.[82] Public disrespect also plays a role in how officers respond to civilians during altercations; that is, disrespect plays a role in an arrest decision sometimes regardless of the seriousness of a crime.

Public Disrespect

John Kavanagh investigated 1,108 arrests made at New York City's Port Authority Bus Terminal.[83] The study found that the most powerful factor related to an arrest was suspect disrespect toward officers; apparently committing a crime and being apprehended does not necessarily translate to an arrest for misdemeanor activities. Also, Robin Engel, James Sobol, and Robert Worden explored whether a suspect's demeanor and characteristics interact and produce differential patterns of citation, arrest, and use of force.[84] The study collected data from 24 police departments in three metropolitan areas: Rochester, New York; St. Louis, Missouri; and Tampa/St. Petersburg, Florida. The findings were that constituent demeanor was a significant predictor of police sanctions.[85] This study, similar to those previously mentioned, is consistent in the conclusion suggesting that public disrespect and hostile demeanor toward the police are more likely to end in an arrest or other police sanction. However, a study also found that blacks were more likely to resist an arrest than Latinos and whites.[86]

Practices of Youth's Disrespect

Practices of youth's disrespect for police can be found within cultural norms of various groups.[87] For example, youngsters learn that disrespecting officers can add to their own reputation. One officer said in confidence, "Kids are just running their mouths at you because you're a cop and ya gotta learn not to take it personal otherwise you'd be arresting everybody."[88] Early police disrespect can turn to subsequent violence. For example, in the inner city, young children learn to play a game that is fairly simple: when officers drive by, juveniles do their best to "punk 'm out."[89] The tougher kids have fathers, brothers, or mothers in jail, and those are the kids who go the furthest. They spit at patrol cars, call the officers filthy names, and wave a one-finger salute with a smile.[90]

Another example is a Swampscott, Massachusetts patrol officer who stood in a courtroom "attempting to swallow his rage and mash his mortification."[91] A youth who was described by the officer as a virtual one-person crime wave had his case dismissed by a judge.[92] The officer had apprehended the youth while he was breaking into a home. The homeowner was a witness to the arrest and came to court numerous times to testify, but the case was delayed several times. She sat in court waiting for the case to be called, and finally in midafternoon her boss said that if she didn't come to work that her job was at risk. The case was called at four o'clock in the afternoon. The judged chewed the officer out for letting the witness leave and dismissed the charges. "I'll never forget how that kid and his mother stood there and laughed, laughed at me," recalls the officer.[93]

Police Discretion

Police officer behavior can also be shaped by *police discretion* (characterized as the freedom to act on one's own choices). Although the law legitimizes the police officer's power to intervene, it does not—and cannot—dictate the officer's response in every given situation when interfacing with the public, unless a mandatory arrest order exists (such as in domestic violence calls when officers must conduct an arrest if probable cause exists).[94] Other factors that shape police officers' responses can include organizational, situational, individual, or environmental factors, and the *police subculture*, which is characterized as learned objectives, shared job activities, and similar use of nonmaterial and material items. Veteran officers are the gatekeepers (as opposed to supervisors) of the police subculture, and they transmit job obligations, responsibilities, and expectations of the job.[95]

Police Organizational Structure

An important factor that influences officer response is the structure that employs the officer.[96] Research supports that the bureaucratic characteristics of the police organization, in addition to the nature of the management style and culture of the department, can explain police officer behavior. For example, one study showed that when they were under the influence of formal and informal organizational characteristics regarding discretionary arrests in larger departments, officers were more likely to base their decisions on the informal culture of their precinct, whereas officers in smaller departments tended to follow written policy.

The war on crime justifies command decisions in some communities that have higher crime rates than other communities, resulting in more frequent deployment of police personnel than in other communities. Serious crime is ascertained by police command priorities; for example, gang violence is more important than sexual assault. An additional study analyzed police–constituent encounters in 60 neighborhoods and found that variations of police use of force and legal authority are also linked to the racial composition of those neighborhoods.[97] This research also detected that people in lower-class black communities were more likely to be arrested than suspects in more affluent white communities. A repetitive perspective is that "Police brutality is a contemporary manifestation of a control . . . that cops never behave in this trigger-happy manner in white communities"[98] or with affluent blacks, such as Michael Jackson, O.J. Simpson, and Kobe Bryant. There are reputable accounts that poor white communities have been victimized by the police, too. For example, residents in a section of Boston known as South Boston or Southie have talked about the Boston police regularly beating the poor Irish in those neighborhoods for decades, yet the popular media stays clear of those allegations.[99,100] The implications of police brutality against poor whites are present in motion pictures such as *Gangs of New York* (2002) and *The Departed* (2006). Were they accurately portrayed? One answer might be they are as accurate as *The Da Vinci Code* (2006), which portrayed a religious mystery that was protected by a secret society for 2,000 years. These factors contribute to urban norms and values, which can demoralize constituents and criminal justice professionals alike, despite the high quality of these and other motion pictures.

Civil Liability Litigation

Some say that the war on crime and aggressive police strategies have aided in the decline of crime, but could the decline also be linked to local police officers' (this does not apply to federal agents) reluctance in conducting an arrest, even when probable cause is present, if an officer feels threatened by litigation?[101] Because American society has become highly litigious and police officers and the agencies that employ them have seen more than their share of lawsuits, officers are vulnerable to becoming defendants in a wide variety of situations.[102]

Lawsuits may arise under claims of negligence, unlawful use of force, false arrest, invasion of privacy, search and seizure, and deprivation of constitutional rights (Title 42, Section 1983).[103] They can also arise under federal prosecution for deprivation of constitutional rights. The end result can be a loss of a career and damages. It could be said that the public is so frustrated by an increase in arrest rates through aggressive police actions—such as zero-tolerance strategies, including the use of tactical units supported by a *broken windows analogy* (discussed next)—that they fight back in courts, which can be called a due process revolution.

The idea of broken windows is simple, logical, and compelling.[104] It is one of many perspectives that influence police policy during the war on crime. A broken window, an alley teeming with debris, and graffiti do little harm to a neighborhood if promptly addressed.[105] Left untended, the signal of broken windows can tell violators that crime will be tolerated in that community. The signal reveals that this neighborhood is a safe place to break things, to litter, and to vandalize.[106] When these miscreants are established in a neighborhood, it is acceptable to be openly drunk, beg, rob, and fight. At its core, the idea is to take back public spaces and make arrests for every minor infraction of the law. One response by police departments, and in this case, the Los Angeles Police Department, was aggressive police zero-tolerance rollouts. These strategies were part of an interlocking set of wider reforms, crucial parts of which had been underway for many years to support the war on crime, yet those aggressive strategies take police power, and if corrupt officers see an opportunity to commit crime, will they? A broken windows metaphor suggests that in those targeted neighborhoods, corrupt police officers can pretty well do as they please; no one of authority is concerned. Years later, such as in the Rampart Scandal in Los Angeles, the city paid $6.5 million in a single suit in 2005 by a man who was falsely imprisoned after being shot and framed by corrupt Rampart gang officers nearly a decade prior.[107]

In New York City, aggressive strategies produced between 40,000 and 85,000 additional adult misdemeanor arrests each year during the period from 1994 to 1998, and the strategies produced an even greater number of stops and frisks during a period of sharply declined crime rates.[108] However, it didn't take long for police officials from New York City to Chicago to Los Angeles to realize that some members of the American public, including urban gangs (more detail is provided later), were fighting back against the war on crime and aggressive police action in the courts.[109] For example, a "police officer is twenty times more likely to be sued than to be shot," argues Carl J. Franklin.[110] With the number of lawsuits on the rise, police officials can no longer ignore suits against their officers or their agencies.

A perspective that can be argued is that police officers may engage in fewer proactive police activities, including a propensity to make a probable cause arrest, use of force (including returning fire), and conduct legal searches and initiate encounters with suspects as a way to insulate themselves from personal accountability, which includes civil liability potentials.[111] Recall the study earlier in this chapter by Jon B. Gould and Stephen D. Mastrofski whereby officers conducted illegal searches of suspects who the officers suspected were involved with drugs (see details earlier in this chapter and in Chapter 11).[112] At first this study seems to contradict the previous findings, but consider that those officers were not threatened with a potential lawsuit by the suspects whom they violated. Consistent with this thought is a study of 658 officers employed by 21 different police agencies across the country.[113] When the officers' data were pooled and examined, distinctive patterns lent support to the idea that the threat of litigation among officers influenced arrest decisions. Police arrested suspects who, by circumstances (drunk driving and immigrants), represented little, if any, threat of litigation. Some scholars might argue that data sets show that attitudes toward civil liability among officers are weak and inconsistent predictors of their behavior.[114] Others argue that "many police officers do not conduct probable cause arrests when both offenders and evidence suggest they should."[115] One implication is that reported crime rates and actual crime rates are highly suspect. When the general public was asked if violent crime in the United States was higher than a year ago, the trend shows that from 1989 to 2007 participants reported that crime was higher.[116]

Experts have cautioned that in the war on crime, through enhanced technology, refined tactics, and specialized tact units, the traditional training provided to officers around the country is inadequate and obsolete. Carl Milazzo and Claire McNaught advise that there are no special rules for special operations or aggressive police policy.[117] The same Fourth Amendment principles governing a lone officer at a traffic stop equally applies to a special unit on a tactical mission. In other words, "it is the facts that change, not the law," argue Milazzo and McNaught.

Litigation and Gangs

In the 1990s, the Chicago City Council stated that an "aggressive [police] action is necessary to preserve the city's streets and other public places so that the public may use such places without fear."[118] As a result, the Chicago Police Department (CPD) practiced zero tolerance against gang loitering.[119] For example, the failure to obey a first-time police directive to disperse was punishable by a fine of up to $500, incarceration of up to six months, community service of up to 120 hours, or any combination of the three.[120] As a result, the CPD vigorously enforced the antigang loitering ordinance, resulting in the issuance of over 89,000 orders to disperse and the arrest of over 42,000 individuals during the period from 1993 to 1995.[121] Eventually the ordinance was challenged by the American Civil Liberties Union (ACLU) and was subsequently ruled to be unconstitutional.[122] Police officials reevaluated aggressive police actions and employed evidence-based (utilizes scientific studies as advanced by researchers such as Lawrence W. Sherman and others)[123] police strategies to aid in furthering their police mission, similar to many jurisdictions across America. For example, evidence-based policing in the Minneapolis Hot Spots Patrol Experiment included 7,542 hours of observations and concluded that substantial increases in police patrol presence can cause modest reductions in crime and more impressive reductions in disorder within high crime locations.[124]

It was also learned through evidence-based police studies that most crime occurs at a few addresses; another researcher adds that 3 percent of 115,000 addresses accounted for 50 percent of calls for service.[125] Further analysis shows that the longer the police stayed at one hot spot, the lower the crime rate would dip—up to a point. More than 10 minutes of police presence in one hot spot produced diminishing returns. As a result, "the optimal way to use police visibility may be to have police travel from hot spot to hot spot, staying about ten minutes at each one."[126] This perspective is not one that receives notoriety on popular television dramas.

In keeping with these and other findings, the city of Chicago employed civil remedies to clean up physical dilapidation, drug trafficking, and social disorder on private property, consistent with the broken windows theory (previously explained). The benefits of code enforcement are substantial because they reduce the window of opportunity of crime; for example, a study found that narcotics crime declined when individual drug houses were closed down.[127]

Legal Injunctions Against Gangs

The CPD generated exponentially higher activity numbers for gun recoveries, hot spot dispersals, and contact cards, to name a few. Recently, Chicago, similar to other cities across the country, departed from the reactive spirit of the war on crime and took a proactive method of dealing with criminals. Chicago, like Fort Worth and San Francisco, prepares and files lawsuits and injunctions against gang members, asking courts to bar gang members from hanging out on street corners, in cars, or anywhere else in certain areas.[128] The injunctions are aimed at disrupting gang activity before it escalates. Police departments have found that controlling criminal activity before it happens (proactive policing) brings their department closer to providing public safety with less chance of litigation; also, more suspects are prosecuted (as opposed to being released) and convicted. Proactive policing provides the police with a legal reason to stop and question gang members who often are found with drugs or weapons in their possession.

During the summer of 2006, 400 Chicago police officers and officers from the US Drug Enforcement Administration (DEA) made a sweep at one of Chicago's projects (Dearborn Homes) and made arrests of 47 Mickey Cobra gang members who distributed heroin and held the community in a "stranglehold."[129]

Dennis Rosenbaum and Cody Stephens report that although the CPD's "hot spot policing, targeted deployment, and enhanced activities were likely key contributors to the overall reduction of public violence and homicide,"[130] there are strong indicators that the proactive arrests and preventive initiatives associated with a broken window analogy can bring police departments closer to their mission of public safety. However, few of these tactics are front-page news, and police commanders tend not to conform to the general media's perceptions; thus, criticism of their professional decisions are an ongoing source of frustration, especially when doing the right thing is the wrong thing, according to the popular media, which lacks a measure of responsibility. For example, the performance of the new police chief in Charlotte, North Carolina (the 21st largest city in the United States), who was previously chief in Richmond, Virginia, is negatively assessed by news reporters at the *Charlotte Observer*. A cofounder of a recent community action group that was looking for funding decided what professional performance is relevant for a police commander and how the commander's field decisions relate to the media's version of the war on crime.[131,132]

■ War on Junkies

In part, the media characterizes junkies as trailer park trash together with their suburban mall-rat "gangsta' wannabes," Hispanic *homies*, and ghetto-storm'en blacks, who seek self-destructive paths because of their inability to fit in with the social–economic middle class expectations.[133] As a by-product of the alleged junkie lifestyle, individually and collectively, junkies, the thinking goes as orchestrated by the popular media, emasculate American traditional values as though they are carriers of the bubonic plague, HIV infections, and other highly-contagious diseases, such as poverty.[134,135] Because junkies are bent upon self-gratification and pleasure, the most effective criminal justice response is aggressive police detection, apprehension, and severe punitive sanctions, which include incarceration or what can be called the war on junkies.[136,137] The media reports that because traditional police units cannot disinfect drug users of the innocuous scent that only junkies radiate, aggressive police action is prescribed by politicians and community activists who take their cues from the *CSI Effect*. However, many competent scholars caution the stereotyping of drug users and addicts because they come from all lifestyles and socioeconomic groups, and there are no single drug–crime relationships (nor is there a simple solution to the challenges faced by drug–crime relationships).[138] Erich Goode and other prominent scholars argue that "even the fact that drugs and crime are frequently found together or correlated does not demonstrate their causal connection."[139] Aside from the use of illegal drugs, illegal drug users do not necessarily engage in other criminal activities. Many are high-functioning individuals who are financially stable and successful at employment pursuits.[140] "Wealth has privilege, and one privilege is obtaining a regular supply of high-end prescription drugs or raiding your own hospital's dispensary for high quality products," a drug enforcer conveyed in confidence.[141]

Nonetheless, some drug experts, such as John Gillis, trekked along heroin smuggling routes from Pakistan to Nigeria, watched addicts put coal tar in their ears to prolong an opium high, and witnessed junkies so desperate for a fix that they resorted to sniffing gasoline and insect spray.[142] Gillis says that drug treatment programs do not work; he gives up on the estimated 20 million people who abuse alcohol and drugs in America.[143] Geraint B. Osborne and Curtis Fogel found that most adult marijuana users regulate use of marijuana to recreational periods and don't live compulsive lifestyles.[144] The researchers advanced the idea that the use of marijuana enhances relaxation and concentration, as reported by their participants, making a broad range of leisure activities more enjoyable and pleasurable.[145] However, there is a chance that this latter perspective has methodological issues associated with its findings, yet many accept this perspective and its implications toward a legalization approach.[146,147] For example, in the spring of 2009 the state of Illinois considered the legalization of marijuana plants in the homes of patients suffering from certain diseases.[148] One thought worth considering is that when alcohol was legalized in the United States in the 1930s, the number of alcoholics drastically increased, as did accidents and family violence, especially among younger individuals.[149] Alcohol kills people, and it encourages antisocial and destructive behavior. Alcohol is used much more frequently than illegal drugs, including marijuana, and the amount of damage it causes is greater; if marijuana becomes legal, the affect on accidents and crime may coincide with its use.

The debate about drug and alcohol abuse continues, and often the criminal justice community is caught between liberal and conservative thoughts.[150] It was asked in the preceding chapter who is responsible for the inadequacies of criminal justice policy, and one answer relates to the popular media through the *CSI Effect*.[151,152]

Drug Problem's Problem

The media capitalizes on junkies' failures and focuses on the *drug problem's problem*: the users pay a high price in stunted lives and physical deficiencies; there are staggering social, psychological, and economic costs of homelessness, unemployment, crime, and disease; and the costs of interdiction (more on this point later) and incarceration are well over $200 billion annually.[153] The annual burden in lost productivity in the workplace, from absenteeism and accidents, will add another $129 billion, and employees' drug- and alcohol-related healthcare costs add up to $16 billion more.[154]

Nonetheless, the media distorts the problem, particularly as drug abuse relates to crime. For example, oxycodone hydrochloride was first introduced in the United States in 1996 and was intended for patients with a terminal disease, such as cancer.[155] It became an overprescribed drug and was trafficked within newly-developed markets. The much-publicized and alleged relationship between oxycodone hydrochloride use and increasing crime rates in Kentucky (and the surrounding Appalachian region) was "propagated by media and government sources, has been socially constructed, and bears little resemblance to empirical reality."[156]

Also consider that the primary focus of the media from 1985 to 1992 was associated with the war on drugs, especially the cocaine epidemic. Research shows that the use of cocaine peaked around 1985 and was on the decline in 1989.[157] President-elect Clinton's political platform included a war on drugs, and the attention of the media shifted to a drug war, which became an important issue continuing into the early 21st century. Intrinsic to this thought is the give and take among policy, media, politics, and public opinion and that the media can, as evidenced by popular television dramas, provide idealistic truths about the justice community.

Media and Cigarette Usage

Another study reports that the positive atmosphere in which cigarettes were used in movies and television in the late 1940s through the 1950s resulted in increased cigarette smoking in America. Decades later, youngsters were introduced to the desirable effects of alcohol and drugs. For example, 5 of 200 movies evaluated by the Office of National Drug Control Policy (ONDCP) and the US Department of Health and Human Services "portrayed no substance use whatsoever (about two percent)."[158] Of those movies, 195 presented positive statements about alcohol and drug use (e.g., expressing longing, desire, or favorable attributes of use). This large amount of substance abuse in the media continues to be of concern because the media desensitizes viewers to responsible and accountable behavior, much as they had done in connection to cigarette smoking.

Another study reported that "none of the young characters who smoked marijuana or cigarettes experienced any apparent consequences of their use."[159] Even some medical doctors proclaim that "there is little or no medical evidence of long term ill effects from sustained, moderate consumption of uncontaminated marijuana, cocaine, or heroin."[160] Motion pictures and television audiences see images of immunity toward the law and little personal responsibility for behavior. Motion pictures and television portray a false reality, and youngsters can easily mistake Hollywood for reality, which can justify their experimenting with drugs and alcohol or use it as an excuse. The Canadian Association of Chiefs of Police (CACP) implies that the media conveys the message to youngsters that smoking marijuana in cannabis clubs can be exciting.

Media and Teen Pregnancy

A study that traced more than 700 12- to 17-year-olds for three years found that those who viewed the most sexual content were about twice as likely to be involved in a pregnancy as those who saw the least such content. Anita Chandra, a RAND researcher, argues that "watching this kind of sexual (such as *Sex and the City*) content on television is a powerful factor in increasing the likelihood of a teen pregnancy."[161] It is unlikely that TV viewing alone explains the outcomes among the participants, but when drugs and alcohol are introduced into any relationship of these young girls, along with images of being cool and mature, pregnancy is more likely.

Music, too, impacts youth with a false representation of reality. In a study conducted by the ONDCP, findings show that more than 35 percent of the 1,000 songs surveyed had "direct reference to alcohol, tobacco, or illicit drugs (and other substance-related [*sic*] actions)."[162] Generally, illicit drug and alcohol use that is depicted in movies and songs is most often linked to the following[163]:

- Wealth or luxury
- Sexual activity
- Crime and violence

Additional findings are as follows:

- Movies were more likely than music to mention consequences of illicit drug use (48 percent versus 19 percent).

- Antiuse statements for illicit drugs were more common in movies (15 percent) than in songs (6 percent).
- Refusal to take illicit drugs when offered was more common in movies (21 percent) than in songs (2 percent).
- Illicit drugs are four times more likely to be shown in movies than depicted in songs.

> Drugs, alcohol, smoking, and sex are glamorized to factious levels by the popular media, suggesting that individuals are invincible to the consequences of wrongful behavior. The media provides a false sense of security about boundaries, standards, and accountability.[164]

Another study that investigated the relationship among news sources, knowledge claims, and the social construction of truth concluded that how the formal media processes constituted "regimes of truth" is centered more in the philosophy of the media agency (consistent with other lead stories and interests) than reality.[165] In fact, many substance abuse counselors would agree that "most often these kids are saying that they didn't think they would become addicted; they said they could control it. They could kick it anytime they wanted, and no one wanted to arrest them for little shit like chipping a little powder on weekends. Now, they're here at a state correctional facility trying to figure out where the last two years of their lives went."[166]

Drug Arrest Rates

The Drug War Clock, from January 1 to June 13, 2009, showed that state and federal drug enforcement conducted almost 837,000 arrests (almost 396,000 for cannabis) and spent an estimated $23 billion.[167] A quick calculation tells us that enforcement arrests a violator for breaking a drug law every 17 seconds and those efforts cost over $1,000 per second.

In 2007 the FBI's Uniform Crime Report (UCR) estimated that there were an estimated 1.9 million state and local arrests for drug abuse violations in the United States.[168] The total estimated state and local drug law violation arrests in the United States have grown from 580,900 in 1980, to 1,089,500 in 1990, to an estimated 1.9 million in 2007 (see Figure 3-1).

According to the UCR, drug abuse violations are defined as state and/or local offenses relating to the unlawful possession, sale, use, growing, manufacturing, and making of narcotic drugs, including opium or cocaine and their derivatives, marijuana, synthetic narcotics, and dangerous nonnarcotic drugs, such as barbiturates (see Figure 3-2). More than four-fifths of drug law violation arrests are for possession.[169]

In 2007 the FBI estimated that 14,209,365 arrests occurred nationwide for all offenses (except traffic violations), of which 597,447 were for violent crimes and

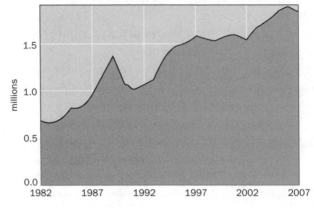

Figure 3-1   Drug abuse violation arrests, 1982 to 2007.

Source: Bureau of Justice Statistics (2008). Arrests and Seizures. Retrieved September 9, 2009, from http://www.ojp.usdoj.gov/bjs/dcf/enforce.htm

1,610,088 were for property crimes. Law enforcement made more arrests for drug abuse violations (an estimated 1.8 million arrests, or 13 percent of the total number of arrests) than for any other offense in 2007.[170] Arrests for drug law violations in 2009 are expected to exceed the arrest rate of 2007.

Additionally, the US Department of Justice, as analyzed through the Transactional Records Access Clearinghouse (TRAC), reported that a consistent 1,000

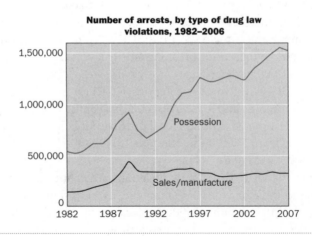

Figure 3-2   Number of arrests by type of drug law violation, 1982 to 2007.

Source: Bureau of Justice Statistics. (2008). Arrests and Seizures. Retrieved September 9, 2009, from http://www.ojp.usdoj.gov/bjs/dcf/enforce.htm

cases or more are referred by the FBI for prosecution each month.[171] In May 2008, the largest number of convictions for these cases was for "Drugs-Drug Trafficking," accounting for 13.6 percent of convictions.

Federal Convictions

In federal drug cases, mandatory minimum sentences range from 5 to 20 years, depending on the type and quantity of drugs involved and whether the offender has a prior felony drug conviction. The maximum sentence allowed is life in prison, and in the federal system there is no parole.[172]

The Daily Flow of Drugs

One count shows that 645 metric tons of cocaine arrives annually in the Unites States through Mexico and the Caribbean, and the US Coast Guard seizes about 11 percent of most incoming illegal products. Approximately 2.9 million pounds of illegal drugs were seized in 2003 within the jurisdiction of the United States by the FBI, DEA, and US Customs and Border Protection (CBP), as well as maritime seizures made by the US Coast Guard, reported the Bureau of Justice Statistics (BJS).[173] Additionally, 420 labs were seized by DEA agents alone, 409 of which manufactured methamphetamines. Keep in mind that the United States has 6,900 miles of border with Canada and Mexico and an estimated 95,000 miles of shoreline. On a typical day in 2007, CBP processed the following[174]:

- 1.13 million passengers and pedestrians
- 844 aliens (found to be inadmissible or withdrew their application)
- 70,200 truck, rail, and sea containers
- 251,000 incoming international air passengers
- 74,100 passengers and crew members arriving by ship
- 304,000 incoming privately-owned vehicles
- 82,800 shipments of goods approved for entry
- $81,834,298 in fees, duties, and tariffs

To provide a better understanding of CBP's drug operations on a daily basis (keep in mind that these statistics are constantly changing), CBP seized 2,250 pounds of narcotics in 69 drug seizures, $77,360 in undeclared or illicit currency, $329,119 worth of fraudulent commercial merchandise, and 4,296 prohibited meat, plant, or animal products, including 147 agricultural pests. On a daily basis, CBP executes the following:

- 70 arrests of criminals at ports of entry
- 2,402 apprehensions between ports for illegal entry
- 146 smuggled alien interceptions
- 1,173 canine enforcement team deployments
- 10,029 vehicles, 267 aircraft, 175 watercraft, and 188 equestrian patrol deployments

- 46,700 employees, including:
  - 18,400 CBP officers
  - 15,000 border patrol agents
  - 2,200 agriculture specialists
  - 760 air and marine agents

Lessons of History Learned During the War on Junkies

According to Harry R. Dammer and Erika Fairchild, the lessons of history we have learned during the war on junkies are as follows[175]:

- If a large number of people want a product or service, someone will supply it.
- Efforts to suppress the supply will result in massive evasion and creation of the criminal syndicates and the reinforcement of gang philosophy and cohesion, such as that among MS-13 gang members.
- Enforcement efforts will generate secondary crime, including the rise of police corruption.
- Intensifying enforcement encourages adaptations, such as the manufacturing of methamphetamines. Shutting down drug trafficking increases local manufacturing of homemade products, such as methamphetamine.

Enforcement Versus Treatment

Overall, the domestic enforcement of drug laws costs four times as much as treatment for a given amount of user reduction, seven times as much as consumption reduction, and 15 times as much for societal cost reduction, reports ONDCP.[176] The following was also suggested[177]:

- Treatment is cost effective when compared to incarceration. Treatment costs about $1,800 to $6,800 per client versus the cost of incarceration at $35,000 to $75,000 per year in 2003.
- Seventy percent of most drug addicts are employed, and their health insurance can pay for treatment.

"One of the greatest myths of this decade is that there is no success in our anti-drug efforts in this country," says Asa Hutchinson, administrator for the US Drug Enforcement Administration.[178] Hutchinson cited several statistics to back his claim, noting that cocaine use has decreased 75 percent during the past 15 years and that overall drug abuse has been reduced by 50 percent since it peaked in the 1970s. These findings are consistent with other reports that drug abuse overall has been reduced by 30 percent in the past 10 years, reports the ONDCP.[179] One reason drug use is declining is because young people are making other choices about their lives and future, and many see the media for what it is because those youngsters see first hand the destruction of their friends and their own family members who have hit bottom.[180] As a university professor and a parent of a teenager, it is encouraging to see so many young people making better decisions than the youngsters from my generation. Additionally, it should be clarified that not every drug abuser has an interest in treatment.

Arrests Deter Crime

There is a general belief among policy makers that arrests deter criminal activity. Maybe they do, but an arrest does not necessarily include rehabilitation, nor are enforcement officers expected to administer treatment. Nonetheless, in part, the behavior of most addicts can be characterized as highly compulsive, and users have few desires to change.[181] Also, most of their possessions are used for drug procurement, and when funds are not available, many addicts commit crimes to obtain their drug of choice.[182] Yet only 16 percent of jail inmates said they committed their offense to get money for drugs.[183] Most drug offenses are never detected by authorities, let alone convicted.[184,185] Nonetheless, studies do not support the arrest–addict–deterrence theory or drug user arrest deterrence because prisoners have access to drugs.[186]

"Drug arrests do not reduce crime."[187] The reality is that drug behavior is resistant to arrest, and a greater number of arrests in a given location might impact the number of addicts in a given location, so they simply go where drugs are available to them. It is clear that offenders of all varieties, including drug abusers and drug traders, are not necessarily motivated by the threat of an arrest or even an actual arrest, but they concentrate on the benefits of their crime.[188] Another way to consider this thought can be found on the streets of Chicago. The reality is that "once a drug trafficker is arrested, there are 10 others who step up to fill the vacancy."[189,190]

Official Drug Policy Changes

Jurisdictions fight back, but public opinion that is reinforced by media sensationalism allows little headway. One response from justice professionals is to change legislation to decriminalize drug possession, for example, for small amounts of drugs, particularly marijuana possession. Proposed changes include making possession of certain amounts of marijuana a misdemeanor instead of a felony, and rather than an arrest, a citation would be written as if the violation were a traffic ticket, such as in Chicago.[191] In California, medical conditions merit marijuana as a legal remedy under specific conditions. Also, since Proposition 36 was voted into legislation, the Los Angeles Superior Court reported that a new sentencing structure for nonviolent drug offenders was mandated. It appears that changing drug possession from a punitive model to a medical model of control is advantageous for all concerned.

Here's How It Works

According to the law, judges in the 19 Proposition 36 courtrooms must place defendants on probation and order them to complete a drug treatment program.[192] If rehabilitation is completed, defendants may ask the judge to dismiss their charges. If defendants don't comply with the ruling, they can be jailed.

During fiscal year 2005 to 2006, the most recent period for available statistics, Proposition 36 courts processed 9,192 participants; 8,540 appeared for their assessment; and 6,597 were placed in treatment.

Other states are watching closely. Up to one-half of most arrests and incarceration of drug possessions are related to simple marijuana violations. The media's war on junkies is entertaining for some, yet its consequences have been that America has employed the most aggressive and expensive antidrug and antigang measures ever conceived. The war on junkies justifies the military-type police aggression models to control local crime and harsh sentences.

"At a time of heightened public awareness regarding excessive penalties and disparate treatment within the justice system, judges' sentencing discretion is critical," said Marc Mauer, executive director of The Sentencing Project.[192] "Harsh mandatory sentences, particularly those for offenses involving crack cocaine, have created unjust racial disparity and excessive punishment for low-level offenses." For example, Alva Mae "Granny" Groves refused to testify against her son and had been implicated in selling crack cocaine in her son's absence. Groves received a 24-year prison sentence at the age of 72 years, explains Randall G. Shelden.[193] Congress passed an unprecedented five-year mandatory minimum sentence for anyone found to have possession of two sugar packets worth of crack, regardless of the person's criminal record. Beyond the minimum are additional sentencing guidelines, which tack on extra months or even years for obstruction of justice (which, in some cases, includes refusing to admit guilt). There are thoughts, however, that major drug suppliers are inadequately dealt with by the justice community because of their economic position in the community.

Some add that while terror alerts rise and fall and states struggle to fund police budgets, the total number of marijuana arrests far exceeds the total number of arrests for all violent crimes combined, including murder, manslaughter, forcible rape, robbery, and aggravated assault.[194] The drug war is more than 90 years old. It originated with the Harrison Anti-Narcotic Act of 1914, and since its inception it has been characterized by contradictory laws, arbitrary enforcement, massive wealth and racial disparities, questionable covert operations, and general media timidity.[195]

As the war continues and people take sides, it is sometimes hard to see the damage that drugs cause, as the Just Think Twice program suggests. There's drug addiction, of course, but there are also families, the medical system, and the environment to consider. "Innocent kids, caught in the crossfire. Drivers killed or injured by those under the influence. Babies found at meth labs, their toys covered with chemicals. Victims of terrorists, whose acts are financed with drug profits."[196]

One estimate reports that in the United States, over 26,000 individuals died from drug-induced causes in 2002, seven times more than the number of people killed in all of the 9/11 attacks. Direct costs include those for drug treatment, health care, costs of goods and services lost to crime, law enforcement, incarceration, and judicial system fees. Indirect costs are those due to the loss of productivity from death, human suffering, drug abuse related illnesses, and victims of crime. Most people who are affected by drugs aren't users. Drug use, the Just Think Twice program articulated, is not a *victimless crime*. Similar to the war on crime, the war on junkies is a reactive war that includes the media's idea that vigilante cops and ruthless prosecutors should be honored. Does the war on crime impact the war on drugs? A thought that can typify the efforts on the reactive war on crime and the reactive war on drugs was expressed by a female prisoner at a state penitentiary: "if a girl wasn't on drugs before she arrived at (this prison), she'd be a worthless whore and desperate junkie when she leaves."[197]

■ Summary

American democracy has been organized and legislated through three distinct branches of government that are articulated in the separation of powers doctrine. This doctrine was intentionally designed to reduce the risk that a single government branch can act independently and abuse its power; however, police officers and prosecutors can abuse their powers through aggressive practices in the name of justice.

Aggressive policing includes the rise of tactical or SWAT deployment, which places officers and the public at risk. Because people tend to respond to things based on the meaning those things have for them, meanings are derived from social interaction, which can be explained by the social interactionist theory. That is, aggressive policing through a tact unit is not seen as a positive police response because that action can enlarge the fear of victimization and helplessness of innocent community members, which gives rise to disrespectful behavior and can lead to civil litigation.

Although many factors played a role, aggressive police strategies produced an increase in stops and arrests, resulting in lower crime rates. However, it didn't take long for police officials from New York City to Chicago to Los Angeles to realize that some members of the American public, including urban gangs, were fighting aggressive police action through litigation. With lawsuits on the rise, police officials could no longer ignore suits against their officers or their agencies, and many jurisdictions developed prosocial strategies, such as legal injunctions against gangs.

The war on junkies is described in terms of the drug problem's problem; the media capitalizes on the failures of individuals who are addicted. Some argue that the use of marijuana enhances relaxation and concentration, making a broad range of leisure activities more enjoyable and pleasurable. However, there is a chance that this latter perspective has methodological issues associated with its findings; nonetheless, many accept this view and its implications toward a legalization approach. When alcohol was legalized in the 1930s, the number of alcoholics drastically increased, as did accidents and family violence, especially among younger persons.

Some reports show that the positive atmosphere in which cigarettes were used in movies and television in the late 1940s through the 1950s resulted in increased cigarette smoking in America. Decades later, youngsters were introduced to the desirable effects of alcohol, drugs, and teen pregnancy.

Law enforcement made more arrests for drug abuse violations than for any other offense in 2007, and it is expected that future arrests will exceed previous arrest rates. It is believed that an arrest deters criminal activity, but most drug use is not detected.

Some of the lessons learned from history are that if a large number of people want a product or service, someone will supply it. Efforts to suppress the supply will result in massive evasion and creation of criminal syndicates and the reinforcement of gang philosophy and cohesion, such as that among MS-13 gang members. Enforcement efforts will generate secondary crime, including the rise of police corruption. Intensifying enforcement encourages adaptations, such as the manufacturing of methamphetamines.

Treatment is more cost-effective than incarceration, and drug policy should change from punitive models to medical models of prevention. Similar to the war on crime, the war on junkies is a reactive war that includes the media's idea that vigilante cops and ruthless prosecutors should be honored.

■ References

1. International Association of Chiefs of Police. Retrieved June 13, 2009, from http://www.theiacp.org/

2. Education World. *Lesson plan: Separation of powers.* Retrieved November 3, 2008, from http://www.education-world.com/a_tsl/archives/00-1/lesson0014.shtml

3. Findlaw.com. (n.d.). *US Constitution: Article 1. Separation of powers and checks and balances.* Retrieved October 14, 2008, from http://caselaw.lp.findlaw.com/data/constitution/article01/01.html

4. Family Guardian Fellowship. (n.d.). *Separation of powers doctrine. US v. Lopez, 514, U.S. 549, (1995).* Retrieved October 31, 2008, from http://famguardian.org/Subjects/LawAndGovt/Articles/SeparationOfPowersDoctrine.htm

5. Barker, T., & Closer, D. (1994). *Police deviance* (3rd ed.). Cincinnati, OH: Anderson.

6. Caldero, M. A., & Crank, J. P. (2004). *Police ethics: The corruption of a noble cause* (2nd ed.). Cincinnati, OH: Anderson.

7. Groeneveld, R. F. (2005). *Arrest discretion of police officers: The impact of varying organizational structures.* New York: LFB Scholarly.

8. Hogan, J. (2008). *The framers and the sovereign. Debates on the sovereignty in the Constitutional convention.* Retrieved August 15, 2008, from http://americanhistory.suite101.com/article.cfm/we_the_people

9. Gould, J. B., & Mastrofski, S. D. (2004). Suspect searches: Assessing police behavior under the Constitution. *Criminology and Public Policy, 3,* 316–362.

10. Skogan, W. G. (Ed.). (2003). *Evidence on policing: Fairness and effectiveness in US law enforcement.* Champaign, IL: National Academy of Code Administration.

11. At the root of the non-Biblical form of this principle is the belief that one of the purposes of the law is to provide equitable retaliation for an offended party. It defined and restricted the extent of retaliation. This early belief is reflected in the *Code of Hammurabi* (the best preserved ancient law code) of 1760 BC in Babylon and in the laws of the Hebrew Bible. Some recall the phrase from the quotation in Exodus 21:23–27 in which a person who has taken the eye of another in a fight is instructed to give his own eye in compensation.

12. Bayley, D. H. (1994). *Police for the future.* New York: Oxford University Press.

13. de Mesquita Neto, P. (2001). *Paths toward democratic policing in Latin America.* Paper presented at the International Workshop Human Rights and the Police in Transitional Countries, Copenhagen, Denmark.

14. de Mesquita Neto, P. *Paths toward democratic policing in Latin America.*

15. Roberts, P. C. (n.d.). The causes of wrongful convictions. *The Independent Review, 7*(4), 569. Retrieved July 14, 2008, from http://www.independent.org/pdf/tir/tir_07_4_roberts.pdf

16. Polikoff, A. (2006). *Racial inequality and the black ghetto.* Retrieved May 4, 2008, from http://www.law.northwestern.edu/journals/njlsp/v1/n1/1/index.html

17. Gilroux, H. A. (2001). Mis/education and zero tolerance: Disposable youth and politics of domestic militarization. *Boundary, 28*(3), 61–94.

18. Franklin, C. J. (1993). *The police officer's guide to civil liabilities.* Springfield, IL: Charles C. Thomas.

19. Sherman, L. (1995). The police. In J. Q. Wilson & J. Petersilia (Eds.), *Crime.* San Francisco: ICS Press.

20. Platt, T. (2003). The state of welfare: US 2003. *Monthly Review.* Retrieved May 30, 2008, from http://www.monthlyreview.org/1003platt.htm

21. Walker, S. (2001). *Sense and nonsense about crime and drugs: A policy guide* (5th ed.). Belmont, CA: Wadsworth.

22. Simon, J. (2007). *Governing through crime, how the war on crime transformed American democracy and created a culture of fear.* New York: Oxford University Press.

23. Parenti, C. (2000). *Lockdown America: Police and prisons in the age of crisis.* New York: Verso.

24. Barlow, M. H. (1998). Race and the problem of *Time* and *Newsweek* cover stories 1946–1995. *Social Justice, 25.* Retrieved June 13, 2009, from http://www.bsos.umd.edu/aasp/chateauvert/raceprob.doc

25. The American Presidency Project. (1982). *President Ronald Reagan, radio address to the nation: Criminal justice reform.* Retrieved May 30, 2008, from http://www.presidency.ucsb.edu/ws/index.php?pid=42952

26. Stevens, D. J. (2003). *Applied community policing.* Boston: Allyn Bacon.

27. According to Dictonary.com, the actual definition of *paramilitary* is "a group of civilians organized in a military fashion (especially to operate in place of or to assist regular army troops)." Because the police are civilians as opposed to military, I will refer to this model as

a paramilitary model. Peter Manning. (1997). *Police work: The social organization of policing.* Prospect Heights, IL: Waveland Press.

28. Kraska, P., & Kappeler, V. (1997). Militarizing American police: The rise and normalization of paramilitary units. *Social Problems, 44*(1), 101–117.

29. Stevens, D. J. (2008). *Police officer stress: Sources and solutions.* Upper Saddle River, NJ: Pearson Education.

30. Klockars, C. L. (1988). The rhetoric of community policing. In J. R. Greene & S. D. Mastrofski (Eds.), *Community policing: Rhetoric or reality.* New York: Praeger.

31. Stevens, D. J. (2009). *Introduction to American policing.* Sudbury, MA: Jones and Bartlett.

32. Federal Bureau of Investigation. (2007). *Law enforcement officers killed and assaulted, 2007.* Washington, DC: US Department of Justice. Retrieved July 30, 2009, from http://www.fbi.gov/ucr/killed/2007/index.html

33. Bureau of Justice Statistics. (2006, June). *Citizens complaints about police use of force.* Retrieved September 21, 2007, from http://www.ojp.usdoj.gov/bjs/pub/pdf/ccpuf.pdf

34. Bureau of Justice Statistics. (2006). *Local police departments, 2003.* Washington, DC: US Department of Justice. Retrieved May 27, 2008, from http://www.ojp.usdoj.gov/bjs/pub/pdf/lpd03.pdf

35. McCampbell, M. S. (2001). Field training for police officers. In R. G. Dunham & G. P. Alpert (Eds.), *Critical issues in policing: Contemporary readings* (4th ed.). Prospects Heights, IL: Waveland.

36. Los Angeles Police Department. Retrieved June 10, 2009, from http://www.lapdonline.org/inside_the_lapd/content_basic_view/848.

37. Walker, *Sense and Nonsense.*

38. Currie, E. (1999). Reflections on crime and criminology at the millennium. *Western Criminology Review, 2*(1). Retrieved May 29, 2008, from http://wcr.sonoma.edu/v2n1/currie.html

39. Kraska & Kappeler, "Militarizing American Police."

40. Kraska & Kappeler, "Militarizing American Police."

41. Kraska, P. B. (1996). Enjoying militarism: Political/personal dilemmas in studying US paramilitary units. *Justice Quarterly, 13*(3), 405–429.

42. Chudwin, J. (2007, February). Active shooters: Training and equipment for first responders. *Law Officer Magazine, 3*, 60–63.

43. Seung-Hui Cho kills 33 people, including himself, in the Virginia Tech massacre, the worst civilian shooting spree in US history and the worst case of mass murder in the United States since 9/11. CNNews.com (2007). Retrieved July 30, 2009, from http://www.cnn.com/SPECIALS/2007/virginiatech.shootings/

44. Fort Dix attack plot in 2007. Six men inspired by jihadist videos are arrested in the United States in a failed homegrown terrorism plot to kill US soldiers. CNNews.com (2007). Retrieved July 30, 2009, from http://www.cnn.com/2007/US/05/08/fortdix.plot/index.html

45. Memphis Police Department. (2004). *History.* Retrieved May 26, 2008, from http://memphis-police.com/History%202004.htm

46. Dries, B. (2008, January 28). Pilot becomes highest-ranked woman in MPD history. *The Daily News.* Retrieved May 26, 2008, from http://www.memphisdailynews.com/editorial/Article.aspx?id=35422

47. Remsberg, C. (2007, January). Seize the moment: Time vs. opportunity in hostage rescue. *Law Officer Magazine, 3*, 40–41.

48. Chudwin, "Active Shooters."

49. Bureau of Justice Statistics. (2001). *Policing and homicide, 1976–98: Justifiable homicide by police, police officers murdered by felons.* Washington, DC: US Department of Justice. Retrieved May 27, 2008, from http://www.ojp.usdoj.gov/bjs/pub/pdf/ph98.pdf

50. Loftin, C., Wiersema, B., McDowall, D., & Dobrin, A. (2003). Underreporting of justifiable homicide committed by police officers in the United States, 1976–1998. *American Journal of Public Health, 93*(7), 1117–1121.

51. Laws vary from state to state, but this is a reasonable explanation and is supplied by *Criminal Law Lawyers Source.* Retrieved May 27, 2008, from http://www.criminal-law-lawyer-source.com/terms/justifiable.html

52. The Florida Senate. (2008). *Statues & Constitution. Title XLVI, Chapter 776. Justifiable use of force.* Retrieved November 11, 2008, from http://www.flsenate.gov/Statutes/index.cfm?App_mode=Display_Statute&Search_String=&URL=Ch0776/SEC012.HTM&Title=->2007->Ch0776->Section%20012#0776.012

53. Cory, P. (2005, October). *Keynote speech by the Honorable Peter deCarteret Cory at the conference.* Paper presented at Unlocking Innocence: An International Conference on Avoiding Wrongful Convictions, Winnipeg, Manitoba, Canada.

54. Stevens, D. J. (1999). American police resolutions and community response. *The Police Journal,* 140–151.

55. Stevens, D. J. (1999, March). Police tactical units and community response. *Law & Order,* 48–52.

56. Bureau of Justice Statistics. (2007). *Contacts between police and public.* Washington, DC: US Department of Justice. Retrieved May 28, 2008, from http://www.ojp.usdoj.gov/bjs/abstract/cpp05.htm

57. Bouza, A. V. (2001). *Police unbound: Corruption, abuse, and heroism by the boys in blue.* Amherst, NY: Prometheus Books.

58. Memphis Tennessee Police Department. (n.d.). *Special operations.* Retrieved May 26, 2008, from http://www.memphispolice.org/special%20Ops.htm

59. US Department of Homeland Security. (2006, March). *Press release. ICE arrests 375 gang members and associates in two-week enforcement action.* Retrieved June 13, 2009, http://www.dhs.gov/xnews/releases/press_release_0878.shtm

60. Callanan, V. J. (Ed.). (2005). *Feeding the fear of crime: Crime-related media and support for three strikes.* New York: LFB Scholarly.

61. Gerbner, G. & Gross, L. (1976). Living with television: The violence profile. *Journal of Communication, 26,* 76.

62. McQuail, D. & Windahl, S. (1993). *Communication models for the study of mass communication.* London: Longman.

63. Newswatch.com, (2005, July 7). Al-Qaeda claims responsibility for London blasts. *News Journal.* Retrieved June 12, 2009, from http://news.dcealumni.com/962/al-qaeda-claims-responsibility-for-london-blast/

64. Stevens, "American Police Resolutions."

65. Stevens, "Police Tactical Units."

66. "No-knock raids can open the door to wrong-door raids. It is impossible to estimate just how many wrong-door raids occur. Police and prosecutors are notoriously inept at keeping track of their own mistakes, and victims of botched raids are often too terrified or fearful of retribution to come forward. During the course of researching a paper for the Cato Institute on the subject, I have found close to 200 such cases over the last 15 years, and those are just the cases that have been reported," says Radley Balko (2006, April 6). *No SWAT*. Retrieved September 12, 2007, from http://www.cato.org/pub_display.php?pub_id=6344

67. Balko, R. (2006, July 17). *Overkill: The rise of paramilitary police raids in America*. Retrieved May 29, 2008, from http://www.cato.org/pub_display.php?pub_id=6476

68. Stevens, "American Police Resolutions."

69. Stevens, "Police Tactical Units."

70. Healy, G. (2003). Deployed in the USA: Creeping militarization of the home front. *Policy Analysis, 503*. Retrieved July 15, 2008, from http://www.cato.org/pubs/pas/pa503.pdf

71. Nall, L. (2005). *Thugs, assassins, and zealots*. Retrieved March 27, 2008, from http://www.americandrugwar.com/

72. Jackman, T. (2006, March 24). No charges in shooting of unarmed man. *Washington Post*. Retrieved March 18, 2008, from http://www.washingtonpost.com

73. Jackman, "No Charges in Shooting."

74. Cassidy, P. (1997). The rise in paramilitary policing. *Covert Action 2005–2028*.

75. Cassidy, "The rise in paramilitary policing."

76. Greg, S. (1975). Kids and coppers. *Australian and New Zealand Journal of Criminology, 8*(3,4), 221–230.

77. This section was researched by Sara Dastoli, a university research assistant to the author at Sacred Heart University, Fairfield, Connecticut during the spring semester of 2008.

78. Federal Bureau of Investigation. (2006). *Crime in the United States*. Washington, DC: US Department of Justice. Retrieved April 8, 2008, from http://www.fbi.gov/ucr/cius2006/arrests/index.html

79. US v. Puerta, 982 F.2d 1297, 1300 (9th Cir. 1992).

80. Mastrofski, S., McCluskey, J., & Reisig, M. (2002). Police disrespect toward the public: An encounter–biases analysis. *Criminology, 40*(3), 519–552.

81. Mastrofski, S., McCluskey, J., Reisig, M., & Terrill, W. (2004). Suspect disrespect toward the police. *Justice Quarterly, 21*(2), 242–268.

82. Mastrofski, et al., "Suspect Disrespect Toward the Police."

83. Kavanagh, J. (1997). The occurrence of resisting arrest in arrest encounters: A study of police–citizen violence. *Criminal Justice Review, 22*(1), 16–33.

84. Engel, R., Sobol, J., & Worden, R. E. (2000). Further exploration of the demeanor hypothesis: The interaction effects of suspect characteristics and demeanor on police behavior. *Justice Quarterly, 17*, 235–258.

85. Engel, R. S. (2003). Explaining suspects' resistance and disrespect toward police. *Journal of Criminal Justice, 31*(5), 475–492.

86. Belvedere, K., & Worrall, J. L. (2005). Explaining suspect resistance in police–citizen encounters. *Criminal Justice Review, 30*(1), 30–44.

87. Stevens, *Introduction to American Policing.*

88. Personal, confidential communication between a New York City police officer and the author during the summer of 2007.

89. Seate, M. (2003, January 24). Disrespect can turn violent. *Pittsburgh Tribune-Review*, p. 7.

90. Belvedere, et al., "Explaining Suspect Resistance."

91. Kelly, P. A. (2002). Stress: The officer killer. In J. M. Madonna, Jr. & R. E. Kelly (Eds.), *Treating police stress: The work and the words of peer counselors.* Springfield, IL: Charles C. Thomas.

92. Stevens, *Police Officer Stress.*

93. Kelly, "Stress: The Officer Killer".

94. Teplin, L. A. (2000). *Keeping the peace: Police discretion and mentally ill persons.* Washington, DC: US Department of Justice. Retrieved June 25, 2007, from http://www.ncjrs.gov/pdffiles1/jr000244c.pdf

95. Crank, J. P. (2003). *Understand police culture.* Cincinnati, Ohio: Anderson Press. Pp. 40–45.

96. Alpert, G., Dunham, R., & MacDonald, J. (2005). Police suspicion & discretionary decision making during citizen stops. *Criminology, 43*(2). 407–434.

97. Alpert, et al., "Police Suspicion & Discretionary Decision Making."

98. Benjamin, C. (2007, March 27). Police brutality, let's take the power. *The Black Star News.* Retrieved November 12, 2008, from http://www.blackstarnews.com/?c=124&a=3160

99. Quinlin, M. P. (2004). *Irish Boston: A lively look at Boston's colorful Irish past, including museums, historic sites, pubs, music, dancing, and much more.* New York: Globe Pequot.

100. MacDonald, M. P. (2007). *All souls: A family story from Southie.* New York: Beacon Press.

101. Kappeler, V. E. (2005). *Police civil liabilities* (2nd ed.). Mt. Prospect, IL: Waveland Press.

102. Sullivan, J. J. (1997). *Guide to the laws of civil liabilities for New York law enforcement officers: Key data you need to know to protect your career.* Flushing, NY: Looseleaf Law.

103. Kappeler, *Police Civil Liabilities.* This is the same legal perspective linked to correctional officers in Chapter 2. Title 42 encompasses all state and local criminal justice personnel but is federally prosecuted, as opposed to prosecution at the state or local level.

104. Wilson, J. Q., & Kelling, G. L. (1982, March). The police and neighborhood safety. *Atlantic Monthly, 249*(2), 29–38.

105. Skyler, R. (2003). *Fixing broken windows.* Retrieved October 15, 2008, from http://www.ambiguous.org/robin/word/brokenwindows.html

106. Wilson, J. Q., & Kelling, G. L. (1982, March). Broken windows: The police and neighborhood safety. *Atlantic Monthly, 127*, 29–38.

107. Blankstein, A. (2005, May 26). Jury awards $6.5 million in frame-up. *Los Angeles Times.* Retrieved November 12, 2008, from http://www.streetgangs.com/topics/2005/052605ramp.html

108. New York State. (2000). *Division of Criminal Justice Services.* Retrieved October 15, 2008, from http://criminaljustice.state.ny.us/

109. Hill, S. J. (2000, May). Civil liability in policing: A proactive view. *Police,* 46–47.

110. Franklin, *Police Officer's Guide.*

111. Kappeler, V. E. (2007). *Critical issues in police civil liability* (3rd ed.). Mt. Prospect, IL: Waveland Press.

112. Gould & Mastrofski, "Suspect Searches."

113. Stevens, D. J. (2002). Civil liabilities and arrest decisions. In J. T. Walker (Ed.), *Policing and the law.* Upper Saddle River, NJ: Prentice Hall.

114. Novak, K. J., Smith, B. W., & Frank, J. (2003). Strange bedfellows: Civil liability and aggressive policing. *An International Journal of Police Strategies and Management, 26*(2), 352–368.

115. Stevens, "Civil Liabilities and Arrest Decisions."

116. Sourcebook of Criminal Justice Statistics Online. (2008). *Attitudes toward level of violent crime in the United States: 1989–2007.* Albany, NY: US Department of Justice. Retrieved November 15, 2008, from http://www.albany.edu/sourcebook/pdf/t2332007.pdf

117. Milazzo, C., & McNaught, C. (2002, March). SWAT team liability. *Law & Order,* 97–100.

118. City of Chicago v. Jesus Morales, et al. (1998). In the Supreme Court of the United States. No. 97-1121. Retrieved July 31, 2009, from http://www.aclu.org/scotus/1998/22520lgl19981001.html

119. Stevens, *Introduction to American Policing.*

120. Chicago Municipal Code § 8–4–015 [added June 17, 1992].

121. City of Chicago v. Jesus Morales, et al. (1998).

122. City of Chicago v. Jesus Morales, et al.

123. Sherman, L. W. (1998). *Evidence-based policing.* Washington, DC: Police Foundation.

124. Faulkner, S. D., & Danaher, L. P. (1997). Controlling subjects: Realistic training versus magic bullets. *FBI Law Enforcement Bulletin.* Washington, DC: US Department of Justice. Retrieved June 13, 2009, from http://www.fbi.gov/publications/leb/1997/feb974.htm

125. Sherman L. (1992). *Preventing homicide through trial and error.* Retrieved May 28, 2008, from http://www.aic.gov.au/publications/proceedings/17/sherman.pdf

126. Sherman, "The Police."

127. Rosenbaum, D. P., & Stephens, C. (2005). *Reducing public violence and homicide in Chicago: Strategies and tactics of the Chicago Police Department.* Chicago: Illinois Criminal Justice Information Authority. Retrieved May 28, 2008, from http://www.icjia.state.il.us/public/pdf/ ResearchReports/ReducingPublicViolenceandHomicideinChicago.pdf

128. Brown, A. K. (2007, July 30). Cities filing civil suits against gangs. *Associated Press.* Retrieved May 28, 2008, from http://www.pantagraph.com/

129. Bond, M. (2006, June 23). *Chicago police narcotics and gang unit assists feds in taking down major drug operation at Dearborn Homes.* Retrieved June 13, 2009, from   http://www. chicagopolice.org/MailingList/PressAttachment/release.snakebite.pdf

130. Rosenbaum & Stephens, "Reducing Public Violence."

131. Kirkpatrick, C. D., Wright, G. L., & Wootson, C. R., Jr. (2009, February 7). Cause of big dip in crime debated: New chief credits boosted patrols, accountability. But some worry about accuracy of latest data. *Charlotte Observer,* p. 1. The community action cofounder is Julie Eiselt, who was the topic of an article written by Cleve R. Wootson, Jr.

132. Wootson, C. R., Jr. (2008, December 27). Setting her sights on crime. *Charlotte Observer*, p. 3.

133. Wooden, W., & Blazak, R. (2000). *Renegade kids, suburban outlaws: From youth culture to delinquency*. Belmont, CA: Wadsworth.

134. Word, C. O., & Bowser, B. (1997). Background to crack cocaine addition and HIV high-risk: The next epidemic. *American Journal of Drug and Alcohol Abuse, 23*(1), 67–77.

135. Satel, S. (2007, July 10). The human factor. *The American*. Retrieved May 26, 2008, from http://www.american.com/archive/2007/july-august-magazine-contents/the-human-factor-2

136. Deans, D. A. (1997). *Human motivations*. Unpublished graduate student paper, California State University at Northridge. Retrieved May 29, 2008, from http://www.csun.edu/~vcpsy00h/psy691.htm

137. Wooden & Blazak, *Renegade Kids, Suburban Outlaws*.

138. Brownstein, H. H., & Crossland, C. (2003). *Toward a drugs and crime research agenda for the 21st century*. Washington, DC: US Department of Justice. Retrieved November 13, 2008, from http://www.ncjrs.gov/txtfiles1/nij/194616.txt

139. Goode, E. (1997). *Between politics and reason—the drug legalization debate*. New York: St. Martin's Press.

140. Thompson, K. (2007). *Moral panics*. New York: Taylor & Francis.

141. Stevens, D. J. (1999). Corruption among narcotic officers: A study of innocence and integrity. *Journal of Police and Criminal Psychology, 14*(2), 1–10.

142. Floyd, M. (1996, May 30). Expert: Billions spent but drug treatment doesn't work. *Oregon State University News and Communication Services*. Retrieved June 13, 2009, from http://oregonstate.edu/dept/ncs/newsarch/1996/96May/drugtreat.htm

143. According to the US Department of Health and Human Services, National Survey on Drug Use and Health (2004), 15.4 million people abuse only alcohol; 3.6 million abuse only drugs; and 3.3 million abuse both drugs and alcohol.

144. Osborne, G. B., & Fogel, F. (2008). Understanding the motivations for recreational marijuana use among adult Canadians. *Substance Use & Misuse, 43*, 3–4, 539–572.

145. This perspective is not one shared by the author because of his experiences in the past with users and criminals.

146. Trebach, A. S. (2005). *The great drug war*. Bloomington, ID: Unlimited.

147. Roe, B. B. (n.d.). *Why we should legalize drugs*. Retrieved May 29, 2008, from http://www.druglibrary.org/schaffer/Misc/roe1.htm

148. Rueff, A. (2009, March 4). Medical marijuana legalization measure passes Illinois House committee for first time. *Chicago Tribune*. Retrieved June 13, 2009, from http://newsblogs.chicagotribune.com/clout_st/2009/03/medical-marijuana-legalization-measure-passes-illinois-house-committee-for-first-time.html

149. Wilson, J. Q. (1990, February). Against the legalization of drugs, commentary, 89(2), 21–28.

150. Walker, *Sense and Nonsense*.

151. Iyengar, S. (1991). *Is anyone responsible? How television frames political issues*. Chicago: University of Chicago Press.

152. Iyengar, S. (1990). Shortcuts to political knowledge: The role of selective attention and accessibility. In J. A. Ferejohn & J. H. Kuklinski (Eds.), *Information and democratic process*. Urbana: University of Illinois Press.

153. Institute for Health Policy. (2001). *Substance abuse: The nation's number one health problem*. Boston: Brandeis University. Retrieved May 29, 2008, from http://www.rwjf.org/files/publications/other/SubstanceAbuseChartbook.pdf

154. Bacharach, S. B. (2007). *Battling addiction: The workplace matters*. Retrieved September 19, 2007, from http://www.hbo.com/addiction/treatment/374_battling_addiction.html

155. Tunnell, K. D. (2005). The OxyContin epidemic and crime panic in rural Kentucky. *Contemporary Drug Problems, 32*(2), 225–258.

156. Tunnell, "OxyContin Epidemic."

157. Reinarman, C., & Levine, H. G. (1989). The crack attack. In J. Best (Ed.), *Images of issues*. New York: Aldine de Gruyter.

158. Office of National Drug Control Policy. (2009, January). *The president's national drug control strategy*. Retrieved June 13, 2009, from http://www.whitehousedrugpolicy.gov/publications/policy/ndcs09/index.html

159. Office of National Drug Control Policy, "President's National Drug Control Strategy."

160. Roe, "Why We Should Legalize Drugs."

161. Chandra, A. (2008). *Does watching sex on television predict teen pregnancy* [videotape]. Retrieved November 2, 2008, from http://www.rand.org/multimedia/video/2008/11/03/anita_chandra_does_watching_sex_on_television_predict_teen_pregnancy.html. View the video at www.rand.org. Search Anita Chandra, *Does watching sex on television predict teen pregnancy?*

162. Singha, S. (2005, March). *The danger of drug use and the media*. Retrieved September 14, 2007, from http://media.www.brockpress.com/media/storage/paper384/news/2005/03/01/Humour/The-Danger.Of.Drug.Use.In.The.Media-881245.shtml

163. National Youth Anti Drug Media Campaign. (2002, August 23). *Substance use in popular movies and songs*. Retrieved June 13, 2009, from http://www.ajph.org/cgi/content/abstract/98/12/2229?andorexacttitleabs=and&HITS=10&sortspec=relevance&hits=10&fdate=%2F%2F&author1=Hornik%2C+R&andorexacttitle=and&maxtoshow=&andorexactfulltext=and&FIRSTINDEX=0&title=media+campaign&resourcetype=HWCIT&searchid=1&RESULTFORMAT=1

164. Adams, R. (2006, November 10). *Sex, drugs, rock & roll: Boundaries and ethical practice*. Presentation at the Legacy of Addictions Conference, Richmond, Virginia.

165. McMullen, J. L., & McClung, M. (2006). The media, the politics of truth, and the coverage of corporate violence: The Westray disaster and the public inquiry. *Critical Criminology, 14*(1), 67–86.

166. Personal communication between a substance abuse counselor and the author at Lakeview Shock Incarceration Correctional Facility, Brocton, New York, summer 2005. For some illuminating pictures on the subject, search Google for "faces of meth."

167. Drugsense.org. (2009). *Drug war clock*. Retrieved June 13, 2009, from http://www.drugsense.org/wodclock.htm. Click on the Drug War Clock for up-to-the-minute expenditures and arrests linked to the war on drugs.

168. Bureau of Justice Statistics. (2008). *Drug and crime facts: Enforcement*. Washington, DC: US Department of Justice. Retrieved June 13, 2009, from http://www.ojp.usdoj.gov/bjs/dcf/enforce.htm

169. Bureau of Justice Statistics, *Drug and Crime Facts*.

170. Easy access to FBI arrest statistics. (2009). Retrieved June 13, 2009, from http://www.ojjdp. ncjrs.gov/ojstatbb/ezaucr/asp/ucr_display.asp.

171. TRAC Reports. (2008). *Convictions for May 2008*. Retrieved September 1, 2008, from http:// trac.syr.edu/tracreports/bulletins/jfbi/monthlymay08/gui/

172. Brown, E. (2007). *Snitch: Informants, cooperators, and the corruption of justice*. New York: Public Affairs.

173. Bureau of Justice Statistics, *Drug and Crime Facts*.

174. US Customs and Border Protection. Retrieved May 29, 2008, from http://www.cbp.gov/

175. Dammer, H. R., & Fairchild, E. (2005). *Comparative criminal justice systems* (4th ed.). Belmont, CA: Wadsworth.

176. Office of National Drug Control Policy, "President's National Drug Control Strategy."

177. McVay, D. A. (Ed.). (2007, June). *Drug war facts*. Retrieved September 14, 2007, from drug-warfacts.com

178. Almond, B. J. (2002, April 25). US drug war has no clear victor. *Rice–News & Media Relations*. Retrieved July 28, 2007, from http://www.media.rice.edu/media/NewsBot. asp?MODE=VIEW&ID=2866&SnID=2

179. Office of National Drug Control Policy, "President's National Drug Control Strategy."

180. Curtis, R. (1998). The improbable transformation of inner city neighborhoods: Crime, violence, drugs, and youths in the 1990s. *Journal of Criminal Law and Criminology, 88*, 1233–1275.

181. Boyum, D. A., & Kleiman, M. A. R. (1995). Alcohol and other drugs. In J. Q. Wilson & J. Petersilia (Eds.), *Crime and public policy*. San Francisco: Institute for Contemporary Studies.

182. Cromwell, P. F., & Olson, J. N. (2004). *Breaking and entering: Burglars on burglary* (2nd ed.). Belmont, CA: Wadsworth.

183. Bureau of Justice Statistics. (2005, July). *Substance dependence, abuse, and treatment of jail inmates, 2002*. Retrieved September 22, 2007, from http://www.ojp.usdoj.gov/bjs/abstract/ sdatji02.htm

184. Glaser, D. (1997). *Profitable penalties*. Thousand Oaks, CA: Pine Forge.

185. Felson, M. (2002). *Crime and everyday life* (3rd ed.). Thousand Oaks, CA: Pine Forge.

186. Stevens, D. J. (1997). Origins and effects of prison drug gangs in North Carolina. *Journal of Gang Research, 4*, 23–35.

187. McCabe, J. E. (2008). What works in policing? The relationship between drug enforcement and serious crime. *Police Quarterly, 11*(3), 289–314.

188. Gottfedson, M. R., & Hirschi, T. (1990). *A general theory of crime*. Stanford, CA: Stanford University Press.

189. Confidential communication between a narcotics officer and the author.

190. Stevens, "Corruption Among Narcotic Officers."

191. Norml Foundation. (2004, September 23). *Chicago considers marijuana decriminalization plan*. Retrieved July 28, 2007, from http://norml.org/index.cfm?Group_ID=6235. Chicago Mayor Richard

Daley voiced approval this week for a proposed plan to encourage police to ticket rather than criminally arrest adults found in possession of small amounts of marijuana. The measure was first proposed by a Chicago police sergeant, who estimated the proposal could annually raise $5 million in city revenue.

192. Los Angeles Superior Court. (2008). *Proposition 36*. Retrieved July 30, 2009, from http://www.docstoc.com/docs/1025018/2008-LA-Superior-Court-Report

193. Shelden, R. G. (2009). *Shelden Says*. Retrieved June 13, 2009, from http://www.sheldensays.com/

194. Nelson, K. (2004, January). *Top ten drug war stories*. Retrieved July 29, 2007, from http://www.alternet.org/story/17515/

195. Chettleburgh, M. C. (2007, June 13). Put the gangs out of business: Legalize drugs. *National Post*. Retrieved September 14, 2007, from http://www.november.org/stayinfo/breaking07/OutOfBusiness.html

196. Just Think Twice. (2003). *Demand reduction: Street smart prevention*. Retrieved May 29, 2008, from http://www.justthinktwice.com/costs/

197. Stevens, D. J. (1999). Interviews with women convicted of murder: Battered women syndrome revisited. *International Review of Victimology, 6*, 117–135.

Wars on Sex Offenders and Poverty

I have a dream that my four little children will one day live in a nation where they will not be judged by the color of their skin but by the content of their character.

Dr. Martin Luther King, Jr.

▶ ▶ CHAPTER OBJECTIVES

- Describe the history of the war on sex offenders and the effects of the labeling phenomenon
- Characterize the sex crime laws and legal levels that are linked to sex crimes
- Articulate the distinctions between sex violent predators and sex offenders
- Describe the political response to sex offenders and the security of sex offender registers
- Characterize the criminalization of poverty

■ Introduction

Chapter 1 characterized the *CSI Effect*; Chapter 2 showed how the *CSI Effect* impacts criminal justice policy and practices, resulting in an emphasis on aggressive reactive police tactics, vigilantism, and fictional accounts of crime and criminal investigations, which weaken constitutional guarantees and target specific groups of individuals through a war on crime and a war on junkies (Chapter 3). Although those wars continue, the rights, reputations, and sense of self-worth of many individuals, particularly those who are wrongfully convicted, have been lost. Yet, on the winning side, conscientious police officials realize that the deployment of an aggressive show of force and vigilante behavior, fueled by retribution through the *CSI Effect*, do not lend themselves to quality policing in a democratic nation; those police officials developed proactive initiatives in an effort to deliver quality police services, enhanced quality of life expectations and arrests, and reduced litigation potentials (defensive policing). The popular media, through the *CSI Effect*, continues its characterization of targeted groups through archaic wars on sex offenders and poverty. In the first decade of a new century, Americans are dramatized by an unstable global economy that enhances poverty, a condition that has been criminalized by the criminal justice community (discussed later), while some of the most popular television programs, such as *Law & Order: Special Victims Unit* (NBC), *CSI: Miami* (CBS), and *Criminal Minds* (CBS), among others, add recognition to the official war on sex offenders.

■ War on Sex Offenders

Looking through the *CSI Effect* lens, another obsession of the popular media comes into view: the war on sex offenders. This war is fueled by the popular media through the CSI Effect promoting aggressive criminal justice police strategies, glorifying vigilantism among justice practitioners and overzealous constituents seeking their moment of fame, and advocating fictionalized accounts of crime and the criminal justice process. For instance, many suspects have been convicted with only DNA evidence, yet in the fall of 2009 some Israeli scientists implied that DNA can be faked by a first year undergraduate student. After convictions and time served (if the offender has not been executed or died in prison), the war on sex offenders continues with probation, parole, registration on a list (sometimes for life) that includes pictures and addresses, and in some cases continued confinement after a sex offender is released from the department of corrections supervision (civil containment).[1] Through it all, going to the root of the crime and aiding the victim of the offender are secondary concerns.

History of the War on Sex Offenders

Prior to the 1900s, crimes relating to sex were not classified separately, nor were those convicted of sex crimes differentiated from those convicted of other crimes.[2] In the 20th century, criminal justice policy was shaped by the following:

- Sexual psychopath laws (1930s to 1940s)
- A focus on domestic sex crimes under the influence of feminism philosophy (which includes mandatory arrest at domestic violent scenes when probable cause is present)
- Renewed attention and laws geared toward sexual predators[3]

These policies acted as milestones in the segregation of sex offenders and their crimes and introduced the war on sex offenders, which was dramatized by the media. Primarily, the renewed attention and regulations were associated with sexual psychopath concepts and definitively described sex offenders as having chronic out-of-control behavior manifested by a mental abnormality. Individuals were referred to as a socially sick people or, at times, they were referred to as patients when they were under correctional supervision, regardless of whether they were institutionalized (imprisoned) or in a community correctional program where they were to be treated, cured, and released into the community.[4,5]

From a criminologist's perspective, Edwin Sutherland identified three stages in the emergence of sexual psychopath laws in the United States:[6]

- Laws are customarily enacted after a state of fear is aroused (i.e., sex murders of children are the most effective in producing hysteria).
- Fear is mobilized across many sectors; people in the most varied situations envisage dangers and see the need of and possibility for control.
- There is the appointment of a committee, which attempts to determine facts, studies procedures in other states, and makes recommendations.

Lyn Hinds and Kathleen Daly argued that Sutherland maintained that these appointed committees dealt with emergencies, and their investigations were generally superficial because they occurred after the crime. Sutherland decried "these dangerous [sex crimes] and futile laws" had "little or no merit" associated with sex offenders or, for that matter, their victims because the laws were not founded in a scientific method of discovery.[7] These thoughts are consistent with current concerns related to the convergence and divergence of antisocial personality disorder or a *psychopathy continuum* that is especially related to courtroom testimony when clinical assessments of sexually violent predators are administered.[8] Those researchers feared that misdiagnosis and incompetent forensic evaluations were likely. They were probably more on target than they realized, especially when a labeling phenomenon is considered for both offenders and victims.

Labeling Phenomenon

When an offender (or a victim) is tagged or labeled a "sex offender" (or a sexual victim), the labeling phenomenon suggests that the manner in which others interact with the labeled person can eventually produce deviant behavior through a self-fulfilling prophecy; the labeled person acts out or behaves within the expected constructs of the label, regardless of his or her previous pattern of behavior.[9] Labeling implies that an individual's audience often responds to the individual's label rather than to the behavior of the individual. For a label to stick, those who provide the label are usually those in authority (such as police, courts, elitists, teachers, parents, and cliques in high schools). For example, teachers and students might respond differently to a student who is labeled as "problematic" as opposed to a student who is labeled as a "jock." In the streets, a person with a "sex offender" label might elicit different behavior from apartment rental agents, pharmacists, and community college admission personnel. The labels most often come from those in authority, such as the criminal justice system, schools, and employers. Howard Becker advises that the audience, not the actor, determines when certain behavior is defined as crime. When the label of "sex offender" is officially provided by the criminal justice community, an individual (regardless of his or her guilt) is likely to experience confrontational behavior from everyone he or she encounters. Jobs, housing, friends, services, and program opportunities disappear. Labeling suggests that the audience holds the power over the labeled person and that professionals from medical doctors to correctional staff to police officers respond to this person as though he or she has the plague.[10,11] This thought is consistent with that of David L. Rosenhan, who applies a labeling perspective to sanity. Rosenhan argues that a failure to discover the sanity of an imposter would mean that "psychiatric diagnoses ... are in the minds of observers and are not valid summaries of characteristics displayed by the observed."[12] That is, reality is in the eyes of the beholder, and what the eyes see is that sex offenders "are universally hated and despised and seen as dangerous sexual predators unless locked up and kept under surveillance," argues Hollida Wakefield.[13] One problem is that individuals lump all sex offenders together without regard for the crime (see the discussion of legal levels later in this chapter).

Statistics

Statistics can aid in an understanding of the war on sex offenders. It can be advanced that an estimated 275,000 convicted sex offenders were under the care, custody, or supervision of correctional agencies across the country, year ending 2009. Approximately 60 percent of those offenders were on parole or probation.[14] Most sex offenders are returned to the community after adjudication. Sex offenders represent almost 4 percent of the estimated seven million offenders convicted yearly. On average, when sentenced to prison, sex offenders serve three years and six months of an eight-year sentence before a conditional release.[15] On the other hand, sex offenders receive harsher sentences than other offenders. For example, under Arizona law, mere possession of pornography involving minors younger than age of 15 is punishable by a 10-year mandatory minimum sentence.[16] Each individual picture is a separate offense, and sentences are served consecutively. Morton Berger, a former high school teacher, received a 200-year sentence without parole: 10 years for each of 20 images on his computer. Berger himself did not victimize anyone, or at least that is what had been revealed from a subsequent investigation into his background.

The problem is that often there is a great deal of confusion stirred through the *CSI Effect* about the nature of sex crimes, sex offenders, apprehension, and convictions, as tragic as those crimes are. For example, in *Dateline NBC*'s special report, "To Catch a Predator," reporter Chris Hansen proclaimed that Web predators are "a national epidemic."[17] Hansen implied that sex offenders are vulnerable to detection, apprehension, and prosecution. Consistent with those fictionalized accounts are popular television dramas, such as *Law & Order: Special Victims Unit*, which suggests that most sexual offenders are easily detected, fall victim to some ingenious plot, and are apprehended or arrested (more details are provided later). Other popular television dramas, such as *Law & Order*, go further and suggest that most sex offenders go to trial (actually, almost 9 of 10 criminal cases end in plea bargains).[18]

Where Sexual Assault Happens

The war on sex offenders through the *CSI Effect* distorts other valuable information and sets offenders up for victimization. For example, in a review of the last 18

Law & Order presentations on either prime time or cable networks (as of July 19, 2008), the last 12 *Law & Order: Special Victims Unit* presentations, the last eight *Criminal Minds* presentations, and the last 14 *CSI: Miami* presentations, an estimated 55 percent (28 of 52 episodes) had characterized sexual assault as occurring outside the home of the victims, and the offenders were depicted as adult strangers to the victims.[19] In reality, nearly 6 out of 10 rape or sexual assault incidents were reported by victims in their own home or at the home of a friend, relative, or neighbor.[20] One implication emerging from the *CSI Effect* is that real-world expectations are altered about who experiences sexual assaults, where these crimes happen, and who committed those crimes. The media depict their version of the facts associated with sexual assault. However, what is known about sexual assault is that violators can be any age, including teenagers or younger, biological fathers and mothers, close relatives, friends of the family, and teachers. For instance, there is an endless stream of reports of female school teachers having sex with underaged students.

Student-Teacher Rape, a federally-funded study, concluded that the problem of school teachers molesting students dwarfs in magnitude the clergy sex-abuse scandal that rocked the Catholic Church.[21]

This thought is consistent with a source that shows 208 images and links of female high school teachers and teacher aids who have been arrested for the sexual assault of students in homes, cars, at school and at hotels, and on the run from largely 2005 to the summer of 2009.[22]

For instance, Abbie Jane Swogger, 34, a teacher's aide at Highlands Senior High School in Harrison, Pa., was arrested in early 2008 for renting a hotel room where police found beer, marijuana, an open condom wrapper, and at least four teenage girls and boys, including several of Swogger's 15-year-old son's friends. Another example is Adrianne Hockett, accused of having sex with a 16-year-old special-needs student in a Houston apartment that she rented for the get-togethers. The boy testified the pair would "have sex, drink beer, and smoke weed." Finally consider, Allenna Ward, 24, a minister's daughter from Laurens County, S.C., who taught at Bell Street Middle School in Clinton, S.C. In early 2007, Ward was arrested for the sexual assault of five boys. Some of the victims, ages 14 and 15, were students at Ward's school. Authorities say the married woman had sex with the boys on campus, at a motel, in a park, and behind a restaurant. Ward pled guilty to three counts of second-degree criminal sexual conduct with a minor and three counts of lewd acts with a minor.

Sex Crime Laws

Although definitions for sex crimes depend on the jurisdiction in which the crimes occurred, they can include attempts and conspiracies and can be characterized as follows:

- *Forcible rape* is forcible intercourse with an adult male or female without the consent of the victim (depending on jurisdiction).[23,24]

- *Statutory rape* is the carnal knowledge of a victim who is usually younger than 16 years of age (age varies by state) and an aggressor older than 17 years of age (age varies by state), regardless of whether force or lack of force existed.
- *Aggravated rape* is a rape committed upon a person aged 65 years or older or when the victim resists the act to the utmost but whose resistance is overcome by more force than necessary or the use of a weapon (including any object used to threaten the victim) and can involve two or more offenders.
- *Lewd acts with children* include fondling, indecent liberties, immoral practices, molestation, and other indecent behaviors with children. Children cannot give sexual consent.
- *Forcible sodomy* includes deviate sexual intercourse, buggery, and oral or anal intercourse by force.
- *Other sexual assault* includes gross sexual imposition, sexual abuse, aggravated sexual abuse, and other acts, such as fondling, molestation, or indecent liberties when the victim is not a child.

Using the Commonwealth of Massachusetts as a guide to provide an understanding of sex offenses, victims who are unable to provide consent include victims who are unconscious, intoxicated by alcohol or drugs, mentally impaired, and children younger than 16 years of age. Each state has a different age of consent statute ranging from 14 to 18 years of age; for instance, Idaho is 14 years of age and California is 18 years of age. There were an estimated 1,700 rapes reported in the Commonwealth of Massachusetts in 2005 associated with Massachusetts General Law Chapter 265 and Chapter 272, Crimes Against Chastity, Morality, Decency, and Good Order.[25] There were an estimated 18,000 offenders residing in Massachusetts who were found guilty of sex offenses in the spring of 2005. The most frequent sex offense for incarcerated males was rape and sexual abuse of a child (29 percent), followed by rape of a child with force (21 percent), aggravated rape (17 percent), and rape of an adult (16 percent).[26] Of 18 imprisoned female sex offenders, 9 were convicted of rape and abuse of a child. However, it is argued that sex offender laws do little to protect children because most sex offenders are known to the child or, worse, related to the child.[27]

Legal Levels

Each state and often each jurisdiction categorize sex offenders into three levels based on future risk assessment (to repeat a crime associated with sexual assault); for example, of the 26,841 convicted sexual offenders in the state of New York as of May 17, 2008, the following levels applied[28]:

- Level 1: Low risk of repeat offense (9,790)
- Level 2: Moderate risk of repeat offense (9,781)
- Level 3: High risk of repeat offense (6,687)
- Level P: Offender is registered but risk of repeat offense is not determined (583)

Arrests

Across the country, there were 23,307 arrests conducted in 2007 for the crime of rape and 83,979 arrests conducted for sex offenses (except forcible rape and prostitution).[29]

Reported Sexual Assault

The *CSI Effect* implies that most sex crimes are reported to the police.[30] In the real world, sex crimes are often not reported, and when they are, an arrest is not an automatic process.[31,32] Generally, across the country 39 percent of 29.4 million violent and property crimes were reported to the police, according to the National Crime Victimization Survey (NCVS).[33] Also, violent crimes that include sexual assault, according to experts, are not reported to the police because they are deemed to be a private or personal matter or because they are reported to another official. Beyond these perspectives, shame, humiliation, fear of retaliation, loss of confidence in the criminal justice community, or personal retaliation might play a role in unreported sex assault cases.[34,35] Other reasons for nonreporting include victims blaming themselves, or the victim is a child or is mentally ill and the aggressor is the victim's father or another close family member. Some children can't speak because they are too young or because there is no one to speak to.[36] The NCVS is one of two statistical series maintained by the US Department of Justice to learn about the incidence and prevalence of crime. For example, in 1995 the Uniform Crime Report (UCR) reported 113,000 rape attacks, and the NCVS showed 355,000 reported victims, or an estimated 314 percent difference.[37] This finding is consistent with criminology experts who argue that sex crimes are among the least reported violent crimes and that sex crimes, including child sexual assault or molestation, are underreported by 20 percent to over 300 percent.[38–40] To put this finding of underreporting into perspective, the Boston Police Department showed 216 rapes reported for the period between January 1, 2007 and October 8, 2007; the San Francisco Police Department showed 166 rapes reported in 2004.[41] Using the official reports (UCR and NCVS) and applying a simplistic calculation (which will probably offer unreliable data because of various reporting policies), Boston could have had another 678 (or 894) rapes, and San Francisco could have had another 521 (or 687) rapes. Additionally, recent data reported by the FBI's UCR showed 92,455 sex crimes across the country in 2006 which can calculate to an additional 291,233 cases or a total of 383,688.[42] In fact, "conservative estimates of sexual assault prevalence suggest that 25 percent of American women have experienced sexual assault, including rape."[43] Reliable data for male rape cases are difficult to find however (see the section on rape in prison).

City data are consistent with these statistics.

Clearance Rates

The *CSI Effect* attempts to convince audiences that when a sex crime is reported that it ends in an arrest. Clearance rates are associated with reported crimes that end in an arrest. A crime is cleared by an arrest or solved for crime reporting purposes, explains the FBI, when a person is arrested, charged with the commission of the offense, and turned over to the court for prosecution (following the arrest, court summons, or a law enforcement notice). A crime can also be cleared by exceptional means. For instance, in certain situations, elements beyond law enforcement's control can prevent the agency from arresting and charging an offender. Law enforcement agencies must meet the following four conditions in order to clear an offense by exceptional means; The agency must have identified the offender; gathered enough evidence to support an arrest, make a charge, and turn over the offender to the court for prosecution; identified the offender's exact location so that the suspect could be taken into custody immediately; and encountered a circumstance outside the control of law enforcement that prohibits the agency from arresting, charging, and prosecuting the offender. For example, exceptional clearances can include, but are not limited to, the death of the offender.

An estimated 40 percent of reported crimes of rape ended in arrests in 2007,[44] which means that 4 of every 10 reported sex crimes end in an arrest. The Boston Police Department's official report (as previously mentioned) showed an arrest rate that equals 30 percent.[45] Making an arrest does not mean that the case ends in a conviction.

Conviction Rates

The *CSI Effect* promises that every sex offender that is detected and arrested is convicted of the crime, but reality tells us that at the state level, three of every four known sex crimes are dropped by station house sergeants, prosecutors, and judges because of a lack of sufficient evidence to prosecute.[46] Of those cases that proceed toward adjudication, a little more than one-half of the defendants are convicted. For example, of 21,840 rapists who were arrested, 12,310 ended in a conviction (56 percent; recall there is a difference between reported and arrested), and conviction does not necessarily translate to a prison sentence.[47,48]

At the federal level, 39 percent of all sex exploitation matters were declined for prosecution by US attorneys in 2006.[49] At the federal level, 30 percent of these cases were dropped because of weak, inadmissible, or insufficient evidence. One-fifth (20 percent) of the cases were declined due to lack of evidence of criminal intent (no crime established), and 15 percent were referred or handled in other prosecutions. In comparison, weak evidence was stated as the reason for 24 percent of declinations for child pornography and 20 percent of declinations for sex transportation (see Chapter 10 for details of why prosecutors reject sexual assault cases). For instance, of the Boston Police Department's 215 arrests for the 715 reported sex crimes (30 percent), 48 were convicted (less than 7 percent of the reported cases or 22 percent of the arrests), and the defendants received an average of 59 months (less than five years) in prison, reports the City of Boston.

Profile of a Sexual Violent Predator

A sexual violent predator (SVP) can be defined as a repeat sexual offender who often uses physical violence and intimidation upon victims, often preys on children, and has many more victims than are ever reported.[50,51] SVPs are prosecuted for only a fraction of their crimes, if they are ever prosecuted at all.[52] A typical characteristic of SVPs is the devastating trauma visited upon their victims.[53-55] However, 47 percent of defendants who are convicted of sex crimes are first-time offenders caught up in a crime of passion (they have an impulsive nature and an inability to understand the consequences of their act), which includes a status offense.[56-59]

Distinctions Between SVPs and Sex Offenders

An estimated 1 in 10 of all convicted sex offenders can be classified as a chronic sex offender or SVP; however, most often the media projects the idea that most sex offenders characterize SVP behaviors or consequences, which similarly do not fit the statistics.[60] Sex offenders of all types, including females and children, vary significantly in age and represent all races, ethnicities, and socioeconomic classes.[61] There are significant distinctions between an SVP and a sex offender, which includes the repetition of the act.[62]

There are similarities in the behavior of sexual predators. Pedophiles or child molesters, as an example, tend to arrive at deviancy via multiple pathways and engage in many different sexual and nonsexual acting out behaviors or episodes with children.[63] However, no single molester profile exists. As expected, child molesters are highly dissimilar in terms of personal characteristics, life experiences, and criminal histories.

An estimated half of all cases of sexual assault and rape involve alcohol consumption by the perpetrator, the victim, or both.[64] In at least 80 percent of sexual assaults, both the perpetrator and the victim knew each other, but alcohol-involved sexual assaults often occur among strangers or people who do not know each other well (e.g., acquaintances or casual dates). Researchers argued that the pathways through which alcohol contributes to sexual assault include the woman's alcohol consumption.[65]

The media tends to report the idea that sexually assaulted children become adult sexual abusers; for example, in Episode 129 ("Quarry") of *Law & Order: Special Victims Unit*, a seven-year-old child is victimized, and the SVU squad investigates a convicted serial killer, Lucas Biggs (John Savage), believing that he molested and murdered the boy. Although Biggs detailed the many children he molested to Detective Benson (Mariska Hargitay) while she interviewed him in prison, it was discovered that he too had been sexually abused when he was a youngster.

The notion that a child sex victim becomes an adult sex abuser is a common theme in many performances offered by popular television dramas, but empirical evidence does not necessarily support that perspective.[66,67] One study shows that a family history of violence, sexual abuse by a female, maternal neglect, and lack of supervision are all associated with a threefold-increased risk that the abused will become an abuser. Twenty-six of the 224 sex abuse victims (12 percent) later committed sexual offenses, and in almost all cases their victims were also children.[68]

SVPs tend to be an extremely heterogeneous population that has not, on the whole, been subdivided into clinically meaningful groups.[69] A sexual offense, whether it be pedophilia, rape, or indecent exposure, is a legal term for describing complex behavior. It tells little about the individual who carries out these complex acts. Yet we tend to think in terms of child molesters or SVPs as members of a group and base our understanding of their behavior on that one aspect of their conduct: victim selection. However, SVPs (both those convicted and those not convicted of sexual assaults)[70,71] are likely to demonstrate the characteristics shown in Table 4-1.

TABLE 4–1 CHARACTERISTICS OF SEXUAL PREDATORS

- Highly manipulative of public and criminal justice personnel[72]
- Victimizes in secrecy[73,74]
- Secretive lifestyles[75]
- Well-planned attack strategies[76]
- Highly functional[77]
- Excellent social skills[78]
- Chronic liars and usually loners[79]
- Developed complicated and persistent psychological and social systems for the purpose of distorting the harm they have brought against others[80]
- Sophisticated rationale to avoid detection[81]
- Established facades designed to hide the truth about themselves[82]
- Commits a wide range and large number of crimes and is highly impulsive[83]
- Has a propensity to reoffend[84]
- Attacks both family and nonfamily victims[85]
- Attacks without regard for the victim's gender, age, or social status[86]
- Attacks without regard for the victim's condition or circumstance[87]
- Sexual assault is their life's work[88]
- Believes that the best victim profile is vulnerability by circumstance or manipulation[89]
- Believes that vulnerability includes victims of other predators
- Believes that vulnerability includes sexual offenders (who are not predators)

In a study of 561 SVPs, rapists reported a lifetime average of seven incidents, and exhibitionists reported more than five incidents.[90] Other researchers suggest that SVPs sexually assault over 100 victims during their lifetime, which can include incarcerated victims.[91]

The Media's Portrayal of Police Response to Sex Offenders

The popular television drama *Law & Order: Special Victims Unit* routinely portrays New York City police detectives administering violent and verbal abuse to registered sex offenders. In Season 6, Episode 140 "Demons", Detective Elliot Stabler (Christopher Meloni) dropped his weapon to physically fight with a sex offender and almost strangled a suspect, Ray Schenkel (Robert Patrick). One truth is that most justice professionals on the streets or in prison (in the author's experience) would not risk fighting with a sex offender when another option is more reasonable and better fits the training of the officer because of litigation, disease (especially HIV), placing other individuals at risk, or losing the battle. Later in the sequence, Detective Olivia Benson (Mariska Hargitay) questioned the suspect, who said to her, "What kind of fool would rape a woman the day he gets out of prison?" Benson responded, "You, Ray, cause there's no cure for sex offenders. So they let you out." Later in the performance, a retired detective told Stabler, "He [Ray] may not have left his DNA, but Ray raped that girl, and he'll rape again till you put him back in jail or he's in a grave." The message is that sex offenders cannot be cured, but it is also implies that when they are incarcerated, sex offenders can and do attack other inmates, correctional personnel, and visitors, which includes volunteers such as chaplains, group leaders, and substance abuse counselors.

Prison Rape

The Uniform Crime Report data reveal that an estimated 92,500 rapes were reported to the police in 2006.[92] On the other hand, a different report shows over 145,000 rapes in male prisons (few of those rapes were investigated, and only 24 percent of the victims received medical care).[93] A little less than one-half of all those incarcerated in state prisons were convicted for a nonviolent offense. The reality is that predators do commit violent crimes while they are incarcerated, but it is equally likely that the inmates and staff members attack sex offenders, too. In most state prison systems, sex offenders (even the ones convicted of sexual assault with their underaged girlfriend) are segregated from the general prison population, but often sex offenders are forced to participate in similar activities and required sex offender treatment programs. Finally, among 10 state facilities across the country with the highest overall inmate sexual assault rates, three had staff sexual misconduct rates that exceeded 10 percent.[94]

Prison Sex Offender Class

An inmate who was convicted of sexual assault (E Class) and incarcerated at Gowanda Correctional Facility in New York was required to complete a year-long course that all other sexual offenders in that facility attended, too. Here is what this first-timer wrote in his journal during one of those classes:

> I can't believe I'm one of them [sexual offenders]. They look at me like I'm a piece of pie. What could I say if they jack me up—the COs [correctional officers] treat us all alike. After growing up, I learned things happened that were in my control. Yes, but the way I dealt with my life issues before this place were [sic] incorrect. My life became a circus, but now. . .. At least I learned the [sic] 3 do's to stop abusive behavior: admit the possibility exists; plan to stop it at the earliest signs; replace the time no longer used abusively with healthy activities. Like what—defend my ass from those maniacs.[95]

Street Cop Response to Sex Offenders

One evening in Portland, Maine, a young man wandered into a church meeting room where church members were involved in a workshop.[96] The young man had been violently attacked as he walked home from a retail establishment between his apartment and the church. He said that he needed help, as his cold fingers wiped blood from his face. It was winter, and soft, white snow had frozen to the ground, the trees, and everything in Portland. The stranger's expression was frozen, too, but he was obviously in pain. One church member pointed to the restroom and another called police about the attack. When officers arrived, they asked for the stranger's identification and called it in. Immediately, the demeanor of the officers changed from helpful to hostile. The officers learned that the stranger was a registered sex offender. More officers arrived, and some checked out the restroom and handcuffed the young man's hands behind his back. The sergeant interrogated the youth in front of the congregation. Eventually, his restraints were removed. Another officer looked at his watch and proclaimed that the sex offender had violated curfew. "But I don't have a curfew," he said, "I'm not on parole or anything."[97] Another officer slapped him in the face and told him to "shag your rotten ass home before I change my mind." The laughter among officers and nervous church members relieved the tension in the room. Several months later, when one of the officers was asked about his conduct during the incident, he said that he "wasn't sure what to do so I followed the Sarg's lead. I sort'a felt sorry for the kid [sex offender] because he really needed [medical] help." Later, some of the other officers said that they would have liked to "beat the crap out of the offender."[98] It appears that officers and the public are confused about sex offenders and respond to an individual's status as opposed to his or her behavior.

Another case clarifies the issue. One of three arresting officers testified at a coroner's inquest in New York City that the officers "didn't think it was necessary" to perform cardiopulmonary resuscitation when they noticed that a rape suspect was having difficulty breathing, but they did use an ammonia capsule and summoned paramedics. The 22-year-old suspect, Ernest Lacy, who died in custody, was "like a man gone berserk" when the police tried to put him in handcuffs, Officer George Kalt says.[99]

Public Response to Sex Offenders

Sex offender registers (discussed later) can lead to harassment and violence against registered sex offenders.[100] For example, a woman who was interviewed on ABC News's *20/20* with John Stossel, who is known as Petra Luna, openly talked about her goal to retaliate against sex offenders so they cannot live normal lives. Luna operates a Web site that threatens nonviolent offenders, lists home addresses of persons on registries, misinforms her followers, and does not preach by statistics. It was learned that Luna utilizes her Web site to promote vigilantism and to sell products, largely her own recorded music. Nonetheless, Luna provides information about sex offenders and promotes harm to registered sex offenders.

Another example relates to Anthony Mullen, who was sentenced to life in prison for killing two sex offenders.[101] Mullen found his victims on Washington's online sex-offender list, posed as an FBI agent to enter their home, and killed Victor Vazquez, aged 68 years, and Hank Eisses, aged 49 years. He said he let a third resident go because he showed remorse. During the trial, Mullen was comforted by several hundred e-mails sent to him, the prosecutor, and the judge, which said that Mullen should receive a medal rather than a trial.[102]

Politicians' Response to Sex Offenders

Confusion comes in many varieties from politicians. For example, in many states, governors declare war on sex offenders and toughen sex crime laws.[103] For example, the governor of New Mexico demanded more sanctions. In a state with capital punishment and a life sentence upon a second offense, a first sexual offense also receives a life sentence. Lifers are ineligible to participate in any programs, such as substance abuse counseling and treatment, general education diploma preparatory courses, manual labor assignments, physical training and drills, training in decision making and personal development, and prerelease skills training.[104]

Other states spend vast resources pursing sexual assault complaints against healthcare professionals, implied medical doctors (the headline seems to say), such as in Washington.[105] Between 1995 and 2005, 1,494 sexual misconduct complaints were filed against licensed healthcare professionals in Washington. Only 1,033 of the doctors were actually investigated, and over one-half (576) of the cases were dismissed, even though in many cases there was enough evidence for a conviction. Of the 457 cases that were not dismissed, charges were filed against 399 licensed practitioners, including 66 MDs. Of those 399, 13.5 percent (202) had their licenses revoked. Of course, the media failed to mention that the state licensed 17,000 registered counselors, which account for the largest number of sex offenders in health care.[106]

Registering Sex Offenders

It has been mandated in most jurisdictions that sex offenders must register with a local sex offender register, which provides information including a picture of the offender to the public.[107] It is the responsibility of the local police to supervise or participate in monitoring a sexual register in their jurisdiction.[108] In many jurisdictions, registration covers a range of offenses, which includes everything from child rape to consensual teenage sex, regardless of the future potential threat. In some jurisdictions, an offender has residency restrictions, which forces the offender to move away from children or the children's parents and can place the offender miles away from their families, jobs, treatment facilities, and even schools.

Primarily, the various types of notification laws are as follows[109]:

- Authorities alert residents of sex offenders who are moving into their neighborhoods.
- School jurisdictions must require sex offenders who commence school attendance in the jurisdiction to appear in person to register or update their registration within three business days.
- Employment jurisdictions must require sex offenders who commence employment in the jurisdiction, or changes employers or places of employment in the jurisdiction, to appear in person to register or update their registration within three business days.
- In all cases in which sex offenders make an in-person appearance in a jurisdiction and register or update their registration as previously described, the jurisdiction must immediately transmit by electronic forwarding the registration information for the sex offenders (including any updated information concerning name, residence, employment, or school attendance) to all other jurisdictions in which the sex offenders are residents, employees, or students.
- Relevant data are made available to residents who seek it.
- Convicted child molesters are required to identify themselves as sex offenders.

At present, America is focused on ways to increase public protection and control of sex offenders, particularly in ways outside the context of criminal law.[110] The perceived harm exaggerated through the *CSI Effect* and the real harm caused by sex offenders, in combination with the persistent nature of some patterns of sex offending, has caused constituents and policy makers to push for specialized remedies and powers.

California enacted the first sex offender registration law in 1944. Other states followed, but it wasn't until the 1990s that registration gained popularity; between 1991 and 1996, 38 states enacted registration laws.[111] The states' efforts have been overtaken by three federal laws that mandated offender registries: Jacob Wetterling Crimes Against Children and Sexually Violent Offender Registration Program, Wetterling as amended in 1996 by the federal Megan's Law, and Wetterling as amended in 1996 by the Pam Lychner Sexual Offender Tracking and Identification Act of 1996. One Web site shows that over 600,000 sex offenders were registered across the nation in 2007.[112]

Current views relate to a sex offender national gap-free network of registration. The idea is that sex offenders who are convicted in one state are mandated to register in another state and that each state is required to provide information on all their sex offenders. Also, Congress authorized the FBI to develop a National Sex Offenders Registry (NSOR). In some states, such as Wisconsin, the community notification statute authorized officials to alert residents about the release and reintegration of sex offenders in their communities, as perceived by residents, law enforcement, probation and parole agents, and sex offenders.[113]

False Security of Sex Offender Registers[114]

The public has been informed that correctional community inpatient and outpatient programs that specialize in treating sex offenders have been enhanced dramatically, yet few incarcerated sex offenders receive treatment.[115] Of those who do, there has been insufficient research to establish consistent estimates of recidivism or identify which treatment is effective for what type of sex offender. However, comparisons between felons convicted of sex crimes and non-sex-offenders released from state prisons show that sex offenders had lower overall rearrest rates; more specifically, 43 percent of sex offenders versus 68 percent of non-sex-offenders were rearrested for any type of crime, not just sex crimes.[116] Prison or prison programs apparently have an effect.

Nonetheless, Peter Finn advises, media attention and school programs may have increased public awareness of the dangers of sex offenders through a series of highly publicized violent sex offenses that were committed on unsuspecting victims by released sex offenders.[117]

Community Notification and Recidivism

Grant Duwe and William Donnay's recent study showed that community notification based on "a tiered risk-management system significantly reduces sexual recidivism."[118] Two components powered this research: (1) SVPs (as opposed to first-time offenders) were the primary participants of this study; and (2) an assumption was made that sexual predators often operate under a veil of secrecy, which enables them to obtain access or networks to unsuspecting victims. Lifting this veil through community notification can limit SVPs' opportunities to form the types of relationships that facilitate sexual offending (assuming they have been identified as such and have been apprehended and convicted).[119] That is, sexual offending and, in particular, sexual recidivism often involve offenders who victimize someone they know, argue many experts.[120] This thought is consistent with the notion that predatory offenders tend to possess the intent to commit sexual assault and merely await an opportunity to act upon their desire.[121,122] Sex offender registration is one answer, but there is no research indicating central registries actually reduce recidivism, argue many scholars.

A study in Washington state during the first years of registration found no statistically significant differences between offenders who were subjected to notification (19% recidivated) and those who were not (22% recidivated). The Washington researcher says, "Driven by revulsion, anger, and fear that far exceed responses to other types of crimes in our society, sexually violent predator statutes may succeed in providing an illusion of public safety. The true efficacy of these laws, however, remains undetermined."[123]

Other ways to control sex offenders can relate to zero-tolerance policies and constituent response to sex offenders, regardless of the original crime that brought the offender to the attention of the police. Then there are constitutional questions about labeling and focusing on a convicted sex offender, which would not provide him or her with an opportunity to resume a reasonable lifestyle that includes personal relationships. However, the media contributes to the congratulations of vigilante behavior in retaliation toward sex offenders. Sex offender registration can be called a *name and shame* program. In this regard, Nevada's sex offender law has been challenged in federal court.[124] Lawyers representing 27 unnamed plaintiffs in a federal civil rights lawsuit claim that a law that creates an Internet-accessible state registry of 4,941 people convicted of sex crimes since 1956 is unconstitutional. The plaintiffs argue that minor offenders, such as those convicted of theft of pornographic magazines, would be unfairly included. Many states will be monitoring this case, which may well impact sex offender programs across the nation.

Finally, many experts argue that sex registers reinforce a sense of false security for the community because of the recidivist rates and because most SVPs are not registered nor have they been apprehended.[125]

Civil Commitment

Are SVPs mentally ill? One group of researchers described several models for the civil commitment after an SVP prisoner serves or maxes out his or her prison sentence.[126] Rather than releasing SVPs, in *Kansas v. Hendricks* (521 U.S., 326, 331) the court deemed that continued detainment (after time served) of an SVP, when the detainment is associated with a mental disorder (such as sexual violence), does not impose a due process issue because an SVP represents a legitimate threat to the public safety, and the SVP can benefit from the treatment.[127]

In most cases, civil commitment follows a psychopathology or mental health civil commitment model whereby the SVP is found to be amenable to treatment and characterizes behavior consistent with dangerous compulsive behavior, consequently representing a continuing danger to the public. That is, the chances of reoffending are likely. Rudolph Alexander, Jr. articulates that contemporary cases asked the question of whether a violent incarcerated sexual predator could be civilly committed to a mental health facility after this prisoner had served his or her entire prison sentence and was about to be released.[128] For both questions, the

Supreme Court answered in the affirmative. The court's rulings that incarcerated sex offenders nearing release may be civilly committed to a mental health facility have potentially ominous implications for both mental health and criminal justice policy, reaffirming *Kansas v. Hendricks.*

One reports shows that in 2007 an estimated 2,700 pedophiles, rapists, and other sexual offenders were held indefinitely, mostly in special treatment centers, under civil commitment programs in 19 states, which on average cost taxpayers four times more than keeping the offenders in prison.[129]

One mission of correctional personnel is to prevent reoffenses.[130] In most jurisdictions, professional supervisors have learned that no single strategy or plan prevents sexual assault because each offender is different. What holds greater promise is the application of multidisciplinary models of sexual offender management.[131] Recent legislation in several states that provide correctional supervision, including rehabilitative treatment or civil containment, has stirred legal, clinical, ethical, and public policy controversies.[132]

Advantages of the Media's War on Sex Offenders

There is little question that high-profile media coverage of crimes against children has heightened public awareness of critical child safety needs and issues, which is a good thing. Yet it also results in blurred realities between heinous sexual predators and young boys and girls who made a single thoughtless decision that, in many cases, changed their lives, the lives of their family members, and the lives of their victims, forever.[133]

Implications

The war on sex offenders promotes aggressive criminal justice policy, vigilantism, and fictionalized accounts of crime and the criminal justice process, including forensic science, in a pursuit to detect, apprehend, and convict sex offenders. After convictions and time served (if the defendant has not been executed, raped, or died in prison), the war on sex offenders continues with a local and national registry, which includes pictures and addresses of an individual, sometimes for life, and in some cases continued confinement after an offender is released from department of corrections supervision (civil containment). The reality is that the war on sex offenders has little to do with changing or controlling sex offenders, similar to the consequences of the war on poverty, or said another way, criminalization of poverty.

■ War on Poverty

One expert advised that, in 2007, poverty translated to less than $16,000 in income for a family of three or $10,300 for a single person, and 36 million Americans lived in poverty. With the economic downturn and many more jobs to be lost in 2009-2010, the economy is the greatest concern of Americans. Largely, it is the children who suffer from the effects of poverty. "Childhood poverty typically means poor health care, high-crime neighborhoods, and lower-quality schools," advises Rebecca Blank.[134] Also, high levels of low-wage jobs are pathways to poverty, and US antipoverty policies do little to compensate low-wage workers and lift those who receive low wages from poverty, argues Timothy M. Smeeding.[135] Many industrial nations around the globe aid poorly-paid personnel, but in America, war has been declared upon those individuals, and as such the *CSI Effect* aids in the *criminalization of poverty*.

Criminalization of Poverty

An issue that led directly to the criminalization of poverty is status laws, which punish individuals for their economic condition rather than their behavior.[136] They justify tactical police control over those in poverty, and one way to describe this un-American conduct is to refer to it as Operation Ghetto Storm, implies Randal G. Shelden.[137] For example, the world's self-professed leading democracy lacks a national healthcare policy, a universal right to health care, and a comprehensive family policy. Welfare applicants are subjected to personal intrusions, arcane regulations, and constant surveillance, all designed to humiliate recipients and deter potential applicants.[138] Welfare recipients of all races, male and female alike, are looked upon with suspicion, and are arrested and convicted more often than individuals who are not on welfare and those employed.[139] There exists a perspective that their personal human rights were waived when they accepted welfare, they should be monitored more often than others because of their dependence on state welfare systems, and they are subject to arrest more often than others as evidenced by arrest rates and, equally important, the rates of incarceration among the poor and the unemployed.[140–142]

Poverty and Incarceration

As evidenced by the 41 percent of all inmates confined in state, city, and federal facilities, one common characteristic, aside from being poor, is that they hadn't completed high school.[143] These statistics imply two distinct yet contradictory perspectives: Uneducated persons commit most of the crimes, and uneducated persons tend to be arrested and convicted more often than an educated population. An education can translate to a higher paying job and better fringe benefits, such as health programs. Then, too, wrongful convictions and wrongful executions might be more pervasive among the poor than other socioeconomic groups. In reviewing the background of America's typical current prisoner, it is seen that Section 8 housing has been redesigned and retooled to include bars and guards, and poor children are subjected to the institutional shuffle—sleeping in alleyways and being sent to foster homes and detention facilities and graduating to prisons. Whether you accept this perspective or not, there are voices who reveal that welfare can be seen as a device of those in charge to control others who are less prosperous, and those in charge encourage those less prosperous souls to rip off the welfare system to find their place on this planet: prison or death row.[144,145]

Root Cause of Crime

A real war on poverty might mean going to the root cause of poverty and enhancing the quality of life experiences and opportunities for individuals who are poor. However, in part through the *CSI Effect*, rather than seeking healthy remedies for poor children and underpaid workers, the United States has criminalized poverty. The roots of poverty and, in particular, urban poverty have yet to be addressed in a similar manner as poverty and its by-products: crime, victimization, the fear of crime, and wrongful convictions. Most criminal justice professionals work hard toward lawful apprehension, prosecution, and supervision of criminals, but through the *CSI Effect*, it's hard to tell who the criminals really are. The media advises that the crimes of the privileged and white-collar crimes go virtually unchecked.[146]

Urban Crime

A study examined how the press emphasizes the urban dimensions of crime and poverty across the nation.[147] Data were obtained from 7,667 separate stories in areas such as crime, human interest, public issues, fires and accidents, government, investigations of President Clinton,[148] politics, consumer news, international stories, and entertainment news. One finding was that the city is a dangerous place and that poverty is more pervasive in the city than the suburbs. These images of the city, crime, and poverty have other implications for the economic and social well-being of local areas and its residents, including poor children. One implication is that poor communities receive fewer civil amenities, such as road repairs, street lighting, and quality police services. Another perspective is that crime in affluent communities does not exist. The concept of fear in relation to crime and criminal victimization is often linked within an historical perspective of poverty, and where poverty is more pervasive, more crime allegedly exists, resulting in more aggressive police initiatives with greater frequency.[149]

American cities, similar to most Western urban communities, have witnessed an increasing divergence in living standards of various socioeconomic groups, and many ethnic and immigrant groups settle in urban areas (see Chapter 5 for more details).[150] One study shows that exposure to victimization, which includes crimes of theft and violence, has followed different trends for poorly-resourced and well-resourced socioeconomic groups, respectively.

Disperse Poor Residents

One perspective is to eliminate Section 8 housing in the inner city and disperse poor residents into other parts of the city.[151] Eliminating areas of concentrated poverty (where more than 40 percent of residents are poor), goes the thinking, should eliminate many of the pathologies associated with poverty. That turned out to be only half true, but the number of areas of moderate poverty (20–40 percent poor) went up, and the crime in these areas went up, too. Inner city gangs and drug traders changed (displaced) where they operated, advises Kevin Drum.

The Fear of Crime

The frequency of victimization and the fear of crime are more pervasive among the poor, and the poor's victimization experiences are more individually devastating because of a lack of resources to aid in their individual recuperation efforts.[152,153] Other studies show a strong relationship among victimization, a fear of crime, health status, mental illness, gender, age, and poverty. This perspective links poverty with the city.[154] For example, to be poor, mentally ill, or have a physical disability means to have a greater fear of crime and to be victimized more often than others; it also can translate to being stopped by the police more often.

Additionally, the fear of crime can be a barrier to participation in health-promoting physical and social activities, which include police community relations initiatives such as community policing, argues Stafford, Chandola, and Marmont.[155] Rather aggressive police initiatives are more frequently deployed in the poorer parts of town than in other areas, as mentioned in Chapter 3 concerning the war on crime.[156] Some argue that the frequency of tact unit deployment in the inner city is necessary because drug traders and gang members are powerfully entrenched there, but others argue that drug traders and gang members operate and live in affluent communities, too.[157]

History of the War on Poverty

The war on poverty is not a new concept. One hundred and thirty some years ago, Charles Loring Brace depicted the fortunes of the street waif in four stages: from homeless child to young thief, drunkard, and imprisoned criminal.[158] There was a new height in the war on poverty from 1964 to 1968, which included a campaign of legislation and social services aimed at reducing or eliminating poverty in the United States. The poverty line was on a sharp decline without a rise or fluctuation when Lyndon B. Johnson was campaigning for president. In his address, he said, "This administration today, here and now, declares unconditional war on poverty in America." As we look at the individuals who remain in poverty, we see that the war was lost. Poverty is pervasive in America, even in light of federal living wage increases, which, by 2009 standards, "will have little effect on the rising costs of goods or services" across the nation.[159] The criminal justice response has been to criminalize those without a political voice by intruding, apprehending, prosecuting, and incarcerating members of that socioeconomic class more often than members of other socioeconomic classes.[160] As Amy K. Glasmeier advises:

> For years now, as a nation we have been debating whether the poor are truly poor given their access to material goods such as housing, washing machines, televisions, and cars. In reality, the nature of life for the truly poor is about "not enough," as in not enough income to eat properly, little access to basic goods such as adequate clothing or shelter and heat. We have finally reached a time when we can all agree that the poor are truly, truly poor. And their numbers are growing rapidly.[161]

Baltimore's Panhandling and Homeless Policy

Through the *CSI Effect*, similar to the war on crime, the police responded to the war on poverty through reactive strategies. Baltimore's panhandling and homeless policy was an ordinance supported by a liberal local government in the latter 1980s and early 1990s.[162] However, Baltimore's violent crime rate jumped 53 percent between 1987 and 1994, and abandoned structures throughout Baltimore became fire hazards. Those to blame included *metal men*—criminals who removed all the aluminum and other valuable metals from churches, homes, and commercial buildings. Pervasive violent crime was blamed on poor people, especially panhandlers and the homeless.

In 1994, Baltimore's city planning committee identified 266 distinct neighborhoods, represented by 400 community associations.[163] Through the aid of community associations, neighborhood residents, and vigorous political leadership from the mayor's office, an attempt to take back public spaces included a new policy to arrest the panhandlers and homeless.

Officers and public guards asked homeless persons and panhandlers to "move along" and "harassed them when they engaged in activities such as sleeping, eating, or tending to personal needs."[164] The police conducted many arrests of individuals they encountered. However, in *Patton v. Baltimore City* (1994), the American Civil Liberties Union argued that the action of the police constituted cruel and unusual punishment, it infringed on the First Amendment right of the homeless to freedom of association, and it attacked their "status" as opposed to their "acts."[165] Baltimore's city lawyers had neglected to inform officers who arrested the homeless that their arrests were an outlawed version of panhandling. The arrests were illegal. The final outcome was that the city had to repeal its vagrancy and homeless ordinance, amend its aggressive panhandling ordinance to read "to redress the constitutional issues," and confidentially settle with the panhandlers and homeless plaintiffs the illegal arrest activity of the police. Similar to many jurisdictions across the country, Baltimore and police officials had to restructure their reactive aggressive police initiatives to meet legal and ethical concerns.

The US Supreme Court had already ruled that solicitation to contribute (begging) money is protected speech in *Schaumberg v. Citizens for a Better Environment* (1980); it also upheld restrictions on where direct solicitations could be made. City regulations on the time, place, or manner of begging have been more resistant to legal challenges than outright bans, argues Patricia K. Smith.[166] Consequently, many US cities have adopted these types of antibegging regulations.[167] For example, a Memphis law states that begging after sunset and before sunrise is a misdemeanor.[168] In 1999, the Supreme Court upheld a Fort Lauderdale law that bans begging on the city's beaches.[169] Los Angeles, Seattle, and many other cities aggressively prohibit begging.

Other experts, such as Stephen R. Covey, imply that we all have crosses to carry, and it could be that some of us, at different times and under certain circumstances, can carry those crosses as well or better than others.[170] Apparently, training, education, and opportunity can make a difference in lifestyle outcomes.

In the final analysis, the war on poverty can lead to wrongful convictions and a continuation of capital punishment; equally important, a war on poverty probably shouldn't be fought by the police but through other means because most of those in poverty are children. In 2009, poverty is a characteristic that justifies another war: the war on immigrants (see Chapter 5 for more details).

■ Summary

Historically, crimes relating to sex were not classified separately from other crimes, nor were those convicted of sex crimes differentiated from those convicted of other crimes. In the 20th century, social policy was shaped by sexual psychopath laws and a focus on domestic violence crimes, which can include mandatory arrest practices. With policy changes, a sex offender (or a victim) is tagged or labeled as a sex offender. The labeling phenomenon suggests that the manner in which others interact with the labeled person can eventually produce deviant behavior through a self-fulfilling prophecy; the labeled person acts out or behaves within the expected constructs of the label, regardless of his or her previous patterns of behavior, and others often respond to the label rather than to the behavior.

There were approximately 275,000 sex offenders under correctional supervision in 2006, and most were on parole or probation. Definitions for sex crimes depend on the jurisdiction in which they were committed. They can include attempts and conspiracies and are generally characterized as forcible rape, which is intercourse with an adult male or female without the consent of the victim. Statutory rape involves a victim, usually 16 years of age or younger, whereby the aggressor is aged 17 years or older and regardless of consent. Also, a low risk to repeat a sexual offense conviction is a Level 1 offender, a moderate risk is Level 2, and a high risk to reoffend is Level 3.

Most sexual assaults are never reported, those that are do not usually end in an arrest, and arrests don't necessarily translate to a conviction. Also, there are major distinctions between a sexual violent predator (SVP) and a sex offender. SVPs are defined as repeat sexual offenders who often use physical violence and intimidation upon victims, often prey on children, and have many more victims than are ever reported. Less than one-half of convicted sex crime defendants are first timers caught up in a crime of passion. However, the media makes little distinction between the types of sex offenders and portrays police response as violent and verbally abusive to all sex offenders. Policies such as a sex offender registry can provide a false sense of security and have little to do with recidivism or rehabilitation. Also, many prison systems, through civil commitment policies, can hold a sex offender after he or she serves a prison sentence if the system decides he or she is a risk.

High-profile media accounts of crimes against children have heightened public awareness of critical child safety needs and issues, but the media, through the *CSI Effect*, has blurred the realities between heinous sexual predators and young offenders who made a single thoughtless decision that changed their lives.

An estimated 36 million Americans live in poverty. The criminalization of poverty justifies tactical police control. Forty-one percent of all inmates confined in state and federal facilities have a common characteristic aside from being poor: They haven't completed high school. These statistics imply two distinctive yet contradictory perspectives: Uneducated persons commit most of the crime, and uneducated persons tend to be arrested and convicted more often than an educated population. The roots of poverty and, in particular, urban poverty have yet to be addressed.

The war on poverty is a concept America has dealt with for a long time. For example, 130 years ago, the fortunes of the street waif were described in four stages: from homeless child to young thief, drunkard, and imprisoned criminal. There was a new height in the war on poverty from 1964 to 1968, which included a campaign of legislation and social services aimed at eliminating poverty. This perspective is continued by the newly-elected administrations. The wars on sex offenders and poverty have encouraged immoral and illegal responses from the authorities in the form of aggressive police strategies, vigilantism, and fictitious accounts of apprehension, conviction, and, among sex offenders, after-conviction strategies. Both wars seem to add to wrongful convictions and justify the continuation of capital punishment.

■ References

1. Wakefield, H. (2006). The vilification of sex offenders: Do laws targeting sex offenders increase recidivism and sexual violence? *Journal of Sexual Offenders Civil Commitment: Science and Law, 1*, 141–149. Retrieved June 14, 2009, from http://ccoso.org/Vilification.pdf

2. Jerusalem, M. P. (1995). A framework for post-sentence sex offender legislation: Perspectives on prevention, registration and the public's right to know. *Vanderbilt Law Review, 48*(1), 219–255.

3. Lueb, R. (2004). Social policy and sexual offenders: Contrasting United States and European policies. *Journal of Criminal Policy and Research, 8*(4), 423–440.

4. La Fond, J. Q. (1998). The costs of enacting a sexual predator law. *Psychology, Public Policy, and Law, 4*(1/2), 468–504.

5. Hinds, L., & Daly, K. (2001). The war on sex offenders: Community notification in perspective. *Australian and New Zealand Journal of Criminology, 34*(3). Retrieved June 14, 2009, from http://www98.griffith.edu.au/dspace/bitstream/10072/3874/1/war_on_sex_offenders.pdf

6. Sutherland, E. H. (1950). The diffusion of sexual psychopath laws. *American Journal of Sociology, 50*, 142–148.

7. Hinds & Daly, "The War on Sex Offenders."

8. Shipley, S., & Arrigo, B. A. (2001). The confusion over psychopathy (II): Implications for forensic (correctional) practice. *International Journal of Offender Therapy and Comparative Criminology, 45*(4), 407–420.

9. Becker, H. (1963). *Outsiders: Studies in the sociology of deviance.* New York: Free Press.

10. Alexander, R., Jr. (2004). The United States Supreme Court and the civil commitment of sex offenders. *The Prison Journal, 84*(3), 361–378.

11. Wakefield, "The Vilification of Sex Offenders."

12. Rosenhan, D. L. (1973). Being sane in insane places. *Science, 179,* 250–258.

13. Wakefield, "The Vilification of Sex Offenders."

14. Bureau of Justice Statistics. (2003). *Sixty percent of convicted sex offenders are on parole or probation: Rapes and sexual assaults decline, 1997* (NCJ 163393). Washington, DC: US Department of Justice, Office of Justice Programs. Retrieved June 10, 2008, from http://www.ojp.usdoj.gov/bjs/pub/press/soo.pr

15. Bureau of Justice Statistics. (2003). *Recidivism of sex offenders released from prison in 1994* (NCJ 193427). Washington, DC: US Department of Justice, Office of Justice Programs. Retrieved October 20, 2008, from http://www.ojp.usdoj.gov/bjs/abstract/rsorp94.htm

16. Sentencing Law and Policy. (2007). *On severe sex offenders sentencing.* Retrieved October 31, 2008, from http://sentencing.typepad.com/sentencing_law_and_policy/2007/03/on_severe_sex_o.html

17. Hansen, C. (2007, December 27). To catch a predator. *MSNBC.* Retrieved June 1, 2008, from http://insidedateline.msnbc.msn.com/archive/category/1035.aspx

18. Bureau of Justice Statistics. (2006). *Violent felons in large urban communities: 1990–2002.* Washington, DC: US Department of Justice. Retrieved June 13, 2009, from http://www.ojp.usdoj.gov/bjs/pub/pdf/vfluc.pdf. The actual estimated percentages for rape defendants include the following: 88 percent of rape cases end in plea bargains, 12 percent went to trial, of which 2 percent were bench (judge only) and 10 percent were by a jury.

19. This study was conducted specifically for this section by the author in the summer of 2008.

20. Kupelian, D. (2005). *The marketing of evil. How radicals, elitists, and pseudo-experts sell us corruption disguised as freedom.* NY: WND Books.

21. WorldNetDaily.com (2009, May 28), *The big list: Female teachers with students Most comprehensive account on Internet of women predators on campus.* Retrieved June 14, 2009, from http://www.wnd.com/index.php?fa=PAGE.view&pageId=39783.

22. WorldNetDaily.com *The big list: Female teachers with students. Most comprehensive account on Internet of women predators on campus.*

23. Bureau of Justice Statistics. (1997). *Sex offenses and offenders: An analysis of data on rape and sexual assault, 1997* (NCJ 163392). Washington, DC: US Department of Justice. Retrieved June 14, 2009, from www.ojp.usdoj.gov/bjs/

24. The Bureau of Justice Statistics defines rape as, "Forced sexual intercourse including both psychological coercion as well as physical force. Forced sexual intercourse means penetration by the offender(s). Includes attempted rapes, male as well as female victims, and both heterosexual and homosexual rape. Attempted rape includes verbal threats of rape." Retrieved August 16, 2008, from http://www.ojp.usdoj.gov/bjs/glance/rape.htm

25. Executive Office of Public Safety and Security, Commonwealth of Massachusetts. (n.d.). *Sex offender registry board*. Retrieved June 14, 2009, from http://www.mass.gov/sorb/community.htm

26. Executive Office of Public Safety and Security, Commonwealth of Massachusetts. (n.d.). *Massachusetts Department of Correction*. Retrieved August 16, 2008, from http://www.mass.gov/doc/

27. Bureau of Justice Statistics, *Recidivism of Sex Offenders Released from Prison* (NCJ 193427).

28. New York State Division of Criminal Justice Services. (2008, May 17). *Registered sex offenders by county*. Retrieved June 2, 2008, from http://www.criminaljustice.state.ny.us/nsor/stats_by_county.htm

29. Federal Bureau of Investigation. (2009). *Estimated number of arrests in US 2007*. Retrieved June 13, 2009, from http://www.fbi.gov/ucr/cius2007/data/table_29.html

30. Stevens, D. J. (2006). Training and management impact sexual assault conviction rates in Boston. *Police Journal, 79*(2), 125–154.

31. Glaser, D. (1997). *Profitable penalties*. Thousand Oaks, CA: Pine Forge.

32. Felson, M. (2002). *Crime and everyday life* (3rd ed.). Thousand Oaks, CA: Pine Forge.

33. Hart, T. C., & Rennison, C. (2003). *Reporting crime to the police, 1992–2001* (NCJ 195710). Washington, DC: US Department of Justice. Retrieved June 12, 2008, from http://www.ojp.usdoj.gov/bjs/pub/ascii/rcp00.txt

34. Stevens, D. J. (2001). *Inside the mind of the serial rapist*. New York: Austin Winfield.

35. Stevens, D. J. (1997). Violence and serial rape. *Journal of Police and Criminal Psychology, 12*(1), 39–47.

36. Leberg, E. (1997). *Understanding child molesters: Taking charge*. Thousand Oaks, CA: Sage.

37. Bureau of Justice Statistics, *Sex Offenses and Offenders* (NCJ 163392).

38. Leberg, *Understanding Child Molesters*.

39. Stevens, D. J. (2002). Three generations of incarcerated sexual offenders. *Journal of Police and Criminal Psychology, 17*(1), 52–59.

40. Stevens, D. J. (2002). Pedophiles: A case study. *Journal of Police and Criminal Psychology, 17*(1), 36–51.

41. San Francisco Police Department. (2004). *2004 annual report*. Retrieved August 16, 2008, from http://www.sfgov.org/site/uploadedfiles/police/information/2004%20annual%20report.pdf

42. Federal Bureau of Investigation, *Uniform Crime Report, 2007*.

43. Abbey, A., Zawacki, T., Buck, P. O., Clinton, A. M., & McAuslan, P. (2001). Alcohol and sexual assault. *Alcohol and Violence, 25*(1). Retrieved June 2, 2008, from http://pubs.niaaa.nih.gov/publications/arh25-1/43-51.htm

44. Federal Bureau of Investigation. (2007). *Clearances*. Washington, DC: US Department of Justice. Retrieved June 14, 2009, from http://www.fbi.gov/ucr/cius2007/offenses/clearances/index.html

45. City of Boston.gov (2009). Boston Police Department Crime Statistics. Retrieved June 14, 2009, from http://www.cityofboston.gov/police/divisions/crimestats.asp

46. Walker, S. (2001). *Sense and nonsense about crime and drugs: A policy guide*. Belmont, CA: Wadsworth.

47. Sourcebook of Criminal Justice Statistics Online. (2007). *Felony convictions and sentences, 2004.* Albany, NY: US Department of Justice. Retrieved June 10, 2008, from http://www.albany.edu/sourcebook/pdf/t500022004.pdf

48. Bureau of Justice Statistics. (2007). *State court convicted felons, 2004: Statistical tables felony sentences in state court.* Washington, DC: US Department of Justice. Retrieved June 10, 2008, from http://www.ojp.usdoj.gov/bjs/pub/html/scscf04/tables/scs04101tab.htm

49. Bureau of Justice Statistics. (2007). *Federal prosecution of child sex exploitation offenders, 2006* (NCJ 219412). Washington, DC: US Department of Justice. Retrieved October 30, 2008, from http://www.ojp.usdoj.gov/bjs/pub/ascii/fpcseo06.txt

50. Alexander, "United States Supreme Court and the Civil Commitment of Sex Offenders."

51. Leberg, *Understanding Child Molesters.*

52. Meadows, R. J., & Kuehnel, J. M. (2005). *Evil minds: Understanding and responding to violent predators.* Upper Saddle River, NJ: Pearson.

53. Leberg, *Understanding Child Molesters.* p. 19.

54. Palmer, C. T., DiBari, D. N., & Wright, S. A. (1999). Is it sex yet? Theoretical and practical implications of the data over rapists' motives. *Jurimetrics, 39*(3), 281–283.

55. Bureau of Justice Statistics. (2005). *Sourcebook of criminal justice statistics online. Table 5.53.* Retrieved June 14, 2009, from http://www.albany.edu/sourcebook/pdf/t5532004.pdf Table 5.53 shows that of the estimated 462 defendants in 2004 for rape, 47 percent of those defendants had a prior felony conviction of which 7 percent had been for a felony, 19 percent for a nonfelony, and 21 percent for a misdemeanor offense. Some would argue that because most predators are not detected that it would be hard to say that 53 percent of those convictions were actually first timers. Because predators engage in many types of crime, they would have been arrested in the past more than once on other charges.

56. Bureau of Justice Statistics, *Sourcebook of Criminal Justice Statistics Online.*

57. Bureau of Justice Statistics. (2002, March). *Summary of sex offender registries, 2001.* Retrieved June 14, 2009, from http://www.ojp.usdoj.gov/bjs/pub/pdf/sssor01.pdf

58. Baker, K. K. (1999). "What rape is and what it ought not to be." *Jurimetrics, 30*(3), 233.

59. Palmer, et al., "Is It Sex Yet?"

60. English, K., Pullen, S., & Jones, L. (1997, January). *Managing adult sex offenders: A containment approach.* Lexington, KY: American Probation and Parole Association.

61. Leberg, *Understanding Child Molesters.*

62. Leberg, *Understanding Child Molesters.*

63. National Institute of Justice. (2000). *Child sexual molestation: Research issues.* Retrieved October 18, 2008, from http://www.ncjrs.org/txtfiles/163390.txt

64. Abbey, et al., "Alcohol and Sexual Assault."

65. Abbey, et al., "Alcohol and Sexual Assault."

66. English, D. J., & Widom, C. S. (2003). *Childhood victimization and delinquency, adult criminality, and violent criminal behavior in a large urban county in the northwest United States, 1980–1997.* Washington, DC: US Department of Justice. Retrieved June 14, 2009, from http://www.icpsr.umich.edu/cocoon/ICPSR/STUDY/03548.xml

67. Weeks, R., & Widom, C. S. (1998). *Early childhood victimization among incarcerated adult male felons.* Washington, DC: US Department of Justice. Retrieved June 2, 2008, from http://www.ncjrs.gov/pdffiles/fs000204.pdf

68. Salter, D., McMillan, D., Richards, M., Talbot, T., Hodges, J., Bentovim, A., et al. (2003). Development of sexually abusive behaviour in sexually victimized males: A longitudinal study. *The Lancet, 361*(9356), 471–476. Of the 224 former victims, only 26 had subsequently committed sexual offenses (victim–abusers), in almost all cases with children, mainly outside their families. Risk factors during childhood for later offending included material neglect, lack of supervision, and sexual abuse by a female. Victim–abusers had more frequently witnessed serious intrafamilial violence and had been cruel to animals.

69. Grubin, D. H., & Kennedy, H. G. (1991). The classification of sexual offenders. *Criminal Behaviour and Mental Health, 1,* 123–129.

70. In this sense, most characteristics of predators are collected from convicted predators. The characteristics offered here include largely those inmates who were not convicted of predatory crimes.

71. Palmer, et al., "Is It Sex Yet?"

72. Felson, M. (2002). *Crime and everyday life* (3rd ed.). Thousand Oaks, CA: Pine Forge.

73. Pithers, W. D. (1990). Relapse prevention with sexual aggressors: A method for maintaining therapeutic gain and enhancing external supervision. In W. L. Marshall, D. R. Laws, & H. E. Barbaree (Eds.), *Handbook of sexual assault: Issues, theories, and treatment of the offender.* New York: Plenum.

74. Kocsis, R. N., & Palermo, G. B. (2004). *Offender profiling: An introduction to the sociopsychological analysis of violent crime.* Springfield, IL: Charles C. Thomas.

75. Douglas, J., & Olshaker, M. (1997). *Journey into darkness.* New York: Scribner.

76. Holmes, R. M., & Holmes, S. T. (1996). *Profiling violent crimes: An investigative tool.* Thousand Oaks, CA: Sage.

77. English, et al., *Managing Adult Sex Offenders.*

78. Thornhill, R., & Palmer, C. R. (2000). *A natural history of rape.* Cambridge, MA: MIT Press.

79. Samenow, S. (1998). *Before it's too late.* New York: Basic Books.

80. Campbell, T. W. (2007). *Assessing sex offenders: Problems and pitfalls* (2nd ed.). Springfield, IL: Charles C. Thomas.

81. Knapp, M. (1997). Treatment of sex offenders. In K. English, S. Pullen, & L. Jones (Eds.), *Managing adult sex offenders: A containment approach.* Lexington, KY: American Probation and Parole Association.

82. Jones, L., Pullen, S., & English, K. (1997). Criminal justice policies and sex offender denial. In K. English, S. Pullen, & L. Jones (Eds.), *Managing adult sex offenders: A containment approach.* Lexington, KY: American Probation and Parole Association.

83. Gottfredson, M., & Hirschi, T. (1990). *A general theory of crime.* Stanford, CA: Stanford University Press.

84. Wakefield, H., & Underwager, R. (1998, May 3). Assessing violent recidivism: Issues for forensic psychologists. Paper presented at the 14th Annual Symposium of the American College of Forensic Psychology, San Francisco, California.

85. Abel, G., & Rouleau, J. L. (1990). The nature and extent of sexual assault. In W. I. Marshall, D. R. Laws, & H. E. Barbaree (Eds.), *Handbook of sexual assault: Issues, theories, and treatment of the offender.* (pp. 9–21). New York: Plenum Press.

86. English, et al., *Managing Adult Sex Offenders.*

87. Egger, S. A. (2002). *The killers among us.* Upper Saddle River, NJ: Prentice Hall.

88. Michaud, S. G., & Hazelwood, R. (1998). *The evil that men do.* New York: St. Martin's Paperbacks.

89. Findings show that most predators will attack a victim based upon the victim's vulnerability as perceived by the offender (as opposed to what the victim thinks).

90. English, et al., *Managing Adult Sex Offenders.*

91. Stevens, D. J. (2000). The problem is that most sexual predators do not keep count after reaching a certain number of victims. One predator told the author at a high-custody penitentiary group encounter, "Who keeps score, ya know?" Leberg (1997) implies a higher number of victims.

92. Federal Bureau of Investigation. (2007). *Uniform crime report.* Retrieved October 18, 2008, from http://www.fbi.gov

93. Human Rights Watch. (2006). No Escape. *Summary and recommendations.* Retrieved October 18, 2008, from http://www.hrw.org/reports/2001/prison/report1.html

94. Bureau of Justice Statistics. (2008). *Sexual victimization in state and federal prisons reported by inmates, 2007.* Washington, DC: US Department of Justice. Retrieved October 29, 2008, from http://www.ojp.usdoj.gov/bjs/abstract/svsfpri07.htm

95. Confidential communication between the author and a sex offender who was incarcerated at Gowanda Correctional Facility in New York and later transferred to Groveland Correctional Facility, where the author often visited as a social service volunteer.

96. Stevens, D. J. (2009). *Introduction to American policing.* Sudbury, MA: Jones and Bartlett.

97. Personal, confidential communication between a church member and the author.

98. The officer was a member of the congregation and confidentially agreed to discuss the matter with the author providing the officer's identity was kept confidential.

99. Articles about police. Rape suspect didn't receive resuscitation from officers. Milwaukee, Wisconsin. (1981, September 18). *New York Times.* Retrieved August 19, 2009, from http://www.nytimes.com/1981/09/18/us/rape-suspect-didn-t-receive-resuscitation-from-officers.html

100. Gardner, T. (2007, September 12). Sex offenders laws do more harm than good: Report. *Reuters.* Retrieved June 15, 2009, from http://www.reuters.com/article/domesticNews/idUSN1258245020070912

101. Ellement, J. R., & Smalley, S. (2006, April 18). Sex crime disclosure questioned: Maine killings refuel debate over registries. *Boston Globe.* Retrieved June 15, 2009, from http://ethics.tamucc.edu/article.pl?sid=06/04/18/2251200

102. Sex *offender issues.* Retrieved August 19, 2009, from http://www.geocities.com/voicism/z-030.html

103. New Mexico Office of the Governor. (2003, August 13). *Governor Bill Richardson "declares war" on sex offenders.* Retrieved August 16, 2008, from http://www.governor.state.nm.us/press/2003/august/081403_4.pdf

104. Justia. (n.d.). *New Mexico criminal codes section 31-18-22.* Retrieved August 19, 2009, from http://law.justia.com/newmexico/codes/nmrc/jd_31-18-22-d117.html

105. *Washington state's war on holistic MDs, Part 2: Sexual predators on the loose.* Retrieved June 15, 2009, from http://www.wachoice.org/theissues/thechallenge.php?aid=2

106. Sommerfeld, J., & Berens, M. J. (2006, May 5). Biggest number of offenders are "registered counselors." *Seattle Times.* Retrieved June 15, 2009, from http://seattletimes.nwsource.com/html/licensetoharm/2002949517_sexmed24.html

107. Zevitz, R. G., & Farkas, M. A. (2000). *Sex offender community notification: Assessing the impact in Wisconsin.* Washington, DC: National Institute of Justice.

108. All 50 states and the District of Columbia's sexual registers and their laws pertaining to registration can be found at http://www.prevent-abuse-now.com/register.htm (retrieved August 16, 2008).

109. Office of the Attorney General. (2008). *The national guidelines for sex offender registration and notification.* Washington, DC: US Department of Justice. Retrieved November 13, 2008, from http://www.ojp.usdoj.gov/smart/pdfs/final_sornaguidelines.pdf

110. Lueb, "Social Policy and Sexual Offenders."

111. Hines & Daly, "The War on Sex Offenders: Community Notification in Perspective."

112. Missing Kids. (n.d.). *Registered sex offenders in the United States.* Retrieved August 16, 2008, from http://www.missingkids.com/en_US/documents/sex-offender-map.pdf

113. Zevitz & Farkas, *Sex Offender Community Notification.*

114. This section was researched by Sarah Olschan, a student assistant of the author from Sacred Heart University, Fairfield, Connecticut, in the spring semester of 2008.

115. Finn, P. (1997). *Sex offender community notification.* Washington, DC: US Department of Justice.

116. Bureau of Justice Statistics, *Recidivism of Sex Offenders Released from Prison* (NCJ 198281).

117. Finn, *Sex Offender Community Notification.*

118. Duwe, G., & Donnay, W. (2008). The impact of Megan's Law on sex offender recidivism: The Minnesota experience. *Criminology, 46*(2), 411–446.

119. Duwe & Donnay, "The Impact of Megan's Law."

120. Leberg, *Understanding Child Molesters.*

121. Levenson, J. S. (2003). Policy interventions designed to combat sexual violence: Community notification and civil commitment. *Journal of Child Sexual Abuse, 12(3/4),* 17–52

122. Stevens, "Pedophiles: A Case Study."

123. Stevens, "Violence and Serial Rape."

124. Ritter, K. (2008, August). Nevada's sex offender law. *Associated Press.* Retrieved June 15, 2009, from http://www.sfgate.com/cgi-bin/article.cgi?f=/n/a/2008/08/16/national/a005139D24.DTL

125. Hall, A. M. (2006, January 28). *Sex offenders: In my neighborhood?* Retrieved May 30, 2008, from http://reliableanswers.com/general/sex_offenders.asp

126. Kendall, W. B. B., & Monit, C. (2004). Sexually violent predators and civil commitment laws. *Child Sexual Abuse, 13*(2), 41–57.

127. American Psychology–Law Society. (2001). *Legal update: Constitutional challenge to sexually violent predator laws post Kansas v. Hendricks.* Washington, DC: American Psychological Association. Retrieved June 12, 2008, from http://www.ap-ls.org/publications/newsletters/spr01.pdf

128. Alexander, "United States Supreme Court and the Civil Commitment of Sex Offenders."

129. Davey, M., & Goodnough, A. (2007). Double rise as states hold sex offenders after prison. *New York Times.* Retrieved October 30, 2008, from http://www.nytimes.com/

130. D'Amora, D. (1999). *Center director: Special services, center for the treatment of problem sexual behavior.* Presentation during the training program "In Defense of the Community: Effective Community-Based Responses to Sex Offenders," Westchester County, New York.

131. American Psychiatric Association. (1999). *Dangerous sex offenders: A task force report of the American Psychiatric Association.* Washington, DC: Author.

132. Grossman, L. S., Martis, B., & Fichtner, C. G. (1999). Are sex offenders treatable? A research overview. *Psychiatric Services, 50*(3), 349–361.

133. Boudreaux, M. C., & Lord, W. D. (2005). Combating child homicide: Preventive policing for the new millennium. *Journal of Interpersonal Violence, 20*(4), 380–387.

134. Blank, R. (2008, Winter). Advising and grading the (presidential) candidates. *Pathways: A Magazine on Poverty, Inequality, and Social Policy,* 14–16. Retrieved June 14, 2008, from http://www.stanford.edu/group/scspi/pdfs/pathways/winter_2008/winter_2008.pdf

135. Smeeding, T. M. (2008, Winter). Poorer by comparison. *Pathways: A Magazine on Poverty, Inequality, and Social Policy,* 3–5. Retrieved June 14, 2008, from http://www.stanford.edu/group/scspi/pdfs/pathways/winter_2008/winter_2008.pdf

136. Platt, T. (2003, October). The state of welfare: US 2003. *Monthly Review.* Retrieved June 27, 2008, from http://www.monthlyreview.org/1003platt.htm

137. Shelden, R. G. (2001). *Controlling the dangerous classes: A critical introduction to the history of criminal justice.* Boston: Allyn Bacon.

138. Platt, "The State of Welfare."

139. Sourcebook of Criminal Justice Statistics Online. (2003). *Characteristics of persons arrested.* Albany, NY: US Department of Justice. Retrieved June 28, 2008, from http://www.albany.edu/sourcebook/tost_4.html

140. DeLisi, M., & Berg, M. T. (2006). Exploring theoretical linkages between self-control theory and criminal justice system processing. *Journal of Criminal Justice, 34*(2), 153–163.

141. For the response of the criminal justice community regarding the poor, see Shelden, *Controlling the Dangerous Classes.*

142. Brace, C. L. (1872). *The dangerous classes of New York and twenty years work.* New York: Wynkoop & Hallenbeck.

143. Bureau of Justice Statistics. (2003). *Education and correctional populations.* Washington, DC: US Department of Justice. Retrieved June 14, 2008, from http://www.ojp.usdoj.gov/bjs/pub/ascii/ecp.txt

144. Piven, F. F., & Cloward, R. A. (1982). *The new class war: Reagan's attack on the welfare state and its consequences.* New York: Pantheon Books.

145. Associated Press. (2002). *Chronology of Clinton investigations.* Retrieved June 16, 2009, from http://www.usatoday.com/news/special/starr/starr005.htm

146. Piven, F. F., & Cloward, R. A. (1997). *The breaking of the American social compact.* New York: New Press.

147. Shover, N., & Wright, J. P. (2000). *Crimes of privilege: Readings in white-collar crime.* Cambridge, UK: Oxford University Press.

148. Yanich, D. (2004). Crime creep: Urban and suburban crime on local TV news. *Journal of Urban Affairs, 26*(5), 535–563.

149. Walklate, S., & Issueen, G. (2008). How scared are we? *The British Journal of Criminology,* 48, 209–225.

150. Nilsson, A. (2006). The inequalities of victimization: Trends in exposure to crime among rich and poor. *European Journal of Criminology, 3*(4), 387–412.

151. Drum, K. (2008, June 10). Crime and poverty. *Washington Monthly.* Retrieved June 14, 2008, from http://www.washingtonmonthly.com/archives/individual/2008_06/013881.php

152. Nilsson, "Inequalities of Victimization."

153. Walklate & Issueen, "How Scared Are We?"

154. Stiles, B. L., Halim, S., & Kaplan, H. B. (2003). Fear of crime among individuals with physical limitations. *Criminal Justice Review, 28*(2), 232–253.

155. Stafford, M., Chandola, T., & Marmont, M. (2007). Association between fear of crime and mental health and physical functioning. *American Journal of Public Health, 97*(11), 2076–2081.

156. Walker, *Sense and Nonsense.*

157. Currie, E. (1999). Reflections on crime and criminology at the millennium. *Western Criminology Review, 2*(1). Retrieved June 27, 2008, from http://wcr.sonoma.edu/v2n1/currie.html

158. Brace, *Dangerous Classes of New York.*

159. Glasmeier, A. K. (2007, July 26). *The poverty in America website.* Retrieved June 27, 2008, from http://www.povertyinamerica.psu.edu/. According to the living wage calculator, an increase in the minimum wage won't offset rising inequality in America.

160. Oehl, D. (2000, February). The American criminalization of poverty. *Peace Work.* Retrieved June 14, 2009, from http://www.peaceworkmagazine.org/pwork/0200/0208.htm

161. Glasmeier, A. K. (2007, February). *The nation we've become.* Retrieved June 14, 2009, from http://www.povertyinamerica.psu.edu/

162. Kelling, G. L., & Cole, K. (1996). *Fixing broken windows.* New York: Free Press. p.186–188

163. Kelling & Cole, *Fixing Broken Windows.* p. 189.

164. Kelling & Cole, *Fixing Broken Windows.*

165. Smith, P. K. (2005). The economics of anti-begging regulations. *American Journal of Economics and Sociology.* Retrieved June 15, 2009, from http://findarticles.com/p/articles/mi_m0254/is_2_64/ai_n13729927/

166. Smith, "Economics of Anti-Begging Regulations."

167. National Law Center on Homeless and Poverty. (1999). *Homelessness.* Retrieved May 30, 2008, from http://www.policyalmanac.org/social_welfare/homeless.shtml

168. US Department of Health and Human Services. (2008). *Homeless home page.* Retrieved May 30, 2008, from http://www.hhs.gov/homeless/

169. James Dale Smith, etc. v. City of Fort Lauderdale, 120 S. Ct. 402 (1999).

170. Covey, S. R. (2008). *The 7 habits of highly effective people: The 8th habit and everyday greatness.* New York: Simon & Schuster.

Terrorism and the War on Immigrants

CHAPTER

5

If liberty and equality, as is thought by some, are chiefly to be found in democracy, they will be best attained when all persons alike share in government to the utmost.

Aristotle

▶ ▶ CHAPTER OBJECTIVES

- Describe the Malthusian and neo-Malthusian perspectives linked to immigration issues
- Explain enforcement, incarceration, and costs of the war on immigrants
- Characterize the consequences of constitutional exclusion of immigrants rationalized through the threat of terrorists
- Describe the proactive practices to aid immigrants and the consequences of those practices, such as labeling and workplace raids
- Characterize the immigration inclusion practices of employers and ethnic organizations
- Describe the positive results of immigration linked to home ownership and a reduction of crime

■ Introduction

A product of the media characterized as a *CSI Effect* shapes criminal justice policy and practice, resulting in aggressive reactive justice strategies, vigilantism, and fictitious accounts of crime and criminal investigations that weaken constitutional guarantees among targeted recipients of the wars on crime, junkies, sex offenders, and poverty. This chapter furthers the descriptions of aggressive targeting of specific groups of individuals through the war on immigrants, which results in inappropriate interactions among individuals and leads to wrongful convictions and the notion that harsh punishment, including capital punishment, can serve a purpose in a democracy. In part, the war on immigrants is rationalized by a fear of terrorism and by limited resources, which include jobs, housing, and education, and is associated with crime and incarceration costs. Patterns of consumption and technology also relate to immigration policy and response. Today, every nation has

121

a population of nonpermanent residents who may or may not work and can be legally or illegally present; yet most often immigrants are not necessarily connected to terrorist organizations. This chapter provides an optimistic perspective regarding immigration, which includes Aristotle's idea as provided at the opening of this chapter that a democracy is best served when everyone shares in government.

> **Native and Foreign-Born Populations**
> - The US Census Bureau uses the term *foreign born* to refer to anyone who is not a US citizen at birth. This includes naturalized US citizens, lawful permanent residents (immigrants), temporary migrants (such as foreign students), humanitarian migrants (such as refugees), and people who are illegally present in the United States.
> - The US Census Bureau uses the term *native* to refer to anyone who is born in the United States or a US island area, such as Puerto Rico, or who is born abroad to a US citizen parent.

■ War on Immigrants

Human beings have migrated throughout history, Teresa Hayter tells us. People and their rulers at various times have tried different ways to exclude migrants, but at other times there were pyramids to build mines to tunnel, and railroad tracks to be laid; sometimes people from the outer regions were enslaved as laborers, and sometimes people were encouraged to settle and to labor for the good of many. Hayter explains that the right of free movement across frontiers is not a right enshrined in any declaration on human rights, but its denial has provided some of the "worst and most vicious abuses of human rights," including imprisonment and execution.[1] Comprehensive legal controls to stop immigration are a fairly recent phenomenon.[2,3] However, immigrants are rarely tied to organized terrorist attacks.

Today every nation has a population of nonpermanent residents who may or may not work and can be legally or illegally present, writes Thomas C. Heller.[4] The size of this population varies depending on opportunities of employment, social benefits, and the likelihood and cost of expulsion for illegal entrants or nonimmigrant overstays. Some nonpermanent residents become legal or permanent residents, with or without the legal right to work, and others collect social benefits, depending in part on the ease of adjusting their status; sometimes immigrants are granted amnesty because they have escaped the atrocities of war, adds Heller. For example, Ethiopian immigrants in Hadera, Israel have been there for over 10 years, and the employment rate of men aged 26–44 years is 77 percent (compared to 84 percent among Jewish men of the same age).[5] The class of permanent residents and workers in any country can increase by the direct admission of immigrants as legal permanent residents.

Affixed to the Statue of Liberty in New York harbor are Emma Lazarus' words from *The New Colossus*, which include, "Give me your tired, your poor, your huddled masses yearning to breathe free, the wretched refuse of your teeming shore."[6] Once those ideals rang true, and immigrants, including illegal new arrivals, were welcomed; today there are serious concerns about an open border policy.

> The primary issue that arises between migration growth and consumption growth is linked to the scarcity of resources, such as food, public amenities (education, health, and welfare benefits), housing, and jobs.

Before discussing the war on immigrants, one issue requires acknowledgment. There is an abundance of information on immigration, but ascertaining the reliability of the information is another matter. Recall from Chapter 1 that many flawed studies are utilized to develop criminal justice policy and that history is largely written by the privileged—those in power.[7] Those in power can include organizations and interest groups that influence policy and public opinion through various strategies which can include information, studies, and legal and professional services such as American Civil Liberties Union (ACLU), National Association for Advancement of Colored People (NAACP), the National Rifle Association (NRA), Immigrationforum.com (green card process)[8] among others (which are discussed at length in this chapter). One definition of an interest group is an organization of individuals who share ideals, values, and goals and attempt to influence policy and opinion. Interest groups can play a positive or negative role in immigration policy and opinion in the United States. When reviewing the abundant but puzzling information, statistics, and legal and professional services focused upon immigrants (in both positive and negative ways), it would be useful to recall that the privileged (i.e., leaders, elitists, powerful academics, interest groups) tend to say whatever they wish to say without justifying or confirming their facts, a thought consistent with the *CSI Effect* characterized in the first four chapters.[9–11]

Malthusian Perspective

A reasonable starting point to understand immigration control or the war on immigrants is in the works of Thomas Malthus:

> We are bound in justice and honor formally to disdain the right of the poor to support. To this end, I should propose a regulation to be made, declaring that no child born from any marriage taking place after the expiration of a year from the date of the law, and no illegitimate child born two years from the same date, should ever be entitled to parish assistance. . . . The infant is, comparatively speaking, of little value to society, as others will immediately supply its place.[12]

Malthusian philosophy implied that if the population increases faster than the food supply, disastrous results are inevitable unless the increase in population is checked by moral restraints or by war, famine, or disease.[13]

Contemporary Malthusians, or neo-Malthusians, focus on the impact of population growth, which includes immigration and the availability of quality environmental resources.[14,15] Neo-Malthusians conceptualize a negative relationship between these two variables.[16] Another way to describe neo-Malthusian concerns is *resource scarcity* (food, job, and energy shortages).

The debate rages about immigration, human rights, change, and resources. For example, Ellen Percy Kraly explains that a general model of immigration has an environmental impact that includes three broad factors[17]:

- A function of population characteristics
- Patterns of consumption and technology
- Consumption and manipulation of energy and natural resources

Concerns about immigration can be grounded in hidden agendas, too, such as racism and racial profiling, imply Kristin F. Butcher and Anne Morrison Piehl.[18] Racism and racial profiling can be interpreted to include greed, pure selfishness, and a lack of self-control—core motivators of criminal behavior as advanced by Michael R. Gottfredson and Travis Hirschi (see Chapter 6 for more details).[19]

Mark Krikorian argues that the differences in immigration in the 21st century are similar to those of earlier periods, but America has changed, offering "different incentives for newcomers."[20] Krikorian adds that immigration once served US national interests, but today immigration is believed to weaken America's national identity, limit opportunity for mobility, and threaten US security and sovereignty; immigration limits resources for social programs and disrupts middle-class norms and values.

Nonetheless, this book argues that through an insecure economy and the distraction of the media, as furthered through the *CSI Effect*, immigrants represent only a perceived threat to the American people and their resources. Michael E. Bonine says that the US Senate wages an "unholy war" against three classes of immigrants: the undocumented persons who are already here, those coming or wishing to come from Mexico and Central America, and all Muslims.[21,22] This unholy war has impacted, among other things, broken dreams, battered hearts, and wrongful convictions; this unholy war has helped to justify aggressive justice strategies, vigilantism, and fictitious accounts of crime and crime control. It has also furthered personal agendas of public officials and members of the public.

That said, typically, some newcomers to the United States arrive with little education (however, see the following section "Managers and Investors"); popular stereotypes tend to associate these newcomers with higher rates of crimes, and as you learned from the war on poverty (see Chapter 4 for details), uneducated individuals are sentenced to prison more often than others. Being poor and a new arrival places an individual on the apprehension and conviction fast track, regardless of innocence, implies Ramiro Martinez.[23]

■ New Arrivals

Aliens in the United States can be divided into permanent residents, *asylees* (individuals who travel to the United States on their own and then request protection from their homeland), *refugees* (people in their homeland who seek protection in the United States on the grounds that they fear persecution), nonpermanent residents, and illegal entrants.[24] Each category is subject to varied conditions of entry, period of stay, and liability to deportation or other removal.[25] The US Census Bureau shows that around 888,000 immigrants arrived in America between July 1, 2007, and July 1, 2008. From April 1, 2000, to July 1, 2008, the net migration into the United States was around 8.1 million individuals. Because of those presently in the United States and migration, the US Census Bureau announced that minorities are expected to become the majority in 2042. The US Census Bureau also announced the following:

- The Hispanic population is projected to triple, from 46.7 million to 132.8 million, from 2008 to 2050. This group's share of the nation's total population is projected to climb from 15 percent to 30 percent; nearly one in three US residents will be Hispanic.
- The black population is projected to increase from 41.1 million, or 14 percent of the population in 2008, to 65.7 million, or 15 percent of the population in 2050.
- The Asian population is projected to climb from 15.5 million to 40.6 million. The group's share of the nation's population is expected to rise from 5.1 percent to 9.2 percent.

The US Census Bureau also shows that 4.8 million immigrants from Ireland have lawfully been admitted to the United States for permanent residence since 1820. By 1870, about half of these immigrants were admitted for lawful permanent residence. Only Germany, Mexico, Italy, and the United Kingdom have had more immigrants admitted for permanent residence to the United States than Ireland.

Managers and Investors

From 2000 to 2008, between 54,000 and 84,000 additional foreigners resided and worked in the United States for a fixed term as managers and investors, temporary workers and trainees, and exchange visitors and intracompany transferees. These individuals used L-1 visas to arrive in the United States, and most of them arrived from England, India, Venezuela, Brazil, and Colombia to work in international companies. For example, Brazilian Renato Rosa opened an Orlando subsidiary of ARTI-PLAC WOOD, a 50-year-old wood import business his father started in Brazil decades ago.[26,27] Many foreigners have taken a similar leap of faith and have arrived in the United States during a difficult economic decline.

Work and Immigrants

US Senators Richard Shelby and Jeff Sessions (Alabama) estimated that the profit to US corporations and businesses that employed illegal aliens in 2005 was more than $2.36 trillion.[28] (In their report, the senators claim that less than 2 percent of illegal aliens pick crops, but 41 percent are on welfare.[29]) Another report shows that by 2014, the Hispanic labor force will reach 25.8 million, due to faster population growth, resulting from a younger population and higher fertility rates and increased immigration levels (see also the previous discussion for more details on the rise of Hispanics in the United States).[30] Whites, despite relatively slow growth, represent the largest group, composing 80.2 percent of the labor force. Blacks represent 12 percent of the labor force. Asians will continue to be the fastest growing racial group, climbing to 5.1 percent of the labor force by 2014. Consistent with these thoughts are results from a two-year study conducted by University of South Carolina (USC) researchers of 181 undocumented immigrants, mostly Mexicans. Sixty percent of the participants reported that they plan to return to Mexico, where they prefer to live.[31] They were in the United States to earn money, and only four of the 181 participants were unemployed.[32]

Despite the economic profits by industries that employ immigrants, the general public continues to believe that terrorist attacks are linked to immigrants. It is posited that the framing of the terrorist problem through the political discourse of new terrorism is built upon an escalated "cultural climate of fear and uncertainty" and the media's enhanced version of imminent danger that leads headlines, argues Gabe Mythen and Sandra Walklate.[33] The media's discussions of terrorists are linked to negative consequences for ethnic minority groups in the United States, the United Kingdom, and France.[34] Mythen and Walklate suggest that:

> The analytical framework utilizes the risk society as the scene in which governmental strategies are parceled up and unpacked and that most of those unpacked packages are represented by Mexicans (they represent strike breakers) or those from Central America (they represent drug pushers) and Muslims (they represent terrorists). At the level of political communication, it will be elucidated that media representations of the terrorist threat have served to further "embed discourses of responsibilization."[35]

Are Immigrants Terrorists?

While Colorado citizens seriously debated the immigrant–terrorist connection, their state legislature passed an ordinance requiring adult applicants for public services to document their citizenship. Colorado Republicans complained that the ordinance wasn't strong enough. One congresswoman wanted the ban to be added to the state's constitution and wanted the ordinance to include individuals under 18 years of age. In the congresswoman's opinion, if immigrant ordinances are not encompassing, such as including youngsters, those ordinances would aid immigrant youth to become terrorists. From the congresswoman's point of view, immigrants and terrorists are one in same. Actually, when some argue that immigration threatens American national security, they cite the example of the 9/11 hijackers. The National Commission on Terrorist Attacks reported that "as we know from the sizable illegal traffic across our land borders, a terrorist could attempt to bypass legal procedures and enter the United States surreptitiously. None of the 9/11 attackers entered or tried to enter our country this way."[36]

Complicating public opinion about immigration can be derived from the efforts of the Movimiento Estudiantil Chicano de Aztlan (MEChA) or Chicano Student Movement of Aztlan. MEChA is an Latino interest group that encourages anti-American activities and civil disobedience. MEChA's radical members refer to themselves as "Mechistas," whose objective is the annexation of Mexico's lost territories which include the Southwestern United States—a Chicano country called Aztlan. The issue of Aztlan is explained by Carlos M. Jimenez in his textbook *The Mexican American Heritage* which was adapted by the Santa Barbara California School Districts.[37] There is a redrawn map of Mexico and the United States (California, New Mexico, and Texas) showing Mexico or Aztlan with a full one-third more territory. It also reports that Latinos hold the power to officially develop the Aztlan dream. Some Americans might view MEChA's intentions as representing a terrorist orientation.

■ Aliens

America's current treatment of immigrants is counter to the concerns of equality and the commitment to the huddled masses on which America was built, argues Kevin R. Johnson.[38] Because noncitizens are afforded few legal and civil rights, they possess few of the protections enjoyed by most Americans (other than those Americans who are targeted through the wars on crime, junkies, sex offenders, and poverty). This differentiation is rationalized in part by classifying noncitizens as *aliens*. The classification of persons as aliens, as opposed to citizens, has legal, social, and political significance (the US Census Bureau's definitions of native and foreign-born populations were provided earlier in this chapter). Citizens are provided with political and civil rights, which include the right of litigation under Section 42, USC 1983, a federal statute that can include local police officers, their trainers, and their departments for civil right violations (i.e., deprivation of any rights, privileges, or immunities secured by the US Constitution) that are secured by the rule of law.[39] A lack of access to constitutional and statutory protections can result in fewer municipal services, which can include, among other things, poor police services, dubious official intervention, and a lack of municipal services to remove garbage, repair roadways and sidewalks, and board up vacant structures (see the section "Plenary Power Doctrine" found later in this chapter).[40,41]

Police Services

From Boston to Los Angeles, immigrants are provided with police services at a different level than services that are provided to others, some would argue.[42] Police officers generally take the position that immigrants keep to themselves and report crime less often than citizens for two reasons: immigrants deal with discrepancies and family disputes internally, and immigrants do not trust the police. Then, too, local police officers cannot enforce federal immigration statutes (more detail below). These findings are consistent with those of the police department in Quincy, Massachusetts, a city with a population of 77,000 residents. The Quincy Police Department is composed largely of Irish officers (who paste shamrocks on their service weapons), despite the city's large Asian and Cape Verdean populations. "You kidd'en? When things happen on this side of town, we never see cops," said a Quincy resident.[43] This anecdote is consistent with the literature. For example, surveys conducted in Chicago by Wesley G. Skogan and colleagues at the Institute for Policy Research found that Latinos were nearly three times more likely than whites to think that the police working in their neighborhoods were impolite, and Latinos were 2.5 times more likely to think that police were unfair, unhelpful, and not concerned about their problems.[44] Chinese immigrants in New York City report that when they had previous contact with New York City police officers, the participants rated those interactions as unfavorable.[45]

In Elizabeth, New Jersey, Hispanics outnumber whites two to one, except at the Elizabeth Police Department (EPD). The mostly white department received a federal grant for $3.2 million in 2001 to enhance community outreach. The Office of Inspector General, Audit Division conducted an audit of grants awarded by the Office of Community Oriented Policing Services (COPS) to the EPD.[46] In the final analysis, the EPD failed in six of the eight basic requirements to accomplish their goals, resulting in a federal investigation into EPD's misuse of those funds. One implication of this finding is that where immigrants are involved, police officials accept federal money for outreach purposes but continue to rely on traditional police practices of isolating immigrants from city decision-making processes or services that are provided to others in the jurisdiction. However, it is equally likely that many immigrants prefer to keep their distance from American police officers and isolate themselves in their communities because of their fear of deportation, their inefficiency to communicate with officers, and their lack of trust (and understanding) of American police because of negative experiences with police in their home countries.[47]

Congruent with this perspective are findings from a survey of 213 residents in Midland, Texas, where 30,000 Hispanics live and work among 70,000 whites.[48] When the 213 participants were asked what country best represented their homeland, the majority (127 or 58 percent) said Central America, South America, or Mexico. Also, 52 participants (24 percent) reported that western Europe represented their homeland, and 27 participants (13 percent) reported that Haiti, the Dominican Republic, or the Caribbean represented their homeland. Fifty-nine participants (28 percent) spoke English at home, 74 participants (35 percent) spoke English and another language, and 70 participants (33 percent) spoke only Spanish or Portuguese. Finally, 83 of the respondents (39 percent) rented their homes, 116 respondents (55 percent) owned their homes, and 14 respondents (7 percent) lived with others. Rarely did Midland participants report an involvement in any of the decision-making processes conducted by the Midland Police Department.[49] The participants reported that their most serious neighborhood issues were fear and lack of trust of the police and home invasion. Remedies toward resolving Midland's most serious neighborhood problems centered on issues of their homes and the business establishments who catered to them. When asked what would be the best way to curb neighborhood problems, 88 of the participants (41 percent) reported home ownership issues and business reinvestment into the neighborhood. When participants were asked how safe it is to live in their neighborhood compared to a year ago, 124 (58 percent) reported they felt unsafe; however, more than one-third reported that the police acted professionally, and 55 percent said the police were effective at their jobs.

There is little evidence that culturally diverse community members engage in police decision-making processes in Midland. This finding is consistent with that of Wesley G. Skogan and Susan M. Hartnett, who add that the Chicago Alternative Policing Strategy (CAPS), the Chicago Police Department's version of community policing, rarely includes participants from Chicago's Mexican communities.[50] It is unlikely that the police departments in Chicago and Midland intentionally exclude Mexicans or other immigrants in community policing initiatives and prevent them from receiving quality services. Nonetheless, the absence or exclusion of immigrants, particularly Mexicans and Central Americans who reside in the United States, is consistent with reports from other community policing observers.

Home Ownership

What is known about immigrants, particularly Hispanics or Latinos, is that "current statistics show that Latino rates of home ownership nationwide have risen faster than the US average since the mid-1990s, with metro areas like Albuquerque, Chicago, and Denver leading the way in Hispanic population growth. Nevada is ranked No. 1 for projected percentage of housing units for Hispanic families needed between 2000 and 2030."[51] The slump in residential home sales and home prices across the United States in 2005 to 2007 moved in a positive direction in late 2008, reports the National Association of Realtors.[52] Many realtors are optimistic about future sales and prices because of many factors that can impact Latino home purchase trends. Home ownership and community stability are related variables, argued John I. Gilderbloom and John P. Markham,[53] and one mechanism toward community revitalization (discussed later) is new immigrant home owners. However, many undocumented immigrants, explains one observer,[54] live below or at the poverty level, are separated from family and friends, deal with the stress of living in a foreign country among people who abuse them, do not have health insurance, and live in overcrowded, substandard housing. However, for all they suffer, if that is the case, many undocumented immigrants possess the motivation to keep going, and that says something about the human spirit despite the difficulties they encounter.[55]

■ Enforcement, Incarceration, and Crime

Enforcement of immigration laws and deportation practices are largely conducted or supervised by US federal agencies (more details later in this chapter); sometimes, federal violations can result in federal incarceration. When immigrants violate state laws, they might be detained in municipal jails and prosecuted in state courts, resulting in confinement at state or county prisons.

US Immigration and Customs Enforcement

US Immigration and Customs Enforcement (ICE), the largest investigative arm of the US Department of Homeland Security (DHS), is responsible for eliminating vulnerabilities on the nation's borders. ICE is composed of four law enforcement divisions and several support divisions. These divisions of ICE combine to form a new investigative approach with new resources to provide unparalleled investigation, interdiction, and security services to the public and law enforcement partners at the federal and local sectors.

Congress passed the USA PATRIOT Act and set other measures in motion, such as the Absconder Apprehension Initiative, making the apprehension of absconders or fugitives a DHS priority. The National Fugitive Operations Program (NFOP) was established under the Office of Detention and Removal (ODR).

The mission of NFOP is to identify, locate, apprehend, process, and remove fugitive aliens from the United States. Also, NFOP's goal is to eliminate the backlog of fugitives and ensure that the number of aliens deported equals the number of final orders of removal issued by the immigration courts in any given year.

The NFOP Fugitive Operations Teams that are strategically deployed around the country are assigned to fugitive cases and attempt to apprehend those persons who will ultimately be removed from the country. Federal agents had a backlog of more than 600,000 persons for whom they could not account as of 2007. A report prepared by the DHS inspector general said that the effectiveness of teams assigned to find the fugitives were hampered by "insufficient detention capacity, limitations of an immigration database, and inadequate working space."[56] More than $204 million has been allocated to 52 Fugitive Operations Teams since 2003, and a backlog of 623,292 cases existed as of August 2006.

In 2007, ICE employed approximately 100 fugitive operations teams who apprehended an estimated 37,000 aliens and doubled that number of arrests in 2006, but there remained 560,000 illegal fugitives in the United States at the end of 2008. Fugitive aliens include individuals similar to President Obama's aunt who sought asylum in America, says Denise Lavoie, "but were rejected and ordered to leave the country."[57] Others were caught illegally entering the country and failed to appear at a hearing. One issue can relate to the concern that many of those backlogged are fugitives by status, not fugitives through the commission of a violent crime; ignoring this distinction has the potential of creating an open door policy of inappropriate and illegal intervention, including wrongful convictions and wrongful detentions. Table 5-1 shows the number of aliens that were formally removed from the United States for violation of immigration laws from 1991 to 2005. Notice the low double-digit entries, which represent the number of immigrants as a national security risk, in relationship to the total number of immigrants who are attempting fraudulent entry or entry without proper documents.

Immigrants Outnumber Federal Agents

One report shows that illegal aliens outnumber federal immigration agents by 5,000 to 1, and one source says there are 10 million illegal immigrants in the country (despite the previous estimate of 560,000 fugitive aliens).[58] The figure of 10 million appears to be weighted with the notion that all aliens are terrorists, drug runners, or "just one more worker eager to join the millions already here driving down the wages of Americans and adding to so many other problems the nation faces."[59] Most immigrants come to the United States to work, to obtain an education, to raise families, to be safe, and to contribute to their communities, says Nicholas DiMarzo.[60]

Foreign-Born Individuals and Incarceration

The ODR estimates that in 2008 there were an estimated 650,000 foreign-born individuals admitted to state correctional facilities and local jails. In California alone, one report shows that the public cost to incarcerate foreign-born individuals in 2004 was approximately $1.4 billion,[61] and $9.1 billion was spent on health care and to school the children of illegal aliens.[62]

Ruben G. Rumbaut and Walter A. Ewing found that among incarcerated males in state and federal penitentiaries across the country, the 3.5 percent incarceration rate of American-born individuals in 2000 was five times higher than the 0.7 percent incarceration rate of foreign-born individuals.[63] The researchers argue that the incarceration rate of foreign-born individuals in 2000 was nearly 2.5 times less than the 1.7 percent rate for native-born non-Hispanic white men and almost 17 times less than the 11.6 percent rate for native-born black men. That is, native-born Hispanic men were nearly seven times more likely to be in prison than foreign-born Hispanics. Also, foreign-born Mexicans

TABLE 5–1　ALIENS FORMALLY REMOVED FROM THE UNITED STATES FOR VIOLATION OF IMMIGRATION LAWS

Fiscal year	Total	Attempted entry with fraud or without proper documents	Criminal	Failed to maintain status	Previously removed or ineligible for reentry	Present without authorization	Smuggling or aiding illegal entry	National security
1991	33,189	3,058	14,475	1,135	735	13,347	28	7
1992	43,671	3,630	20,098	1,076	1,008	17,403	177	31
1993	42,542	2,968	22,470	783	913	15,018	208	54
1994	45,674	3,482	24,581	716	1,052	15,500	218	57
1995	50,924	5,822	25,684	611	1,432	17,069	196	34
1996	69,680	15,412	27,655	708	2,006	23,522	275	36
1997	114,432	35,738	34,113	1,031	3,340	39,297	385	30
1998	173,283	79,328	35,984	996	7,201	48,531	498	15
1999	181,194	91,891	42,028	811	9,483	35,089	409	10
2000	186,391	89,935	41,155	748	11,906	40,501	494	13
2001	178,207	76,292	40,196	729	10,827	48,150	511	12
2002	150,788	41,392	37,816	1,257	13,239	55,733	582	11
2003	189,856	52,728	40,356	1,334	18,595	75,329	624	15
2004	204,290	50,727	42,835	1,125	21,504	86,313	729	12
2005	208,521	75,532	40,018	1,042	18,203	72,229	540	10

Source: Sourcebook of Criminal Justice Statistics Table 4.47 (2005).[64] Categories not included: Missing, Unknown, Other.

had an incarceration rate of only 0.7 percent in 2000—more than eight times lower than the 5.9 percent rate of native-born males of Mexican descent. Also, foreign-born Salvadoran and Guatemalan males had an incarceration rate of 0.5 percent, compared to 3.0 percent of native-born males of Salvadoran and Guatemalan descent.

The New York State Department of Correctional Services (NYS DOCS) reports that between 1985 and 2006, the overall inmate population increased 83 percent; the number of inmates born in the United States increased by 81 percent in New York prisons, and those born in other countries increased by 157 percent.[65] (Keep in mind that in 1985 the war on immigrants was not in full swing, and there were few foreign-born inmates in the prison system.) This huge percentage increase translates to a total of 6,791 foreign-born inmates as of December 31, 2006, reports NYS DOCS; it represents an estimated 11 percent of the NYS DOCS' 61,000-inmate prison population. Although 117 countries are represented by foreign-born inmates, largely the increases of foreign-born inmates were born in Mexico, El Salvador, and Ecuador. Also, NYS DOCS reports that largely foreign-born inmates were convicted of violent crimes more often than other inmates. However, a clear signal that emerges from this chapter is that immigrants might be at a greater risk of wrongful convictions when compared to others, especially if those immigrants represent individuals in poverty (see Chapter 4 for more details). It is likely that there are many immigrants confined who are not guilty of crimes that would normally produce a jail sentence for native-born individuals.

Incarcerated Alien Statistics

One study of 55,322 illegal aliens who were incarcerated at federal, state, and local correctional facilities in April 2005 revealed the following statistics regarding alien–inmates[66]:

- Each inmate was arrested an average of eight times, or about 460,000 times total.
- Each inmate was arrested for an average of 13 offenses, or 700,000 offenses total.
- 49 percent had previously been convicted of a felony.
- 20 percent had previously been convicted of a drug offense.
- 18 percent had previously been convicted for a violent offense.
- 56 percent of those charged with a reentry (in confinement) offense had previously been convicted on at least five prior occasions.

Illegal aliens, in addition to all laws that are applicable to American citizens, are required to conform to immigration laws, which can be included in felony arrests and convictions.

Crime and Illegal Aliens

The following data is provided by the 2006 (First Quarter) INS/FBI Statistical Report on Undocumented Immigrants[67]:

- 95 percent of all warrants in Los Angeles are for illegal aliens.
- 83 percent of all warrants for murder in Phoenix are for illegal aliens.
- 86 percent of all warrants for murder in Albuquerque are for illegal aliens.
- 24.9 percent of all inmates in California are Mexican nationals who are here illegally.
- 40.1 percent of all inmates in Arizona are Mexican nationals who are here illegally.
- 53 percent of all investigated burglaries reported in five western states were perpetrated by illegal aliens.
- 50 percent of all gang members in Los Angeles are illegal aliens.
- 71 percent of all apprehended cars stolen in five western states were stolen by illegal aliens, or Transport Coyotes (human smugglers or human traffickers).

Nine of every 10 warrants in Los Angeles are linked to illegal aliens; therefore, only 1 of every 10 warrants are issued to a native-born person, but this is a difficult statistic to document. The Superior Court of California, Los Angeles County reported over three million cases in 2007, and warrants include homeless and vehicle violations, among others.[68] Professor Daniel Mears, a Florida State University criminologist, argues that such statistics and reasoning linked to illegal aliens can be turned on their heads. "If someone is here illegally," Mears asks, "why would they call attention to themselves by committing a crime?"[69] One answer might be that some would commit crimes, but Mears's perspective implies that because many illegal aliens worked so hard to arrive in this country in the first place, it seems curious that they now would draw attention to themselves.

■ Costs of Immigration

In 1997 (the last known calculation by Professor Donald Huddle, Rice University) immigration was estimated to cost American taxpayers a net of $70 billion per year, after subtracting taxes paid by immigrants. That is, the estimated annual expense for an illegal alien's use of public services is approximately $11,000. (Note: These statistics cannot be documented.) Also, 62 percent of all undocumented immigrants in the United States, Huddle claims, are working for cash and not paying taxes; illegal aliens are predominately working without their green card. However, another study reports that immigrants pay their fair share of taxes.[70] Even the undocumented immigrants pay into Social Security, many through false Social Security numbers. According to a 2005 study by Physicians for a National Health Program (PNHP), immigrants, including undocumented aliens, use fewer healthcare resources than native-born citizens. Immigrants (not illegal aliens) accounted for 10 percent of the US population but only 8 percent of total healthcare spending and only 8 percent of government healthcare spending. Their per capita expenditure is less than half that of nonimmigrants. Thirty percent of immigrants used no healthcare services at all in the course of a year.

■ Immigration Control Advocates

Advocates of immigration control say that the high crime rate among immigrants would never happen if the United States maintained "a serious program of deportation of the illegal aliens already here and proper border security to prevent both entry and re-entry."[71] These ideas are reinforced by the media and enhanced through congressional legislation that provides funds for enforcement of immigration laws by federal and local agencies. For example, a US congressman asked Congress for an electrical fence similar to livestock fences along the border to control the immigration flow.

Also, the inability of most recent legislation to effectively control illegal immigration from Mexico into the United States has resulted in myriad difficulties for immigration enforcement officials, policy makers, and migrants.[72] Despite various increases in US Customs and Border Protection (CBP) funding, technology, and personnel, the deaths of migrants caused by enforcement officers at the border have escalated to an estimated 320 per year. Migrants are forced to attempt border crossings in increasingly remote areas with harsh conditions; because of the heightened risk, many would-be migrants enlist the help of smugglers. It has been reported that some of these smugglers have raped and beaten many of their clients. International human rights groups have charged the United States government with implementing immigration enforcement programs that put migrants in grave danger, but these charges seem to have little effect on US policy, explains Kiera LoBreglio.

Legislation was signed into law by President George W. Bush (Public Law 109-367; Secure Fence Act of 2006[73]) that provided $33.8 billion to pay for, among other things, a border fence along the United States–Mexico border and all the high-tech gadgetry it would take to attempt to control illegal immigration (see the section "287(g) Agreement with DHS" for more details).

Exclusion: Historic Political Policy

The constitutional exclusion of immigrants is closely tied to the historic Chinese Exclusion Act of 1882 (while Chinese laborers helped build American railroads), which describes the gradual shift from state to federal immigration laws and law enforcement.[74] Most immigration and citizenship laws have centered on federal law since the 19th century, including the passage of the Hart-Celler Act in 1965, which represented a reduction in racist policies that had underpinned immigration law for many decades. The Hart-Celler Act eliminated the national origins quota system that was erected in the 1920s, a system that had discriminated against all immigrants from countries outside the northern or western regions of Europe, advises Carolyn Wong.[75] The Hart-Celler Act produced some unexpected consequences: it expanded legal immigration from Asia and the movement of undocumented workers across the US–Mexico border, and it expanded the influence of ethnic rights groups. Hart-Celler brought together the interests of business and union leaders because there was a concern that employment-based immigrants would impact American workers.

The Immigration Act of 1990 once again revised US immigration law, including Hart-Celler. This legislation affected the US–Mexico migration relationship, says Kiera LoBreglio.[76] It established a higher, more flexible annual ceiling on immigration levels and instituted a permanent diversity program. The Immigration Act of 1990 encouraged immigration from countries that were poorly represented in the United States. Congress later amended the act to provide specifically that no person from a foreign state "contiguous to the United States" was eligible for a diversity visa, thereby excluding Mexicans.

Congress viewed the North American Free Trade Agreement of 1992 (NAFTA) as a possible solution to illegal Mexican immigration. US interests in reducing illegal immigration from Mexico, NAFTA states, would be realized by stimulating economic development in Mexico. Although NAFTA did produce positive effects on the Mexican economy, it failed to resolve the severe economic problems of the border region, and it failed to decrease the rate of illegal migration from that area. For example, under a 1996 statute, "legal" immigrants were routinely detained without bond, deported without consideration for discretionary relief, restricted in their access to counsel, and barred from appealing to the courts, largely by federal personnel.[77] Laws allow additional grounds for deportation and subject long-term immigrants to mandatory detention and automatic deportation for offenses such as shoplifting, disturbing the peace, or possession of a "joint" (marijuana). Low-level federal immigration officials act as judge and jury (no jury of their peers is allowed), and the federal courts are allowed no power to review most deportation decisions and federal government activities (see the section "Plenary Power Doctrine" later in this chapter). However, the Web site of the US Citizenship and Immigration Services (USCIS) shows a number of legal settlements among immigrants who litigated against the United States, although the numbers are small.

287(g) Agreement with DHS

State and local governments can apply for a 287(g) agreement to enforce federal immigration laws. The Illegal Immigration Reform and Immigrant Responsibility Act (8 USC § 1357g) provides that a partnership can be formed between local law enforcement and the federal immigration enforcement agency, the US Department of Homeland Security (DHS).[78] For example, former Arizona Governor Napolitano signed HB 2779 into law on July 2, 2007. HB 2779 suspends the business license of employers who hire and employ unauthorized aliens. For a second intentional violation, state and local agencies must permanently revoke all business-related licenses.

Maricopa County, Arizona and Civil Rights Violation Investigation

In Maricopa County, Arizona, Sheriff Joe Arpaio terrorized communities for years through police brutality, forced family separation, racial profiling, unjustified arrests, inmate abuses, and more. His latest action is linked to HB 2779 and the 287(g) agreement with DHS (Napolitano is its new director); it is alleged that he forcibly marched an estimated 200 undocumented immigrants through the streets in chains to a tent city surrounded by an electric fence, disregarding human rights. According to the US Department of Justice (DOJ), its Civil Rights Division will investigate Sheriff Joe Arpaio and his department for violations of due process practices such as discrimination and unconstitutional searches and seizures.

Nonetheless, it is argued that many of these strategies are promoted through the *CSI Effect*, which applauds official zero-tolerance initiatives, vigilantism (citizens, police, sheriffs, and federal agents who violate human rights), and political and personnel intervention, with or without the consent of the immigrants.[79]

■ Plenary Power Doctrine

The US Constitution includes no clause for any branch of the US government on immigration, although it does invest the power of "naturalization" to Congress. Historically, the US Supreme Court has taken a hands-off approach when asked to review the political branches' immigration decisions and policy making. The Center for Immigration Studies advises that federal policy on immigration has been focused by the plenary power doctrine, which holds that the legislative branch and the executive branch retain sole power to regulate all aspects of immigration as a basic attribute of sovereignty (see the section "Separation of Powers Doctrine" in Chapter 3 for more details).[80] There is an attempt to erode political-branch control over immigration in favor of a judge-administered system based on the right of a foreigner to immigrate. When the plenary power doctrine's authority is limited, immigrants would have the opportunity to test their individual rights in court because the judicial branch would extend constitutional prerogatives to all exclusion and deportation cases.

Here's How It's Beginning to Work

Discretionary relief is granted at the discretion of a judge, advises Lawyer Central.[81] If granted, it will eliminate or postpone the execution of a deportation order. In most cases, the alien must apply for discretionary relief during the deportation hearing, although some forms of relief may be sought before the hearing begins. In a two-part process, the judge first determines whether the alien is eligible under statutory requirements and then decides whether to grant it.

The crux of the matter is that immigrants can be deported and, in some cases, forfeit all their holdings and personal property, whereas citizens cannot. In one respect, federal law enforcement and local traditional police policy (some local jurisdictions are training officers to arrest immigrants based on federal immigration regulations) offer a promise of public safety through aggressive immigration intervention initiatives that may or may not widen the gap of alleged criminal activities of immigrants.

■ Proactive Practices and Violations of Human Rights

In an effort to regulate immigration, federal and local police agencies often pursue proactive practices to aid and protect newcomers (see the USCIS' guide for citizenship and employment verification available at: http://www.uscis.gov/portal/site/uscis). For example, the Chicago Alternative Policing Strategy (CAPS) was developed to improve police effectiveness by identifying and prioritizing problems leading to crime by partnering with the various community groups, including Latinos.[82] However, despite the best efforts, research showed that "Latinos are one of Chicago's most troubled populations, and they have reaped comparatively fewer benefits than those enjoyed in many other city neighborhoods, such as declining crime rates and generally improving conditions."[83(p1)] Another study conducted in jurisdictions with large immigrant populations included the California cities of Long Beach, Garden Grove, San Jose, and Stockton. Police agencies strove to provide civic participation among their immigrant populations through community initiatives, including citizen police academies, hiring, youth programs, and other programs.[84] However, those agencies were not as successful as anticipated for numerous reasons, and police agencies that are engaged in 287(g) agreements can open the door to wrongful convictions and human rights violations (as evidenced in the previous Maricopa County, Arizona discussion).

Also, in New York City, more than one-third of the population is foreign born, and those residents originated from approximately 200 different countries; aiding those residents in participating with police and civic matters is a huge challenge.[85] Few attempts are successful at building trust and providing police services, particularly in areas of the city where large numbers of immigrants reside. Police departments across the country face many barriers, including[86]:

- Fear that contact with police could lead to deportation
- Imported distrust of police and judicial systems carried over from countries of origin
- Language and communication barriers
- Cultural misunderstandings
- Unfamiliarity with the local justice system

One study describes immigrant clients who were enrolled in Massachusetts batterer intervention programs from 2002 to 2004.[87] The research shows that immigrants in a mandated intervention group were more likely to complete the program than nonimmigrants, but the consequences of just being in the program helped further the label of batterer or criminal (whether or not the client had battered is unclear), and the clients who failed the program faced the consequences of the court and social services. Nonetheless, it appears that proactive practices are flawed because they tend to label immigrants as criminals.

Labeling Immigrants

Labeling immigrants as criminals increases their fear of victimization by the public and the police. For example, a group that includes immigrants whose mission is associated with social justice, the Idaho Community Action Network, presented strong police roundup scenarios, which included polarizing language.[88] The program created so much fear of immigrant roundups that immigrants in Idaho stayed home and sent their children to do the grocery shopping.[89]

Workplace Raids

ICE raids of Latinos at places of employment might have a similar effect: immigrants stop working. For example, on August 25, 2008, a raid at Howard Industries in Laurel, Mississippi netted 600 workers suspected of being undocumented,[90,91] and in Postville, Iowa ICE conducted arrests of 700 undocumented workers at the world's largest kosher meat packing company.[92] At the House of Raeford Farms in Greenville, South Carolina, a raid in October 2008 resulted in the arrest of 331 workers, but six of those workers were 15 and 16 years of age.[93] One of the youths said that no one asked his age when he was hired. This facility processes 750,000 chickens per week and is one of the nation's largest chicken producers.

Also, a class action lawsuit in Tacoma, Washington was filed against Zirkle Fruit in 2005 for allegedly conspiring to hire thousands of illegal immigrants to keep wages low.[94] William Zirkle, the company's president, admitted no wrongdoing, but he decided to settle the case out of court for $1.3 million.

Roadblocks, Racial Profiling, and The Danbury Nine

Additionally, vigilante citizen groups have forced vehicles carrying day laborers off the roads. Refugees have been awakened in the middle of the night to someone banging on their doors telling them to get out of the country, and the white supremacist interest group called the National Alliance has set fires at a local university to defend the flag. Members of the National Alliance developed flyers that read: "Stop Immigration! Non-Whites are turning America into a Third World slum. They are messy, disruptive, noisy, and multiply rapidly. Let's send them home now!"[95]

In addition, alleged racial profiling by various police departments in Ohio and elsewhere have resulted in lawsuits,[96] and police roadblocks to enforce motor vehicle laws against undocumented Mexican workers in Kentucky sparked strong controversy.[97,98] Anti-immigrant sentiments and hate crimes have also grown in cities as they have experienced the emergence of Mexican migrant communities.[99] Upstate New York, for example, has seen hate crimes typified by vigilante groups directed at Mexican immigrants.[100] As the Southern Poverty Law Center outlines,

"The raging national debate over immigration is stoking the fires of racist extremism across the country. Neo-Nazis and other white supremacists are ratcheting up the intensity of their bloodthirsty 'race war' rhetoric, and violent hate crimes against Hispanics, regardless of their immigration status, appear to be on the rise."[101]

The Southern Poverty Law Center suggests that the following events have been recorded in 2005:

- The National Knights of the Ku Klux Klan held an anti-immigration rally in Russellville, Alabama that drew more than 300 Klansmen and Klan supporters, including members of the neo-Nazi hate group Aryan Nations, another interest group. At the rally, robed Klansmen burned a 22-foot-high cross and yelled, "Let's get rid of the Mexicans!"
- When Hispanic families in Tucson gathered in a park to celebrate Cinco de Mayo, anti-immigration extremist Roy Warden arrived, strapped with a pistol, and led a demonstration. "Listen up, Mexican invaders," Warden said. "We will not permit you, the ignorant, the savage, the unwashed, to overrun us, as happened in Rome. . . . Land must be paid for in blood. If any invader tries to take this land from us we will wash this land and nurture our soil with oceans of their blood!" Warden later e-mailed a death threat to Isabel Garcia, a Tucson public defender who cochairs the human rights group Derechos Humanos. The e-mail was titled, "Warden to Isabel Garcia: I will blow your freaking head off!"
- A neo-Nazi in East Hampton, New York was arrested for threatening two Hispanic teenagers with a machete and chainsaw, holding the blade to the throat of one while threatening to kill them.
- A 17-year-old Hispanic high school football player was dragged from a suburban house party in Texas and savagely attacked by two white assailants, one of them a neo-Nazi skinhead, according to Harris County law enforcement officials.

African Americans have joined whites in expressing concern about the impacts of Latino immigration and in particular Mexican immigration.[102] Vigilante groups comprised of whites and blacks have used force against undocumented Mexican immigrants, frequently with tragic results.[103]

The Danbury Nine, as they are called, are day laborers who filed a federal lawsuit challenging the legality of a sting operation in Danbury, Connecticut that led to their arrest on immigration charges.[104] The plaintiffs, including an individual who had been deported to Ecuador, contend that their arrests were illegal and part of a campaign based on racial profiling. The complaint said that a Danbury police officer posed as a contractor, drove an unmarked van belonging to the federal Immigration and Customs Enforcement agency, and parked where day laborers, many from Ecuador, gather. Pretending to offer $11 per hour to demolish a fence, the officer transported 11 would-be workers to a fenced-in lot where they were arrested, handed over to federal immigration agents, and eventually placed in deportation proceedings. They argued that the City of Danbury acted to enforce federal immigration law without an ordinance to support their pursuit or authority. Clearly, some argue that racism is the wedge conservatives use to distract many from real questions that need answers.[105]

One implication is that these and other accounts of proactive practices end in unlawful and immoral behavior toward immigrants and wrongful imprisonment. A contemporary trend focuses on how the judiciary, through case law and the influences of what can be described as the *CSI Effect*, has influenced the nation's official response and the public's response to new arrivals in America.[106] Yet because immigrants, especially illegal immigrants, lack the full latitude of protections of the Constitution, little is accomplished to aid the individual.

■ Statistics of Deportation and Criminalization of Immigrants

Statistics show that an estimated 173,000 aliens were deported in 1998 (114,000 were deported in 1997 and 69,000 were deported in 1996). Almost one-half (79,000) attempted entry without proper documentation; 36,000 were deemed to be criminals; and 7,100 had been previously removed.[107] A criminal label now applies to those 79,000 individuals. Therefore, it comes as no surprise that over a 10-year period (1994 to 2003), the federal government's annual increase of incarceration for all convictions was greatest among immigration defendants (ranging from 14 percent for arrests to 25 percent for prison sentences imposed).[108] Other factors that contribute to the criminalization of immigrants might have to do with environmental contributions, which consist of the following approaches[109]:

- Opportunity structure
- Cultural approach
- Social disorganization

Opportunity Structure

New immigrants tend to settle in urban neighborhoods, which, as previously suggested, tend to be dominated by underpaid and undereducated workers; those neighborhoods also give rise to substandard housing and fewer municipal amenities, such as police services and road repairs.[110,111] Immigrants may become blocked from wage earning potentials and turn to illegal avenues to earn a living—such as working without a green card or house cleaning, office cleaning, working at children's centers and at tailoring enterprises—which can translate to criminal prosecution. Other authors argue that isolated immigrants might be contaminated by criminal opportunities, and culture and crime are more or less functions of pre-existing structural factors, such as poverty.[112] Many immigrants, especially young gang members, find the potential benefits of the underground economy attractive, so the thinking goes, but stereotypes produced by the *CSI Effect* might be different from the actual accomplishments of gangs, although this thought should in no way minimize the destructive nature of some gang activity. Nonetheless, it is clear that the rise of MS-13 and other youth gangs has much to do with discrimination and exploitation of immigrants, as have been the historic accounts of youth gang development throughout American history.[113]

Cultural Approach

The culture of poverty thesis, whereby low-income individuals adapt to their structural conditions in ways that give rise to perpetuate their disadvantaged condition, is an example of the cultural approach. A variation of this perspective can be understood from the *subculture of violence* perspective, whereby violence can be seen as both normal and an expected means of dispute resolution among disadvantaged community members.[114,115] Yet it appears that the cultural perspective, regardless of variation, tends to blame the victim as opposed to looking at the root causes of crime.

Social Disorganization

Social disorganization implies that the community social institutions have broken down because of the change in the community due to the migration of the immigrant, explains a prominent researcher.[115-118] Robert Bursik describes socially disorganized communities as possessing an "inability to realize the common values of their residents or solve commonly expressed problems." Therefore, the thinking goes, weak social controls among community members (such as an immigrant neighborhood) enhance criminal opportunities. One implication of this idea is that one of the functional processes of social change allows violent crime to thrive. Abundant in the literature are studies suggesting that the functions of structural (e.g., poverty) and cultural (e.g., subculture of violence) forces are tied to social change, and a product of social change (e.g., immigration) is social disorganization, which leads to violent crime because the social institutions have broken down or have been devalued.[119]

In part, devalued social institutions are related to the language a resident speaks, some say. For example, the English language will create unity among community members. Mayor Tom Macklin of Avon Park, Florida developed a new law based on a Pennsylvania precedent, making English the city's official language, in addition to fining landlords and denying business licenses to those who accommodate immigrants.[120] However, a woman in Avon Park reported that a bartender refused to serve her sister, who had a Puerto Rican driver's license. He said, "I can't read that." In Bogota, New Jersey, Mayor Steve Lonegan campaigned to force a McDonald's restaurant to remove a Spanish-language billboard. The mayor might want to consider changing the name of the community, too.

However, one study shows that among 581 residents of a city in Texas, Spanish-speaking Hispanics and whites were more likely to cooperate with the police than English-speaking Hispanics.[121] Also, Spanish-speaking Hispanics were more likely to agree with the concept of a house visit by a police officer.

Another explanation for violence suggests that inner-city law-abiding community members arm themselves; they see violence as an appropriate response if they are attacked because of a lack of municipal services, including public safety services.[122] That is, the fear of victimization that hovers over some individuals— immigrants or natives—is associated with the fear of crime, argues Nancy E. Marion and Willard M. Oliver,[123] and ultimately they use violence to protect themselves because municipal services are perceived to be lacking or inadequate.

■ An Optimistic Perspective

A more optimistic perspective emphasizes the "enhanced potential inherent in positive population growth for social, economic, and technological progress" and therefore a means to solve environmental problems, advances Ellen Percy Kraly.[124] For example, population growth can enhance technological advances through such techniques as land-use intensity[125,126] and enhanced municipal services through advanced training (and paychecks), which can include the delivery of police services through evidence-based (scientific discovery methods) policing.[127]

Immigrants and Education

Confusing perspectives about immigrants and American education exist. Statistics show that more than 34 percent of Arizona's students in grades 1–12 are illegal aliens, and 24 percent do not speak English. More than 39 percent of California students in grades 1–12 are illegal aliens, and more than 42 percent are non-English speaking. At first glance, the statistics might show a drain of resources, but unexpectedly, the drain can have other effects. Immigrants and education can be typified in the action taken by the school district in St. Paul, Minnesota, whereby the district supported the actions taken by a public school bus driver who stranded three children (10-year-old twin girls and their 8-year-old brother) because the children spoke English.[128] The bus driver specifically told the children that the route was only for non-English-speaking students. The children attended a public school in the St. Paul School District where an estimated 30 percent of the 41,000 students are Hmong (from China and Southeast Asia). Hmongs also make up one of the city's largest ethnic groups.

Another example originates in the New York City educational system, where almost 14 percent of elementary school pupils are foreign born, and roughly half of these students are "recent immigrants."[129] The impact of immigrant students on school resources is an issue: immigrant advocates suggest that inequitable treatment of immigrant students could exist, and others imply that immigrants drain resources from native-born students.[130] The researchers showed that although schools' resources decreased the representation of immigrants, this relationship largely reflects differences in the educational needs of immigrant students. Although analyses that link resources to the representation of foreign-born students in 12 geographic regions within the

New York City educational system found some disparities, researchers found that some resources increased over time when there were large increases in the percentage of immigrants in a school. Thus, "elementary schools appear not to be biased either against or for immigrants per se, although differences in the needs of particular groups of immigrant students may lead to more (or fewer) school resources."[131]

■ Inclusion

Carolyn Wong takes exception to the exclusion issue and argues that the existence of a proimmigration coalition of cultural and economic interests is at the core of a positive pattern of immigration policy in the United States.[132] For example, federal judges are asked to review cases that involve immigrants.[133] During the summer of 2007 in Pennsylvania, a federal judge struck down ordinances adopted by the City of Hazleton to bar illegal immigrants from working or renting homes there.[134] The judge's verdict said that the city was not entitled to implement a law that would impose fines on businesses that hired illegal immigrants and penalize landlords who rented rooms to them.

Another example occurred in Riverside, New Jersey when residents received more than they bargained for after passing a get-tough immigration law.[135] Proponents of the law blamed Latino newcomers for crowding, scarce parking, increased crime, and strained public services. Although the get-tough law was never enforced, hundreds, if not thousands, of Brazilians and other immigrants fled Riverside. Then the town had different problems: a deserted downtown, economic malaise, and lingering resentment. Riverside repealed the law in the face of mounting legal bills and lawsuits. Riverside's dynamics were predictable. Wary of strangers who spoke a different language and brought different customs, residents rebelled. They feared the sudden influx of strangers. "Why can't they speak English?" "They are taking our jobs." Ironically, Riverside had experienced many immigrant waves before. The Portuguese settled there in the 1960s and built businesses. This made the town attractive to Brazilians, who began arriving in 2000. It is unknown how many of the new arrivals had legal status.

A coalition composed of interest groups, including churches, ethnic organizations, civil rights groups, and employer associations, have played a fundamental role in advancing civil rights linked to immigration, advises Debra L. DeLaet.[136] It is the development of due process rhetoric that has liberalized US immigration policies that are often funded by national employer associations in spite of growing evidence that the public opposition to immigration grew during the same period. Carolyn Wong adds that a consensus exists among many Americans to better control immigration, yet Congress has developed immigration reform that enhances immigrant opportunities.[137] Wong supports her claim with two central ideas:

- American employer associations that are made up of businesses that rely heavily on immigrant labor are very effective at lobbying lawmakers to provide them with access to permanent and temporary foreign workers.

- Latino and Asian American organizations strongly influenced policy outcomes, even before their constituencies gained political clout in the voting booth.

American Employer Associations

Business lobbyists are mainly interested in economic outcomes; they have a strong voice and the funding to secure their favored outcomes, such as congressional politics that led to the passage of three immigration bills[138]:

- Immigration Reform and Control Act of 1986 (IRCA)
- Immigration Act of 1990
- Illegal Immigration Reform and Immigrant Responsibility Act of 1996 (IIRIRA)

Lawmakers are highly responsive to American employers' demands for access to permanent and temporary foreign workers. Associations of employers rely on immigrant labor funded by powerful lobbying machines. Although Wong's idea about employer associations that are actively engaged in encouraging immigration is notable, the fact remains that persons who violate federal law (including a group of persons, businesses, organizations, or local government) commit a federal felony when they do any of the following[139]:

- Assist an alien who they should reasonably know is illegally in the United States or who lacks employment authorization by transporting, sheltering, or assisting the alien to obtain employment
- Encourage the alien to remain in the United States by referring him or her to an employer or by acting as an employer or agent for an employer in any way
- Knowingly assist illegal aliens due to personal convictions

Conviction penalties include criminal fines, imprisonment, and forfeiture of vehicles and real property used to commit the crime. For example, the federal government has cracked down on employers who hire undocumented workers.[140] Specifically, federal immigration enforcement officers arrested the owners of Kawasaki Sushi Restaurant in Baltimore, Maryland for hiring 24 undocumented workers and providing them and their families with housing. The owners were indicted for money laundering and alien harboring, crimes that carry penalties of 10 years imprisonment in a federal facility. Their business went into bankruptcy after the arrest. In 2006, immigration officials conducted raids on large corporations, such as Swift & Company, the third largest meat packing company in the country; IFCO Systems, a large pallet manufacturer; and Fischer Homes, a leading home builder in Indiana, Kentucky, and Ohio. The federal government doubled their investigative agents and added $41.7 million toward work site enforcement in 2007.

Latino and Asian American Organizations

Latino and Asian American organizations framed immigration issues as a matter of universal rights and formed alliances with other civil rights and humanitarian organizations. They also linked human rights with the maintenance of family reunification—family members who were left behind by the immigrant now residing in America.

To further characterize the work of Latino and Asian American organizations and interest groups, in 2006 thousands of marchers dotted the American urban landscape in Charlotte, Chicago, Denver, Los Angeles, and New York City, among others, to protest against a legislative bill that would drastically strengthen immigration enforcement, including extending a fence along the Mexican border and severe punishment for those who would aid undocumented workers. The Latino American marchers, in particular, crammed the streets carrying signs that said, "No human being is illegal" and "We are not criminals." Critics say that the Sensenbrenner Bill (HB 4437) would turn millions of undocumented workers into felons for crossing the border without permission.[141] Nonetheless, by a 239 to 182 vote, the House of Representatives approved the Border Protection, Antiterrorism, and Illegal Immigration Control Act (HR 4437) on December 16, 2007.

In their coverage of the marchers, television news channels (i.e., CNN, MSNBC, and FOX News) and leading newspapers (i.e., *New York Times*, *Chicago Tribune*, and *Los Angeles Times*) added their drumroll to the marchers' thoughts by draping their own tinsel onto the events. For example, "Unlike earlier protests in Los Angeles and other cities when protestors waved flags from Mexico and other countries, activists Monday around the country waved American flags, an obvious response to criticism that illegal immigrants aren't interested in assimilating into American culture and have no allegiance to this nation."[142] It's as though many illegal immigrants suddenly accepted the implications revealed by the media and those immigrants decided it would be advantageous to wave an American flag.

Often the media provides news space to dissenters. Someone held a sign that said, "Mexicans need special favors."[143] A scuffle involving the San Antonio Police Department officers and protesters started near the person who was carrying the sign. Police officers provided traffic control and tried to keep people on the sidewalks. Some resisted, and a struggle ensued. Officers were manipulated into the struggle between protesters and hecklers. Pepper spray was released into the crowd, an event that even police officials were unclear about. Four marchers were arrested at the scene, three for assault on a public servant and one for inciting a riot and disorderly conduct. Later in the day in Dallas, it was emphasized that immigrant children crowded the school systems, and in Chicago and Washington, DC, immigrant marchers were compared to Arab protesters in Britain and Paris, suggesting an absurd link between terrorists and Mexicans.[144]

■ Immigrants and Crime

Immigration and crime dominate the political debate in most nations that experience frequent immigration.[145] Researchers advise that there is little systematic evidence supporting this perspective or stereotype. What is supported in the literature is a trend that shows an increase in immigrant crime rates and that immigrants disregard American laws and therefore should be subjected to American legal procedures without the right to defend themselves.[146]

However, the weight of the evidence suggests that concentrated immigration has little, if any, association with aggregate homicide, whereas the concentration of blacks has long predicted homicide rates.[147] Robert Sampson and Lydia Bean explain that while the number of illegal immigrants in the country doubled between 1994 and 2005, violent crime declined by nearly 35 percent, and property crimes declined by 26 percent over the same period.[148] Yet the undocumented population has doubled to 12 million since 1994. The Public Policy Institute of California (PPIC) determined that, on average, between 2000 and 2005 the cities that had a higher share of recent immigrants experienced greater violent crime declines than cities with a lower influx of illegal immigrants.

The broad pattern of secular declines in violence at the same time that immigration skyrocketed suggests a plausible hypothesis to be added to the race–ethnic theory of invariance. In fact, an implied thesis, perhaps the most intriguing of all, argues John Hagan and Alberto Palloni, is that[149]:

> The broad reduction of violence in the United States over the last decade was due in part to increasing diversity and immigration.

That is, local and federal police agencies reported a huge decline in the violent crime rate during the same period of time that immigration, especially from Mexico and South American nations, was unparalleled in US history.

Furthermore, the Bureau of Justice Statistics reports that based on current rates of first incarceration, an estimated 32 percent of black males will enter state or federal prison during their lifetime, compared to 17 percent of Hispanic males and almost 6 percent of white males.[150]

Robert Sampson and Lydia Bean examined over 3,000 violent acts committed in Chicago from 1995 to 2003, analyzing police records, census data, and a survey of more than 8,000 residents.[151] They said that a *Latino Paradox* exists, "whereby Latinos do much better on various social indicators, including violence, than blacks and apparently even whites given relatively high levels of disadvantage."[152] That is, first-generation Mexican immigrants were 45 percent less likely to engage in violence than third-generation Americans. The concentration of immigrants also appears to tell a very different story with respect to violence than the concentration of African Americans. This finding challenges the myth that increasing immigration is linked to increasing violence. The evidence from this study suggests that concentrated immigration has little, if any, association with aggregate homicide, whereas the concentration of blacks has long predicted homicide rates. Similar trends have been seen in New York and Miami, both of which have large immigrant enclaves. Most often, immigrants or new arrivals tend to settle in urban communities, explains Waldinger.[153] "Immigrant communities are often responsible for revitalizing the urban neighborhoods that they live in," Sampson and Bean add.

President Obama and Workplace Raids

On March 17, 2009, ICE agents raided a workplace in Bellingham, Washington and arrested 28 immigrants. This was the first major workplace raid since President Obama took office, reports the Immigration Reform Law Institute in Washington, DC.

■ Summary

The war on immigrants provides a label of enemies for immigrants; consequently, the public and some officials see immigration as a holy war and utilize policy and legalized violence as means to resolve the immigrant threat. The contemporary or neo-Malthusian perspective focuses on the impact of population growth and the negative relationship between immigration and the availability of quality environmental resources or resource scarcity. The debate continues about immigration, human rights, change, and resources. A general model of immigration has an environmental impact that includes the broad factors associated with a function of population characteristics, patterns of consumption and technology, and the consumption and manipulation of natural resources. However, racism and racial profiling powered by greed, pure selfishness, ignorance, and a lack of self-control influence the models of immigration, too.

Immigrants in the 21st century are similar to those of earlier periods, but America has changed. Immigration once served US national interests, but today it's believed to weaken America's national identity and threaten US security and sovereignty. This book argues that through an insecure economy and the distraction of the media, immigrants represent a perceived threat.

Aliens in the United States can be divided into permanent residents, asylees, refugees, nonpermanent residents, and illegal entrants. Approximately 888,000 immigrants arrived in America between July 1, 2007, and July 1, 2008. From April 1, 2000, to July 1, 2008, the net migration into the United States was around 8.1 million individuals. Also, between 600,000 and 700,000 individuals reside and work for a fixed term as managers and investors, temporary workers and trainees, exchange visitors, and intracompany transferees. Despite the economic profits by industries that employ immigrants, the general public continues to believe that terrorist attacks are linked to immigrants. Consequently, America's current treatment of immigrants is counter to the concerns of equality and the commitment to the huddled masses on which America was built.

The US Department of Homeland Security (DHS), through US Immigration and Customs Enforcement (ICE), is responsible for eliminating vulnerabilities on the nation's borders. Congress passed the USA PATRIOT Act and set other measures in motion to identify, locate, apprehend, process, and remove fugitive aliens from the United States.

The US Constitution provides no clause for any branch of the US government on immigration, and the US Supreme Court has taken a hands-off approach to the question. Most policy is powered by the plenary power doctrine, which holds that the legislative and executive branches retain sole power to regulate immigration. When the plenary power doctrine's authority is weakened, immigrants have a greater opportunity to test their individual rights in court because the judicial branch extends constitutional prerogatives to all exclusion and deportation cases.

The immigrant population explosion over the past 15 years appears to have impacted a decline in crime in urban America because immigrants, especially Latinos, revitalize their communities, and there are few indicators that immigrants and terrorists are linked.

■ References

1. Hayter, T. (2000). *Open borders: The case against immigration controls.* London: Pluto Press.

2. Sutcliffe, B. (2001). *100 ways of seeing an unequal world.* New York: Zed Books.

3. Sutcliffe, B. (1998). *Nacido en otra parte: Un ensayo sobre la migración internacional, el desarollo y la equidad.* Bilbao, Spain: Hegoa.

4. Heller, T. C. (2001). Change and convergence: Is American immigration still exceptional? In A. Kondao (Ed.), *Citizenship in a global world: Comparing citizenship rights for aliens.* Gordonsville, VA: Palgrave Macmillan.

5. King, J., & Efrati, R. (n.d.). *Survey of Ethiopian immigrants in three Hadera neighborhoods.* Retrieved March 18, 2009, from http://brookdale.jdc.org.il/default.asp?catid=%7B91983569-194E-4E02-860B-4997E3DEDDA7%7D

6. Jewish Women's Archive. *Exhibit: Women of valor.* Retrieved March 18, 2009, from http://www.jwa.org/exhibits/wov/lazarus/el9.html

7. Shelden, R. G. (2008). *Controlling the dangerous classes: A critical introduction to the history of criminal justice* (2nd ed.). Boston: Allyn & Bacon.

8. National Immigration Forum. *Green Card.* Retrieved August 21, 2009, from http://www.immigrationforum.org/

9. Motomura, H. (2006). *Americans in waiting: The lost story of immigration and citizenship in the United States.* New York: Oxford University Press.

10. Muradian, R. (2006). Immigration and the environment: Underlying values and scope of analysis. *Ecological Economics, 59*(2), 208–213.

11. Yoshihama, M. (2001). Immigrants-in-context framework: Understanding the interactive influence of socio-cultural contexts. *Evaluation and Program Planning, 24*(3), 207–318.

12. Malthus, T. (1797). *An essay on the principle of population.* London: St. Paul Church Yard.

13. *TheFreeDictionary.* Retrieved June 16, 2008, from http://www.thefreedictionary.com/Malthusians

14. Ehrlich, P. R., & Ehrlich, A. H. (1994). *Optimum human population size.* Retrieved June 23, 2009, from http://dieoff.org/page99.htm

15. Ehrlich, P. R., & Ehrlich, A. H. (1998). *Betrayal of science and reason: How anti-environmental rhetoric threatens our future.* New York: Island Press.

16. Hogan, D. J. (1992). The impact of population growth on the physical environment. *European Journal of Population, 8,* 109–123.

17. Kraly, E. P. (1995). *US immigration and the environment: Scientific research and analytic issues.* Washington, DC: US Commission on Immigration Reform.

18. Butcher, K. F., & Piehl, A. M. (1998). Recent immigrants: Unexpected implications for crime and incarceration. *Industrial and Labor Relations Review, 51*(4), 654–679.

19. Gottfredson, M. R., & Hirschi, T. (1990). *General theory of crime.* Stanford, CA: Stanford University Press.

20. Krikorian, M. (2008). *New case against immigration, both legal and illegal.* New York: Penguin Group.

21. Bonine, M. E. (1997). *Population, poverty, and politics in Middle East cities.* Gainesville: University of Florida Press.

22. Lendman, S. (2006, May 5). *A nation addicted to the need for enemies.* Retrieved October 20, 2008, from http://www.populistamerica.com/the_war_on_immigrants___part_iii

23. Martinez, R. (2006). Coming to America: The impact of the new immigration on crime. In R. Martinez, Jr. & A. Valenzuela, Jr. (Eds.), *Immigration and crime: Race ethnicity and violence.* Albany: New York University Press.

24. Latina Lista. (2007). *Undocumented immigrants are easy targets.* Retrieved September 12, 2008, from http://www.latinalista.net/palabrafinal/2007/09/undocumented_immigrants_are_easy_targets.html

25. Kondao, A. (2001). *Citizenship in a global world: Comparing citizenship rights for aliens.* Gordonsville, VA: Palgrave Macmillan.

26. Sarmah, S. (2009). Foreigners use L-1 visas to open businesses. *Orlando Sentinel,* p. 4.

27. Lawyer Central. (2009). *Foreigners use L-1 visas to open businesses.* Retrieved March 2, 2009, from http://immigration.lawyercentral.com/Foreigners-use-L-1-visas-to-open-busines-Legal-News-14-70885.html

28. Congress.org. (2007, August). *2006 (first quarter) INS/FBI statistical report on undocumented immigrants.* Retrieved October 28, 2008, from http://www.congress.org/congressorg/bio/userletter/?id=158&letter_id=1354780601

29. Congress.org. *INS/FBI statistical report on undocumented immigrants.* Also note that the $2.36 trillion in profits for companies that employ illegal aliens cannot, similar to the rest of the report, be documented.

30. Bureau of Labor Statistics. (2004). *Employment projections: 2006–16 summary.* Retrieved October 28, 2008, from http://www.bls.gov/news.release/ecopro.nr0.htm

31. Lacy, E. (2006, November). *Four issues about undocumented immigrants dispelled.* Retrieved September 12, 2008, from http://www.sph.sc.edu/cli/

32. Lacy, *Four Issues About Undocumented Immigrants Dispelled.*

33. Mythen, G., & Walklate, S. (2005). Criminology and terrorism: Which thesis? Risk society or governmentality? *British Journal of Criminology, 45*(1), 1–20.

34. Mythen & Walklate, "Criminology and Terrorism."

35. Mythen & Walklate, "Criminology and Terrorism."

36. National Commission on Terrorist Attacks. (n.d.). *Entry of the 9/11 hijackers into the United States.* Retrieved June 24, 2009, from http://govinfo.library.unt.edu/911/staff_statements/staff_statement_1.pdf

37. Jimenez, C. M. (1997). *The Mexican American heritage: With writing exercises.* (2nd ed.). Berkeley, CA: TQS Publications.

38. Johnson, K. R. (2003). *Huddled masses myth: Immigration and civil rights.* Philadelphia: Temple University Press.

39. Kappeler, V. E. (2006). *Critical issues in police civil liability* (4th ed.). Mount Prospect, IL: Waveland Press.

40. Stevens, D. J. (2003). *Case studies in applied community policing.* Boston: Allyn & Bacon.

41. Stevens, D. J. (2003). *Applied community policing.* Boston: Allyn & Bacon.

42. Escobar, E. J. (2001). Race, police, and the making of a political identity: Mexican Americans and the Los Angeles Police Department, 1900–1945. *The American Historical Review, 106*(2), 578–579.

43. Personal, confidential communication with a Quincy resident who was also a university student. January 2007.

44. Skogan, W. G., Steiner, L., DuBois, J., Gudell, J. E., & Fagan, A. (2002). *Community policing and the new immigrants: Latinos in Chicago.* Washington, DC: US Department of Justice, National Institute of Justice. Retrieved August 17, 2008, from http://www.ncjrs.gov/pdffiles1/nij/189908.pdf

45. Chu, D., Song, J. H. L., & Dombrink, J. (2005). Chinese immigrants perceptions of the police in New York City. *International Criminal Justice Review, 15*(2), 101–114.

46. US Department of Justice. (2001, March 23). *Office of community oriented policing services grants to City of Elizabeth, New Jersey police department.* Retrieved October 18, 2008, from http://www.usdoj.gov/oig//grants/g7001003.htm

47. Stevens, D. J. (2003), *Applied community policing in the 21st century,* Boston: Allyn Bacon.

48. Stevens, *Case Studies in Applied Community Policing.*

49. Stevens, *Case Studies in Applied Community Policing.* See p. 110-119. More specifically, those areas included deployment of routine police auto, bike, and boat patrols, decisions on ministations, building owner notification, use of police force, priorities of calls for service, police officer disciplinary actions, and police training and promotions.

50. Skogan, W. G., & Hartnett, S. M. (1999). *Community policing, Chicago style.* New York: Oxford University Press.

51. Cisneros, H. G. (2006). *Casa y comunidad: Latino home and neighborhood design.* New York: Builderbooks.com. (Cisneros is the former secretary of HUD.)

52. National Association of Realtors. Retrieved June 26, 2008, from http://www.realtor.org/research/research/ehsdata

53. Gilderbloom, J. I., & Markham, J. P. (1995). The impact of homeownership on political beliefs. *Social Forces, 73*(4), 1589–1607.

54. Lacy, *Four Issues About Undocumented Immigrants Dispelled.*

55. Latina Lista. (2006, November 15). *Four issues about undocumented immigrants are dispelled in new university study.* Retrieved June 23, 2009, from http://www.latinalista.net/palabrafinal/2006/11/four_myths_about_undocumented_immigrants.html

56. Malkin, M. (2007, May 1). *May day: Open-borders math.* Retrieved September 13, 2008, from http://michellemalkin.com/2007/05/01/may-day-open-borders-math/

57. Lavoie, D. (2008, November 15). 560,000 illegal immigrants defying deportation orders. *Charlotte Observer*, p. 14A.

58. Kobach, K. (n.d.). *State and local authority to enforce immigration law. CLEAR Act.* Retrieved November 15, 2008, from http://www.numbersusa.com/hottopic/clearact.html

59. Kobach, "State and Local Authority."

60. DiMarzio, N. (2006). *Labor Day statement.* Retrieved June 24, 2008, from http://www.usccb.org/sdwp/national/LaborDay2006.pdf

61. Federation for American Immigration Reform. (2003). *The cost of immigration.* Retrieved June 26, 2008, from http://www.fairus.org/site/PageServer?pagename=iic_immigrationissuecenters87d3

62. Longley, R. (2004). *Illegal immigrants cost California over 10 billion annually.* Retrieved June 26, 2008, from http://usgovinfo.about.com/od/immigrationnaturalizatio/a/caillegals.htm

63. Rumbaut, R. G., & Ewing, W. A. (2007). *The issue of immigrants criminality and the paradox of assimilation: Incarceration rates among native and foreign-born men.* Washington, DC: Immigration Policy Center, American Immigration Law Foundation.

64. Sourcebook of Criminal Justice Statistics Online. (2005). *Table 4.47.* Albany, NY: US Department of Justice. Retrieved November 15, 2008, from http://www.albany.edu/sourcebook/pdf/t4472005.pdf

65. New York Department of Correctional Services. (2007). *Executive summary.* Retrieved November 20, 2008, from http://www.docs.state.ny.us/Research/Reports/2007/Impact_of_Foreign-Born_Inmates.pdf

66. US Government Accountability Office. (2006, May 9). *Information on certain illegal aliens in the United States.* Washington, DC: Author. Retrieved September 13, 2008, from http://www.gao.gov/new.items/d05646r.pdf

67. Congress.org, *2006 (First Quarter) INS/FBI Statistical Report.*

68. Los Angeles Superior Court. (2008). *Annual report.* Retrieved October 28, 2008, from http://www.lasuperiorcourt.org/courtnews/Uploads/142008311101628AnnualReport2008Issue.pdf

69. Kingsbury, K. (2008, February 27). Immigration: No correlation with crime. *Time.com.* Retrieved June 22, 2008, from http://www.time.com/time/nation/article/0,8599,1717575,00.html

70. Sen, R. (2006, July 24). *Six immigration lies, dispelled.* Retrieved September 26, 2008, from http://www.alternet.org/module/printversion/39269

71. Illegal Immigration ProCon.Org: Illegal immigrants kill more Americans than Iraq War. (2007, February 16). *Family Security Matters.* Retrieved August 21, 2009, from http://immigration.procon.org/viewanswers.asp?questionID=782

72. LoBreglio, K. (2004, Summer). Border Security and Immigration Improvement Act: A modern solution to a historic problem. *St. John's Law Review.* Retrieved June 30, 2008, from http://findarticles.com/p/articles/mi_qa3735/is_200407/ai_n9416910/pg_2

73. US Citizenship and Immigration Services. (2009). *Public laws amending the INA.* Retrieved June 24, 2009, from http://www.uscis.gov/propub/ProPubVAP.jsp?dockey=2b289cf41dd6b70a61a078a9fbfbc379

74. Motomura, *Americans in Waiting.*

75. Wong, C. (2006). *Lobbying for inclusion: Rights politics and the making of immigration policy.* Stanford, CA: University of Stanford Press.

76. LoBreglio, "Border Security and Immigration Improvement Act."

77. Lendman, S. (2006, April 11). *The war on immigrants. ZNET.* Retrieved July 30, 2007, from http://www.zmag.org/content/showarticle.cfm?ItemID=10077

78. Immigration Reform Law Institute. (n.d.). *Writing good legislation.* Retrieved March 18, 2009, from http://www.irli.org/bulletin707.html

79. Johnson, *Huddled Masses and Myth.*

80. Center for Immigration Studies. (2009, February). *Plenary power: Should judges control US immigration policy?* Retrieved March 1, 2009, from http://www.cis.org/plenarypower

81. Lawyer Central. (n.d.). *Discretionary relief.* Retrieved March 2, 2009, from http://immigration.lawyercentral.com/Discretionary-Relief-Relief-from-Removal-10-13546-61.html

82. Skogan, et al., "Community Policing and the New Immigrants."

83. Skogan, et al., "Community Policing and the New Immigrants."

84. Bennett, B. R. (1995). Incorporating diversity: Police response to multicultural changes in their communities. *FBI Law Enforcement Bulletin.* Retrieved August 17, 2008, from http://findarticles.com/p/articles/mi_m2194/is_n12_v64/ai_17885493?tag=artBody;col1

85. Vera Institute of Justice. (2005). *Building strong police–immigrant community relations: Lessons from a New York City project. (COPS, 2005).* Retrieved June 23, 2009, from www.vera.org/download?file=83/300_564.pdf

86. Vera Institute of Justice, *Building Strong Police–Immigrant Community Relations.*

87. Rothman, E. F. (2007). Batterer intervention program enrollment and completion among immigrant men in Massachusetts. *Violence Against Women, 13*(5), 527–543.

88. Idaho Community Action Network. Retrieved June 24, 2009, from http://idahocan.org/

89. Johnson, *Huddled Masses Myth.*

90. Confidential communication between author and Linda Moss of Laurel, August 26, 2008. The Howard Industries raid was, in part, the result of union workers complaining that undocumented workers were taking jobs and overtime from them. After the raid, a resident of Laurel, Mississippi (Linda Moss, a MS candidate at the University of Southern Mississippi) informed this author that hundreds of American workers lined up to apply for the jobs vacated because of the raid. A similar event followed the raid in Postville, Iowa, informed sources reported to this author. A question left unanswered is why American employers hired undocumented workers in the first place when unemployment among citizens is sweeping the nation.

91. Haller, J. (2008, August 25). Hundreds of workers held in immigration raid. *New York Times.* Retrieved August 31, 2008, from http://gangbox.wordpress.com/2008/08/26/dragnet-in-laurel-mississippi-350-latino-electrical-workers-arrested-by-ice-at-howard-industries-transformer-plant/

92. Duara, N., & Petroski, W. (2008, May 12). Hundreds arrested in Iowa immigration raid. *USA Today*. Retrieved August 31, 2008, from http://www.usatoday.com/news/nation/2008-05-12-iowa-immigration_N.htm

93. Ordonez, F., & Alexander, A. (2008, November 9). Critics: Raid shows need to investigate. *Charlotte Observer*, p. 12A.

94. Lawyers and Settlements. (2005, December 5). *William Zirkle*. Retrieved November 16, 2008, from http://www.lawyersandsettlements.com/settlements/04741/immigrant_wages.html

95. Johnson, *Huddled Masses Myth*.

96. Farm Labor Organizing Committee v. Ohio State Highway Patrol, 308, F.3d 523 (6th Cir. 2002).

97. Tagami, T. (2000, November 21). INS arrests fourteen Hispanics at courthouse in Monticello. *Herald-Ledger*. p. 2.

98. Farm Labor Organizing Committee v. Ohio State Highway Patrol, 308, F.3d 523 (6th Cir. 2002).

99. Pressley, S. A. (2000, March 3). Hispanic boom rattles South. *Washington Post*, p. A3.

100. LeDuff, C. (2000, September 20). Immigrant workers tell of being lured and beaten. *New York Times*, p. B1.

101. Southern Poverty Law Center. (2006). *Immigration fever fuels racist extremism*. Retrieved June 24, 2009, from http://www.splcenter.org/news/item.jsp?aid=186

102. Miles, J. (1992, October). Browns vs. blacks. *Atlantic Monthly*, 41.

103. Fuchs, L. H. (1990). The reactions of black Americans to immigration. In V. Yans-McLaughlin (Ed.), *Immigration reconsidered: History, sociology, and politics*. New York: Oxford University Press.

104. Bernstein, N. (2007, September 27). Challenges in Connecticut over immigrants arrest. *New York Times*. Retrieved June 23, 2009, from http://query.nytimes.com/gst/fullpage.html?res=9E03EFD81E31F935A1575AC0A9619C8B63.

105. Motomura, *Americans in Waiting*.

106. Motomura, *Americans in Waiting*.

107. Sourcebook of Criminal Justice Statistics Online. (2007). *Aliens deported from the United States, 1991–1998*. Albany, NY: US Department of Justice. Retrieved August 21, 2009, from http://www.albany.edu/sourcebook/pdf/sb1999/sb1999-section4.pdf

108. Bureau of Justice Statistics. (2006). *Federal criminal justice trends, 2003*. Washington, DC: US Department of Justice. Retrieved October 29, 2008, from http://www.ojp.usdoj.gov/bjs/pub/pdf/fcjt03.pdf

109. Martinez, Jr., R. (2002). *Latino homicide: Immigration, violence, and community*. New York: Routledge Press, Taylor & Francis Group.

110. Martinez, *Latino Homicide*.

111. Stevens, *Case Studies in Applied Community Policing*.

112. Yeager, M. G. (1997). Immigrants and criminality: A review. *Criminal Justice Abstracts, 29*, 143–171.

113. National Geographic. (2006). *World's most dangerous gang: MS-13*. Washington, DC: Author.

114. Wolfgang, M. E., & Ferracuti, F. (1967). *The subculture of violence: Towards an integrated theory in criminology*. London: Tavistock.

115. Dixon, J., & Lizotte, A. J. (1989). The burden of proof: Southern subculture-of-violence explanations of gun ownership and homicide. *The American Journal of Sociology, 95*(1), 182–187.

116. Bursik, R. J. (1988). Social disorganization and theories of crime and delinquency: Problems and prospects. *Criminology, 56,* 519–551.

117. Skogan, W. G. (2000). *Disorder and decay.* Evanston, IL: Northwestern University Press.

118. Skogan, W. G. (1992). *Disorder and decline: Crime and the spiral of decay in American neighborhoods.* Berkeley: University of California Press.

119. Martinez, *Latino Homicide.*

120. Sen, *Six Immigration Lies.*

121. Cheurprakobkit, S. (2000). University of Texas of the Permian Basin at Odessa. Data analysis was based on a telephone survey of residents at Midland and Odessa, Texas.

122. Stevens, D. J. (1997). Urban communities and homicide: Why American blacks resort to murder. *Policing and Society, 8,* 253–267.

123. Marion, N. E., & Oliver, W. M. (2008). *The public policy of crime and criminal justice.* Upper Saddle River, NJ: Pearson Prentice Hall.

124. Kraly, *US Immigration and the Environment.*

125. Boserup, E. (1981). *Population and technological change: A study of long-term trends.* Chicago: University of Chicago.

126. Brookfield, H. (1995). Postscript: The "population-environment nexus" and PLEC. *Global Environmental Change, 5*(4), 281–393.

127. Stevens, D. J. (2009). *Introduction to American policing.* Sudbury, MA: Jones and Bartlett. Because of enhanced immigration and general population physical mobility, technological advances have forced policing initiatives to meet current needs through artificial intelligence advances such as COPLINK: http://www.coplink.com/. Retrieved June 24, 2009.

128. Corruption Chronicles: A Judicial Watch Blog. (2007, January 10). *English forbidden on public school bus.* Retrieved June 23, 2009, from http://www.corruptionchronicles.com/2007/01/english_forbidden_on_public_sc.html

129. Schwartz, A. E., & Stiefel, L. (2004). Immigrants and the distribution of resources within an urban school district. *Educational Evaluation and Policy Analysis, 26*(4), 303–327.

130. Stiefel, L., Schwartz, A. E., Rubenstein, R., & Zabel, J. (2005). *Measuring school performance and efficiency: Implications for practice and research.* New York: Yearbook of American Education Finance Association: Eye on Education.

131. Schwartz & Stiefel, "Immigrants and the Distribution of Resources."

132. Wong, *Lobbying for Inclusion.*

133. Lacy, *Four Issues About Undocumented Immigrants Dispelled.*

134. Preston, J. (2007, July 27). *Judge voids ordinance on illegal immigrants.* Retrieved June 23, 2009 from, http://www.smalltowndefenders.com/public/node/209.

135. Belson, K., & Capuzzo, J. P. (2007, September 26). Towns rethink laws against illegal immigrants. *New York Times.* Retrieved June 23, 2009, from http://www.nytimes.com/2007/09/26/nyregion/26riverside.html

136. DeLaet, D. L. (2000). *US immigration policy in an age of rights.* Westport, CT: Greenwood.

137. Wong, *Lobbying for Inclusion.*

138. Wong, *Lobbying for Inclusion*.

139. Federation for American Immigration Reform. (1999). *The law against hiring or harboring illegal aliens*. Retrieved July 2, 2008, from http://www.fairus.org/site/PageServer?pagename=iic_immigrationissuecentersbcdd

140. Tsai, R. (2007). The immigration crackdown on employers. *Business Law Today, 16*(6). Retrieved July 3, 2008, from http://www.abanet.org/buslaw/blt/2007-07-08/tsai.shtml

141. Goodman, A. (2006, March 13). *Over 100,000 march in Chicago*. Retrieved October 3, 2007, from http://www.democracynow.org/article.pl?sid=06/03/14/1456247

142. Associated Press. More immigrants take to streets to protest proposed laws. (2006, April 11). *FOX News*. Retrieved October 3, 2007, from http://www.foxnews.com/story/0,2933,191142,00.html

143. Cima, C. (2006, May 18). Protest 2006: Different cause, same passion. *The Ranger*. Retrieved June 23, 2009, from http://media.www.theranger.org/media/storage/paper1010/news/2006/05/18/TheFourthWrite/Protest.2006.Different.Cause.Same.Passion-2131754.shtml?norewrite200612010914&sourcedomain=www.theranger.org

144. Immigrant Protest March. (2006, April 10). Retrieved June 23, 2009, from, http://www.cnn.com/2006/US/05/01/immigrant.day/index.html

145. Bianchi, M., Buonanno, P., & Pinotti, P. (2008). *Do immigrants cause crime?* Bergamo, Italy: University of Bergamo. Retrieved May 31, 2008, from http://www.unibg.it/dati/bacheca/783/30504.pdf

146. Bianchi, et al., *Do Immigrants Cause Crime?*

147. Martinez, *Latino Homicide*.

148. Sampson, R. J., & Bean, L. (2005). *Cultural mechanisms and killing fields: A revised theory of community-level racial inequality*. Cambridge, MA: Harvard University. Retrieved May 31, 2008, from http://www.wjh.harvard.edu/soc/faculty/sampson/Cultural%20Mechanisms%20and%20Killing%20Fields.pdf

149. Hagan, J., & Palloni, A. (1999). Sociological criminology and the mythology of Hispanic immigration and crime. *Social Problems, 46*, 617–632.

150. Bureau of Justice Statistics. (2001). *Criminal offender statistics*. Washington, DC: US Department of Justice. Retrieved June 15, 2008, from http://www.ojp.usdoj.gov/bjs/crimoff.htm#lifetime

151. Sampson & Bean, *Cultural Mechanisms and Killing Fields*.

152. Sampson & Bean, *Cultural Mechanisms and Killing Fields*.

153. Waldinger, R. (1989). Immigration and urban change. *Annual Review of Sociology, 15*, 211–232.

Crime Scene Investigations, Forensics, and Junk Science

Too much mercy . . . often results in further crimes which are fatal to innocent victims who need not have been victims if justice had been put first and mercy second.

Agatha Christie

▶ ▶ CHAPTER OBJECTIVES

- Describe the process and personnel who participate in crime scene investigations (CSI)
- Explain profiling associated with criminal minds
- Provide the history of forensic science and its objectives
- Describe police reluctance to use crime labs
- Clarify the chain of custody and its process
- Characterize CSI procedures and challenges

■ Introduction

Contemporary policing in the United States relies upon three strategies to provide police services[1]:

- Police patrols
- Rapid response to emergency (accident) assistance, crime control, and troubled persons
- Retrospective investigation of crimes and evidence (the focus of this chapter)

Detection is the discovery of a crime. Although much depends on a number of factors (explained later), most often patrol officers detect a crime through observation or in response to a 911 emergency call, detectives investigate the detected crime, field personnel or field technicians collect what appears to be evidence, forensic lab technicians or lab technicians and medical examiners (ME) evaluate materials collected by field technicians, and eventually, assuming a suspect emerges and the evidence is enough to charge a violator, prosecutors indict or charge a suspect.

Detectives are plainclothes investigators who can be employed by local, state, or federal enforcement agencies. They usually specialize in investigating one of a wide variety of violations, such as homicide or fraud, depending on the size of the agency.[2] This chapter examines crime scene investigations (CSI) with an emphasis on the process, which includes forensic (or crime lab) science participation because it is from this body of evidence that police can conduct an arrest, and it is assumed that prosecutors will follow through with a criminal charge or indictment, leading to a conviction of a defendant (most often through plea bargaining and least often through a trial). However, recently with the rise of technology and an increase of awareness of forensic science, crime lab participation in some cases has been moved to the beginning of an investigation while detectives are attempting to build a case to eliminate individuals as suspects or to move an individual to a person of interest status.

Consistent with Agatha Christie's thought at the opening of this chapter, professional criminal investigators and prosecutors have to find a balance between justice and mercy, yet relevant to any decision about a case is the fundamental principle of *justice*, which entails "the constant and perpetual will to render everyone his (or her) due."[3] Providing mercy without justice can derail justice. For example, a mother murders a 23-year-old female she caught sexually assaulting her four-year-old child. How much mercy should be provided? The concept of justice from a democratic perspective conveys the significance of the rule of law or a lawful (due process) policy and practice to investigate suspects and prosecute defendants in an attempt to punish the guilty and protect the innocent.[4,5]

■ Crime Scene Investigative Units

Overall, 9 of every 10 local police departments have investigative personnel or detectives; they investigate crimes related to sexual assault, robbery, homicide, arson, cybercrime, and hate crimes, to name a few.[6] State police, constables' offices (in Texas), and sheriffs' offices often have investigative personnel to examine crimes in their jurisdiction; often these investigative units aid smaller police departments that lack investigative units. For example, the Massachusetts State Police investigates most crimes of violence throughout the state, with the exception of Boston and Springfield. The number of detectives responsible for investigating specific crimes depends upon the size of the agency, the seriousness of the crime, the number of detectives in a unit, and the priorities of the department. Often, police agencies have special policies or procedures to deal with specific crimes but no regularly assigned personnel to investigate those crimes; other times agencies have full-time sworn officers and staff assigned to specific crime categories.[7] For example, the Huntington

Beach (California) Police Department has full-time personnel assigned to child abuse, domestic violence, drug education in schools, gangs, juvenile delinquency, missing children, youth outreach, hate crime, crime analysis, crime prevention, and internal affairs, but the department has only policy to deal with repeat offenders (at least at the writing of this book). The Fairfield (Connecticut) Police Department has policy but no assigned personnel to address child abuse, domestic violence, or gangs (at least at the writing of this book). Other departments have policy or procedures and designate personnel as needed, such as the Waukesha (Wisconsin) Police Department in dealing with child abuse.

Units can be assigned to interagency task forces to combat specific types of crime, such as drug trafficking and gangs.[8] Additionally, when evidence (or what appears to be evidence) is gathered from crime scenes, and depending on the type of evidence (i.e., blood stains, bullets, hair, fibers, fingerprints), it can be processed through a crime lab, which can be public or private, or through another police agency. As technology advances, some bits of evidence, such as fingerprint identification, can be evaluated in the field.[9] There are many variables, few standards, and little surplus funds available, depending on the jurisdiction, policies, personnel, expertise, history, priorities, and relationships with other federal, state, and private agencies.

■ The Players

Although detectives are the primary investigators at crime scene investigations, the popular media depicts CSI personnel as field investigators or criminalists who, oddly enough, are also the primary investigators who chase down suspects, interview witnesses, gather evidence, "tag and bag it," and in their spare time conduct laboratory tests and are chemists, biologists, and forensic scientists.[10] Television programming in the spring of 2009 continued to glorify tactical units (*Flashpoint*, CBS) and unruly personal police behavior (*Saving Grace*, TNT), and many new television programs capitalize on characters who read minds (*The Mentalist*, CBS; although the primary character denies that he can read minds), detect lies from across miles (*Lie to Me*, FOX), and move through time to the past (*Life on Mars*, ABC). Hollywood does everything to enhance the appeal and capacity of those occupations, but as of yet, police investigators strictly investigate crime scenes and have difficulty in living up to the media's expectations of being able to perform in many more areas because of case loads, training, jurisdiction, and civil liabilities (discussed later in the chapter).

In reality, police can do nearly everything that is done on popular CSI performances. However, it takes a great deal of time, and the expense is often prohibitive. Nonetheless, 1 percent of all serious crimes are resolved through forensic science alone. Usually, forensic results are part of the evidence package developed by detectives and prosecutors.

The popular media has socially defined the titles and work styles of investigative personnel, which can be a good thing because many find those occupations attractive, and the media encourages investigative units to find alternative ways to examine criminal events. However, they can also instruct criminals in what do during the commission of a crime.

Standards, initiatives, and authority among CSI and forensic units (crime labs) are administered through various local (municipal), state, county or parish (such as in Louisiana), and federal law enforcement agencies. Crime labs are often under the authority of a police agency, yet many crime labs are privately owned and operated.[11] When crime labs are private enterprises, their method of operation, including their analysis, can be altogether different from that of public labs. There is no definitive standard for police agencies in employing one lab over another, and if funds permit, particularly in high-profile cases, more than one lab might be utilized to examine the same evidence. Keep in mind that some labs have many other clients, which can include police departments and other state and private agencies, such as hospitals and clinics. However, crime labs are largely operated or supervised by law enforcement agencies.

Field personnel and lab technicians across the country are distinctively different from one another and from police officers; each can possess distinctively different training and experiences, and they are administered through a different chain of command. For example, one of the nation's largest municipal crime labs is the Hertzberg-Davis Forensic Science Center in Los Angeles, which maintains its own standards that can be different from other forensic facilities.[12] The five-story, 209,080-square-foot facility was a collaborative effort among the Los Angeles Police Department, the Los Angeles Sheriff's Department, and California State University, Los Angeles (CSULA), and it was operational in 2007. Top management is responsible to the chief of the Los Angeles Police Department and employs 400 technicians. Its hiring requirements, process, and training can be different from other labs across the state and country. One method of raising income for the county is to offer services to other police departments across the nation. Just as a reference, it costs an estimated $3 million to produce one CSI television performance, such as *CSI: Miami*, and although it is difficult to estimate the costs of a single investigation because of the various factors, it probably is unlikely that police departments spend that amount of money on any single case.[13]

Field Technician

Field technicians are police personnel who collect evidence for laboratory analysis, but the detectives assigned to a case could collect evidence, depending on the agency size and the case circumstances.

Lab Technician

Collected evidence is sent to a forensic science unit or crime lab where an analyst, a biologist, a chemist, a criminalist, a forensic nurse, a medical doctor, or another type of specifically-trained person examines or tests the evidence collected by field technicians and detectives, or at least that is the hope. From the point of collection and identifying or tagging evidence, to transporting, storing, and distributing the evidence to others is referred to as chain of custody (discussed later in the chapter). Five job descriptions require further explanation: criminalist, forensic nurse, police psychologist, forensic psychologist, and criminal profiler.

Criminalist

A criminalist can also be called a crime scene technician, examiner, field technician, or investigator. Generally, a criminalist is a person who searches for, collects, and preserves physical evidence in the investigation of crime and suspected criminals.[14] Offenders are referred to as suspects because investigators do not indict or judge an individual. Criminalists typically work in city or regional crime labs and are expected to do more than the forensic scientists and crime lab technicians. They are expected to be available 24 hours a day to investigate crime scenes. In some jurisdictions, assuming budgeting is available, the presence of a criminalist is required at all major crime scenes. CSI units can be described as employing criminalists or field investigators who gather evidence. A criminalist is largely employed at the end of a case and is the individual who testifies or signs off on the results of an evaluation of the evidence. Yet, in some cases, criminalist (and forensic personnel) participation during the process of a case can aid detectives as they attempt to build a case.

Forensic Nurse

Forensic nurses deal with the care of crime victims, collecting evidence, and provide health services. They are also qualified to aid in the investigations of death and domestic violence, and are eligible to complete a sexual assault nurse exam (SANE) and administer a rape kit.[15] SANE programs have been developed throughout the United States to better meet the needs of sexual assault survivors. Sommers, Schafer, Zink, Hutson, and Hillard argue that prompt medical care for sexual assault survivors is critically important because of the physical and emotional effects of sexual assault and to collect forensic evidence to legally pursue the offender.[16] The researchers advance that SANE programs consistently offer forensic evidence collection, sexually transmitted infection (STI) prophylaxis, information about HIV, information about pregnancy risk, and referrals to community resources. Also, Sommers, Schafer, Zink, Hutson, and Hillard clarify that the methods of sexual assault injury identification include:

- *Gross, direct visualization*
  In this method, injuries are identified through simple observation by a health care professional during a standard gynecological or forensic examination. It was the primary method used in examining female victims after sexual assault from about 1970 to 1990.

- **Staining techniques**

  Several staining solutions have been used: Gentian violet, Lugol's solution, toluidine blue, and flurorscein. A health care professional applies a staining solution in and around the female genitals. The solution makes injured tissues stand out from uninjured, surrounding tissues. For example, with Lugol's, tears in the epithelium appear as unstained, lighter areas than surrounding, uninjured genital tissues; with toluidine blue, tears or injured genital tissues pick up the stain and appear darker than uninjured tissues.

- **Colposcopy**

  Colposcopy, the preferred and most effective technique for identifying genital injuries of sexual assault survivors, refers to the use of a technical device, the colposcope, to illuminate and magnify the part of the body being inspected by a health care professional. Green lens filters make scars or abnormal patterns of blood vessels stand out from normal genital tissue. Colposcopy enables examiners to detect microscopic injury, and it reduces the need for repeated examinations of rape victims; the colposcope can be attached to a 35mm or video camera for documentation when evaluation by other medical experts is needed, or as evidence for prosecuting cases.

Finally in this regard, Sommers, Schafer, Zink, Hutson, and Hillard reveal that the findings of the literature linked to sexual assault injuries include the following types of injuries or patterns of injuries:

- Injury detection varies depending on both the method used to examine a sexual assault survivor and the experience and knowledge of the examiner. Thus, human error is possible.
- Not all women sustain injuries from sexual assault other than the assault itself.
- Non-genital injuries predominate in sexual assault survivors; the majority of women sustain non-genital injuries from sexual assault.
- When sexual assault involves anal intercourse proportionately more non-genital injuries result.
- The posterior fourchette, identified by staining and colposcopy, is the anatomic (genital) site most often injured when women are sexually assaulted.

Two other issues are relevant before moving on: the length of time between the victimization and the examination and the question of consensual versus non-consensual sex (aside from an individual who by law can not provide consent, see Chapter 4 for details).

Some programs do not routinely offer particular services (e.g., STI cultures, HIV testing and prophylaxis, and emergency contraception) because of financial constraints and difficulties balancing medical care with legal prosecution.[17]

However, there are barriers that can cause the survivor to have a negative experience in seeking medical care, such as backlogged cases which include the availability of a forensic nurse to conduct the examination, and the consequences of forensic nursing participation. Forensic nursing examinations can be conducted in ways that inadvertently add to survivor trauma, such as in blaming or insensitive treatment of survivors.[18] Health practitioners may not be knowledgeable about the special circumstances and needs of sexual assault survivors, and as a result victims do not get the health care they need.[19] Additionally, sexual assault survivors may be billed for services, resulting in a financial burden that adds to the overall trauma.[20]

Police Psychologist

For most police personnel, the few times they have contact with a psychologist is during prehire screening, before police academy training, or for a fitness-for-duty evaluation after a critical incident. "The very nature of how our system is set up [makes] officers wary of being involved with psychologists," explains Joel Fay, a police officer and psychologist.[21]

If a police department employs a police psychologist, he or she is usually on retainer as a consultant and may have a private practice of some type. Some psychologists are retained or contracted with several jurisdictions and ration their time according to need or to the contracted dollars. The kinds of collaborative programs portrayed by *CSI* and *Law & Order*, as characterized by Dr. George Huang and Dr. Emil Skoda (described later in more detail), are not the norm within departments. Few police departments that employ 100 sworn officers or less (this is the average size department in the United States) have the resources to aid stressed officers, let alone to operate prevention programs or hire psychologists to assist in crime investigations.[22] However, more departments are contracting with psychologists for consulting services, and larger departments often employ full-time clinical psychologists.

One impression is that police psychologists often perform the tasks of a forensic psychologist in many departments; however, state-licensed and certified psychologists or psychiatrists are not necessarily trained police officers or investigators, let alone criminal profilers (detailed later).[23] (Psychologists are certified by the American Psychological Association. Psychiatrists are medical doctors with a psychiatry specialty, and they are certified by the American Psychiatric Association and the American Medical Association).

Forensic Psychologist

Although it is new to criminal justice, forensic psychology is any application of psychological knowledge or methods to a task faced by the legal system.[24] Some say that it is both the research related directly to the legal profession (i.e., eyewitness memory and testimony, jury decision making, or criminal behavior) and the practice linked to criminal and civil law.[25] Most often forensic psychologists are academically trained psychologists who enter criminal justice professions or privately contract with police departments, whereas a criminal profiler (discussed next) is different. In this regard, a relationship with a general clinical psychologist is not encouraged in most departments because the work police perform is different from mainstream occupations.

This description does little to inform the CBS television drama *The Mentalist*, which premiered on September 23, 2008. *The Mentalist* tells the tale of Patrick Jane (Simon Baker), who is employed as an independent detective (whatever that is) working with the California Bureau of Investigation to solve crimes.[26] Previously, Jane was a psychic and assisted the police on cases until two family members were killed by a serial killer he was helping to track. He uses refined observation skills to help solve cases, but often in the presentation it appears that Jane reverts back to his psychic experiences to solve crime.

Criminal Profiler

Criminal profilers can be included in forensic psychology, but most often profilers, unlike forensic psychologists, generally have not participated in graduate work at a university but rather were moved through various police jobs such as patrol officer and detective to become a profiler. Experienced, self-professed profilers, such as John Douglas, who had been a special agent with the FBI, acknowledges that profiling is more of an art than a science.[27] One way to characterize profiling is as a "broad, hard-to-pin-down term that covers a variety of procedures and operating assumptions."[28] Think about it this way: profiling is an educated attempt to provide specific information about a certain type of suspect.

■ About Profilers

Profilers usually attempt to ascertain the suspect's physical characteristics—gender, age, race, height, weight, whether the suspect is right or left handed—and other demographics, such as occupation and education. However, some argue that most profilers are more sociological than psychological in orientation.[29] Some profilers emphasize personality traits and motivations, which can include the ways offenders treat their victims. This is a very consistent approach taken on popular television dramas, such as *Law & Order: Special Victims Unit*, as portrayed by a character named Dr. George Huang (Brad D. Wong), who appeared in 138 episodes. Huang is a forensic psychologist who is also an expert on the criminal mind. According to his media history, Huang (not Wong) joined the SVU after becoming frustrated with attempts at sex offender rehabilitation techniques and found that the offenders didn't want to participate in his therapy.[30] There are times his opinions clash with the detectives, especially when he agrees with a defendant's diagnosis on metal illness. Huang serves as both an FBI special agent and psychiatrist for the SVU. *Law & Order* (the original series), *Law & Order: Special Victims Unit*, and *Law & Order: Criminal Intent* feature Dr. Emil Skoda (J. K. Simmons), who appeared in 43 episodes as a police psychiatrist (his qualifications are that he is a medical doctor and has a PhD in psychology, assuming he has his certifications and licenses). He evaluates the personalities of defendants before and during trials. As you can imagine from the previous descriptions, most profilers and the American public, as evidenced by the Nielsen ratings, are infatuated with popular television dramas and the occupation of a profiler. It is exciting to have a job that pursues bad guys using advanced technology and cool multicolored gadgetry.

However, most profilers are not in agreement about appropriate methods and standardized tools. For example, there is a debate surrounding whether to use a statistical analysis of the findings or to use clinical approaches of single cases to make inferences about the perpetrator's unconscious personality process.[31] Equally important, in court the battle of the experts has withered down the process of court proceedings, steering attention away from the offender's criminal acts and the welfare of the victim(s). For these and other reasons, expert testimony on profiling is not likely to be admitted in court because it fails to meet the *Daubert* test of merit, as well as subsequent Supreme Court cases inspired by *Daubert*, as judged by the scientific community.[32] That is, profiling can open the door for serious legal challenges, and when prosecutors are working hard toward a conviction, it is not in the best interest of the case to encourage anything that can be challenged.

Sex Offenders and Profiling

Courts have consistently banned expert testimony that comments on so-called *profiles* of sex offenders during the guilt phase of trials.[33] These decisions have excluded such testimony because it invades the province of the jury, amounts to improper character evidence, is scientifically unreliable, and is premised on assessment devices that are not scientifically reliable or capable of determining guilt or innocence.[34] A Wisconsin decision in *State v. Richard A.P.2* held that exclusion of proffered expert testimony profiling the defendant's character was reversible error. The Wisconsin Supreme Court denied review, and this verdict set a precedent in Wisconsin. Other jurisdictions observed the model with interest to enhance their own potential of winning convictions. Regardless of a high court's decision, it is not in the best interests of the people to pursue a legal argument that can further litigation, as previously mentioned. For every expert who reports one perspective, there are other experts with similar or better credentials to present another perspective.

Criminal Minds

A CBS television performance, *Criminal Minds*, revolves around an elite team of FBI profilers who analyze the country's alleged most twisted criminal minds, anticipating their next moves before they strike again.[35] There are communications in episodes that merit attention; for example, when *Criminal Minds'* Dr. Spencer Reid was asked if he is a genius, he replied, "I don't believe that intelligence can be accurately quantified, but I have an IQ of 187, an eidetic memory, can read 20,000 words per minute." If that were true, then Dr. Reid would have an IQ greater than that of Microsoft CEO Bill Gates (over 160) and Microsoft cofounder Paul Allen (over 160), and it would place Reid at the same IQ level as former World Chess

Champion Bobby Fischer (187). Gates and Allen earn a substantial income, but the FBI's Web site reports that a newly assigned special agent starts out at a GS-10, step 1 pay rank, which is $43,441 plus locality pay. If the agent merits it and it would certainly seem Reid would, the pay can be moved through a number of steps to step 10, whereby the agent can expect $56,973 per year plus great benefits. The length of time on the job can also increase the grade level. Based on available information about *Criminal Minds'* Reid, who is on call 24/7 for 12 months per year, the GS income grades suggest that Reid would be earning a similar income as a college assistant professor (beginning) who works nine months, teaches three classes per semester (two breaks during each semester, but no holidays or weekends) with grant and research potentials (and no one is shooting at them for the most part).[36] In private industry, Reid's potential is unlimited, thus a question about his choice of employment had not been addressed for over a year. In *Criminal Minds*, Season 4, Episode 7, "Memoriam," the question again comes up about Dr. Reid's IQ and his employment choice, and his answer was that he wanted to help people. The writers of *Criminal Minds* apparently pay attention to their audience because the question of Reid's choice of jobs buzzed on blogs for several months. Most cops want to help people and put away the bad guy.

Another *Criminal Minds* FBI profiler, Elle Greenaway, reports that "the people I go after are cowards. They often prey upon the weaker members of society, such as women and children. There is nothing I would rather do than put the bastards away." In the real world of predators, there are many predators who are neither weak nor cowards, and they are so shameless and confident that they commit crimes of violence in public places and continue to remain at-large, the FBI reveals through clearance rates.[37] Another concern might be with the FBI itself, which states on their Web site that they do not have a job title called "Profiler." They add that, "The tasks commonly associated with profiling are performed by Supervisory Special Agents assigned to the National Center for the Analysis of Violent Crime (NCAVC) at Quantico, Virginia. Despite popular depictions, these FBI Special Agents don't get 'vibes' or experience 'psychic flashes' while walking around fresh crime scenes." Too bad, because most of my university students want to become criminal profilers.

■ The National Center for the Analysis of Violent Crime

One unit of the FBI is the purported employer of the *Criminal Minds* cast. The mission of the real National Center for the Analysis of Violent Crime (NCAVC) is to combine investigative and operational support functions, research, and training to provide assistance, without charge, to federal, state, local, and foreign law enforcement agencies that are investigating unusual or repetitive violent crimes. One of its divisions is the Behavioral Science Unit, which is primarily the instructional component of the FBI's Training and Development Division at Quantico, Virginia.[38] Its mission is to develop and provide programs of training, research, and consultation in the behavioral and social sciences in furtherance of the FBI's strategic priorities in support of the law enforcement and intelligence communities' operational effectiveness. This work includes conducting high-impact research and presenting a variety of cutting-edge courses. The unit's personnel are primarily supervisory special agents, experienced instructors, and veteran police officers with advanced degrees in the behavioral science disciplines of psychology, criminology, and sociology. The Behavioral Science Unit professional personnel also includes a clinical forensic psychologist, a research analyst, a management analyst, and a technical information specialist.

Requests for Psychological Assistance

Requests for psychological assistance often come from specific investigative units within a police department, such as the homicide unit, sex crimes unit, or violent crimes committed against persons division, for the purposes of criminal investigative analysis or criminal psychological personality profiling. Crime scene analysis, criminal investigative analysis, or what is often referred to as "profiling" can involve detailing the crime scene area identified by officers, detectives, coroners, medical examiners, criminalists, forensic scientists, and evidence technicians, advises the American Academy of Experts in Traumatic Stress.[39] Most often, typical profilers might not be clinical psychologists as presented in the popular media; they are investigators who specialize in forensic psychology or techniques because of their experience and professional understanding of most street crimes.

■ Most Street Crimes

It should be clarified before discussing forensic labs that any discussion about criminal profiling should include a description of street crimes. Most crime is not brilliantly executed nor is it performed by an intellectual giant such as Hannibal Lecter in *The Silence of the Lambs*. A district attorney shares his thoughts about the psychological motivation of a criminal:

"[M]ost perps [criminals] do what they do because it's all they know. They're stupid. They hate, they want, and they do things to other people because that's what they know how to do. Robbers rob, muggers mug, rapists rape. . . . it's their job. All that talk about sociopathic patterns, the messed-up childhoods, the resentment of the father–authority figure. I think it's a crock."[40]

These thoughts are consistent with criminologists (people who study criminals and how to control them), such as Michael R. Gottfredson and Travis Hirschi,[41] who argue that most crime is amazingly simple, largely unplanned (although the intent to commit the act is present), and performed by individuals who have little self-control and are highly impulsive (see Chapter 3 for more details).[42] Crime can be defined as "acts of force or fraud undertaken in pursuit of self interest."[43] Many violent crimes are situational and occur in the life of an offender once; for example, a wife who has been battered for 10 years and murders her spouse or a parent who murders a sexual predator caught in the act of assaulting his or her child. Criminal lifestyles are another matter and represent a smaller percentage of most offenders. Chronic offenders can be characterized as individuals who are consistent with behaviors that demonstrate antisocial personality disorders (see Chapter 4 for details); nonetheless, most offenders tend to think in terms of the benefits of the crime: What will I get if I do it? Fulfilling self-interests or pure selfishness characteristics when linked to a lack of self-control could explain why some individuals smoke, drink, abuse drugs, gamble, speed, engage in irresponsible sex, or commit violent crimes.[44] Other motivations or triggers for violent crimes are jealously, envy, greed, rage, ignorance, and lust.[45]

With so many variables and so many more possibilities, it is easy to see how profiles can be inaccurate and push police in the wrong direction. Thus, the importance of forensic units is to provide trustworthy evidence toward apprehension and conviction of the guilty party and exoneration of the innocent.

■ Forensic Units

The services provided by real forensic crime laboratories can include the following[46]:

- Anthropologists who specialize in bones can deduce the deceased's gender, age, height, and race, as well as medical history and manner of death.[47] Note: FOX's *Bones* is a popular television drama (82 episodes in the fall of 2008) about Dr. Temperance Brennan (Emily Deschanel) and her constant colleague, FBI Special Agent Seeley Booth (David Boreanaz). The character of Dr. Brennan is a highly skilled forensic anthropologist who works at the Jeffersonian Institute in Washington, DC and writes novels as a sideline. When the standard methods of identifying a dead body are useless—when the remains are so badly decomposed, burned, or destroyed that local police give up—they call in Brennan for her uncanny ability to read clues left behind in the victim's bones. In real life, the Jeffersonian is the Smithsonian Institution's division of physical anthropology that examines human remains; however, their personnel are not FBI employees or sworn police officers, nor do they carry weapons or interview persons of interest linked to crimes as Dr. Brennan does. During many episodes, Dr. Brennan is out of the laboratory more than she is in the lab. In some episodes she has not hesitated to strike a suspect, an action that could result in her arrest in real life.
- Biology unit (biochemists who identify and perform DNA examinations).
- Document examination unit (handwriting and typewriting experts).
- Firearms unit (discharged bullets, cartridge casings, and ammunition of all types).
- Latent fingerprint unit.

- Entomology unit (insect and other arthropod biology helps to determine the time of death and can detect drugs and poisons).
- Pathology unit (the cause of death can be determined by examining the cadaver and can include an autopsy).
- Photography unit (a photographic lab that also examines and records physical evidence).
- Physical science unit (applies principles and techniques of chemistry, physics, and geology to the identification and comparison of crime scene evidence).
- Pathologist or coroner who performs an autopsy of the remains, which can reveal the cause of death, the weapon(s) used (if any are involved), and the length of time since death.
- Polygraph unit (lie detector).
- Toxicology unit (body fluids and organs).
- Voiceprint analysis unit (telephone and tape recorded messages).

After the material (evidence) is delivered to a crime lab, the process in the laboratory is often referred to as forensic science. The crime scene analyst endeavors to arrange and collate numerous individual events, details, and observations that present themselves in an order that might become a part of a comprehensive picture associated with the crime, victims, and suspects.[48] Depending on the size of the department, field and lab personnel are different individuals; however, sometimes their tasks overlap. Joe Clayton, who is employed by the State of Colorado's forensic lab, advises that:

> Depending on what scientific examinations are needed or requested, I may be involved in the actual "bench work" once the evidence is submitted to the laboratory. I have expertise in blood pattern identification (blood spatter), trajectory determination, serology (blood and body fluids), and photography. I also have knowledge in many other areas (firearms, fingerprints, questioned documents ...) that may assist me at the scene. As a primary crime scene responder at the CBI, my role at the scene may involve one or more of my particular disciplines. While I would not do a functionality test on a firearm here at the laboratory, my role at the crime scene would be to collect the gun and understand its potential evidentiary significance.[49]

There are concerns about which crime lab is appropriate for a specific evaluation. Some jurisdictions do not have the equipment, new technology, or trained personnel to perform blood spattering evaluations, for example, and some jurisdictions might contract work to another forensic lab, sometimes a private agency or a state lab and other times to a federal agency. It is highly unlikely that *CSI: Miami's* or *Bones's* labs exist because most police departments have small budgets, but also because some of the gadgets they use are fictional. It is also unlikely that forensic personnel use the expensive police vehicles as those driven by *CSI: Miami's* staff and Horatio Caine (David Caruso) in 148 episodes.

Television crime labs can be summed up by Naren Shankar, executive producer of *CSI: Crime Scene Investigation*: "We are in a funny position. We demand scientific realism in techniques, results, and conclusions, but we take dramatic license with how these things are rendered on film because it has to look beautiful and cool."[50] And it does. The Las Vegas crime lab depicted in the television show has supersaturated colors and moody lighting, large flat-panel screens scroll numbers at hyperspeed, and the liquids that drop from pipettes into test tubes always have a gorgeous hue. Sometimes the camera even swoops into an experiment to show you a macro close-up of a tiny spot sticking to a carpet fiber, then swoops back out to show deep concentration on the face of a stylish young investigator with perfect hair. Anyone would want to work in a place like that. Shankar adds, "The appeal of the show is empirical analysis. People love to know how things work and they like to be taken into those roles. That's why we push the camera into carpet fibers and through cadavers. Going into things is part of the appeal."[50]

■ Forensic Goals

Evidence from a crime scene is sent to a forensic lab because the forensic scientist's goal is the "evenhanded use of all available information to determine the facts and, subsequently, the truth," advises the American Academy of Forensic Sciences.[51] This thought is consistent with the FBI's *Handbook of Forensic Services*,[52] and it may have nothing to do with appeal (as Shankar previously noted) depending on how the process is evaluated. In addition, CSI services often vary (similar to investigative units, discussed earlier) because of the following[53]:

- Variations in local laws
- Different capabilities and functions of the organization to which a laboratory is affiliated
- Budgetary and staffing limitations

Many crime labs, especially private enterprises, tend to specialize in specific evaluations, such as blood stains or skeleton analysis.

■ History of Forensic Science

Forensic science had its beginnings in the eighth century, when the Chinese used fingerprints to establish the identity of documents and clay sculptures.[54] The basic principle they refined was linked to the theory of transfer: when two objects meet, some evidence of that meeting can later be found and verified. In 1248, a Chinese book, *Hsi Duan Yu* (the washing away of wrongs), described how to distinguish the differences between drowning and strangulation. It was the first recorded application of medical knowledge to the solution of crime. In 1609, the first treatise on systematic document examination was published in France. In 1784, one of the first documented uses of physical matching saw an Englishman convicted of murder based on the torn edge of a wad of newspaper in a pistol that matched a piece remaining in his pocket.

The world's first crime laboratory was established by Edmond Locard at Lyon, France in 1910. The famous Locard Exchange Principle, which says that every contact leaves a trace, was named for him after Locard solved a strangling case by using fingernail scrapings.[55] Locard believed that when any person comes into contact with an object or another person, a cross-transfer of physical evidence occurs (refer to the previously mentioned theory of transfer). Locard was influenced by Bertillonage philosophy which suggests that every living thing on the planet is unique. Therefore, the priority of modern police investigations is to secure the crime scene before performing any other task (other than aiding an injured person, reducing a dangerous threat, or conducting an arrest) to protect the trace evidence that is present.

■ Secure the Crime Scene

Most police investigations begin at the scene of a crime. The crime scene (CS) is simply defined as the actual site or location at which the incident or crime took place. The first responder's priority (largely patrol officers) at the crime scene is to secure the crime scene and protect the evidence. The entire investigation hinges on that first responder's skill to properly identify evidence, isolate it from onlookers, and secure the scene by establishing a restricted perimeter. One way to accomplish this task is to rope off the area with police tape. Securing a crime scene means to restrict access and prevent evidence from being destroyed or altered. Some say that even the presence of police officers and investigators can compromise a crime scene because their presence alone changes the environment. It goes without saying that witnesses, suspects, or participants of the circumstance must be detached from the crime scene as soon as possible. When the CS is secured, restrictions extend to all nonessential police personnel, too. An investigation may involve a primary scene as well as several secondary scenes at other locations.

At a serious CS (sexual homicide, decapitated victims), a designated area is identified for the purpose of briefing investigators, storing needed equipment, and as a break area for officers and investigators. Critical incident management, the protocol taught in law enforcement academies, identifies a three-layer or -tier perimeter, as described by Detective Mike Byrd[56]:

- The outer perimeter is established as a border larger than the actual crime scene to keep onlookers and nonessential police personnel and news reporters away.
- The inner perimeter allows for a command post and comfort area just outside of the crime scene.
- The core or crime scene itself is established.

Criminal Investigation Process

The forensic personnel's crime investigation participation begins when they receive a call from detectives (often through police dispatch) or command personnel or if policy dictates forensic personnel's automatic participation at specific crimes. Field personnel might take the following steps after the crime scene has been secured[57]:

- Make notes of all emergency personnel (police, fire, and medical technicians) who visited the crime scene and note the reports they wrote, including any action taken.
- When crime scene investigators define the CS, the district attorney's office might be contacted, depending on the merits of the case, because if evidence is collected illegally, it is of little value if it is not admissible in court.
- A walk-through process can aid in determining the scope of the case, and forensic personnel take note of anything that was moved and anything that can be considered evidence.
- If not certified in a particular area (i.e., blood spatter on a ceiling or maggot activity on a corpse), field personnel might enlist specialists or obtain additional tools to gather evidence. Transporting a section of a ceiling to the lab for blood spatter analysis is difficult, and maggot activity changes with each passing moment.
- Photographs, sketches, and video aid the documentation process and are important responsibilities of field personnel.
- Systematically, field personnel collect all potential evidence, tag it, log it, and bag or package it to ensure safety. Evidence is rarely analyzed at the CS, but new technology is beginning to change that process. (Note: An unexpected advantage of popular television dramas is that having real technicians and scientists use equipment to process evidence at the CS results in fewer concerns about human error and chain of custody issues, described later.)
- Electronically or in writing, field personnel record conversations with first responders, detectives, witnesses, and victims (if any).
- The crime lab processes the evidence collected by field personnel. The results are generally distributed to the lead detective.

Rationale of Forensic Science Results

Crime scene investigation forms a vital part of the justice and regulatory system. CSI is the meeting point of science, logic, and law.[58] Crime scene investigators create a hypothesis based on physical evidence of the actions of the victim(s) and suspect(s) before, during, and after a criminal event. Hopefully, the material (evidence) that was collected and evaluated will support an investigator's hypothesis, eliminate innocent persons, guide the detective toward a person of interest (a possible suspect), and aid in obtaining a recorded legal confession. The analysis should play a key role in a prosecutor's decision to indict and convict a suspect. The reconstruction of the circumstances and behaviors of individuals (which include victims, survivors, and suspects) who are involved in a crime is an important aspect of forensic science.[59] Despite the scenarios offered on the preceeding pages, keep in mind that:

> The vast majority of forensic laboratories and their personnel are highly professional and eager to give an honest and objective voice to physical evidence regardless of whose case the final results tend to bolster.[60]

■ Burden of Proof

All the training, resources, and experiences of forensic personnel (and prosecutors) come down to one final component: a lawful conviction. In court, prosecutors have "responsibility of affirmatively proving the allegations on which it has based its accusation."[61] This feature is supported by the US Constitution and its Amendments and places the *burden of proof* upon the people (the government), represented by the prosecutor. The prosecutor's task is to show "beyond and to the exclusion of every reasonable doubt" that the defendant is guilty of the crime charged and the evidence was legally collected, appropriately evaluated, and that the chain of custody (details later) has not been compromised. The innocence of a suspect is presumed. There are exceptions, but what is relevant to an understanding of a conviction (which includes a guilty plea) will depend upon the performance of police, particularly those officers who investigated the case, collected and provided legal evidence, and interrogated suspects, but it is the prosecutor who charges or indicts a suspect and prosecutes the defendant.

■ Objectives of Crime Scene Processing

The objective of CS processing and documentation is to create a visual record that allows the crime analyst, police investigator, and prosecutor to easily recreate an accurate view of the crime.[62] That said, it is easy to understand that field personnel are designated to collect, preserve, package, transport, and document physical evidence from a crime scene, Mike Byrd of the Miami-Dade Police Department advises.[63] However, before evidence can be assessed, the CS must come to the attention of forensic science personnel. Therefore, police detectives and first responders are often faced with a series of dilemmas, which start with the primary components of evidence and the chain of custody.

■ Primary Components of Evidence

In the United States, the four primary components associated with forensic science as a tool in crime control are also strongly related to the burden of proof, as previously discussed.

- Laws and regulations: Pertain to evidence and how it can be collected and distributed.
- Collection of evidence: Methods used to tag and bag evidence and how it is transported and stored while transported.
- Evaluation of the evidence: Methods used, which include the integrity of the equipment that was utilized to assess evidence, the expertise of the evaluators, and the storage of evidence and equipment.
- Chain of custody: Evidence cannot have been compromised.

■ Chain of Custody

Whether or not a detective, patrol officer, lab technician, or medical health practitioner (i.e., a medical doctor or a forensic nurse conducting a rape exam) has formal training in handling forensics or evidence, he or she must ensure proper collection, maintenance, and disposition of the evidence.

> The chain of custody is a chronological, documented record of those individuals who have had custody of the evidence from its initial acquisition until its final disposition.[64]

The chain of custody begins when an item is collected.[65] Every person involved with the evidence must be identified. Every person in the chain of custody is responsible for the care, safekeeping, and preservation of the evidence while it is under his or her control. The chain is maintained until the evidence is disposed of or obtained by another individual. The chain of custody assures continuous accountability. This accountability is important because, if it is not properly maintained, an item may be inadmissible in court or lost or misused. Because of the sensitive nature of evidence, an evidence custodian has the responsibility to control the evidence when not in use by the investigating officer or other competent individuals who are involved in the investigation. In some agencies, an evidence custodian can be a sworn officer or a civilian. Maintaining the chain of custody involves preserving the integrity of evidence by documenting its possession from the moment of collection until the moment it is introduced in court.

Think of it this way: the chain of custody is a documented paper trail that describes the seizure, custody, control, transfer, analysis, and disposition of physical and electronic evidence.[66] For example, if a bloody knife is recovered at a murder scene, Officer A carefully collects the knife (wearing evidence-handling gloves) and places it into a container, then gives the container to Field Technician B, who transports it to the lab. Field Technician B gives the container with the bloody knife in it to Lab Technician C, who collects fingerprints and other evidence from the bloody knife. Lab Technician C gives the knife and the reports gathered from examining the knife to Evidence Clerk D, who stores the knife and the reports until they are needed and documents everyone who has accessed the original evidence (the knife and the original copies of the lifted fingerprints). It's as easy as A, B, C, and D.

■ Chain of Custody and the Courtroom

In the courtroom, if the defendant's lawyer questions the chain of custody linked to the bloody knife previously described and the prosecutor can show that the knife in the evidence room is the same knife found at the crime scene with the defendant's fingerprints on it, then it is more likely that a conviction would be forthcoming. However, if there are discrepancies and it can be shown that the chain of custody was compromised, then the evidence can be declared inadmissible. Obviously, the chain of custody takes priority during the training process of officers and other personnel (i.e., medical examiner, forensic nurse, and forensic psychologist) who are likely to handle evidence.

■ Priority of Gathering Evidence

Every crime scene is different, and therefore every crime scene investigation is different. For example, a sexual assault homicide that occurred indoors requires a search confined to a specific, relatively smaller area compared to an abduction at a shopping plaza that ended in a sexual assault homicide miles from the abduction site. Joe Clayton of the Colorado Bureau of Investigation implies that there is no typical crime scene, there is no typical body of evidence, and there is no typical investigative approach.[67] Physical evidence and its assessments are merely part of the equation toward truth and justice. However, there are certain general rules that guide the plans for searching a crime scene.[68]

First, the type of crime can often point out the appropriate order of the search. This means that indoor crime zones take a secondary precedence to outdoor crimes because the weather is likely to cause damage or alteration to evidence, and public access to outdoors is easy, making outdoor areas more difficult to protect. Second, if a body cannot be taken from the scene until the area around it is searched, then that search is given priority. A body might not be able to be removed from a scene because removing it may affect or destroy important evidence that must be collected first.

■ Protocols Beyond the Crime Scene and Crime Lab

Protocols for the chain of custody go beyond the CS and a crime lab; often those protocols are not clearly established. For example, when a victim (or suspect) is taken to a hospital's emergency unit for removal of a bullet, what happens to the bullet when it is turned over to the hospital's or police's pathology unit is relevant.[69] The bullet must be guarded continuously or locked in a controlled area. Hospital and police personnel must be able to provide certainty that the chain of custody remained unbroken and that the evidence has not been tampered with. In this example, bullets, in particular, are pieces of evidence that can be altered by pathology procedures, and many times the proper chain of custody is not maintained during the process.

Also, items such as clothing can be used as criminal evidence. For example, using a bullet hole as a convenient starting place, clothing is commonly cut off and tossed aside or placed under a stretcher. When the patient (victim or suspect) is transferred to or from the emergency care unit, the clothing might be misplaced. Identifying, collecting, preserving, and securing evidence (in this case, clothing), even at the hospital, are crucial steps to establishing and maintaining the chain of custody. The most common types of physical evidence are weapons; drugs; bullets; pieces of glass, wood, or paint; bloodstained clothing or jewelry; and stolen property, which includes cars, boats, weapons, furniture, and appliances.

■ Police Reluctance to Use Crime Labs

Before evidence can be assessed by crime lab technicians, the crime has to come to the attention of forensic personnel. First responders and their superiors, which can include detectives, are often faced with a series of dilemmas.

Backlog of Unsolved Rapes and Homicides

Nationally, the backlog of unsolved rapes and homicides are massive.[70] There are more than 221,000 violent crimes with possible biological evidence that local police agencies have not submitted to a laboratory for analysis. This number consists of an estimated 52,000 homicides and 169,000 rape cases, which are not solved. There are more than 264,000 property crime cases with possible biological evidence that local law enforcement agencies have not submitted to a laboratory for analysis, and there are more than 57,000 unanalyzed DNA cases reported by state and local crime laboratories. That means that detectives realize the time lapse involved if they send evidence to a lab, and it also means that, contrary to popular media interpretation of crime, many crimes of violence are never solved, let alone processed by detectives.

Rape Backlog in New York City

Howard Safir, former police commissioner of New York City, found there were 16,000 untested rape kits in storage when he was in office. Now a consultant for a DNA testing lab, Safir estimates there are 300,000–500,000 untested kits across the country. He says, "Not testing a woman's kit is like telling her 'You are not worth $500.'"[71]

Reality of Lab Turnaround Time

The delayed lab turnaround time is not on the police's side when they are investigating criminal activities because apprehending a perpetrator is less likely as more time passes after a crime has been committed.[72] Therefore, backlogs of unsolved crimes and lab turnaround time problems seem to make investigators reluctant to use labs.

The reality of crime lab turnaround time is different from the way the media presents it. For example, the 50 largest labs in the country began in 2002 with about 117,000 backlogged requests for forensic services, and they ended the year with over 93,000 backlogged cases, including about 270,000 requests for forensic services.[73] One estimate is that about 930 additional full-time equivalents would have been needed to achieve a 30-day turnaround for all requested forensic services in 2002.

Turnaround Time at the Arizona Department of Public Safety

The Arizona Department of Public Safety (DPS), known as the crime lab, analyzes physical evidence submitted by police agencies throughout the state.[74] Fewer than 2,000 of the 7,623 blood samples (26 percent) received by DPS on offenses have been analyzed with current DNA techniques and uploaded to the database. Initially, another 38 percent were analyzed but are awaiting quality control reviews. This significant backlog is caused by changes in forensic DNA analysis methods, requiring additional training for lab personnel. The toxicology unit had a backlog of 1,189 samples for 30 days or more primarily because of the large increase of samples submitted during 1998 and 1999. Alcohol submissions increased 42 percent, and drug screen requests increased 31 percent.

Some of the problems that impact delayed lab time in Arizona are similar across the country. For example, the state's own budgetary problems have encouraged its state legislature to slash the DPS's budget by $7.8 million and suggest that one of the ways to make up for it is to charge counties and cities for use of the crime labs.[75] In 2008, the City of Nogales took a wait-and-see approach to the issue of paying crime lab fees to the State. Similarly, Santa Cruz County is withholding payment to the state for lab services. Santa Cruz County was going to be assessed $46,301 for the year, but the amount had been reduced to $14,544. The sheriff says that beyond the legality of the fee, there was concern that it would become a yearly assessment instead of a one-shot deal to financially help out the State.

Turnaround Time in Baltimore

To investigate lab turnaround time in Baltimore, ABC's *20/20* paid the Baltimore Police Department half of the money required to test 50 rape kits.[76] Their investigation solved five major cases and exonerated a wrongfully imprisoned man. Brian Ross, a correspondent for ABC News, says that it would take an estimated $4.5 million to process Baltimore's backlog and to enhance their turnaround time.

Police Reluctance Study

In a Michigan study among police officers, it was found that they were generally reluctant to utilize crime labs for various reasons, such as the following[77]:

- 51 percent said DNA was not considered to be a tool for crime investigations.
- 31 percent said no suspect had been identified.
- 24 percent of the police agencies had no funds for forensics.
- 10 percent of the suspects who were stopped were not charged.
- 9 percent said prosecution had not required testing.

■ Police Reluctance Is Consistent with Evidence-Based Literature

Many perspectives held by the police are consistent with the literature. For example, it is widely accepted that actuarial risk instruments that evaluate sexual offenders outperform clinical assessments and judgments.[78] Also, a Texas study reviewed 155 capital cases in that state in which prosecutors used behavioral experts to predict a defendant's future dangerousness, and the only problem was that in 95 percent of the cases, the experts were wrong, reports the Texas Defender Service.[79] Another study reveals that first responders in Boston (see Chapter 1 for details) inadequately safeguard evidence, inadequately secure the CS, and withhold their own theory of the crime because of their inadequate training and the supervisors' inappropriate manipulation of police personnel.[80]

Decisions to process crime scene evidence in forensic labs are directly related to budgetary issues. There are four additional factors that influence the detectives' use of crime labs, researchers argue[81]:

- Attitudes of officers and investigators
- Institutional support
- Personnel
- Networks

Also, there is a need to reconcile the consequences of resource allocation if forensic services departments want to become an investigator's standard to help solve a case.[82] Then, too, defendants are employing forensic science technology to aid them in their own defense. A Mississippi judge ordered that several thousand dollars of public funds should be available for a defendant to hire a forensic expert to examine the evidence in his murder trial of a Jackson State University coed.[83] If this becomes a common judicial response, the costs to prosecute a defendant will increase substantially.

Some departments mandate the employment of forensic science or crime lab participation, and other departments leave decisions to investigative discretion. The handling of a case normally proceeds in accordance with informal understandings shared among detectives,[84] which include an individual investigator's initiatives and interpretations of the crime, especially if the investigator sees less value of forensic assessment than his or her own theory of the crime or if a detective is simply out of time or energy to pursue a case.[85] Perhaps the case should be processed quickly because suspects; victims, and witnesses leave or die; crime scenes environmentally change; budgets decrease for cold cases; the personnel ratio is directed to more cases or more serious cases; and investigators age out (retire) or transfer out.[86] One way to understand investigator discretion associated with caseload is first to acknowledge that most detectives spend most of their time at their desks reviewing paperwork and online reports, talking on the telephone, interviewing, and e-mailing colleagues, witnesses, and victims. A Police Executive Research Forum study reports that a detective's caseload consists of three components[87];

- Normal caseload (all assigned cases)
- Workable caseload (cases with sufficient leads that are worth pursuing)
- Actual caseload (cases actually worked)

There are other forensic lab issues linked to detective discretion that are worth mentioning, such as if a lab is employed, how much of the analysis finds its way into a case? One assumption held by many observers is that all of the forensic analysis findings are automatically part of a case, but a case can proceed to adjudication without forensic findings for various reasons, which can include lab backlog time (previously discussed), a confession (see Chapter 8 for details on false confessions), a preponderance of evidence, or a guilty plea.[88] Nonetheless, numerous studies suggest that there are many questions left unanswered about the employment of forensic science; eight of those concerns follow, although there are many more (see Scientific Fraud and Incompetence at Crime Labs in Chapter 8 for more details):

- Differences of forensic science opinions can derail investigative interviews among child abuse victims.[89] The problems created through the investigative process and the parallel difficulties of the law can create more problems than answers.
- Forensic pathologists confront vague results when investigating various violent crimes, such as child homicide.[90]
- Natural disease can masquerade as trauma, especially among children, and the fatal event is usually not witnessed by anyone other than the accused. There are problems distinguishing accidental injury from assault, e.g., instances of multiple injuries, including the timing of different injuries; ascertaining the relationship between old injuries and death; and the relationship between shaken baby syndrome and subdural hemorrhage.[91]
- Suicides diagnosed through CS initiatives can subsequently be revealed as homicide cases, as discovered in Arizona when over 10,000 bodies were reviewed by the five boards of certified forensic pathologists after receiving precremation examinations over a two-year period.[92]

- Private labs that perform DNA assessments are criticized for their failure to use appropriate and adequate standards (similar criticism applies to local public labs and even county and state labs) that can aid prosecutors in winning convictions.[93]
- Analysis arising from trace evidence after a fire depends more on the field personnel's interpretation than the crime lab's assessment.[94]
- When forensic experts testify and present their forensic assessments, there is little evidence that their scientific expertise and trial presentations are similar or vise versa, as revealed in one study that also suggests that criminal defendants do not always benefit from those presentations.[95] Developing high-quality assessments might have less to do with judicial outcomes than expected, depending upon the witnesses' capacity and expertise of trial delivery.
- Early goals of the National Institute of Justice research program to develop an organized body of knowledge about police matters, which includes forensic science standards, has yet to be fulfilled.[96]

The previous studies suggest that caution should be exercised in the employment of forensic assessment. Another concern is that:

> Forensics cannot successfully validate every piece of evidence, nor is every piece of evidence, evidence at all.[97]

Although mentioned previously, it merits repetition that forensic analysis can guide but not necessarily confirm the degree of intent exercised to commit a crime, and each jurisdiction has varying degrees. For example, first-degree murder is defined as an unlawful killing that is both willful and premeditated, meaning that it was committed after planning, or lying in wait, for the victim.[98] First-degree murder can be categorized as deliberate—that is, the defendant made a premeditated, clear-headed decision to kill the victim—and the defendant thought about the killing before it occurred (the period for this can be very brief).[99] Some states consider murder committed in a specific way to be first-degree murder, other states disagree; first-degree murder in California is not necessarily first-degree murder in Ohio. Then, too, there's first-degree felony murder, which is a killing that happens during the course of the commission of a felony. Even if the death is accidental, the case will be considered felony murder by many states. However, if the killing happens during certain felonies, again determined by the state, it can be considered first-degree felony murder.[100] We previously learned that crime scenes, laws, and circumstances can vary, suggesting that any forensic analysis process or its personnel can be scrutinized, but another part of a conviction equation comes from the burden of truth.

Forensics and Burden of Truth

The centerpiece of a criminal trial is linked to the presumption of innocence until proven guilty.[101] Specifically, the irony is the government's burden to prove, beyond a shadow of a doubt, that a defendant possesses the intention to commit the crime, or mens rea (a guilty mind; a guilty or wrongful purpose; a criminal intent). This thought is consistent with the notion that it is not necessary to find that the defendant deliberately intended (see the previous discussion about felony murder) to injure the plaintiff. It is sufficient if the plaintiff proves by the greater weight of the evidence that the defendant intentionally acted in such a way that the natural and probable consequence of his or her act was injury to the plaintiff.[102]

> Forensic practices cannot satisfy the guilty mind constitutional standard and often distort or avoid justice realities.

For example, jurors heard closing arguments in a 22-year-old San Francisco murder–rape case in which the only evidence against the defendant was DNA found at the crime scene.[103] John Davis was convicted. Prosecutor Claudia Phillips said the odds that someone other than the defendant committed the December 4, 1985, burglary, rape, and fatal stabbing of 28-year-old Barbara Martz were in the quadrillions-to-1 and quintillions-to-1, based on the rarity of his DNA pattern (a quadrillion is a 1 followed by 15 zeroes; a quintillion is a 1 followed by 18 zeroes). Conversely, "modern science has finally caught up with Mr. Davis," the prosecutor told the jury. "Modern science tells you who raped and murdered Barbara Martz." However, Davis's defense attorney challenged the reliability of the DNA evidence and at the same time suggested several competing theories of the crime, which included the idea that Martz may have had consensual sex with Davis sometime before the slaying and that someone else committed the killing. Deputy Public Defender Gabriel Bassan called the case "very troubling," saying the passage of time since the killing had prevented him from finding witnesses to testify on Davis's behalf, provide an alibi, and for that matter the prosecutor had not shown a guilty intent. Could there have been other possible killers, such as an unknown stalker, relatives of Davis, or even Martz's domestic partner? "There are no witnesses to cross-examine," the defense said. "You cannot under these circumstances prove that this man didn't do it." She was raped, stabbed several times, and her throat was slashed to the point of near decapitation. The killer took her purse, which was later found in a crawlspace to a housing project where Davis lived.[104] A question linked to the guilty mind or mens rea is, Did the defendant have the intent to commit the crime or was the crime committed for another reason (self-defense, justifiable homicide, crime of passion, an accident, to name a few)?

What punishment is appropriate for a person who causes great harm without intent but recklessly, even to the point of disregarding specific warnings? Matt Rupp served two years in prison for starting a fire by using a riding mower on dry grass. The penalty for starting one of California's colossal wildfires was severe, even if it was an accident.[105]

However, forensic evidence is only one of many tools employed to indict and convict a defendant, but it can also lead to an acquittal. Popular television dramas validate this perspective. For example, in *Bones*, Season 3, Episode 56, "The Verdict in the Story,"[106] Dr. Brennan's (Emily Deschanel) father, Max Keenan (Ryan O'Neil), is on trial for the alleged murder of FBI Deputy Director Kirby. Everyone on the forensic team, except for Brennan who is the team supervisor, is called as a witness for the prosecution during the trial. Brennan, on the other hand, is the forensics advisor for the defense, and she must rely on both her dedication to her television family and her skill as an anthropologist to help free her father. Although all the evidence, including the elaborate forensic analysis (most of which had been conducted in Brennan's lab by Brennan's subordinates), showed that Keenan had committed the murder, an alternate theory of the murder was presented, resulting in Keenan's acquittal. The alternate theory was that Dr. Brennan did it. In light of these thoughts, prosecutors, too, have their challenges among judges and jurors whose beliefs are shaped by the media as opposed to the law, similar to John Davis's conviction that was previously detailed.

■ The Media's Bit

There is a strong relationship between what appears on television dramas and the illegal behavior of police officers who investigate crimes, forensic personnel who evaluate evidence (see the following discussion for details), and the prosecutors who indict innocent individuals (see Chapter 7 for prosecutor misconduct). For example, Santa Cruz, California detective Lieutenant Joe Haebe says he's hooked on both *CSI* and *Law & Order*.[107] Part of the fun of watching is seeing how little the shows resemble his own job, he says. "It gives people the perception that all this stuff can be solved in an hour, and that every single police department has all this amazing technology at their disposal. That's just not the case," Haebe adds. "They don't show police laboring over evidence and filling out reports." Haebe says it's not uncommon for investigators to find themselves working overtime clear through the night on a crime. He also estimated that for every hour he spends processing evidence at a crime scene, he spends more than two hours documenting that effort with the proper paperwork. "Everybody goes home at night on these shows." Detective Haebe says detectives on shows such as *Law & Order* take too many liberties with suspects. There's no smacking around suspects such as demonstrated by detectives on those shows. "Their philosophies and rules of engagement are different," Haebe says wryly. "We have ethics and rules." See Chapter 8 for more details about human error and human incompetence in forensic science and its link to wrongful convictions.

Many popular television presentations contribute, at some level or another, to the poor quality of forensic practices across the country. Earlier it was demonstrated that the quality of a television presentation outweighs knowledge, competence, and common sense. Here are a few examples:

- *CSI: Miami*, Season 2, Episode 44, "The Oath": Horatio says, "A .22 [caliber gun] is registered to Gary Nielson's wife." Florida law (similar to many southern states) neither requires nor provides a method to register handguns. Florida does issue a Concealed Weapon or Firearm License, which legally permits the licensee to carry a concealed handgun, but an application for the license does not require divulging any information about the gun. This was not the first time this error and similar errors about weapons and licenses were made.[108]

- *CSI: Miami*, Season 2, Episode 45, "Not Landing": Toward the middle of the episode, a lab technician makes the comment, "Since oil is heavier than water." However, oil is lighter than water. Also in the same episode, in an early analysis of a plane crash, Horatio goes through the sequence of events leading to the crash with a model airplane in his hand. He incorrectly states that after the valve is detonated to release the chemicals, the center of gravity shifts aft (toward the back of the aircraft), causing the plane to pitch up, stall, and then crash. In fact, it is quite the opposite. Because the cargo was loaded in bladders in the aft end of the airplane, the center of gravity would already be aft, compared to an empty plane with just the pilot. With the cargo gone, the center of gravity shifts forward, causing a pitch down. This effect would have been compounded by the fact that the airplane would have had some nose-down trim added to counteract the aft center of gravity. The real result would have been a nose dive to the ground—not a stall—with the angle depending on the nose-down trim setting.[109]

- *CSI: Miami*, Season 3, Episode 69, "Recoil": It is expected that a sworn officer who also doubles as a forensic scientist and supplies prosecutors with evidence would know the difference between weapons. Wolfe mentions after a shooting that Horatio's weapon is a "department-issued 9 mm." Horatio's weapon is a Sig Sauer P229 that is only made in .40 and .357 calibers.[110]

- *Law & Order: Special Victims Unit*, Season 7, Episode 144, "Strain": At the first murder scene, the CSI officers are shown photographing the storefront with flash photography. Because it is dark outside, the resulting photographs will consist of a reflection of the light from the flash rather than the crime scene inside the store display. Carolyn Maddox talks hypothetically about a "dirty bomb" turning Manhattan into a "nuclear wasteland." Dirty bombs contain radioactive material, but they are much smaller than nuclear warheads and they have much lower levels of radioactive fallout. These types of bombs are dangerous, but they are not powerful enough to create a nuclear wasteland.[111]

■ Junk Science

In 1974 the Forensic Sciences Foundation performed a series of 21 tests at forensic laboratories. The labs showed unacceptable proficiency in the following:

- Identifying animal hair specimens
- Determining that paint, soil, glass, blood, and handwriting samples shared a common origin

Other dated findings showed that crime labs lacked analysis techniques for discriminating bloodstains. An analysis identified the following causes of forensic science inadequacies[112]:

- Misinterpretation of test results
- Examiners who were careless or lacked training or experience
- Mislabeled or contaminated standards
- Inadequate databases
- Faulty testing procedures

Recently, researchers examined 390 crime laboratories' analyses that were produced over a 13-year period (firearms, tool marks, hair, footwear, physiological fluids, glass, paint, fibers, and latent fingerprints).[113] The findings produced error rates ranging from 0.5 percent for latent print cards to a high of 23 percent for automotive parts. In tests of controlled substances, hair, flammables, explosives, fibers, blood, and body fluids, results showed many misidentifications or failure to accurately identify evidence in each of those areas.[114]

> Some forensic practitioners and researchers say that forensic science laboratories are reluctant to monitor themselves and make necessary reforms.[115,116]

The police and prosecutors cannot rely on crime labs' assistance as much as they would like for the previously mentioned reasons because the truth is that most crime forensic units are underfunded, undercertified, and under attack.[117,118] Crime labs cannot or will not do the following[119,120]:

- Standardize their operations
- Control their excessive objectives
- Change techniques that often rely on some element of censorship or manipulation, either omitting significant information or distorting it
- Meet the judicial responsibilities of their mission

Chapter 8 reveals forensic lab failures in Oklahoma, Chicago, Boston, Richmond, New York City, and even in Washington, DC at FBI Headquarters that produced wrongful convictions, including capital punishment case convictions. Subsequently, some of those labs were shut down and their forensic personnel were fired; in some cases forensic personnel were indicted at criminal proceedings, and others were involved in civil suits. The real misery is that many defendants were sentenced to prison, and some were exonerated if they weren't already executed. For now, consider the implications for guilt and innocence provided by the following accounts:

- Federal experts who were evaluating the reliability of forensic science tests heard evidence against the most common techniques (analysis of finger-prints, tire tracks, and bite marks), which were shown not to be as reliable as believed. Because of these findings, the panel of crime-scene specialists referred to forensic science as "junk science" in the fall of 2008.[121] Another study showed that the FBI's crime lab produced the following results[122]:
  - Not properly examining physical evidence
  - Failing to file and maintain critical notes
  - Not checking work done by an incompetent examiner
  - Using DNA typing science and research that has fundamental flaws
  - Failing to take sufficient precautions against contamination
  - Disposing of pivotal evidence
  - Failing to follow protocols
  - Destroying a computer drawing that implicated an FBI sniper in a fatal shooting
- The Michigan State Police's audit of the Detroit Police Department's gun lab (discussed later) produced rampant problems, resulting in the shutdown of the department's entire crime lab in the fall of 2008, says George Hunter.[123] Wayne County Prosecutor Kym Worthy (who was a participant in the study for this book) was quoted by George Hunter as saying that "If the quality system is failing in one forensic discipline, it is highly likely to be an indicator of a severe problem that affects other forensic disciplines as well." Once the Detroit City Council closed the crime lab, many reliable personnel were out of work with worthless reputations.[124]
- The Houston (Texas) Police Department's crime laboratory was closed after a 2003 University of California study discovered numerous problems with the lab's results. The primary researcher reported that "DNA tests sometimes produce ambiguous results that are subject to multiple interpretations," thus introducing "subjective judgments" to the forensic process.[125] For example, when recovered DNA of criminals and their victims are mixed together, which is a frequent occurrence, DNA analysts typically have a suspect's DNA profile before them to help sort out the evidence "correctly." That is, they go

into the test with a cheat sheet, similar to a criminal lineup in which a potential witness is told, "Number 4 is our suspect, does he look familiar?"

- A study of crime lab proficiency found incorrect matches between recovered
evidence and reference samples more than 10 percent of the time in areas
such as fibers, paints, glass, and body fluid mixtures.[126] The rate of errors in
real casework might be higher because crime labs are probably most careful
to screen out false positives when they know they are being tested themselves.
The same study suggested a false positive rate of 2 percent for fingerprints,
creating the potential for thousands of false convictions each year.

Of the 200 cases reviewed during the Detroit, Michigan forensic science audit,
10 percent were found to have errors, one expert reveals. Most labs have an error rate
almost 10 times less than what state police auditors found in Detroit. "When you're
dealing with human beings, you can expect some errors. But a decent lab would have
an error rate of under one percent. A 10 percent rate is absolutely shocking," says
George Hunter.[127] A forensic expert sums up the implications of forensic science errors in general: "Worst of all, in some cases," forensic science has been "manipulated
to guarantee convictions instead of justice."[128] Each time a forensic lab's performance
is flawed, every conviction case that had been evaluated by that lab could be challenged, and those who were set up because of it cannot be tried again. On the other
hand, laws make it difficult, if not impossible, to retry all the O. J.s.

■ Experts Make Mistakes, Misjudgments

It is not surprising that the many forensic personnel have different training,
education, and experiences from one another, which can produce different outcomes that apparently lack accuracy, validity, or reliability, and it is difficult to verify
data from one lab to another because of the differences among processes, personnel, and policies. The forensics profession lacks a truly scientific culture—one with
sufficient written protocols and an empirical basis for the basic procedures, experts
say. This results in an environment in which misconduct can easily thrive.[129] That
said, this is aside from the criminal and lazy behavior described in Chapter 8 among
forensic personnel, including police examiners such as Pamela Fish (Chicago), Joyce
Gilchrist (Oklahoma City), and Paul Ferrara (State of Virginia). A quick look at
the following reveals the limits of relying on forensic science:

- In an examination of the criminal convictions of 62 men who were later
exonerated by DNA evidence, it was learned that a third of the cases involved
"tainted or fraudulent science."[130] Although in some cases rogue experts were
directly to blame, a much larger problem exists.
- Rogue experts, such as Fred Zain, a chemist for the West Virginia police crime
lab, testified in many cases about tests he never actually did.[131] Also, Texas
pathologist Ralph Erdmann, Mississippi forensic dentist Michael West, FBI

Special Agent Thomas Curran, a serologist, and others falsified evidence, faked autopsies, falsified toxicology and blood reports, and some faked training and college degrees. They all committed perjury.

Roy Taylor, a forensic pathology expert and attorney, says, "the public perception is that faking science is rare. The truth is it happens all the time."[132] Other researchers argue that forensic science shows a bias in favor of the prosecution.[133] On one hand, while real-time forensic DNA analysis at a crime scene using a portable microchip analyzer has advanced forensic science outcomes; on the other hand scientists claim that there is a strong possibility that DNA evidence can be faked.[134,135] Supposedly, anyone with basic equipment and know-how can alter or fake DNA. If this perspective has scientific merit, then many cases where criminal convictions were produced through DNA analysis can be contested.

■ Another Way to Describe Forensics

"Forensics is a way to make science relevant," argues Bobby Fisher, director of the crime laboratory for the Los Angeles County Sheriff's Department.[136] "I am a chemist, and I know that it is hard to get young people interested in the field by simply talking about molecules. But if you can give them a real-world example of what organic chemistry can do, they begin to think it's cool. Forensics is an antidote to the idea that scientists are nerds." However, through the advances in forensic science technology, thousands of unsolved cases, such as serious sex offenses, have been adjudicated, and that itself is an accomplishment, claims the American Academy of Forensic Sciences.

■ Summary

Contemporary policing relies upon police retrospective investigation of crimes and evidence, which starts with detection or discovery of a crime. Crime scene investigative personnel consist of field technicians, lab technicians, detectives, criminalists, forensic nurses, police psychologists, forensic psychologists, and criminal profilers, as well as patrol officers who are first responders.

Profilers attempt to ascertain physical characteristics of violators. Some emphasize personality traits and motivations, which can include ways offenders treat victims, a consistent approach taken on popular television dramas. Most profilers are not in agreement about appropriate methods and standardized tools, which has withered the court process, moving attention away from the offender's heinous criminal acts and the welfare of the victim(s). Thus, expert profiling testimony is not encouraged in court because it fails to meet the *Daubert* test of merit and opens the door for legal challenges. Most often the typical profiler might not be a clinical psychologist, as presented in today's popular media dramas.

Most crime is amazingly simple, largely unplanned, and performed by impulsive individuals with little self-control. Crime is defined as acts of force or fraud undertaken in pursuit of self-interest; some crime is situational and occurs in the life of an offender once. Criminal lifestyles are another matter and represent a smaller percentage of most offenders. Chronic offenders can be characterized as individuals who have behaviors that are consistent with antisocial personality disorders. Fulfilling self-interests or pure selfishness characteristics, when linked to a lack of self-control, could explain why some individuals smoke, drink, abuse drugs, gamble, speed, engage in irresponsible sex, or commit violent crimes. Other motivations or triggers are jealously, envy, greed, rage, ignorance, and lust.

Real services provided by forensic crime laboratories can include anthropology services, biology units, document examination units, latent fingerprint units, and pathology units. Television's crime labs can be summed up as taking dramatic license with how these things are rendered visually because they have to look beautiful and cool. The goal of a forensic lab is the evenhanded use of all available information. Crime labs vary because of variations in local laws, different capabilities and functions of the organization that are linked to budgetary and staffing limitations, and specific areas of expertise.

Forensic science had its beginnings in the eighth century, when the Chinese used fingerprints to establish the identity of documents and clay sculptures. The basic principle they refined was linked to the theory of transfer: when two objects meet, some evidence of that meeting can later be found and verified.

The forensic investigation process might include taking note of everyone who assisted at the crime scene; contacting the district attorney's office, depending on the merits of the case; walking through the scene to aid in determining the scope of the case; contacting experts if field personnel are not certified in a particular area; and other techniques. It all comes down to a lawful conviction through the burden of proof. The prosecutor's task is to show beyond and to the exclusion of every reasonable doubt that the defendant is guilty and the evidence was legally collected.

The reasons for police reluctance to use crime labs includes the backlog of unsolved rapes and homicides, the reality of lab turnaround time, and evidence produced by alleged experts whose calculations can be in error and sometimes criminal. Forensic science cannot successfully validate every piece of evidence, nor is every piece of evidence actually evidence at all. Also, forensic science practices cannot satisfy the guilty mind constitutional standard. There is a relationship between what appears on television dramas and the illegal behavior of investigators, forensic personnel, and prosecutors. Some forensic practitioners and researchers say that forensic science laboratories are reluctant to monitor themselves. However, forensics is a way to make science relevant, despite the errors, and has resolved thousands of unsolved cases. Yet some scientists advance the idea that DNA can be faked.

■ References

1. Moore, M. H., Trojanowicz, R., & Kelling, G. L. (1988). *Crime and policing*. Washington, DC: National Institute of Justice.

2. Bureau of Labor Statistics. (2008). *Occupational outlook handbook.* Washington, DC: US Department of Labor. Retrieved March 19, 2009, from http://www.bls.gov/oco/ocos160.htm

3. This is the Roman definition of justice as set out in the Justinian Code, according to Justice David Miller in *The Blackwell Encyclopedia of Political Thought,* (1987). Oxford: UK.

4. Digeser, P. E. (2003). Justice, forgiveness, mercy, and forgiving: The complex meaning of executive pardons. *Capital University Law Review, 31,* 161–178.

5. Digeser, P. E. (2001). *Political forgiveness.* New York: Cornell University Press.

6. Bureau of Justice Statistics. (2006). *Local police departments, 2003* (NCJ 210118). Washington, DC: US Department of Justice. Retrieved March 19, 2009, from http://www.ojp.usdoj.gov/bjs/pub/pdf/lpd03.pdf

7. Bureau of Justice Statistics. (2004). *Law enforcement management and administrative statistics, 2000. Data for state and local agencies with 100 personnel and more officers.* Washington, DC: US Department of Justice. Retrieved March 19, 2009, from http://www.ojp.usdoj.gov/bjs/pub/pdf/lema005a.pdf

8. For a description of detectives and their roles in crime scene investigations, see Stevens, D. J. (2009). *Introduction to American policing.* Sudbury, MA: Jones and Bartlett.

9. Valenzuela, B. E. (2008, August 17). Gang member arrested after portable scanner identifies him: Device allows law enforcement to check fingerprints in the field. *The Daily Press.* Retrieved November 16, 2008, from http://www.policeone.com/police-products/investigation/evidence-management/articles/1726526-Scanner-identifies-Calif-gang-member/

10. Harrold, M. (2007, July 17). Everyone's an expert as TV's CSI craze raises the bar for police. *The Gazette.* Retrieved March 19, 2009, from http://www.canada.com/montrealgazette/news/story.html?id=e06d7f34-a809-4266-ac66-1808d1435c49

11. Saferstein, R. (2006). *Criminalistics: An introduction to forensic science* (9th ed.). Upper Saddle River, NJ: Prentice Hall.

12. Los Angeles Police Department. (n.d.). *Hertzberg-Davis Forensic Science Center.* Retrieved November 1, 2008, from www.lapdonline.org

13. Harrold, "Everyone's an Expert."

14. City of Los Angeles. (n.d.). *The city has a job for you: Criminalist.* Retrieved March 19, 2009, from http://www.ci.la.ca.us/per/exams/exam2234.htm

15. Logan, T. K., Cole, J., & Capillo, A. (2007). Sexual Assault Nurse Examiner program characteristics, barriers, and lessons learned. *Journal of Forensic Nursing, 3*(1), 24–34.

16. Sommers, M. S., Schafer, J., Zink, T., Hutson, L., & Hillard, P. (2001). Injury patterns in women resulting from sexual assault trauma violence abuse. *Pediatrics, 2*(3), 240–258.

17. Campbell, R., Patterson, D., & Lichty, L. F. (2005). The effectiveness of Sexual Assault Nurse Examiner (SANE) program: A review of psychological, medical, legal, and community outcomes. *Trauma, Violence, & Abuse: A Review Journal, 6*(4), 313–329.

18. Ullman, S. E., Townsend, S. M., Filipas, H. H., & Starzynski, L. L. (2007). Structural models of the relations of assault severity, social support, avoidance coping, self-blame, and PTSD among sexual survivors. *Psychology of Women Quarterly, 31*(1), 23–37.

19. Campbell, R., Townsend, S. M., Long, S. M., Kinnison, K. E., Pulley, E. M., Adames, S. B., et al. (2005). Organizational characteristics of Sexual Assault Nurse Examiner programs: Results from the National Survey of SANE Programs. *Journal of Forensic Nursing, 1*(2), 57–64.

20. Logan, et al., "Sexual Assault Nurse Examiner Program."

21. American Psychological Association. (2002, June). A psychological force behind the force. *Monitor on Psychology, 33*(6). Retrieved July 9, 2008, from http://www.apa.org/monitor/jun02/force.html

22. Stevens, D. J. (2008). *Police officer stress: Sources and solutions.* Upper Saddle River, NJ: Prentice Hall.

23. Douglas, J., & Olshaker, M. (1995). *Mind hunter: Inside the FBI's elite serial crime unit. The evil men do.* New York: Pocket Star Books.

24. Wrightsman, L. S. (2001). *Forensic psychology.* Belmont, CA: Wadsworth.

25. Bartol, C. R., & Bartol, A. M. (2007). *Criminal behavior: A psychological approach.* Upper Saddle River, NJ: Prentice Hall.

26. TV.com. *The Mentalist.* Retrieved November 1, 2008, from http://www.tv.com/the-mentalist/show/75200/summary.html

27. Douglas & Olshaker, *Mind Hunter.*

28. Wrightsman, L. S. (1999). *Judicial decision making: Is psychology relevant?* New York: Kluwer Academic/Plenum.

29. Holmes, R. M., & Holmes, S. T. (1996). *Profiling violent crimes.* Thousand Oaks, CA: Sage.

30. NBC.com. (2007). Retrieved July 9, 2008, from http://www.nbc.com/Jump/

31. Bekerian, D. S., & Jackson, J. L. (1997). Critical issues in offender profiling. In J. L. Jackson & D. S. Bekerian (Eds.), *Offender profiling: Theory, research and practice.* New York: John Wiley.

32. The *Daubert* test arose from *Daubert v. Merrell Dow Pharmaceuticals Inc.* (509 U.S. 579, 113 S.Ct. 2786, 1993). A *Daubert* hearing begins its explanation of the criteria that trial courts should use to screen "purportedly scientific evidence" by parsing Rule 702, focusing on the meanings of "scientific" and "knowledge." An important key to understanding the court's reliability-based analysis of the admissibility of expert testimony lies in the court's focus on the requirement that, for expert testimony to be admissible, "[t]he subject of an expert's testimony must be 'scientific . . . knowledge'" because it is "the requirement that an expert's testimony pertain to 'scientific knowledge'" that "establishes a standard of evidentiary reliability." However, "in order to qualify as 'scientific knowledge,' an inference or assertion must be derived by the scientific method." In brief, because only scientific knowledge can be offered as expert testimony, and the court regards as scientific knowledge only that which is derived by the scientific method, only inferences that are derived by the scientific method can be offered as expert opinion testimony. The courts of 19 states have adopted *Daubert*, and the courts of 11 states, including Florida, have apparently rejected it, but those numbers are constantly changing. See Mahle, S. (1999, April). *The impact of Daubert v. Merrell Dow Pharmaceuticals, Inc., on expert testimony: With applications to securities litigation.* Retrieved August 12, 2007, from http://www.daubertexpert.com/basics_daubert-v-merrell-dow.html. Under *Kumho Tire Co. v. Carmichael* (526 U.S. 137, 119 S.Ct. 1167, 1999), courts are now

responsible for winnowing out unreliable nonscientific expert testimony, along with their task, imposed by *Daubert v. Merrell*, of deciding which scientific expert testimony is acceptable. Kumho holds that the *Daubert* factors of admissibility apply to all expert testimony, including testimony by such experts as vocational specialists and economists. Under Kumho, no longer will expert testimony be acceptable on the ipse dixit (the say-so) of the expert. Courts must now don lab coats and scrutinize, under the *Daubert*-test microscope, all testimony based on "scientific, technical, or other specialized knowledge."

33. Holmgren, B. K. (1999). Expert testimony profiling sex offenders—a dead issue rears its head again. *American Prosecutor Research Institute, 4*(12). Retrieved March 19, 2009, from http://ndaa.org/publications/newsletters/apri_update_vol_12_no_4_1999.html

34. Holmgren, "Expert Testimony Profiling Sex Offenders."

35. CBS.com. (2007). *Criminal Minds.* Retrieved June 25, 2009, from http://www.cbs.com/primetime/criminal_minds/recaps/

36. Chronicle of Higher Education. (n.d.). *Average annual salary by academic rank, 2007–2008.* Retrieved October 31, 2008, from http://chronicle.com/stats/aaup/index.php?action=result&search=Enter+an+institution+name&state=&year=2008&category=&withRanks=1&limit=

37. Federal Bureau of Investigation. (2007). *Clearances.* Washington, DC: US Department of Justice. Retrieved August 20, 2008, from http://www.fbi.gov/ucr/cius2006/offenses/clearances/index.html

38. Federal Bureau of Investigation. (2007). *Behavioral science.* Washington, DC: US Department of Justice. Retrieved August 20, 2008, from http://www.fbi.gov/hq/td/academy/bsu/bsu.htm

39. American Academy of Experts in Traumatic Stress. (2007). The emergence of psychologists and behavioral scientists as human factors and performance consultants to law enforcement. Retrieved August 24, 2009, from http://www.aaets.org/index.html

40. Weisman, J. (1980). *Evidence.* New York: Viking, p. 221.

41. Wrightsman, *Forensic Psychology*, p. 74.

42. Gottfredson, M. R., & Hirschi, T. (1990). *A general theory of crime.* Stanford, CA: Stanford University Press, pps. 115–117.

43. Gottfredson & Hirschi, *A General Theory of Crime.*

44. Akers, R. L. (1991). Self-control as a general theory of crime. *Journal of Quantitative Criminology, 7*, 201–211.

45. Samenow, S. E. (2004). *Inside the criminal mind.* New York: Crown.

46. Saferstein, *Criminalistics.*

47. Forensic Science. (2004). *The autopsy.* Retrieved October 31, 2008, from http://library.thinkquest.org/04oct/00206/autopsy.htm

48. Ruslander, H. W. (2006). *The role of the crime scene investigator.* Retrieved August 18, 2008, from http://www.criminalistics.us/thumbnails.html

49. Layton, J. (2006). *How crime scene investigation works.* Retrieved August 20, 2008, from http://science.howstuffworks.com/csi.htm. Joe Clayton of the Colorado Bureau of Investigation participated in gathering technical data for Layton's article.

50. Edmondson, B. (2007, May 5). *CSI: Realistic, except cool.* Retrieved June 25, 2009, from http://expertvoices.nsdl.org/tvscience/2007/05/05/csi-realistic-except-cool/

51. American Academy of Forensic Sciences. (2007). *Resources: Choosing a Career.* Retrieved August 24, 2009, from http://www.aafs.org/default.asp?section_id=resources&page_id=choosing_a_career

52. Federal Bureau of Investigation. (2007). *Handbook of forensic services.* Washington, DC: US Department of Justice. Retrieved August 20, 2008, from http://www.fbi.gov/hq/lab/handbook/forensics.pdf

53. Saferstein, *Criminalistics.*

54. New York State Division of State Police. (n.d.). *Forensic science: The early years.* Retrieved June 25, 2009, from http://www.troopers.state.ny.us/forensic_science/Forensic_Science_History/

55. Chisum, W. J., & Turvey, B. E. (2000). Evidence dynamics: Locard's Exchange Principle and crime reconstruction. *Journal of Behavioral Profiling, 1*(1). Retrieved March 19, 2009, from http://www.profiling.org/journal/vol1_no1/jbp_ed_january2000_1-1.html

56. Byrd, M. (2000). *Duty description for the crime scene investigator.* Retrieved March 19, 2009, from http://www.crime-scene-investigator.net/dutydescription.html

57. Stevens, *Introduction to American Policing.*

58. Layton, *How Crime Scene Investigation Works.*

59. Chisum & Turvey, "Evidence Dynamics."

60. Crime Lab Report. (2008, October). Crime labs under police—unresolved issues. *Crime Lab Report, 2*(10). Retrieved October 20, 2008, from http://www.crimelabreport.com:80/library/monthly_report/10-2008.htm

61. Swanson, C. R., Chamelin, N. C., & Territo, L. (2008). *Criminal investigation* (8th ed.). Boston: McGraw Hill.

62. Saferstein, *Criminalistics.*

63. Byrd, M. (ND). *Crime Scene Investigations.* Miami-Dade (Florida) Police Department. Retrieved August 24, 2009, from http://www.geocities.com/cfpdlab/photos.htm

64. Waegel, W. B. (2004). Case routinization in investigative police work. In S. Stojkovic, J. Klofas & D. Kalinich (Eds.), *The administration and management of criminal justice organizations: A book of readings* (pp. 420–437). Long Grove, IL: Waveland Press.

65. Stevens, *Introduction to American Policing.*

66. Stevens, *Introduction to American Policing.*

67. Layton, *How Crime Scene Investigation Works.*

68. Forensic Science Library. Retrieved June 25, 2009, from http://www.trutv.com/library/crime/criminal_mind/forensics/

69. Evans, M. M., & Stagner, P. A. (2003). Maintaining the chain of custody: Evidence handling in forensic cases. *AORN Journal, 78*(4), 563–567.

70. Lovrich, N. P., Pratt, T. C., Gaffney, M. J., Johnson, C. L., Asplen, C. H., Hurst, L. H., et al. (2004). *National forensic DNA study report. Final report* (NIJ 203970). Washington, DC: US Department of Justice. Retrieved October 8, 2006, from http://www.ncjrs.gov/pdffiles1/nij/grants/203970.pdf

71. Oprah.com. (2007). *The rape kit controversy.* Retrieved June 25, 2009, from http://www.dancinginthedarkness.com/articles.php?show=5&arc=220

72. Lumb, R., & Wang, Y. (2006). The theories and practice of community problem-oriented policing: A case study. *The Police Journal, 79*(2), 177–193.

73. Bureau of Justice Statistics. (2004). *Fact sheet: 50 largest crime labs, 2002* (NCJ 205988). Washington, DC: US Department of Justice. Retrieved June 26, 2007, from http://www.ojp.usdoj.gov/bjs/pub/pdf/50lcl02.pdf

74. Arizona Office of the Auditor General. (2000). *Performance audit, Department of Public Safety: Scientific Analysis Bureau.* Phoenix, AZ: Author.

75. Coppola, M. C. (2008, October 10). Battle over crime-lab fees for cities, towns is on. Nogales International.

76. Oprah.com, *Rape Kit Controversy.*

77. Lambert, E., Nerbonne, T., & Watson, P. L. (2003). The forensic science needs of law enforcement applicants and recruits: A survey of Michigan law enforcement agencies. *Journal of Criminal Justice Education, 14*(1), 67–81.

78. Craig, L. A., Browne, K. D., Stringer, I., and Beech, A. (2005). Sexual recidivism: A review of static, dynamic, and actuarial predictors. *Journal of Sexual Aggression, 11*(1), 65–84. Retrieved June 25, 2009, from http://pdfserve.informaworld.com/289916_714030565.pdf

79. Based on the disciplinary records of those inmates while incarcerated. Texas Defender Service. (2004). *Deadly speculation: Misleading Texas capital juries with false predictions of future dangerousness.* June 25, 2009, from http://www.texasdefender.org/DEADLYSP.PDF

80. Stevens, *Police Officer Stress.*

81. Cheurprakobkit, S., & Pena, G. T. (2003). Computer crime enforcement in Texas: Funding, training, and investigating problems. *Journal of Police and Criminal Psychology, 18*(1), 24–37.

82. Berger, M. A. (2002). Raising the bar: The impact of DNA testing on the field of forensics. In A. Blumstein, L. Steinberg & C. C. Bell (Eds.), *Perspectives on crime and justice: 2000–2001 lecture series.* Washington, DC: National Institute of Justice. Retrieved June 25, 2009, from http://www.ojp.usdoj.gov/nij/pubs-sum/187100.htm

83. Koppl, R., & Krane, D. (2008, September). Potentially flawed science deciding many cases. *OnlineAthens.* Retrieved March 19, 2009, from http://www.onlineathens.com/stories/091408/opi_331950086.shtml

84. Waegel, "Case Routinization in Investigative Police Work."

85. Saverio, F. R., & Pierre, M. (2001). Identification of gunshot residue: A critical review. *Science International, 119*(2), 195–211.

86. Walker, S., & Katz, C. M. (2008). *The police in America: An introduction* (6th ed.). Boston: McGraw Hill.

87. Eck, J. E. (1983). *Solving crimes: The investigation of burglary and robbery.* Washington, DC: US Department of Justice, Police Executive Research Forum.

88. Cheurprakobkit & Pena, "Computer Crime Enforcement."

89. Sternberg, K. J., Lamb, M., & Davies, G. M. (2001). The memorandum of good practice: Theory versus application. *Child Abuse and Neglect, 25*(5), 669–681.

90. Cordner, S. M., Burke, M. P., & Dodd, M. J. (2001). 11 cases. *Legal Medicine, 3*(2), 95–103.

91. Cordner, et al., "11 Cases."

92. Nelson, C. L., & Winston, D. C. (2006). Detection of medical examiner cases from review of cremation requests. *American Journal of Forensic Medicine & Pathology, 27*(2), 103–105.

93. Ginsberg, L. D. (1997). And the blood cried out. A prosecutor's spell-binding account of the power of DNA. *American Journal of Forensic Medicine & Pathology, 18*(2), 218–237.

94. Hagimoto, Y., & Yamamoto, H. (2006). Analysis of a soldered wire burnt in a fire. *Journal of Forensic Sciences, 51*, 87–94.

95. Saks, M. J., & Faigman, D. L. (2005). Expert evidence after Daubert. *Annual Review of Law and Social Science, 1*, 105–130. Daubert stands for a trilogy of Supreme Court cases as well as revisions of the Federal Rules of Evidence. Together they represent American law's most recent effort to filter expert evidence offered at trial.

96. Melnicoe, S., Sulsbury, W, Arnesen, N, and Caplan, M. (1982). *Police research catalog: Police-related research supported by the National Institute of Justice 1969–1981.* Washington, DC: National Institute of Justice. NCJ 082138.

97. Saks & Faigman, "Expert Evidence After Daubert."

98. Findlaw.com. (n.d.). *Murder: First degree.* Retrieved August 21, 2008, from http://criminal.findlaw.com/crimes/a-z/murder_first_degree.html

99. Free Advice. (2008). *Are there different degrees of murder?* Retrieved August 21, 2008, from http://criminal-law.freeadvice.com/violent_crimes/degrees.murder.htm

100. Findlaw.com. (n.d.). *First degree murder.* Retrieved August 24, 2009, from http://criminal.findlaw.com/crimes/a-z/murder_first_degree.html

101. Colb, S. F. (2002). *Allen Iverson and the presumption of innocence.* Retrieved October 10, 2008, from http://writ.news.findlaw.com/colb/20020617.html

102. Posey, A. J., & Wrightsman, L. S. (2005). *Trial consulting.* New York: Oxford University Press.

103. Van Derbeken, J. (2007, August 17). Closing arguments in 1985 rape–murder trial in San Francisco. *San Francisco Chronicle.* Retrieved August 22, 2008, from http://www.sfgate.com/cgi-bin/article.cgi?file=/c/a/2007/08/17/BALURK067.DTL

104. Van Derbeken, "Closing Arguments."

105. Bulwa, D. (2008, August 10). Accidental fire-starter furious at punishment. *San Francisco Chronicle.* Retrieved August 21, 2008, from http://www.sfgate.com/cgi-bin/article.cgi?f=/c/a/2008/08/10/MNOI125JRQ.DTL

106. *Bones,* Season 3, Episode 56, "The Verdict in the Story." First aired May 5, 2008.

107. Schultz, J. (2002, November 10). True crime is nothing like TV. *Santa Cruz Sentinel.* Retrieved June 25, 2009, from http://www.scsextra.com/story.php?sid=21176&storySection=Local&fromSearch=true&searchTerms=

108. TV.com. (n.d.). *CSI: Miami, show trivia, season 2.* Retrieved October 26, 2007, from http://www.tv.com/csi-miami/show/8460/trivia.html?season=2&tag=season_nav;next

109. TV.com, *CSI: Miami, Show Trivia, Season 2.*

110. TV.com. (n.d.). *CSI: Miami, show trivia, season 3*. Retrieved October 26, 2007, from http://www.tv.com/csi-miami/show/8460/trivia.html?season=3&tag=season_nav;next

111. TV.com. (n.d.). *Law & Order: Special Victims Unit, show trivia, season 7*. Retrieved October 26, 2007, from http://www.tv.com/law-and-order-special-victims-unit/show/334/trivia.html?season=7&tag=season_dropdown;dropdown;6

112. Peterson, J. L., Fabricant, E. L., Field, K. S., & Thornton, J. I. (1978). *Crime laboratory proficiency testing research program*. Washington, DC: US Government Printing Office.

113. Peterson, J. L., & Markham, P. N. (1995). Crime laboratory proficiency testing results, 1978–1991, II: Resolving questions of common origin. *Journal of Forensic Sciences, 40*(6), 994–1008.

114. Taupin, J. (2001). Forensic hair morphology comparison—a dying art or junk science? *Science & Justice, 44*(2), 95–100.

115. Lynch, M. (2003). God's signature: DNA profiling, the new gold standard in forensic science. *Endeavour, 27*(2), 93–97.

116. Taupin, "Forensic Hair Morphology Comparison."

117. Roane, K. R. (2005, April 25). The CSI effect. *US News & World Report*. Retrieved August 22, 2008, from http://www.usnews.com/usnews/culture/articles/050425/25csi_2.htm

118. Saferstein, *Criminalistics*.

119. Cheurprakobkit & Pena, "Computer Crime Enforcement."

120. Willing, R. (2004, August 5). CSI effect has juries wanting more evidence. *USA Today*. Retrieved August 22, 2008, from http://www.usatoday.com/news/nation/2004-08-05-csi-effect_x.htm

121. Hamilton, B., & Cohen, S. (2008, September 21). Clueless crime labs: Pros slam CSI techniques as junk. *New York Post*. Retrieved October 2, 2008, from http://www.nypost.com/seven/09212008/news/nationalnews/clueless_crime_labs_130091.htm

122. Wearne, P., & Kelly, J. (2002). *Tainting evidence: Inside the scandals at the FBI crime lab*. New York: Free Press.

123. Hunter, G. (2008, September 26). Detroit shuts down error-plagued crime lab. *Detroit News*. Retrieved June 25, 2009, from http://netk.net.au/Forensic/Forensic33.asp

124. Schmitt, B., & Swickard, J. (2008). *Crime lab shutdown slammed as too fast*. Retrieved June 25, 2009, from http://lawprofessors.typepad.com/crimprof_blog/2008/10/crime-lab-shutd.html

125. University of California Newsroom. (2003, April 7). *DNA expert offers inside look at the case overhauling justice system: University of California Professor William Thompson reveals how DNA evidence was abused and manipulated for wrongful conviction of Josiah Sutton*. Retrieved March 19, 2009, from http://www.universityofcalifornia.edu/news/article/5300

126. Koppl, R., & Krane, D. (n.d.). *Fairness in forensics*. Retrieved March 19, 2009, from http://www.bioforensics.com/news/Koppl_Krane_Olympian_8-08.html. Dr. Roger Koppl is a professor of economics and finance and director of the Institute for Forensic Science Administration at Fairleigh Dickinson University, New Jersey. His updated vitae (May 2008) is available at http://alpha.fdu.edu/~koppl/vita.htm.

127. Hunter, "Detroit Shuts Down Error-Plagued Crime Lab."

128. University of California Newsroom, *DNA Expert Offers Inside Look.*

129. Koppl & Krane, "Potentially Flawed Science Deciding Many Cases."

130. Giannelli, P. C. (n.d.). Crime labs need improvement. *Flaws in Forensic Science, Issues in Science and Technology.* Retrieved March 19, 2009, from http://www.issues.org/20.1/giannelli.html

131. Wearne & Kelly, *Tainting Evidence.*

132. Frank, L., & Hanchette, J. (1994). Convicted on false evidence? False science often sways juries, judges. *USA Today.* Cited in State of Kentucky, Fund Manuel. Department of Public Advocacy. (n.d.) Chapter 4, pp. 13–15. Retrieved June 25, 2009, from http://www.dpa.state.ky.us/library/manuals/funds/ch4.html

133. Burns, D. C. (2001). When used in the criminal legal process forensic science shows a bias in favour of the prosecution. *Science & Justice, 41*(4), 271–277.

134. Liu, P., Yeung, S., Crenshaw, K., Crouse, C., Scherer, J., & Mathies, R. (2008). Real-time forensic DNA analysis at a crime scene using a portable microchip analyzer. *Forensic Science International: Genetics, 2*(4), 301–309.

135. Frumkin, D., Wasserstrom, A., Davidson, A., & Grafit, A. (2009). Authentication of forensic DNA samples. *Forensic Science International: Genetics.* In press.

136. Edmondson, B. (2007, May 16). *Forensic fever spins off scientists.* Retrieved March 19, 2009, from http://expertvoices.nsdl.org/tvscience/

Prosecutors

Nearly all men can stand adversity, but if you want to test a man's character, give him power.

Abraham Lincoln

▶ ▶ CHAPTER OBJECTIVES

- Describe the discretion of prosecutors and their amazing official powers
- Identify the origins of public prosecutors and explain their role
- Provide prosecutor statistics and describe their traditional responsibilities
- Offer a perspective of why some lawyers became prosecutors
- Describe the ethics of prosecutors and rules of professional conduct
- Characterize the influence of the *CSI Effect* on prosecutor conduct

■ Introduction

One way to introduce this chapter is to repeat the words so many viewers have heard from the popular television series *Law & Order*: "In the criminal justice system, the people are represented by two separate and important groups: the police who investigate crime and the district attorneys who prosecute the offenders." One prosecutor reveals that the primary responsibility of a prosecutor is to seek truth and justice, regardless of where the search might lead—whether it results in prosecution and conviction or release of a suspect.[1] This thought is consistent with the National District Attorneys Association's description of the primary function of prosecutors: "to seek justice."[2(p9)] Yet a "try'm and fry'm" prosecutorial attitude (indict and convict) typified by popular television performances helps to enhance wrongful convictions of innocent individuals (see Chapter 8) and enhances capital punishment as a sanction[3] (see Chapter 9).

A prosecutor is one of the most critical building blocks upon which democracy has developed because violent crimes are crimes against the people (local, state, and federal), and a prosecutor's primary task is to administer justice to violators by the people and for the people.[4] However, prosecutors are faced with heavy caseloads and long delays by forensic laboratories and courts, and the public demands swifter and more effective justice; therefore, prosecutors make hard choices in allocating resources to accomplish their mission.[5] This can mean that prosecutors legally hold enormous discretion about which suspects, what crimes, and which sanctions (i.e. capital punishment, mandatory sentences, and probation) to pursue often without supervision or consequence.

As a result, Americans have witnessed two separate and distinctive patterns: (1) the violent (reported) crime rate is down because prosecutorial discretion is productive and amazingly flawless, and (2) law enforcement (largely prosecutors) engage in a wholesale betrayal of their "sworn duties to the nation,"[6] the rule of law, and, equally important, to the unswerving pursuit of justice even at the risk of wrongful convictions (see Chapter 8) and wrongful executions (see Chapter 9). It can be argued that judicial betrayal and the risk of wrongful convictions and wrongful executions have been fueled by the popular media through the *CSI Effect*, explained in Chapter 1. That is, while the *CSI Effect* reinforces aggressive reactive strategies, glorifies vigilantism as an American tradition, and promotes fictitious accounts of crime, crime control, and its process, the criminal justice community (cops, courts, and corrections) widens its violator net through superfluous intrusion into the private lives of constituents. The justice community is attempting to evolve greater immunity from the rule of law, producing an autonomous yet significant amount of unchecked discretionary power as documented in the wars on crime, junkies, sex offenders, poverty, and immigrants (see Chapters 3–5). Finally in this regards, it is the primary law enforcement officer in a jurisdiction—the prosecutor—who holds the most autonomy and power within the justice system.[7] Despite the best (and brave) police efforts toward detection, apprehension, and detainment of a violator, a prosecutor can alter or reject a case with or without the influence of others, including the police, courts, or oversight public groups; there are exceptions, but most often a prosecutor can do as he or she pleases without consequence.

■ Most Prosecutors Behave Ethically

"For all the talk prosecutors like to engage in about how their number-one priority is to seek justice, not just win trials, it's the number [of] trials completed, trials won, and trials lost that means everything."[8] A former district attorney (DA) believes this thought is in error. He says that although the verdicts are sometimes imperfect, the overall perspective of prosecutors is that justice is usually accomplished. Another DA agrees that the prosecutor's duty is more than one side of an adversarial process; the duty is toward justice.[9]

Most prosecutors conduct themselves professionally and rarely, if ever, behave un-ethically, but legal wrongdoers are not always as visible as Michael Nifong, the ex-North Carolina prosecutor who was disbarred for misconduct in a rape case against three Duke University lacrosse players in 2008.[10] Nifong filed for bankruptcy and listed the lacrosse players among his major creditors. The players accused Nifong of withholding evidence and said he pressed the case to boost his reelection in a contested primary.

The fact remains that most prosecutorial abuse is tied to practices of both federal and state prosecutors, reflected in their application of the death penalty (see Chapter 9), basic indictment methods, the issues of victims, and plea bargaining; in fact, prosecutors have "virtually unfettered discretion in their plea negotiations with defendants."[11] Prosecutor misconduct has created a context that facilitates abuse and little, if any, accountability. This gives rise to *judicial blindness* (see Chapter 11), which opens the door to wrongful convictions and wrongful executions. In keeping with Abraham Lincoln's thoughts about power and performance, let's examine some of the power held by prosecutors and see how they measure up. First, it would be helpful to review the origins of prosecutors.

■ British and Colonial Origins of Public Prosecutors

Four hundred years ago, a system of private prosecution dominated England. Public prosecutors did not exist, either locally or nationally, although the local justice of the peace sometimes assumed the role of a public prosecutor.[12] The at-torney general (AG) of England had the power to initiate a prosecution but only in matters that affected the Crown and in guiding public prosecution practices. By filing a writ of nolle prosequi (not to prosecute), the AG could dismiss any prosecution, and his decisions were final.

In the beginning, criminal procedure in the American colonies followed the English practice. There was an AG in each colony; the first was appointed in Virginia in 1643. Similar to their English counterparts, the American AG represented the Crown but left criminal prosecution to the victim. It was quickly learned that private prosecution was unsuited to the democratic process, especially when the victim was poor. If a grand jury was required, the expenses, expertise, travel to the colonial capital from a village, and time away from work or loved ones made it impractical for many citizens to represent themselves. If an offender was found guilty, how would the public prosecutor provide criminal sanctions upon the defendant? Thus, most people settled their affairs privately, and usually that meant financially.

American populations grew, as did crime, and with independence from Eng-land, a single criminal court in each colony was replaced by county courts and by county attorneys in each court. This occurred as early as 1704 in Connecticut. County prosecutors came to be regarded as local officials rather than agents of a central colonial authority. In their counties, they were treated as if they were at-torney generals, although they held the role of the colony's attorney.

In England today, any member of the public can prosecute, but the attorney general has complete authority to dismiss the charge, and the local police conduct many prosecutions, although this is changing to become more Americanized (only prosecutors prosecute). That is, until recently in the U.K. (England, Northern Ireland, Scotland, and Wales), the function of prosecution was largely in the hands of the police, and larger police agencies had prosecution divisions as part of their organizational structure.[13]

In minor cases, police officers were the only prosecution representatives in court. In continental Europe, the initiative lies almost entirely with the state acting through a public prosecutor or an investigating magistrate; charging discretion is nonexistent or subject to judicial review. American criminal prosecution is a hybrid. Like continental systems, it is an institutionalized and public function; like its English ancestor, it places extraordinary emphasis on local autonomy and charging discretion.

■ What Is an American Prosecutor?

For a democratic nation like the United States to succeed, it is essential to distinguish between legal (the state's use of force and detainment) violence from illegal (citizen or criminal) violence. Specifically, the state's exercise of force and detainment through its criminal justice apparatuses (cops, courts, and corrections) within the rule of law or constitutional due process guarantees can be considered legal violence; conversely, illegal violence is exercised by constituents for their own ends (i.e. fraud, robbery, rape, murder, and so on). A public prosecutor aids in differentiating legal violence from illegal violence.

> An American *prosecutor* is a licensed government lawyer who initiates legal action and possesses the authority to investigate, indict, and prosecute violators in both criminal and misdemeanor matters.[14]

A government lawyer who prosecutes organizations and arrested suspects for crimes is typically known as a district attorney, state's attorney, county attorney, US district attorney, assistant district attorney, and so on. Public prosecutors can be appointed, hired, or elected, and they can prosecute all criminal offenses and initiate various services as prescribed by law or ordinances. In every state and jurisdiction, laws and ordinances can vary about prosecutors. For example, Nevada defines a prosecutor as any of the following:

1. The Attorney General or a deputy attorney general who prosecutes a contested case pursuant to this chapter
2. If the Attorney General and his deputies are disqualified to act in such a matter, an attorney appointed by the Attorney General to prosecute a contested case pursuant to this chapter

3. If the regulatory body is authorized to employ or retain attorneys other than the Attorney General and his deputies, an attorney employed or retained by the regulatory body to prosecute a contested case pursuant to this chapter[15]

There is more to a prosecutor's responsibility than initiating a legal case, depending on the jurisdiction. For example, the Trumbull County, Ohio prosecutor's office has five divisions[16]:

- Administrative
- Appellate
- Civil (child support, tax collection, real estate foreclosures)
- Criminal (child assault, gun violence, vehicular homicide, drug prosecutions, elderly abuse, juvenile division, welfare fraud)
- Victim–witness (victim–witness advocate, victim–witness juvenile advocate)

The focus of this chapter relates to criminal prosecutors and their assistant attorneys at the municipal, county, and state levels of government.

■ The Job of a Prosecutor

One of the first jobs of a prosecutor is the authorization of criminal warrants. Each jurisdiction has different ideas of how to get from the police investigation to the formal institution of bringing a criminal charge or indictment against a suspect arrested by police (prosecutors can charge a suspect with a crime after an individual has been arrested; see the sections "Separation of Powers Doctrine" in Chapter 3 and "Prosecutor Discretion and the Media" in Chapter 8). Some jurisdictions allow police, for some violations, to issue a citation and proceed on that action to the point where the defendant enters a formal plea of not guilty. In other jurisdictions, this is where the prosecutor becomes involved with a case. Some states allow minor offenses or offenses of a specified type (e.g., traffic or fish and game violations) to proceed to completion without a prosecutor's involvement. Usually, these are offenses where there is no right to a jury trial. For felonies (a serious crime, such as murder, that is punished more severely than a misdemeanor), the prosecution process tends to be more similar from jurisdiction to jurisdiction. One reason for these similarities relates to constitutional limits on how long police can detain a suspect before they must bring him or her before a judicial officer and what the judicial officer is supposed to do when the miscreant is before him or her.

As you already know, the burden of proof (see Chapter 6) is on the government, or specifically it is the prosecutor's job to prove the defendant's guilt. A prosecutor's task is to prove beyond and to the exclusion of every reasonable doubt that the defendant is guilty of the felony charged and the evidence was legally gathered and appropriately evaluated. Innocence is presumed. However, in a democratic nation the rule of law is very specific, yet the gray areas are very gray, just like the process that governs a prosecutor who decides to indict a suspect with a crime or release him or her based upon prosecutorial discretion. If a suspect is holding a smoking gun when police arrest him, and the lab confirms that the bullet that pierced the body of a night watchman came from that weapon and killed him during the commission of a robbery, it is expected that a prosecutor will indict the suspect with felony murder and armed robbery, among other charges as prescribed by law. Also, it is expected that in a death penalty state, the prosecutor will seek capital punishment when legally sanctioned. What we are about to learn is that prosecutors do not always do what is expected for whatever reason, despite the fact that they are public servants bound by the rule of law and ultimately answerable to the constituents whom they serve.[17]

■ Role of Prosecutors

The previous description of prosecutors suggests that there are few single models that adequately describe every prosecutor. A prosecutor is the principal representative of the state, city, or county in all matters related to the adjudication of criminal offenses.[18] The prosecutor's office has a hand in virtually every decision made in the legal course of every case that comes before the criminal courts. There are 54 jurisdictions comprised of 50 states; the federal government; the military (beyond the scope of this book); American self-governing commonwealths, such as Puerto Rico and some American Indian tribes (also beyond the scope of this book); and the District of Columbia. Maybe there are only 53.5 jurisdictions because it is uncertain if the District of Columbia is really all that separate from the federal system in general. Typically, state prosecution is organized along county lines under the direction of an elected and autonomous prosecutor, variously designated as county attorney, district attorney, or state attorney. Rarely is he or she part of a statewide department of justice, but even state prosecutors have limited functions because cities and towns have their own prosecutors. However jurisdictions are counted, there are a number of large-scale ways of providing justice at the prosecutor's level: defining crimes; setting procedural rules; establishing responsibilities for different functions; and deciding what the functions are and who will perform those functions.[19]

Next, within most jurisdictions there are smaller units of government in charge of the day-to-day practices of providing frontline criminal justice services. Most often these smaller units are counties (they are called parishes in Louisiana, boroughs in Alaska, and geographic regions in Connecticut and Rhode Island). There are an estimated 3,033 counties plus 33 city–county combined governments, reports the National Association of Counties. What this means is that there are at least 3,066 ways of providing justice in the United States, including the way prosecutors process offenders. That means that prosecutions occur on behalf of the state or the people of the state or commonwealth. This number of 3,066 does not include prosecutions initiated by cities, towns, townships, villages, or other attorneys and the infinite number of ways those prosecutions can proceed.

One key to understanding prosecutors (other than at the US district level) is that their powers and authority are fragmented and linked somehow within a nonhierarchical system that reports to no one in particular. However, the power of the prosecutor to determine whether charges should be filed or dismissed has made the prosecutor the critical link between the state's criminal code, its judicial system, and local police agencies.[20] There are similar roles and expectations of prosecutors across the country with guidance by their respective state laws and regulations, the US Constitution and its Amendments, and jurisdictional ordinances. Some common ground among prosecutors can be seen among the prosecutor models (described next), including prosecutors' discretion and responsibilities.

■ Prosecutor Models

There are many prosecutor models worth examining; however, this section discusses district attorneys (DA) in several states. Also discussed is the attorney general's (AG) position in several cities across the United States.

District Attorney

District attorney (DA) is, in some jurisdictions, the title of the local public official who represents the government in the prosecution of criminals. The district attorney is the highest officeholder in the jurisdiction's legal department and supervises a staff of assistant district attorneys. Similar functions are carried out at the local level in other jurisdictions by officers called commonwealth's attorney, state's attorney, county attorney, or county prosecutor. Depending on the system in the particular jurisdiction, district attorneys can be appointed by the chief executive of the region or elected by the people. Because different levels of government in the United States operate independently of one another, there are many differences between individuals who perform this function at each level of government. Most states also have an attorney general who oversees specific prosecutions throughout the state and may play a role in the selection of the state attorney to represent the state.

Occasionally, a district attorney is informally referred to as the state's attorney. In large urban environments, DAs employ numerous assistant district attorneys (ADAs), many of whom are primary prosecutors and researchers, such as *Law & Order*'s ADA Jack McCoy (Sam Waterston) and ADA Casey Novak (Diane Neal) in *Law & Order: Special Victims Unit*. Care should be taken not to confuse the two. Variations are numerous and can depend upon the jurisdiction, as illustrated in the following examples:

- California: In Long Beach, the district attorney's office is a department under the authority of Los Angeles County. This office engages in the criminal prosecution of felonies (such as murder, rape, and robbery), misdemeanors, and public personnel infractions. The city prosecutor's office deals only with misdemeanors and infractions committed within the city of Long Beach. In Long Beach, the city prosecutor, not the district attorney, prosecutes all adults charged with misdemeanors or infractions. These offenses range from serious crimes—such as vehicular manslaughter, domestic abuse, drunk driving, and burglaries—to minor infractions.

- Connecticut: Although the state has an attorney general who is elected (see the next section for details), it also has a chief state's attorney who is the administrative head of the Connecticut Division of Criminal Justice, the independent agency of the executive branch of state government that is responsible for the investigation and prosecution of all criminal matters in the state. The chief state's attorney is appointed and governed by a board of commissioners (one member is the attorney general) that, in turn, appoints state's attorneys for each of the state's 13 judicial districts. "The prosecutorial power of the state shall be vested in a Chief State's Attorney and the state's attorney for each judicial district."[21]

- Florida: In Fort Lauderdale, Broward County, the office of the county attorney is appointed and governed by the Broward County Board of County Commissioners. The Broward County board provides that the county attorney shall be the chief legal counsel to the county and direct and supervise the office of the county attorney. The county attorney represents the county, the county commission, the county administrator, the department heads, all departments and divisions of the county, and all boards, committees, agencies, and authorities in all legal matters that affect the county.

- New York: The county attorney's office provides all civil legal services for the county and represents county personnel in connection with county business, which can include building and zoning issues. The board of supervisors appoints the county attorney to that position. The district attorney is the criminal prosecutor and is elected.

- Texas: In 221 counties, a county attorney is elected for a four-year term. In 33 counties, there is no county attorney, so an elected criminal district attorney performs the duties of the county attorney. Their duties vary depending on whether the county has a district attorney. If there is no district attorney, the county attorney represents the state in all civil and criminal cases in both the district and county courts. If there is a district attorney, the county attorney is responsible for cases in the courts below the level of the district attorney. The county attorney also acts as legal advisor for the county.

Attorney General

In many states, attorney generals or district attorneys and other executive-level prosecutors are elected, and their employees serve at their pleasure, that is, if the boss is not reelected, the staff could be out of work. For example, the California Department of Justice carries out the responsibilities of the attorney general through 10 main divisions. The department operates statewide with major offices in Sacramento, San Francisco, Los Angeles, Oakland, San Diego, and Fresno. In California attorney generals are elected statewide to serve as the chief law enforcement officials. It is the duty of the attorney general to see that the laws of the state are uniformly and adequately enforced. Under the state Constitution, the attorney general is elected to a four-year term in the same statewide election as the governor, lieutenant governor, controller, secretary of state, treasurer, superintendent of public instruction, and insurance commissioner. In 1990, voters imposed a two-term limit on these statewide offices.

In Connecticut, the chief state's attorney is the administrative head of the Division of Criminal Justice, the independent agency of the executive branch of state government that is responsible for the investigation and prosecution of all criminal matters in the state. The division includes the offices of the state's attorney for each of the 13 judicial districts and the office of the chief state's attorney. It is the desire of the Division of Criminal Justice to serve the public; therefore, prosecutors are public servants. The appellate bureau is the largest group of attorneys in the division; its practice is limited to the research and authorship of legal briefs and the presentation of oral arguments before the Connecticut Supreme Court and the Connecticut Appellate Court. Other specialized units investigate and prosecute corruption in government, white-collar crime, abuse of the elderly, fraud, and other high-profile crimes. The state's attorneys are responsible for the investigation and prosecution of all criminal matters within their respective judicial districts— matters from motor vehicle infractions to homicide cases.

■ Prosecutor Statistics

In the United States in 2005, an estimated 2,344 state court prosecutors' offices employed over 78,000 attorneys, investigators, and support staff. This is a 27 percent increase from 1992 and a 9 percent increase from 1996.[22] One-half of the state prosecutors' offices employed nine or fewer people and had a budget of $355,000 or less. Each year, state and local prosecutors dealt with over 2.3 million felony cases.[23] This represents approximately 95 percent of all criminal prosecutions in the country, thus most criminal prosecutions are conducted by state and local prosecutors as opposed to federal prosecutors (detailed later in the chapter).

In 2005, state court prosecutors reported facing an increasingly complex composition of cases and issues with staff and budget resources essentially unchanged since 2001.[24] The average state prosecutor's office closed 976 criminal cases during 2001, varying from an average of more than 48,000 cases in large offices, to 13,450 cases in medium-sized offices, to 1,100 cases in small offices, to about 300 cases per year in offices with a part-time prosecutor. Overall, an estimated 2.3 million cases were litigated by state court prosecutors. Generally, over 90 percent of all charged felonies end in a plea bargain, a percentage that varies across the nation.[25] A jury tried 3 percent of the felony cases, and 2 percent were bench (judge) trials.[26]

The policies and practices of these offices vary from state to state and county to county, but nearly all of them share one common trait: the chief prosecutor or district attorney is usually an elected position.[27] Two-thirds of the offices of prosecutors used DNA evidence during plea negotiations or felony trials in 2001, compared to about one-half of the offices in 1996.[28] In 2001, these state and local prosecutor offices experienced combined total budgets of over $4.6 billion, an increase of 61 percent over the preceding five years. One-fourth of the prosecutor offices reported that their district maintained an offender DNA database. Unlike their appointed federal counterparts, the local district attorneys who prosecute the vast majority of criminal cases in this country must respond to the populist demands of politics.[29] State prosecutors are elected officials, and all but three of the 50 states (Alaska, Connecticut, and New Jersey) plus the District of Columbia do not elect their local prosecutors.

■ Federal Prosecutors

Although this book emphasizes state and local prosecutors, a brief description of federal prosecutors will aid in understanding their role in the scheme of things. There are 94 federal judicial districts that employ a US attorney and assistant US attorneys who litigated over 70,000 criminal cases in 2005.[30] Also, in July 2006, 25 additional federal prosecutors were added to US–Mexico border districts, advises the US Courts Web site. United States Attorneys are appointed by the President with the advice and consent of the Senate for a four-year term. Assistant United States Attorneys are appointed by the Attorney General and may be removed by that official. The Deputy Attorney General exercises the power and authority vested in the Attorney General to take final action in matters pertaining to the employment, separation, and general administration of Assistant United States Attorneys.

Data from the US Department of Justice shows that during May 2008, 1,118 new prosecutions were referred by the FBI to federal prosecutors.[31] The largest number of prosecutions in May 2008 were for "Drugs-Drug Trafficking (as opposed to drug possession)"(11.4 percent of prosecutions; see Chapter 3 for federal drug conviction details). Prosecutions were also filed for "Bank Robbery" (10.8 percent), "Drugs-Organized Crime Task Force" (10.8 percent), "Other-Not Specified" (7.2 percent), "Withheld by Government from TRAC (Freedom of Information Act [FOIA] challenged)" (7.2 percent), "Other Criminal Prosecutions" (5.4 percent), "Fraud-Financial Institution" (5.2 percent), "Violent Crime in Indian Country" (4.5 percent), "All Other Violent Crime" (3.4 percent), "Fugitive Crimes" (3.3 percent), "Immigration" (3.3 percent), "Weapons-Operation Triggerlock Major" (2.9 percent), "Pornography-Child" (2.4 percent), and "Organized Crime-Traditional Organization" (2.2 percent).

Also, federal prosecutors are authorized by department rules and custom to reject agency recommendations for prosecution when, for whatever reason, federal prosecutors choose not to file charges against a suspect.[32] A study of federal prosecutorial discretion linked to the process of federal involvement with capital cases from 1995 to 2000 found that federally-related homicides are frequently involved with drug, gang, and organized crime investigations. "The findings make clear that no one factor likely predicts whether homicide cases are brought to the federal system[33(p3)] [in the first place]." The frequency of homicide prosecutions was dependent on how wide the window to federal involvement was opened by federal and local officials working together to solve crime. However, this openness was influenced by the perception of local authorities that there was a local crime problem with which they needed help solving and that the federal system was capable of providing that needed assistance. Similarly, federal authorities had to have the resources, capabilities, and willingness to handle these offenses.

However, unlike the *CSI Effect* that depicts federal jurisdiction over many cases, the researchers found that local authorities could not be pushed into working with federal officials or turning cases over to federal authorities (other than cases that fall under federal jurisdiction, such as those previously listed, particularly when those cases involve interstate activities).[34] Most often, criminals in the United States are prosecuted through state jurisdictions.

US attorneys can shape the demographics of federal death row when they define their prosecution priorities. For example, in one district "it was only after the focus turned to drug trafficking on the southwest border that almost every defendant, including those prosecuted in death penalty cases, was Hispanic."[35] Generally, a smaller number of federal prosecutorial *declinations* would suggest a higher quality of investigative work. Yet when it comes to the FBI and international terrorism cases, the percentage of those cases turned down by federal prosecutors "has been generally increasing and reached a peak of 87 percent year ending 2006."[36]

■ Traditional Responsibility of a Prosecutor

The traditional responsibility of an American prosecutor is highly infused through the moral judgment of the following two components, reports the Commission on Behavioral and Social Sciences and Education[37]:

- A prosecutor is to see that justice is done to those who engage in reprehensible illegal conduct by convincing the court to convict the defendant.[38]
- A prosecutor is to impose an independent judgment between arrest and prosecution by deciding which cases to prosecute.[39]

The prosecutor presents the government's case at trial and bargains over guilty pleas that could reflect the likely outcome of a trial without requiring the costs of prosecution of an actual trial. One alternative would be to have the police prosecute suspects, similar to the English system, a system that is in rapid change, as previously mentioned.

> The primary responsibility of a prosecutor is to ensure that justice is served by administrating the laws and ordinances of the jurisdiction in a fair and impartial manner, a responsibility owed to everyone, including the defendant.[40]

In terms of role definition, a prosecutor is more than an avenger and an order maintainer; a prosecutor has an equal concern about the justice system that imposes punishment. A defendant is usually represented by a defense lawyer whose sole responsibility is to his or her client. This is clearly illustrated by the rule that requires the prosecutor to turn over any evidence that might benefit a defendant at trial. If prosecutors present more and weaker cases of a given type, the ratio of conviction to prosecutions (the conviction rate) falls. If the budget of a prosecutor's office increases, he or she can choose either to prosecute more cases or to put more effort into existing cases.[41] Depending on the particular circumstances, either decision can be rational, but do prosecutors make decisions about which cases to move forward in the court system based on the knowledge that a case does not meet mythical perspectives presented through and reinforced by the media?

In Germany, when a suspect is formally accused in a judicial proceeding, the case goes to trial whether the individual pleads guilty or not guilty (in the U.S. accepted guilty pleas end the judicial process).[42] However, the Bureau of Justice Statistics reports that in Germany the percentage of cases actually indicted and convicted is similar to the U.S. for offenses examined.[43] However, the German system has a percentage of more trials, more acquittals, but fewer dismissed cases than the U.S. Recall that in the U.S., most guilty cases are obtained through the plea bargain process. This is a changing trend in that German prosecutors are being provided with increasingly more judicial discretion.

Prosecutors are more likely to face technology-related issues as they deal with DNA evidence and computer-based crimes. In 2001, two-thirds of the nation's prosecutors' offices used DNA evidence during plea negotiations or felony trials, compared to about one-half in 1996. Their offices encountered high-tech offenses, such as computer crime, credit card fraud, and identity theft. In addition, state prosecutors have the following homeland security responsibilities:

- One-fourth of prosecutors participated in a state or local homeland security task force.
- One-third of prosecutors reported that an office member attended homeland security training.

State and county prosecutors' offices litigated against a broad range of felony criminal matters that can include murder, rape, aggravated assault, armed robbery, kidnapping, and other crimes of violence such as domestic violence; many of their cases included nonfelony cases such as misdemeanors, juvenile matters, traffic violations and child support enforcement; state prosecutors also litigated against electronically-related crimes which can include the following:

- Credit card fraud
- Bank card fraud
- Identity theft
- Transmission of child pornography
- Computer forgery
- Cyberstalking
- Unauthorized access (computer hacking)

There are a number of factors that can characterize effective prosecutors, including their individual attitudes (discussed later) as they attempt to meet the responsibilities and goals of their office.

■ Meeting Goals

Prosecution programs are intended to aid prosecutors with meeting the following goals, as proposed by Marcia R. Chaiken and Jan M. Chaiken[44]:

- Conviction of the most serious applicable charge; for example, conviction for burglary rather than possession of stolen property
- Increased likelihood of incarceration of convicted offenders as opposed to probation
- Increased length of sentence; the maximum allowable sentences for specific convictions
- Increased pretrial detention; jail rather than released on one's recognizance
- Reduced time until the case is disposed

■ Attitudes of an Effective Prosecutor

Five attributes of an effective prosecutor are as follows, ranked in order[45]:

1. Credible: The prosecutor must be an achiever in and out of the courtroom; for example, the goal of a prosecutor during trial is to persuade a jury to convict a defendant through credible evidence and presentations.

2. Intelligent: The prosecutor must have common sense and street smarts and be analytical and creative. Getting a job as a prosecutor has to do with networks, and many networks are established at law school. Local government

jobs tend to favor specific law schools; for example, most City of Chicago prosecutors, public defenders, judges, and personnel in top managerial city government are DePaul University College of Law or Loyola University Chicago School of Law graduates. New York City government jobs favor New York Law School or Fordham; Boston favors Suffolk University, but the Commonwealth of Massachusetts favors Boston University School of Law graduates. Depending on the jurisdiction where a potential law graduate wants to work, it is advised to discover the law schools most often represented by the individuals in the jobs and individual desires before making a decision about which law school to attend (assuming the student has a choice).[46]

3. Diligent: Thorough preparation is absolutely critical to successful execution inside the courtroom, which depends on preparation outside the courtroom. The police usually build a case to the level of probable cause but often stop there. Prosecutors and their investigators and assistants have the burden of finding additional evidence necessary to prove the case beyond a reasonable doubt.

4. Self-sufficient: The prosecutor must work alone in an extremely stressful environment. How an issue is dealt with during jury selection affects the opening, the direct (a legal strategy), and the summation regarding the issue.

5. Compelling or convincing: Presenting a case in the courtroom is a performance like that of an actor in the theater. Being brilliant helps, but if a prosecutor has low orator (verbal) skills, the chances of presenting a case and winning are less likely.

■ Why Some Lawyers Became Prosecutors

There are many reasons lawyers became prosecutors and some of those reasons follow.

Patricia M. Froehlich, Connecticut State's Attorney (Judicial District of Windham)

Patricia M. Froehlich informs us that "[I] went to law school only because I wanted to be a prosecutor. To me, it's not just a job or a career, but a calling, a way of life. Being appointed state's attorney is the greatest professional honor I could achieve. I am proud to be a representative of the criminal justice system and to work to uphold the rights of both persons charged with crimes and those who are crime victims."[47]

Ray Larson, Fayette County Commonwealth (Lexington, Kentucky)

Ray Larson has been in his job since 1985.[48] He represents a jurisdiction with a population of 250,000. Larson's office has 17 prosecutors (six men and 11 women, of which 41 percent represent minorities), and more than 1,500 felony crimes are prosecuted annually. "I don't recruit diversity," states Larson, "I recruit people of character. Diversity is a bonus." His career began in 1972 when he was appointed city prosecutor of Paducah, Kentucky. In 1974, he became an assistant deputy attorney general and was elected to become the Fayette County Commonwealth's attorney in 1985. Larson says that he became a prosecutor because "the apple doesn't fall far from the tree." He says that his father (an Air Force officer) taught him that "everyone should be treated equally, everyone must be responsible for their behavior, and people who violate the rules suffer consequences." Prosecutors deal with those who break the rules, and prosecutors make sure those people suffer the appropriate consequences.

US Attorney Daniel A. Saunders (Los Angeles)

Nearly two decades ago, Saunders graduated from Princeton University and moved to Los Angeles with the hopes of becoming a headliner and motion picture actor.[49] He wrote a play (*The Death of William Shakespeare*), and after a brief run, the play died its own death.

"Saunders, only a bit daunted, decided that his future was not in pounding out words but rather in speaking them. He had acted at Princeton, always to good notices, and an objective glance in the mirror revealed leading-man good looks—a mop of curly black hair, chiseled jaw, and piercing eyes." Saunders reached some success, including some appearances on the network television soaps. He performed at theater clubs and later as a comedian. Saunders eventually enrolled at UC Berkeley's Boalt Hall Law School, and after graduation he landed a job as an assistant prosecutor in the US Attorney's Office. He was assigned to the Los Angeles Terrorism and Organized Crime section. However, in the summer of 2002 his reputation changed. One case that placed Saunders on the Hollywood map was the conspiracy and wire tapping case against ex-Hollywood private investigator Anthony Pellicano and Terry Christensen, the managing partner of the powerhouse entertainment law firm Christensen, Glaser, Fink, Jacobs, Weil & Shapiro.[50] Apparently, Dan Saunders finally became a headliner.

Kym L. Worthy, Wayne County (Detroit) Prosecutor

Setting goals and maintaining the discipline needed to achieve them is something Kym L. Worthy learned from her father, a retired Army colonel.[51] "My father was very rigid and very disciplined," she confides, "but he made me feel I could do anything I wanted to do." [52] She wanted to prosecute offenders and presently has a win ratio of over 90 percent for the people of Wayne County, Michigan. With her colorful business suits, multicolored painted fingernails, and long black tresses, Worthy is a college-educated "home-girl," she calls herself, and works in an ultra-conservative, white, male-dominated legal system. One of her early victories was with the convictions of two white Detroit police officers who were charged with second-degree murder in the beating death of black motorist Malice Green. The

Wayne County prosecutor's office prosecuted 64 percent of all serious felony jury trials and 40 percent of all juvenile cases in the state of Michigan.[53]

■ Similarity in Prosecutor Responsibilities

Marcia R. Chaiken and Jan M. Chaiken studied prosecutors in two jurisdictions: Los Angeles (LA) and Middlesex County, Massachusetts (MCM).[54] The study resulted in 10 findings experienced by prosecutors that were similar more often than different, despite the estimated 3,000 mile distance between the two jurisdictions, population mix and density, socioeconomic differences in the populations, lifestyle standards and expectations, laws and ordinances, weather, and urbaneness.[55] For example:

- LA and MCM prosecutors evaluated four dimensions of a defendant's criminality on a case-by-case basis:
  - Rates of committing crimes
  - Dangerousness (violence committed before, during, and after a crime)
  - Persistence (determination to overcome obstacles in committing the crime)
  - Professionalism of criminal act (planning, high gain)
- Defendants who were identified as high rate and dangerous in LA were also identified as high rate and dangerous in MCM.
- Written office guidelines concerning selection criteria for career criminals promote consistency in deputy district attorneys' judgments about the kinds of defendants who are high rate and dangerous offenders.
- Long-term, persistent offenders may or may not be high-rate and dangerous offenders. Chronic or habitual criminality should not be confused with high-rate, dangerous criminals (i.e., an offender with a criminal history is a valid indicator of persistence but bears little relationship to the type of offender the prosecution units want to target for prosecution).
- Although some existing guidelines for identifying high-rate, dangerous offenders are valid, greater accuracy means understanding state laws that can conflict with practical outcomes, and visa versa. "The study found that information used because of formal rule or state laws does help focus resources on high-rate, dangerous, and persistent offenders." The strongest official record of high-rate offending was linked to offenders' previous adult convictions, drug abuse, and currently being on pretrial release (bail or own recognizance) when they were arrested, among other variables.
- When a group of high-rate offenders was identified, the subset demonstrated similar characteristics, such as wants and warrants, crimes committed in public places against a female, and juvenile convictions for robbery (armed or unarmed).

- Characteristics that are not typically linked to high-rate offenders but are perceived to be indicators include display or use of guns, alcoholism, prior arrests, adult convictions, probation or parole revocation, or previous incarcerations. These factors were not dependable indicators of high-rate dangerousness or persistence.
- Some factors may preclude the selection and priority prosecution of defendants who are in fact dangerous, such as an instant charge for a crime that carries a light penalty, constraints on resources, constraints on forensic resources, and backlogs.
- The most criminally active defendants in MCM and in LA commit crimes at essentially the same frequency (i.e., 30 percent of most active defendants in both jurisdictions who committed burglary, forgery, fraud, and drug dealing continued to commit these crimes at essentially the same rates, but car theft was an exception in LA—four times as many cars were stolen in LA compared to Middlesex).

A recommendation that emerged from Marcia R. Chaiken and Jan M. Chaiken's study is that "prosecutors planning priority prosecution programs should target dangerous offenders who commit crimes at high rates."[56] Dangerous offenders can be identified more accurately than nondangerous, high-rate offenders. Prosecutors should prepare a checklist that flags cases, and jurisdictional policies should allow prosecutors discretion in making decisions about which offenders to indict and the extent of the resources to be employed, the researchers add.

A Broad Perspective of Prosecutors' Work and Failures

There are numerous descriptions of the job prosecutors perform and numerous reasons why some of them fail. Following are some of those descriptions and reasons for failure.

Lisa Madigan of the Office of the Illinois Attorney General

To provide a perspective about the workload at an attorney general's office, the following information about the Office of the Illinois Attorney General was provided by Illinois Attorney General Lisa Madigan in 2007[57]:

- Received 32,577 complaints from constituents to prosecute
- Collected $841,873,553.23 on behalf of the State of Illinois
- Successfully mediated 2,000 healthcare coverage complaints for consumers
- Assisted in the prosecution of more than 234 criminal cases
- Regulated more than 28,000 charities that operate in Illinois
- Analyzed and recommended an estimated 4,804 compensation claims be awarded to victims of violent crimes
- Handled more than 120 environmental protection cases

- Represented state government in over 23,000 cases
- Received more than 16,000 case referrals from state government agencies and constitutional officers

Cono Caranna, Chief Prosecutor in Hancock, Harrison, and Stone Counties, Mississippi

Cono Caranna is the elected chief prosecutor in three Mississippi counties. The prosecutor's office handled 2,193 cases in 2006; seven were prosecuted before a jury, and 950 were resolved through a plea bargaining process.[58] Caranna's ADA Sean Tindell helped prosecute nearly 20 cases in the district attorney's office. The remainder of the cases (1,216) were dropped or are still pending, it can be assumed from all available information.

San Francisco Prosecutor's Office

San Francisco's prosecutors convicted less than one-third of all adult felony suspects arrested in the city in 2001, according to the most recently available California Department of Justice statistics. The prosecutors' office disputes the accuracy of the justice department's statistics and says that factors beyond its control—such as the city's liberal jury pool and sloppy police work—contributed to the comparatively low rate of felony convictions in San Francisco, reports Bill Wallace of the *San Francisco Chronicle*.[59] The city prosecutor said that he was elected, in part, because of his commitment to employing rehabilitative justice initiatives that divert narcotics and other nonviolent crime offenders into programs aimed at breaking cycles of recidivism as alternatives to incarceration. San Francisco prosecutors obtained convictions against 29 percent of all adult felony suspects in 2001. Statewide in 2001, prosecutors convicted 68 percent of all felony cases. Apparently, different prosecutors possess different judicial styles of prosecuting suspects, resulting in different performance levels, including indictment and conviction rates.

Prosecutor Commits Suicide

Michael F. Burns, chief of the criminal division of the Rhode Island attorney general's office, committed suicide.[60] His body was discovered in a wooded area across the street from his house in Johnston, Rhode Island. Burns had been dogged in the past year by accusations of prosecutorial misconduct, resulting from the dismissal of a sweeping corruption case against a former governor of the state. He was also the overseer of a narcotics strike force that became the target of a federal investigation. Before his death, Burns complained to friends about various professional and personal setbacks that had bedeviled him since his promotion to chief of the criminal division, including embarrassing publicity over a domestic abuse complaint by the woman who was then his wife.

O. J. Simpson's Prosecutor

Marcia Clark painstakingly recounted the trial proceedings from jury selection to final summation and concluded that nothing could have saved her case, given the prominent role of race in the defense's strategy and the hostile jury who heard it. In Clark's opinion, the mountain of evidence should have convicted Simpson many times over. Clark says, "But it didn't because of a judicial system wracked by race and overly impressed by a celebrity."[61] One implication arising from Clark's book about the case was that the media played a vital role in the outcome of O. J. Simpson's case. She admits to some mistakes; one of those mistakes was a false sense of complacency about the competence of the criminalist, Dennis Fung, who was assigned to the case, rather than following her thoughts about replacing him. Clark neglected to mention that racism does play a role in officers' responses to suspects, and one of the results of Simpson's trial led to a priority on training officers about due process practices, which can be considered a positive result from the trial.

Margita Dornay, King County Prosecutor

Margita Dornay, a King County prosecutor in Seattle, Washington, was a seasoned domestic violence prosecutor until she fell victim to domestic violence herself.[62] During a rough patch in her marriage, she became interested in a King County sheriff's deputy, David Hick. Dornay was the daughter of a police officer and admired officers, referring to them as "good guys." Starting in spring 2001, Hick and Dornay began a relationship that seemingly spun out of control. Dornay said that Hick warned her that she was in danger in their relationship. "He alluded to having Mafia connections, talked about doing hits," Dornay reported. Hick was increasingly monitoring her movements. For example, Hick told Dornay the shade of nail polish she should use. When Dornay tried to end the relationship, Hick threatened to commit suicide. One time he forced her hand onto his gun, aimed it at his head, and screamed at her to pull the trigger. Dornay implies that she finally learned, despite all her trial experience and dealings with criminals that she was really inexperienced about how things worked until she ended her relationship with Hick.

Nicholas L. Bissell, Jr., Somerset County Prosecutor

The late Nicholas L. Bissell, Jr., former prosecutor of Somerset County, New York, was convicted in 1996 of tax fraud, embezzling, and abuse of power. He had prompted calls for a statewide code of ethics for prosecutors.[63]

In Response to Prosecutor Failures

The previous discussions illustrate that prosecutors are human beings with their own problems and shortcomings. However, many of the problems of the office are antecedent to a lawyer considering a prosecutor's job. For example, Newman Flanagan, the executive director of the National District Attorneys Association, says that in "hundreds of communities throughout the United States, local prosecutors—the people's attorneys—cannot afford to hire or retain top quality assistants. The cost of getting married, having a family, or buying a home is almost impossible when they are saddled with the debt of their law school education."[64]

Consistent with Flanagan's thoughts, and despite overall increases in budgets, about one-third of all prosecutors' offices, particularly those serving a district with a population over 250,000, reported to the Bureau of Justice Statistics that they had problems recruiting and retaining enough staff attorneys, largely because of low salaries. One implication is that the brightest and best young men and women who graduate from law school cannot economically pursue a prosecutor's job because they require higher salaries to make student loan payments and to afford suitable lifestyles after the life of a university student; it could be reasoned that lower-level graduates from law school apply for prosecutors jobs. For example, the average salary for state and local attorneys, which includes prosecutors, is $62,398, compared to $75,677 for private-practice attorneys.

For example, the city of Phoenix, Arizona advertised the following:

Prosecutor Supervisor Wanted: job description includes to supervise the prosecution of cases filed in the Phoenix Municipal Court within the jurisdiction of the Office of the City Attorney, which includes all violations of the City Charter, City ordinances, and Arizona statutes which are within the original or concurrent jurisdiction of the Phoenix Municipal Court. Work is performed under the direction of the City Attorney within the limits of general policies of the City and established standards and practices of the legal profession. Supervision is exercised over all professional and administrative support staff members of the Criminal Division.

Some of the essential functions of this job include:

- Plans, organizes, directs, implements, and seeks alternative approaches to prosecution activities as well as administrative functions
- Reviews legislation affecting criminal prosecution
- Works with police department to coordinate efforts and provide training;
- Trains new attorneys through key subordinates
- Reviews reports received from supervising attorneys and follows up on unusual or critical items
- Prepares standards and procedures for and coordinates work of professional and administrative support staff

Some of the required knowledge, skills, and abilities of this position include: Knowledge of:

- City codes and state statutes, with emphasis on criminal law
- Judicial procedures and rules of evidence
- Principles of criminal law and appeal procedures related to violations of municipal ordinances and state statutes

Ability to:

- Analyze, appraise, and organize facts, evidence, and precedents and present them in oral and written reports
- Work cooperatively with other employees, customers, clients, and the public

Some the additional requirements of this position include:

- Performance of other essential and marginal functions, depending upon work location, assignment, or shift
- Admission to the State Bar of Arizona

The position calls for at least 4 years of experience as a practicing criminal attorney, including two years of substantial involvement in the management process and policy making function of a law office (or two years at the Assistant City Attorney III level), and graduation from an accredited school of law.[65]

In August 2008, one western state advertised for a prosecutor with experience to manage a state office with a pay range of $50,000 to $55,000. Another state also in August 2008 sought a deputy prosecutor with experience with a starting salary of $39,000.

The implications of low salaries can lead to the assumption that many cases reaching a prosecutor's office are not necessarily processed in a judicial manner, resulting in incompetent or inconsistent processes and wrongful convictions (the topic of Chapter 8). At other times, prosecutors make decisions founded upon cultural or popular expectations rather than truth. For example, increasingly, state and federal hate crime policies include the status category of gender. One study assessed the knowledge of prosecutors about gender-bias hate crimes and their willingness to charge violence against female victims as hate crimes.[66] The surveyed prosecutors revealed that generally they attribute violence against women to motivations of power and control rather than hate. They thought that hate crime prosecutions were problematic, especially with female victims.

■ Ethics of Prosecutors

The legal battle to develop and enforce ethics and rules for prosecutors is unlikely to occur despite all the rhetoric from the National Center for Prosecution Ethics created in 2001 by the National College of District Attorneys (NCDA).[67] The NCDA is dedicated to the promotion of the highest ethical standards for prosecutors; for example, Mathias (Mat) H. Heck, Jr., president of the National District Attorneys Association (NDAA), says that:

> The actions of the district attorney (DA) in the Durham rape case are an anomaly and inexcusable. The false accusations of rape by members of the Duke Lacrosse team were abhorrent, dishonest, and self-serving, and fly in the face of the ethical conduct that prosecutors not only accept and endorse, but adhere to. We are deeply sorry for the pain this has caused them and their families. He misled the defendants, their attorneys,

the public, the media, and the residents of the community he serves. Mr. Nifong's actions and intentional prosecutorial misconduct have cast a shadow on America's approximately 30,000 prosecutors who daily strive to adhere to strict ethical standards in their search for truth and justice for victims of crimes and their families.[68]

How many other prosecutors have performed similar to Nifong is a question yet to be answered.

Model Rules of Professional Conduct

The American Bar Association (ABA) offers a model of professional conduct for lawyers which includes prosecutors; following are some of those highlights of the ABA's ethical expectations:

In a criminal case a prosecutor should not indict a suspect without probable cause; a prosecutor should protect the rights of a suspect to obtain counsel in a timely fashion; a prosecutor should not allow a waiver of important pretrial rights such as a preliminary hearing until a suspect is represented by counsel; a prosecutor should make timely disclosures to the defense of all evidence or information obtained through investigations and other sources; a prosecutor should refrain from making extrajudicial comments that can heighten public condemnation of the accused and exercise reasonable care to prevent others involved with the prosecution (for example, investigators and clerks) from making any extrajudicial statement that the prosecutor would be prohibited from making.[69]

Rules of Conduct for a District Attorney

To add to the preceding thoughts concerning the conduct of a prosecutor, a district attorney[70] reports that in *Berger v. United States*,[71] the seminal case defined the prosecutor's legal and ethical role as a minister of justice. The Supreme Court implied that the prosecutor's duty to serve justice includes the avoidance of conduct that deliberately corrupts the truth-finding process. The prosecutor's conduct, both in presenting evidence and argument to the jury, was characterized by the court as an "evil influence" that was "calculated to mislead the jury." The misconduct during the evidence phase included misstating facts during cross-examination; falsely insinuating that witnesses said things they had not said; representing that witnesses made statements to him personally out of court when no proof of this was offered; pretending that a witness had said something that he had not said and persistently cross-examining him on that basis; and assuming prejudicial facts that were not in evidence. The prosecutor's closing argument contained remarks that were "intemperate," "undignified," and "misleading," including assertions of personal knowledge, allusions to unused incriminating evidence, and ridiculing of the defense counsel.

Despite *Berger v. United States*, the rules of conduct promoted by the ABA and the ideas of the NDAA, and 50 state bar associations, rigorous rules and standards that govern the actions of prosecutors appear to be pervasive. However, if, at the very heart of his or her performance, a prosecutor contradicts all the rules of conduct, then it can be wondered exactly how ethical the profession might be in the first place. For example, the lecture is an ancient device that prosecutors use to coach their clients so that a victim who testifies at trial will not quite know that he or she has been coached, and the prosecutor can preserve the face-saving illusion that he or she has not done any coaching. Coaching victims, or clients for that matter, like robbing them, is not only frowned upon, it is downright unethical.[72] Linking this to television dramas, especially in 393 episodes of *Law & Order*, a quick review of Executive ADA Jack McCoy's directives to his numerous assistants over the years—Jill Hennessy as ADA Claire Kincaid; Carey Lowell as ADA Jamie Ross; Angie Harmon as ADA Abbie Carmichael; Elisabeth Rohm as ADA Serena Southerlyn; Annie Parisse as ADA Alexandra Borgia; Richard Brooks as ADA Paul Robinette (the only male); and Alana De La Garza as ADA Connie Rubirosa—amounted to the words "prep 'em" instead of "book 'em, Dano." McCoy directed his assistants to prompt the state's victims and witnesses for trial. New York City Medical Examiner Dr. Elizabeth Rodgers (Leslie Hendrix) was crossed-examined on the witness stand and later told McCoy that she was wrong about information she presented at trial regarding the contents of a book. McCoy knew that this new information could cast a light on acquittal for the defendant; nonetheless, his assistant used the information in the case during closing arguments, resulting in a murder conviction.

■ Prosecutors Are Immune from Civil Lawsuits

In *Imbler v. Pachtman* (District Attorney USC 424, 1976),[73] the petitioner, who was convicted of murder, unsuccessfully petitioned for state habeas corpus on the basis of the respondent's prosecuting attorney's revelation of newly discovered evidence and charged that the respondent had knowingly used false testimony and suppressed material evidence at the petitioner's trial. The petitioner thereafter filed a federal habeas corpus petition based on the same allegations and ultimately obtained his release. He then brought an action against the respondent and others under 42 U.S.C. § 1983 (litigation that plagues many police practices), seeking damages for loss of liberty allegedly caused by unlawful prosecution, but the district court held that the respondent was immune from liability under § 1983, and the court of appeals affirmed. A state prosecuting attorney who, as in this example, acted within the scope of his or her duties in initiating and pursuing a criminal prosecution and in presenting the State's case is absolutely immune from a civil suit for damages under § 1983 for alleged deprivations of the constitutional rights of the accused.

US Supreme Court Justice Jackson noted in 1940 that "the prosecutor has more control over life, liberty, and reputation than any other person in America."[74] The reality is that nearly all of the decisions to prosecute or not to prosecute, nearly all the influences toward release or offering a plea or trial, and, in fact, more than nine-tenths of local prosecutions are supervised or reviewed by no one except for an occasional case that may be publicized.[75] In part, researchers explain why so many individuals are freed after an arrest and why police investigative personnel refrain from forensic participation with their cases (as discussed in Chapter 6).

Because prosecutors suffer no personal or professional penalty for participating in framing people, there is no downside for them. The US Supreme Court, for example, granted prosecutors absolute immunity from civil liability when exercising their prosecutorial functions in *Imbler v. Pachtman* (424 U.S. 409, 1976). Likewise, they face no criminal responsibility for their actions because history has shown that with very rare exceptions, prosecutors do not prosecute fellow prosecutors. This can mean that a prosecutor can withhold evidence tending to show that someone who is accused of murder is innocent, and if it is brought to light after the person is convicted, sentenced, and executed that the information was withheld, the prosecutor does not have to worry about being criminally charged.[76] Prosecutors are also protected from prosecution when they leak secret grand jury testimony to the news media. There is a small ray of light within this otherwise bleak scenario concerning prosecutorial discretion, which is the Citizen Protection Act of 1998 (28 USC 530B). It makes federal attorneys subject to the state bar ethics, rules, and disciplinary proceedings that apply to all other lawyers in the state where they are located. However, because bar associations loathe to discipline private attorneys who lack the political pull of a US attorney, the protection provided by the Citizen Protection Act is more symbolic than real.

Prosecutors are well aware of their privileged position, and they are opposed to being constrained from exercising their power in any way. The US Department of Justice, for example, vigorously lobbied against the minimal restraints imposed on its behavior by the Citizen Protection Act. A congressional aide explained this by remarking that US attorneys "get hysterical about being subjected to external ethical standards. They don't want to have to live by rules."[77]

■ Summary

A prosecutor is one of the most critical building blocks upon which democracy has developed because violent crimes are crimes against the people; thus, a prosecutor's job is to administer justice. This means that prosecutors make choices about which offenders, what crimes, and what criminals receive attention and resources.

Four hundred years ago, a system of private prosecution dominated England. Public prosecutors did not exist. In the beginning, criminal procedure in the American colonies followed the English practice. There was an attorney general (AG) in each colony. Similar to their English counterparts, the American AG represented the Crown but left criminal prosecution to the victim. However, private prosecution is unsuited to a democratic process. Today, prosecutors are licensed government lawyers who initiate legal action and possess the authority to investigate, indict, and prosecute violators in both criminal and misdemeanor matters.

Prosecutors initiate a legal case, and depending on the jurisdiction, their duties can include administrative, appellate, civil, criminal, and victim witness duties. A prosecutor is the principal representative of the state, city, or county in all matters of adjudication of criminal offenses.

The district attorney (DA) is the highest officeholder in the jurisdiction's legal department and supervises a staff of assistant district attorneys. In many states, attorney generals or DAs and other executive-level prosecutors are elected, and their employees serve at their pleasure. In the United States, an estimated 2,341 state court prosecutors' offices employ over 78,000 attorneys, investigators, and support staff who annually try 2.3 million felony cases. At the federal level, there are 94 federal judicial districts that employ a US attorney and assistant US attorneys who annually litigate over 70,000 criminal caseloads. Recently, 25 additional federal prosecutors were added to US–Mexico border districts.

The primary responsibility of a prosecutor is to ensure that justice is served by administrating laws and ordinances of the jurisdiction in a fair and impartial manner, even on behalf of the defendant. Rank-ordered attitudes of an effective prosecutor can include credibility, intelligence, diligence, self-sufficiency, and being convincing.

The American Bar Association (ABA) provides rules of conduct that include refraining from prosecuting a charge that the prosecutor knows is not supported by probable cause and making reasonable efforts to ensure that the accused has been advised of the right to, and the procedure for, obtaining counsel and has been given reasonable opportunity to obtain that counsel. However, a prosecutor who has acted within the scope of his or her duties in initiating and pursuing a criminal prosecution is absolutely immune from a civil suit for damages for alleged deprivations of the constitutional rights of the accused. Because prosecutors suffer no personal or professional penalty for participating in wrongful convictions, there is no downside to making an error.

■ References

1. McCulloch, R. P. (2008). *What do prosecutors do?* Retrieved March 20, 2009, from http://communities.justicetalking.org/blogs/day17/archive/2007/02/13/what-do-prosecutors-do.aspx

2. National District Attorneys Association. Strengthening forensic science in the United States: A path forward. Retrieved August 24, 2009, from http://www.wininteractive.com/NDAA/NAS.html

3. This statement was made by the prosecutor (Amy Carlson) on *Criminal Minds*, Season 3, Episode 19, "Tabula Rasa," which aired on May 14, 2008. After a suspected serial killer wakes up from a coma, the BAU reopens the case and uses brain fingerprinting to determine if the suspect really doesn't remember the crimes he could have committed four years earlier. Brain fingerprinting is a controversial technique that is advocated as a way to identify a terrorist or other dangerous person by measuring the brainprint of that person when he or she is shown a particular body of writing or an image that was previously familiar (such as of a training

camp or manual). The brainprint is based on the P300 complex, a series of well-known brain wave components that can be measured. The technique is said to be more accurate than a lie detector test. The inventor of the technique, Dr. Lawrence Farwell, has used the technique in at least one court case to determine the innocence of a man convicted of murder and the guilt of his accuser. Farwell showed each person pictures of the crime scene and measured their brain wave responses to determine which person had seen the crime scene before. Claiming that the test is 99.99 percent infallible, Farwell's test convinced the court to free the convicted person. The real perpetrator pleaded guilty.

4. Horton, S. (2007, September 8). The federal prosecutor: A calling betrayed. *Harpers.* Retrieved November 19, 2008, from http://www.harpers.org/archive/2007/09/hbc-90001135

5. Chaiken, M. R., & Chaiken, J. M. (2000). Priority prosecution of high rate dangerous offenders. In B. W. Hancock & P. M. Sharp (Eds.), *Criminal justice in America* (2nd ed.). Upper Saddle River, NJ: Prentice Hall.

6. Horton, "The Federal Prosecutor."

7. Spohn, C., Beichner, D., & Davis-Frenzel, E. (2001). Prosecutorial justifications for sexual assault case rejection: Guarding the gateway to justice. *Social Problems, 48*(2), 206–235.

8. Delsohn, G. (2003). *Prosecutors: A year in the life of a district attorney's office.* New York: Dutton.

9. Davis, A. J. (2007). *Arbitrary justice: The power of the American prosecutor.* New York: Oxford.

10. McCarty, D., & Feeley, J. (2008). Nifong, Duke lacrosse prosecutor, files bankruptcy (update 3). *Bloomberg.* Retrieved September 17, 2008, from http://www.bloomberg.com/apps/news?pid=20601079&refer=home&sid=aCZsc7aJFP5k

11. Ball, J. D. (2006). Is it a prosecutor's world? Determinants of count bargaining decisions. *Journal of Contemporary Criminal Justice, 22*(3), 241–260.

12. Goldstein, A. S. (2002, July). Prosecution: History of the public prosecutor. *Crime and Violence Encyclopedia.* Retrieved November 19, 2008, from http://law.jrank.org/pages/1863/Prosecution-History-Public-Prosecutor.html

13. Dammer, H. R., & Fairchild, E. (2006). *Comparative criminal justice systems* (3rd ed.). Belmont, CA: Wadsworth Thomson.

14. Lectric Law Library. (n.d.). *Prosecutor.* Retrieved November 19, 2008, from http://www.lectlaw.com/def2/p101.htm

15. Nevada Legislature. (n.d.). *NRS 622A.070 "Prosecutor" defined.* Retrieved August 23, 2008, from http://www.leg.state.nv.us/NRs/NRS-622A.html#NRS622ASec010

16. Trumbull County Prosecutor's Office. (n.d.). Administrative Division. Retrieved August 26, 2009, from http://www.prosecutor.co.trumbull.oh.us/pr_admin.htm

17. Heymann, P., & Petrie, C. (2001). *What's changing in prosecution? Report of a workshop.* Washington, DC: National Research Council.

18. Mister District Attorney. (2004, October 12). *So, what do prosecutors do, anyway?* Retrieved November 18, 2008, from http://misterda.blogspot.com/2004/10/so-what-do-prosecutors-do-anyway.html

19. Mister District Attorney, *So, What Do Prosecutors Do, Anyway?*

20. Goldstein, "Prosecution: History of the Public Prosecutor."

21. Article XXIII Connecticut Constitution. Adopted November 28, 1984.

22. Bureau of Justice Statistics. (2005). *Prosecution statistics.* Washington, DC: US Department of Justice. Retrieved June 26, 2009, from http://www.ojp.usdoj.gov/bjs/pros.htm

23. This is the total number of cases closed by local prosecutors in 2001; the case may have been closed without an indictment, or it may have proceeded all the way to a jury verdict. Id. at 6. Local prosecutors also handle over seven million misdemeanor cases each year.

24. Bureau of Justice Statistics. (2006). *Prosecutors in state courts in 2005.* Washington, DC: US Department of Justice. Retrieved August 31, 2008, from http://www.ojp.usdoj.gov/bjs/pub/pdf/psc05.pdf

25. Bureau of Justice Statistics. (2005). *Criminal case processing statistics.* Washington, DC: US Department of Justice. Retrieved August 31, 2008, from http://www.ojp.usdoj.gov/bjs/cases.htm

26. Bureau of Justice Statistics. (2004). *Sourcebook of criminal justice statistics 2003. Table 5.9.* Albany, NY: US Department of Justice. Retrieved November 18, 2008, from http://www.albany.edu/sourcebook/pdf/t546.pdf

27. ODeFrances, C. J. (2002). *Prosecutors in state courts, 2001* (NCJ 193441). Washington, DC: US Department of Justice, Bureau of Justice Statistics. Retrieved June 27, 2009, from http://www.ojp.usdoj.gov/bjs/pub/pdf/psc01.pdf>

28. DeFrances, C. J. *Prosecutors in state courts, 2001* (NCJ 193441).

29. DeFrances, C. J. *Prosecutors in state courts, 2001* (NCJ 193441).

30. US Courts (2006). *The federal judiciary.* Washington, DC: US Department of Justice. Retrieved November 18, 2008, from http://www.uscourts.gov/caseload2005/front/mar05toc.pdf

31. TRAC Reports. (n.d.). *Prosecutions for May 2008.* Retrieved September 1, 2008, from http://trac.syr.edu/tracreports/bulletins/jfbi/monthlymay08/fil/

32. TRAC Reports. (n.d.). *National profile and enforcement trends over time.* Retrieved September 1, 2008, from http://trac.syr.edu/tracfbi/newfindings/current/

33. Newton, P. J., Johnson, C. M., & Mulcahy, T. M. (n.d.). *Investigation and prosecution of homicide cases in the United States, 1995–2000: The process for federal involvement.* Retrieved November 16, 2008, from http://www.icpsr.umich.edu/cocoon/NACJD/STUDY/04540.xml

34. Newton, et al., *Investigation and Prosecution of Homicide Cases.*

35. Newton, et al., *Investigation and Prosecution of Homicide Cases.*

36. TRAC Reports. *National Profile and Enforcement Trends.*

37. Commission on Behavioral and Social Sciences and Education. (2001). *What's changing in prosecution?* Retrieved June 26, 2009, from http://books.nap.edu/catalog.php?record_id=10114#orgs

38. Raghav, M., Ramseyer, J. M., & Rasmusen, E. (2005, September). *Prosecutors' choices of prosecution and conviction rates: Theory and evidence.* Retrieved November 18, 2008, from http://www.law.northwestern.edu/news/fall05/MLEA/EricRasmussenandRaghav-Prosecutors.pdf

39. Rasmusen, E., Raghav, M., & Ramseyer, M. (2008). *Convictions versus conviction rates: The prosecutor's choice.* June 26, 2009, from http://www.rasmusen.org/papers/prosecutors-raghav-ramseyer-rasmusen.pdf

40. Bugliosi. J. (2000). *The art of prosecution: Trial advocacy fundamentals from case preparation through summation,* Fleshing, NY: Looseleaf Law Publishers.

41. Raghav, et al., *Prosecutors' Choices of Prosecution and Conviction Rates.*

42. Dammer & Fairchild, *Comparative Criminal Justice Systems.*

43. Bureau of Justice Statistics. (1998). *German and American prosecutions: An approach to a statistical comparison.* Washington, DC: US Department of Justice. Retrieved August 31, 2008, from http://www.ojp.usdoj.gov/bjs/abstract/gap.htm

44. Chaiken & Chaiken, "Priority Prosecution of High Rate Dangerous Offenders."

45. Bugliosi, *The Art of Prosecution: Trial Advocacy Fundamentals from Case Preparation through Summation.*

46. This information was developed by the author in his role of adviser of university students who wanted to pursue law school.

47. State of Connecticut Division of Criminal Justice. (n.d.). *Patricia M. Froehlich, Connecticut State's Attorney (Judicial District of Windham).* Employment/Career Opportunities. Retrieved June 26, 2009, from http://www.ct.gov/csao/cwp/view.asp?a=1797&q=305518&csaoNav=|

48. Larson, R. (2007). *In profile.* National District Attorney Association: Retrieved June 26, 2009, from http://www.ndaa.org/ndaa/profile/ray_larson_may_june_2003.html

49. Finke, N. (2006, May 6). *Pellicano prosecutor: Hollywood wannabe*! Retrieved October 10, 2007, from http://www.deadlinehollywooddaily.com/pellicano-prosecutor-hollywood-wannabe/

50. Finke, N. (2008, August 28). *15 WGA writers incubating TV pilots on Internet.* Retrieved June 26, 2009, from http://www.deadlinehollywooddaily.com/

51. Worthy, K. L. (2009). *Wayne County Prosecutor's Office.* Retrieved June 26, 2009, from http://www.waynecounty.com/mygovt/Prosecutor/default.aspx

52. BNET. (1993). *Detroit's dramatic prosecutor—Kym Worthy, lawyer in Malice Green police brutality case.* Retrieved November 18, 2008, from http://findarticles.com/p/articles/mi_m1077/is_n2_v49/ai_14680137

53. Worthy was one of the prosecutors who included a letter with her returned questionnaire. See Chapter 10 and Appendix 1 for more details.

54. Chaiken & Chaiken, "Priority Prosecution of High Rate Dangerous Offenders."

55. This author is responsible for any errors in the descriptions of the two jurisdictions because they were compiled by this author to help in understanding the two jurisdictions.

56. Chaiken & Chaiken, "Priority Prosecution of High Rate Dangerous Offenders."

57. Lisa Madigan About Us. Retrieved August 26, 2009, from http://www.illinoisattorneygeneral. gov/about/index.html

58. LaFontaine, R. (2007, October 25). District attorney candidates clash on statistics. *Sun Herald Newspaper,* p. 4.

59. Wallace, B. (2003, October 17). San Francisco ranks last in convictions: State figures show relatively low rate for D.A.'s office. *San Francisco Chronicle.* Retrieved November 18, 2008, from http://www.sfgate.com/

60. Malinowski, W. Z., Stanton, M., & Breton, T. (1997, November 25). Top criminal prosecutor takes his own life. *Providence Journal.* Retrieved November 18, 2008, from http://www.projo.com/words/burns.htm

61. Clark, M., & Carpenter, T. (1998). *Without a doubt*. New York: Penguin.

62. Teichroeb, R. (2003, July 24). Tables turn: Prosecutor says she became a victim. *Seattle Post Reporter*. Retrieved September 1, 2008, from http://seattlepi.nwsource.com/local/132082_dv-dornay24.html

63. Newman, A. (1997, February 10). Setting ethics for prosecutors. *New York Times*. Retrieved June 26, 2009, from http://www.nytimes.com/1997/02/10/nyregion/setting-ethics-for-prosecutors.html

64. National District Attorneys Association. (2007). *Message from the executive director, Newman Flanagan*. Retrieved September 1, 2008, from http://ndaa.org/ndaa/about/executive_director_message_mar_april_2003.html

65. City of Phoenix, Arizona. *Job Description*. (2009). Retrieved June, 25, 2009, from http://phoenix.gov/JOBSPECS/10170.html

66. McPhail, B. A., & Dinitto, D. M. (2005). Prosecutorial perspectives on gender-bias hate crimes. *Violence Against Women, 11*(9), 1162–1185.

67. National Center for Prosecution Ethics. Retrieved August 26, 2009, from http://www.ethicsforprosecutors.com/

68. National Center for Prosecution Ethics. (2007, June 17). *Press releases: There is not an epidemic of rogue prosecutors in America*. Retrieved November 19, 2008, from http://www.ethicsforprosecutors.com/press_releases_3.html

69. American Bar Association. (2007). *Model rules of professional conduct*. Retrieved September 1, 2008, from http://www.abanet.org/cpr/mrpc/mrpc_toc.html

70. Gershman, B. L. (2001). Prosecutor's duty to truth. *The Journal of Legal Ethics*. Retrieved September 1, 2008, from http://findarticles.com/p/articles/mi_qa3975/is_200101/ai_n8949921

71. Berger v. United States, 295 U.S. 78 (1935).

72. Posey, A. J., & Wrightsman, L. S. (2005). *Trial consulting*. New York: Oxford.

73. Imbler v. Pachtman, District Attorney 74-5435; USC 424 U.S. 409, 96 S. CT. 984. March 1976.

74. Davis, K. C. (1969). *Discretionary justice: A preliminary inquiry*. Chicago: University of Illinois Press.

75. Gordon, S. C., & Huber, G. A. (2002). Citizen oversight and the electoral incentives of criminal prosecutors. *The American Journal of Political Science, 46*, 334–351.

76. Yost, P. (1999, September 14). Court order to prosecute Starr overturned. *Seattle Post-Intelligencer*, p. A4.

77. Kaminer, W. (2002). Games prosecutors play. *The American Prospect, September/October*(46), 26.

Wrongful Convictions

You can only protect your liberties in this world by protecting the other man's freedom. You can only be free if I am free.

Clarence Darrow

▶ ▶ CHAPTER OBJECTIVES

- Identify the consequences of resources and energies engaged to control stereotypes produced through the wars on crime, junkies, sex offenders, poverty, and immigrants
- Articulate the difficulties of determining the wrongful conviction rates
- Describe the role of public defenders
- Characterize the causes of wrongful convictions
- Identify scientific fraud and incompetence at crime labs
- Clarify an interrogator's role as it is linked to confessions
- Articulate prosecutor misconduct associated with wrongful convictions

■ Introduction

Previous chapters in this book described the popular media's success of the *CSI Effect*, which helps define crime, describes the perpetrator of those crimes, and provides initiatives to apprehend perpetrators. This scenario isn't necessarily a bad thing, but specific populations are targeted through the wars on crime, junkies, sex offenders, poverty, and immigrants. Consequently, public resources and energies are engaged to control stereotypes while the following situations occur:

- Real violators operate under the radar of justice and continue to viciously attack others without consequence (see Chapter 4, War on Sex Offenders).[1,2]
- A false sense of security is felt by the public whereby some people now choose inattentive lifestyles (research shows a strong relationship between inattentive or careless lifestyles and victimization).[3]
- Corruption among criminal justice practitioners, policymakers, and the public is glorified in their pursuit of justice.[4,5]
- Pathways to wrongful convictions and executions are more likely (see Chapter 9).
- Wrongful convictions ruin the lives of innocent men and women, destroy families and friends, and require complex psychological and sociological adjustments if and when the innocent person is released from prison.[6]
- Public resources pay for the original apprehension and judicial process, the false imprisonment, and release procedures.[7]
- Public resources often pay hundreds of millions of dollars in legal settlements to wrongfully convicted individuals (if they haven't been murdered in prison or executed) or their survivors.[8]
- About 4 in 10 wrongfully convicted persons receive little, if anything, for the years they were incarcerated, including after-the-fact medical or mental health care for issues resulting from confinement, such as HIV, TB, or any other condition.[9–11]
- A single wrongful conviction has the potential to destroy the spirit of the democratic system, as implied by Clarence Darrow's observation at the beginning of this chapter: everyone's freedom is connected.

This chapter will examine wrongful convictions and their causes. The reader is cautioned that there is an enormous amount of information available in the press and the literature on each topic addressed in this chapter, and there was a serious attempt to weed-out unreliable sources. However, sometimes invalidated information appears to be objective because of its source (see Supreme Court Judge Antonin Scalia's statistics below). Recall from Chapter 1 and Chapter 5 that history is written largely by those in power—the privileged, which includes interest groups, in this case the Innocence Project (of several states), the Just Science organizations, and RAND. Their perspectives can lack reliable data, producing a flawed inference about reality. A challenge of invalid materials is often perceived as a challenge of the source of the invalid materials or knowledge such as experienced by Galileo (1564–1642), who revolutionized astronomy and paved the way for the acceptance of new knowledge, but his advocacy of that knowledge eventually resulted in an Inquisition process against him.

Let's start by asking, how many wrongful convictions occur in America?

■ Error Rate and Wrongful Convictions

One issue before accepting an error rate associated with wrongful convictions is that there is no accepted standard or method to calculate the rate at which defendants have been wrongfully convicted. Those who attempt to make such a calculation differ widely in their results, argues a Mid-Atlantic Innocence Project executive. For instance, US Supreme Court Justice Antonin Scalia, concurring in *Kansas v. Marsh* (June 29, 2006), said that "the error [in the felony convictions] rate is .027 percent which suggests a success rate of 99.973 percent."[12] Justice Scalia was citing Josh Marquis, an Oregon prosecutor who was running for public office. Marquis utilized every felony conviction in his equation and included exonerations in his calculations.[13] This error rate implies that 27 factually wrong felony convictions occurred in every 100,000 felony convictions.

We've learned a lot about false convictions (and unreliable sources) in the past years, says Samuel R. Gross.[14] For example, an unreasonable equation results when one attempts to determine a wrongful conviction ratio utilizing all convicted felons. That is, the Bureau of Justice Statistics reported that in 2004, an estimated one million convictions occurred in state courts, consisting of approximately 195,000 felony convictions that included 8,400 murderers and 12,000 rapists.[15] Most felony arrests are not contested because of plea bargains, adds David Feige, who relied on government statistics, such as the following[16]:

- Ninety-seven percent of convictions that occurred within one year of arrest were obtained through a guilty plea. About 9 in 10 guilty pleas were to a felony indictment.[17]
- Murder defendants (25 percent) were the most likely to have their cases adjudicated by trial. Seventy-one percent were convicted.
- An estimated 5 percent of defendants who were indicted for rape went to trial. Fifty-two percent were convicted.[18]
- Fifty-nine percent of all felony defendants were convicted.[19]

In 19 of every 20 felony cases, there is no contested issue of guilt and no real claim of error; on the other side of the coin, an estimated 4 in 10 felony defendants were not convicted. Shawn Armbrust, the executive director of the Mid-Atlantic Innocence Project, says that a number of wrongful convictions in Virginia were "proven by re-testing of DNA samples maintained by the state laboratory. A comparison of that number against all the Virginia cases in which results could be determined yields a wrongful conviction rate of closer to 9 percent."[20] Armbrust's study consistent of a few dozen cases suggesting that that sample was too small to be reliable. Nonetheless, others estimated lower false conviction percentages, specifically for rape and murder cases. For example, Michael D. Risinger argues that:

> Using DNA exonerations for capital rape-murders from 1982 through 1989 as a numerator, and a 406-member sample of the 2,235 capital sentences imposed during this period, [Risinger's study] . . . shows that 21.45 percent, or around 479 of those, were cases of capital rape-murder (death penalty for defendants who rape children under a specific age such as age 12; *Kennedy v. Louisiana* struck down capital rape-murder in Louisiana in 2008). Data supplied by the Innocence Project . . . and

[Risinger's study] shows that only 67 percent of those cases would be expected to yield usable DNA for analysis. Combining these figures and dividing the numerator by the resulting denominator, a minimum factually wrongful conviction rate for capital rape-murder in the 1980's emerges: 3.3 percent.[21]

Adding difficulty to the computation of an error or wrongful conviction rate, criminologists have not yet devised a standard to estimate the extent of such errors in the justice system, argues Tony Poveda.[22] He provides data from the New York State Department of Correctional Services that indicates an error rate of 1.4 percent in murder convictions.[23] Also RAND researchers surveyed inmates and asked about their innocence; it came as a surprise that only 85 percent said they were guilty.[24]

Competent researchers report that wrongful felony convictions occur more often than expected, but they would be hard pressed to accept RAND's findings[25]; in an attempt to offer a workable description, a conservative ratio seems suitable. That is, researchers show that for every 200 defendants who are convicted of a felony, one or two of those defendants could be innocent of that crime.[26] Using this ratio, it is possible that 10 to 20 convicted murderers out of 2,100 murder defendants could be falsely convicted (of that crime). Because exonerated defendants we know about were most likely convicted at trial rather than by guilty plea, the number of false convictions in other crime categories, which could include those who accepted a plea bargain, will never be known.[27]

A recent editorial in Lincoln, Nebraska's *Journal Star* expressed shock at how the death penalty distorted a state criminal investigation to the extent that six innocent people were convicted of murder.[28] Defendants were pressured by an overzealous prosecutor to offer erroneous testimony through the threat of facing the death penalty (see Chapter 9 for more details). Five of the defendants pleaded guilty and testified against the sixth defendant.

Bennett L. Gershman (a former prosecutor) argues that misconduct among prosecutors in the plea bargaining process is more commonplace than expected. Gershman cites hundreds of cases where prosecutors produced inducements to defendants to plead guilty, which included vindictive behavior in the plea process, deliberately eliciting inadmissible and prejudicial evidence, making false promises, threatening the defendants' family and friends, and making open-ended bargains that prosecutors could never fulfill.[29]

There are some researchers who argue that innocent defendants should be shielded from erroneous legal maneuvers, implying that prosecutors hinder those ideals (more detail about prosecutor misconduct later in this chapter).[30] There are serious questions pertaining to whether an honest person could actually perform well as a prosecutor.[31] However, one study revealed who most often influenced a defendant's guilty plea.[32] Of 724 defendant participants who pleaded guilty, 26 were influenced by the judge, 116 by the district attorney, 411 by their own defense counsel, and 120 by their wife (the balance included probation officer, psychiatrist, friends, police, fellow inmate, others, and no response). Additionally, 86 reported that they were "conned," but 395 participants reported that they either wanted to get the proceedings over with or they pleaded guilty as a matter of convenience.

Some popular television performances, through the *CSI Effect*, help explain wrongful convictions. For example, the story line of *Law & Order*, Episode 393, "The Family Hour," includes the murder of US Senator Randall Bailey's (Harry Hamlin) ex-wife. The family's alleged secrets of torture and sexual exploitation are revealed through the investigation and trial process. While on the witness stand, the medical examiner (ME, Leslie Hendrix) identified a novel that influenced Bailey's (Hamlin's) motive of self-defense, and that novel had been inventoried in Bailey's library. However, before final legal arguments were presented by the prosecutor and the defense, the ME admits to ADAs Jack McCoy (Sam Waterston) and Connie Rubirosa (Alana De La Garza) that she had been in error about the novel. The DA (Arthur Branch), McCoy's boss, advises McCoy to ignore the error and explains that Hamlin's character (Senator Bailey) is guilty of other grievous crimes that would render a similar prison sentence in a New York state penitentiary. The senator was convicted of murder, and the ME's error was never disclosed.

■ Wrongful Convictions and Exoneration

Consistent with the Center on Wrongful Convictions, the terms *wrongful conviction* and *exoneration* are employed to synonymously describe cases in which a defendant is convicted of a crime and later restored to the status of legal innocence.[33] There is a difference between *legal innocence* and *actual innocence* and between *legal guilt* and *actual guilt*. The emphasis of this chapter is on actual innocence associated with a substantial majority of wrongful conviction cases.

> Actual innocence is a claim made in an appeal of a criminal conviction when the convicted defendant presents (through appropriate channels) additional significant or exculpatory (defined later) evidence that was not available at the trial.[34]

To prove actual innocence, the prisoner must submit evidence that undermines the court's confidence in the verdict by a jury or a judge in the case of a bench trial. Appellate rules largely require that this evidence must not have been available to the defendant at the time of the trial. Also, a national registry of exonerations does not exist, nor is there a simple way to distinguish from official records which dismissals, pardons, etc. are based on innocence. Also, the Death Penalty Information Center advises that it is necessary to distinguish between the concepts of actual innocence and legal innocence; the former is when a defendant is simply the wrong person, not the actual violator or person culpable (responsible) for the crime[35]; legal innocence means a defendant cannot legally be convicted of the crime, even if that person was the actual violator or was somehow responsible for the offense. That is, a defendant is only convicted if a jury or court finds the defendant guilty of murder beyond a reasonable doubt. Implicit in the reasonable doubt standard is that the conviction does not require absolute certainty as to guilt.

> The least likely reason defendants are acquitted is innocence.[36]

A defendant can be acquitted if critical evidence of his or her guilt is inadmissible because the police violated the constitutional rights of the defendant in obtaining the evidence through, for example, an unlawful search or coercive interrogation (explained later in this chapter).[37] Also, a jury acquittal can be a product of a sympathetic jury finding for the defendant even though his or her guilt clearly had been proven by the evidence. Therefore, many guilty defendants will be acquitted, rather than convicted, because the proof or evidence does not eliminate reasonable doubt.[38] A jury must acquit (declare innocence) "someone who is probably guilty but whose guilt is not established beyond a reasonable doubt."[39] An acquittal means that the defendant is legally innocent but not necessarily actually innocent.[40] A distinction between acquittal and innocence or actual and legal innocence can include O. J. Simpson, who was acquitted of criminal charges, but the court found him responsible for his wife's and Ron Goldman's deaths in a civil proceeding based on the preponderance of the evidence (the level of proof required in a civil case; one side's case must simply be considered more provable than the other's).[41]

Juries are not the last word in capital murder trials, which become especially risky in states where the trial judge has the authority to disregard the jury's sentence recommendation, as in Alabama, Delaware, Florida, and Indiana.[42] When researchers interviewed 54 jurors from a dozen Florida capital juries, it was concluded that "the existence of some degree of doubt about the guilt of the accused was the most often recurring explanatory factor in the life [imprisonment] recommendation cases studied."[43] Even when jurors believe that certain defendants are guilty beyond a reasonable doubt, lingering doubts often remain about whether the defendant is guilty of a capital crime, and those doubts understandably make the jurors reluctant to recommend the extreme penalty.

■ History of Wrongful Convictions

Russell Colvin disappeared from his Manchester, Vermont home in 1812.[44] Suspicion fell upon Colvin's brothers-in-law, Jesse and Stephen Boorn, who worked with him. Several years passed, then a family member revealed recurring dreams that suggested Colvin was murdered by the Boorn brothers. His bones could be found whole in an old cellar, which was later excavated, but no remains were found. However, a dog unearthed large bones from a nearby tree stump. Physicians said the bones were human. Jesse Boorn was arrested. Silas Merrill, who was a cell mate with Boorn, claimed that Boorn confessed that he had committed the murder. In return for agreeing to testify, Merrill was released from custody. Jesse Boorn confessed to the crime but blamed his brother. A posse found Stephen in New York and returned him to Vermont, where he claimed self-defense. After the brothers were charged with Colvin's murder, the physicians reexamined the bones and recanted their original story because the bones were animal bones. Nonetheless, based on Merrill's testimony and the Boorns' admissions, the prosecution won two convictions. The Vermont legislature commuted Jesse Boorn's sentence to life in prison, but Stephen had already been hung. Russell Colvin was eventually found alive in New Jersey.

■ Wrongful Convictions 1989 to 2003

On August 14, 1989, the Cook County Circuit Court in Chicago, Illinois vacated Gary Dotson's 1979 rape conviction and dismissed all charges.[45] Dotson had spent 10 years in and out of prison because the victim recanted her rape victimization, only to claim later that she was a victim; this case was a breakthrough because Dotson was the first convict cleared by DNA identification technology. It was the beginning of a revolution in the American criminal justice system. Until then, exonerations of falsely convicted defendants were seen as aberrational. Since 1989, these once-rare events have become disturbingly commonplace. One study shows that the rate of exonerations increased sharply over a 15-year period, from an average of 12 per year (1989 to 1994) to an average of 43 per year since 2000.[46] The rapid increase in reported exonerations reflects the combined effects of three interrelated trends[47]:

- Growing availability and sophistication of DNA identification technology
- DNA revolution has made exonerations newsworthy
- More resources devoted to wrongful convictions, for example, 41 Innocence Project efforts in 31 states

In a longitudinal study conducted from 1989 through 2003, 340 exonerations were revealed[48]: 327 men and 13 women; 144 were cleared by DNA evidence and 196 were cleared by other means; most had served terms of 10 years or more; 80 percent had been imprisoned for at least five years. As a group, they spent more than 3,400 years in prison, an average of more than 10 years each, for crimes for which they never should have been convicted. Exoneration occurred in four ways:

- 52 cases (16 percent) in which governors (or other appropriate executive officers) issued pardons based on evidence of the defendants' innocence.[49]
- 252 cases (74 percent) in which criminal charges were dismissed by courts after new evidence of innocence emerged.

- 32 cases (9 percent) in which the defendants were acquitted at a retrial on the basis of evidence that showed they had no role in the crimes for which they were originally convicted.
- 4 cases (1 percent) in which the states posthumously acknowledged the innocence of defendants who had already died in prison—Frank Lee Smith was exonerated in Florida in 2000; Louis Greco and Henry Tameleo were exonerated in Massachusetts in 2002; and John Jeffers was exonerated in Indiana in 2002.

The Innocence Project reports that "throughout New York State, 23 people have been exonerated through DNA testing after their conviction. Each one was arrested, jailed, convicted and served years in prison before DNA evaluations proved their innocence. Combined, they served 260 years in prison. Only two other states in the nation, Texas and Illinois, have seen more convictions overturned by DNA evidence."[50] Interestingly, in 10 of those 23 DNA exonerations, the actual perpetrators were later identified. Nine of the 10 offenders who eluded apprehension and an innocent person were incarnated in their stead, and the innocent person was eventually exonerated. Before they were apprehended, they had committed more crimes, including five murders, seven rapes, two assaults, and one robbery.[51] In perspective, the Criminal Court of the City of New York Annual Report shows an estimated 61,000 felony finings, 358,000 arraignments, almost one million calendared cases, 464 trial verdicts, and a budget exceeding $123 million.[52] Highlights of 282,684 total cases in 2007 include 144,000 guilty pleas, 217 convictions, 190 acquittals, 44,000 dismissals, and 13,000 cases sent to the grand jury.

■ Public Defenders

Many defendants imply that they did not possess the means to afford quality counsel.[53] Consistent with constitutional guarantees, indigent defendants are provided a public defender or a court-appointed attorney from the private sector at the government's expense.[54] The traditional defender's office is lawyer-driven and case oriented. However, there are many public defenders and court-appointed lawyers who rarely have enough funds to provide an adequate defense for their clients.[55] For example, in Alabama, the state has no public defender system; indigent defendants receive appointed lawyers from the private bar.[56] The total compensation the private lawyer receives is limited by statute from $1,500 to $3,500 per case (as of 2005). On Alabama's death row, 72 percent of the inmates were represented by appointed lawyers who received $1,000 to prepare their case. Legal scholars criticize the quality of the representation for indigent defendants, suggesting that hard-working public defenders are the primary contributors toward wrongful convictions.[57,58] For example, a notice that read "PLEASE HELP. DESPERATE" was posted in a Covington, Kentucky courthouse in the hopes of attracting a lawyer to defend Gregory Wilson in his capital case.[59] The manager of the indigent defense program asked the presiding judge, Raymond E. Lape (First Division, 16th Judicial

Circuit), to order additional compensation to secure a defense lawyer. "The judge refused and suggested that the program rent a river boat and sponsor a cruise down the Ohio river to raise money for the defense."[60]

Government statistics show that over 80 percent of felony defendants who are charged with a violent crime in America's largest counties and 66 percent of defendants in US District Courts are represented by publicly-financed lawyers.[61] Statistics show that in the largest county courts, 75 percent of the defendants with either court-appointed or private counsel were convicted; in federal courts, 90 percent of the felony defendants with public or private lawyers were also convicted.

In federal court, almost 9 of every 10 felony defendants with public lawyers and 8 of every 10 defendants with private lawyers received a prison sentence.[62] Furthermore, an implication offered by those statistics is that except for state drug offenders, federal and state inmates received about the same sentence on average, regardless of whether their lawyer was a public defender or paid by the defendant. Lastly, defendants who were represented by public defenders pleaded guilty more often than hired lawyers (see above for details about who influenced defendants to accept a guilty plea). Thus, public defenders, appointed council, and paid lawyers are not significantly correlated with wrongful convictions, which begs the question, what are the causes of wrongful convictions?

■ Causes of Wrongful Convictions

Previous studies have identified several factors that contribute to wrongful convictions.[63] It should be acknowledged that modern jurisprudence can and does lapse into bureaucratic routines and statistical cost–benefit formulas that mean little more to honorable intentions than the ancient rules of retaliation and vengeance.[64] Justice can be blinded (see Chapter 11) by bureaucratic routines, which include a lack of prosecutorial control and the popular media's perseverance as sensationalized through aggressive criminal justice initiatives, vigilantism, and fictitious accounts of crime and the criminal process, leading to wrongful convictions and justification of capital punishment. That said, a recent study shows that faulty forensic evidence or testimony was a contributing factor in 6 of 10 wrongful conviction cases.[65] These results can be manipulated by redefining specific areas; therefore, those specific areas are reduced to 10 categorical factors that can aid in understanding how each impacts wrongful convictions:

- Eyewitness testimony
- Scientific fraud and incompetence at crime labs
- The interviewer effect
- False confessions
- Voluntary false confessions
- Coerced-compliant false confessions
- Coerced-internalized false confessions

- Snitches
- Police misconduct
- Prosecutor misconduct

■ Eyewitness Testimony

Eyewitness testimony relies on the accuracy of human memory, and eyewitness testimony has an incredible impact on the outcome of a trial.[66] Aside from the smoking gun in the hand of the accused, a jury strongly considers the testimony of a witness. The memory of a witness is crucial because it can help establish who is at fault for the crime. Yet implicit in the acceptance of testimony is the assumption that the human mind is a "precise recorder and storer of events," argues Elizabeth Loftus and Katherine Ketcham. Supposedly, eyewitness testimony offers the truth about events and circumstances. For example, in the climactic scene of Rob Reiner's 1992 film *A Few Good Men*, Tom Cruise slams his fist on the table and demands, "I want the truth!"[67] In response, Jack Nicholson defiantly bellows, "You can't handle the truth!" Although this is Hollywood's dramatic rendition, erroneous witness testimony, whether in good faith or intentionally perjured, is the most common cause of wrongful convictions in the United States.[68] In the movie, the truth prevails and the suspects are acquitted of a murder charge.

In real life, military trials are distinctively different from public criminal trials; nonetheless, an evaluation of 86 legally exonerated inmates found that over 50 percent of the wrongful convictions were the result of eyewitness testimony. In just over one-third of the cases, eyewitness testimony was the sole determinant in the conviction.[69] Eyewitnesses are short on memory and long on misidentification, which is when a witness mistakenly (or intentionally) identifies the accused as the perpetrator of the crime which can be explained through imagination inflation.[70]

■ Imagination Inflation

The criminal justice system has historically relied on the testimony of eyewitnesses, but policies and practices of interviewing witnesses are as different as the individual agencies and investigators (discussed later) who conduct the interview and the policy of each individual jurisdiction.[71] That said, even an honest witness can characterize imagination inflation.

> *Imagination inflation* is a distorted identification of an event, individual(s), and account(s) of eyewitness testimony, which is an uncontrollable natural state of human memory.[72]

The way imagination inflation works can be characterized through the power of suggestion; hearing the details of an incident or seeing a picture of an aggressor can alter memory. In one study, participants were asked if certain events happened in their childhood; two weeks later they were again asked the same questions.[73] The participants then rated the likelihood of occurrence for each event a second time. The results showed that the act of imagining the target events led to increased ratings of likelihood. This finding has been interpreted as indicating that false events can be suggestively planted in memory by simply having people imagine them. The present study tests and confirms the hypothesis that the results that have been attributed to imagination inflation are simply a statistical artifact of regression toward the mean. This can also suggest that when prosecutors (or defense lawyers) prepare a witness, reviewing certain facts prior to trial may or may not suggest that certain events actually took place. Therefore, it can be argued with a great degree of confidence that when popular television dramas offer inaccuracies about justice principles and foundations, the viewing public can easily mistake fantasy for reality. Recall from Chapter 1 that juries often believe that if the evidence has not been developed similar to how they have seen it on TV, it's not real.[74]

When attempting to identify faces, witnesses can fail to identify the face that they claim to have seen and often incorrectly identify a face they have never before seen.[75] "Not only does a generally accepted theory for eyewitness identification not exist, but the evidence in many areas is inconsistent, the procedures and measures used to study various relationships are not well tied to legal procedure, and there is no evidence that the experts who testify would be any better at detecting witness inaccuracy than uninformed jurors."[76]

The longer you stare into someone's eyes, the more reasonable it is to believe you could identify that person in the future. However, the duration of a crime, along with other factors such as weapons and the violence of the crime, tend to attract attention to details other than the physical description of the suspect.[77]

Eyewitness Testimony

On May 2, 2007, Jeff Miller was the 200th person to be exonerated by DNA testing after being wrongfully convicted. According to the Innocence Project, his case is not unusual. Of those who were exonerated after a rape conviction, 85 percent were black men accused of assaulting a white woman. In contrast, black men are accused in 33.6 percent of rapes or sexual assaults of white women.

Eyewitness testimony is close to useless and often confuses judges and jurors when offered into evidence, say experts.[78,79] Eyewitness testimony, even in good faith, is useless when identifying a person of a different race, when the light is bad, and when a subject is under stress, all of which usually come into play in violent crimes. Has a victim or a witness really had an opportunity to study the face of the attacker?

Definition of the Situation

Often it doesn't matter if the person making the identification (ID) is really, really sure. The confidence of an ID is uncorrelated with whether the ID is actually correct. Modern memory researchers advise that although false testimony can be deliberate, "it is much more sincere."[80] Motivations and biases pervasively influence memory so that witnesses very sincerely believe the false reports they provide to a jury—they become honest liars.[81] This new research on memory strikes an old chord linked to research conducted in the last century by W. I. Thomas and his notion of the *definition of the situation*.[82,83] "If men [and women] define things as real, they are real in their consequences," explains Thomas. For example, if an individual is afraid of the dark and walks down a dark street, the individual is inclined to act in a defensive manner. Another example is when a driver believes that the neighborhood streets he is riding on are crime ridden, he will check the car locks and tighten the windows. When something is believed to be true (regardless of the truthfulness), an individual will behave according to his or her own understanding of the situation. W. I. Thomas and others talk about human beings in such a way that humans can see and feel and hear what they think they see and feel and hear. Each of us develops our own social reality or definition of the situation, which is influenced by beliefs and culture but limited by physical attributes (such as age and strength). Sometimes that can lead to a self-fulfilling prophecy by accepting our own social definition as real, and eventually it becomes real. For example, when a university student thinks that he or she will fail a course, the student alters his or her behavior to fit the prediction and tends to study less and turns in poor-quality, incomplete assignments. At semester's end, when an F grade is received, the student might actually say, "See, I knew I would fail the course, so it's a good thing I didn't work hard in that course."

Robert Merton coined the term *self-fulfilling prophecy* some 60 years ago and explained it this way: the prophecy or prediction is actually false but is made true by a person's actions.[84] More on point, do jurors have preconceptions about the way witnesses and victims should behave? A victim of sexual assault, for example, can also invoke victim behavior. When a juror hears unemotional testimony and observes the behavior of the victim that does not match the juror's idea of a victim, the verdict would probably be different than if the victim cried.

This is not quite like TV where eyewitnesses take center stage and play vital roles in a prosecutor's performance. For example, during cross-examination a prosecutor can employ a series of prosodic questions that can become a vehicle for changing the interpretation of evidence and controlling a defendant's testimony and behavior.[85] By asking leading questions that project expected answers, framing questions as statements of fact that invite a defendant's agreement, and building propositions step by step, prosecutors can simulate a monologue and control the path of the testimony, which manipulates what jurors hear or think they hear.

Jurors, too, have their own affect on the good faith testimony that in the end may not be completely accurate. Jurors make eight basic mistakes when considering the testimony of eyewitnesses[86]:

- Jurors overbelieve the testimony and quickly accept it as accurate.
- Jurors fail to understand the individual interpretations that affect the accuracy of the testimony and are unlikely to adjust their own beliefs to look at the evidence objectively.
- Jurors are unable to discern between honest and dishonest witnesses.
- A confident witness (forensic scientist or police officer) can lead a juror to a false conclusion about the relationship between the evidence and the defendant (see the following discussion about Pamela Fish and forensic scientists who lie on the stand but are compelling witnesses).
- Jurors generalize a witness's statement about being uncertain of a detail as being uncertain of all the other details and may discount the witness's entire statement.
- If a defendant testifies and the jury doesn't believe him or her, they tend to convict.
- Most jurors grossly underestimate the amount of prison time a defendant would serve if not sentenced to death, and the sooner jurors wrongly believe a defendant would return to society if not given the death penalty, the more likely they are to vote for death.[87]
- Juries in civil trials tend to find for the defendant more than a judge in a bench trial. In 2005 plaintiffs won in more than half (56 percent) of all general civil trials that concluded in state courts. The plaintiff was significantly more likely to win in a bench trial compared to a jury trial.[88]

The reality is that many jurors are not regularly confronted with witnesses and suspects who lie and are good at it.[89] Whether an eyewitness attempts to hide his or her own behavior or attempts to retaliate against the defendant, perjury by any witness hinders the chances of a fair trial.

In 1998, retired farmer William Dulan was found dead in his home. Police arrested Gayle Potter when she attempted to cash one of Dulan's personal checks. Found in Potter's possession was the murder weapon, and she had an injury on her head with blood consistent with the crime scene circumstances. Potter implicated Joseph Burrows and a mildly retarded friend, Ralph Frye.[90] No physical evidence linked Burrows to the crime, and four other witnesses placed Burrows at least 60 miles away at the time of the crime. After a lengthy interrogation, the mildly retarded Frye began to affirm Potter's story. Potter, Frye, and Burrows were all sentenced to prison. Later, Burrows was granted a new trial with Potter and Frye recanting their stories. During the trial, Potter admitted that she alone was responsible for the murder and lied in the previous trial. Burrows and Frye were released.

How often do eyewitnesses misidentify a defendant? In one study of 283 cases that demonstrated probable systemic failure, eyewitness misidentifications were responsible in 54 percent (153) of those cases.[91] A final acknowledgement about eyewitness testimony is that although it is strongly linked to wrongful convictions, it cannot result in wrongful convictions on its own. For example, in Texas, faulty eyewitness testimony helped secure wrongful convictions because police and prosecutors ignored safeguards and built cases with flimsy corroboration.[92]

■ Scientific Fraud and Incompetence at Crime Labs

Forensic science analysis can be faulty, especially when human error and human incompetence are considered.[93] In an Innocence Project study of 283 felony cases, forensic science malpractice accounted for 21 percent (59) of those cases that led to wrongful convictions.[94] Also, in an examination of the 200th DNA and death row exoneration case since 1986, including numerous interviews and a review of court transcripts and appellate opinions, it was discovered that more than a quarter of those cases involved faulty crime lab work or forensic personnel testimony.[95] In both felony and capital crime wrongful conviction cases, 2 of every 10 are linked to malpractice or incompetent personnel.

Evidence of problems ranging from negligence to outright deception has been uncovered at crime labs in 17 states (discussed later). Among the failures were faulty blood analyses, fingerprinting errors, flawed hair comparisons, the contamination of evidence used in DNA testing, and outright lies. The following six cases will help clarify scientific fraud:

Case 1: Oklahoma City

Disgraced police chemist Joyce Gilchrist changed and destroyed trial evidence during her 21-year career with the police department. Gilchrist had been involved with an estimated 3,000 cases, some of which included capital punishment cases.[96] The state reexamined 196 cases, including those of nine defendants who had already been executed. One defendant on death row (Robert Lee Miller, Jr.) was convicted of murdering and raping two elderly women, based in part on Gilchrist's testimony that crime-scene hairs were consistent with Miller's hair samples. He spent 10 years in prison. Gilchrist never examined Miller's hair.

Case 2: Chicago

Governor George Ryan of Illinois established a moratorium on capital punishment, converted the death penalty to life sentences for 167 death row prisoners, and got shorter sentences for four inmates.[97] The City of Chicago was plagued with fraudulent forensic analysis. For example, the governor had no confidence in the Chicago police interrogation process and the state forensic lab. One case that eventually led to the moratorium was that of Larry and Calvin Ollins, Marcellius Bradford, and Omar Saunders, who were convicted of the abduction, rape, and murder of 23-year-old Lori Roscetti.[98] Saunders was a 17-year-old black male who had confessed to the crime after being interrogated for many hours. At trial, Bradford testified that the four teens abducted Roscetti and drove her to a remote location and assaulted her. When Roscetti tried to escape, Bradford testified, Saunders crushed her head with a chunk of concrete and raped her. Bradford later recanted his testimony and claimed that the police investigators coerced him (see the section "False Confessions" later in this chapter). However, sealing the fate of the young defendants was Pamela Fish, the Illinois State Police crime analyst who testified that semen taken from the victim's body belonged to Saunders. "He looked good for it," Fish compellingly informed the jury. Fish never examined the evidence or matched the semen samples. She was the state's star witness in over 2,000 cases, of which over 20 were capital murder cases.

Case 3: Boston

A crime analysis unit was blamed for the wrongful conviction of Stephan Cowans, who was convicted of attempted murder of a police officer.[99] Boston police admitted that two fingerprint examiners linked Stephan Cowans to the shooting, even though a later review found that the fingerprints were not Cowans'.[100]

Case 4: Richmond

As Earl Washington, Jr. neared his execution date, a leading DNA expert suggested that an analyst in the Virginia state crime lab might have made a mistake in the case.[101] The lab's director, Paul Ferrara, rejected the criticism. A second expert hired by Washington's lawyer questioned another round of tests. Ferrara dismissed him as a "hired gun" and rebuffed calls for an outside review. Several months later, three other experts—this time not paid by the defense—reached a similar conclusion: the lab's analyst had misinterpreted the evidence. Nonetheless, after an audit of the lab's work on the Washington case, the governor intervened, raising doubts about the reputation of labs as unbiased advocates for scientific truth.

Case 5: New York City

The inspector general for the State of New York closed a seven-month investigation into allegations that police chemists reported results for drug cases that were either not analyzed or not sufficiently analyzed, a practice called *dry-labbing*.[102] A former New York Police Department lab director faced criminal charges for allegedly covering up the scandal. The state's inspector general recommended that the Queens district attorney file charges against W. Mark Dale, who is no longer employed by the New York Police Department.

Case 6: FBI

Scandal also hit the FBI crime lab in the mid-1990s. A lab whistle-blower touched off a broad inquiry over allegations of improper handling of evidence. It led to the firing of several lab officials and the overhaul of protocols and procedures. Recently, an FBI analyst, Jacqueline Blake, pleaded guilty to a misdemeanor charge of making false statements about following protocol in some 100 DNA analysis reports. Though the FBI said its review found no wrongful convictions resulting from her work, the US Department of Justice's inspector general concluded that the lab's failure to detect her misconduct "has damaged intangibly the credibility of the FBI laboratory."[103]

See Chapter 9 for more details on forensic science malpractice that contributes to wrongful convictions among defendants who are sentenced to death.

■ The Interviewer Effect

The memory of the investigator is just as influential in an investigation as that of the witness. An investigator is likely to be called as a witness to testify about the collected evidence. So how would a trained professional make the same mistakes as another witness? People can hold only about five to nine items in their conscious memory, making it difficult to recall information stored in long-term memory in a complex case. Even when the information is recalled, it is perceived and interpreted through the past experiences of the investigator. How investigators collect witness statements along with physical and forensic evidence is determined by the controlled experiences in the training environment. The investigators' training is of utmost importance in the overall objectiveness and credibility of an investigation.[104] A trained interrogator could obtain a confession from an innocent person; investigators tend to work hard to avoid false confessions.

■ False Confessions

In a society governed by law, an interrogation is an integral part of an investigation. Interrogations are largely conducted by a professional and unbiased investigator; otherwise the number of unsolved crimes would increase, offenders would be released more often, and false confessions could lead to more wrongful convictions.[105] In a criminal court, the mere mention of a confession sways a jury, even when a judge orders the jury to ignore the evidence. A suspect's confession during any phase of the investigative or judicial process would eliminate all doubts of guilt from the minds of investigators, judges, and jurors. One estimate is that as many as 80 percent of criminal cases are solved through confessions.[106] Are all confessions authentic? Consider the Omar Saunders case (previously discussed) where his confession aided his conviction (along with Fish's testimony). Lori Roscetti, the young victim, was a nurse at Rush Presbyterian St. Luke's Hospital in Chicago, a hospital near where seven nursing students were beaten, raped, and killed (not necessarily in that order) by Richard Speck. The pressure on the Chicago Police Department to resolve Lori Roscetti's rape and murder was enormous.[107] Interstingly, Saunders was incarcerated at Stateville Penitentiary, as was Speck at the same time this writer conducted college courses there.

Confessions, some argue, are in truth, products of an interrogator who either provides the written account of the alleged facts or supervises the suspect's written accounts of the crime and coerces the suspect into signing the confession. An analysis of cases where convicted suspects were later cleared by DNA evidence found that not only are false confessions a serious reality, but they also account for many wrongful convictions.[108] For example, a former Chicago police commander, Jon Burge, was arrested in late 2008 on charges of obstruction of justice and perjury.[109] The charges stemmed from a lawsuit alleging police torture, electric shocks, and death threats against dozens of interrogated suspects. (Also see the section "Case 2: Chicago" for an example.)

When Costanzo, Gerrity, and Lykes reviewed 125 (false) confessions that eventually led to exoneration, two consistent characteristics emerged:

- False confessions tend to occur in serious violent cases. Of many reviewed cases, 81 percent were confessions of murder, and another 9 percent were confessions of rape.
- Because information about confessions is derived from proven false confessions, the actual number of false confessions could be substantially higher.[110]

There are four reasons as to why it is difficult to estimate the number of false confessions:[111]

- Interrogations are conducted in private circumstances and are largely unrecorded.
- Even in cases where confessions are recorded, those recordings can be manipulated.
- Records of interrogations are not necessarily logged.
- If interrogations are not recorded, there is little evidence supporting the interrogator's integrity.

Detective Stoney Brook says that interrogations on popular television dramas bear little resemblance to reality.[112] "You see these guys take a suspect into a room [on *Law & Order* and *CSI*] and in 4½ minutes they get a confession—even if they have to beat it out of him." Brook adds, "That's just not the way it works." Watsonville, California police Sergeant Bob Montes adds that "the [popular television dramas] depict a fraction of what we do. They don't show us sitting on stakeouts for days. They show five detectives assigned to one case when the reality is one detective can have as many as 25 open cases at a time. It's good television." He adds, "But I'm more of a critic when I watch. Boy, it would be nice if we could do things that way."[113]

Evidence of a Wrongful Confession

Detective Jim Trainum of the Washington, DC Metropolitan Police Department says that he could never understand why a suspect would confess to a crime he or she never committed.[114] Trainum says that he stepped into the interrogation room one day believing that he had hard evidence linking the suspect to a murder. He used standard and approved interrogation techniques, "no screaming or threats, no physical abuse, no 12-hour sessions without food or water." Trainum obtained what he thought was a solid confession. At the beginning of the interrogation, the suspect said she was innocent, but as time passed she became cooperative, and in her confession she included details of the crime, Trainum writes. The suspect described the beating and dumping of the victim's body in a river. She made several purchases with the victim's ATM card. "Surveillance video from the ATM showed a woman who resembled the suspect," and her signature was verified on the victim's credit card receipts. Confident in their evidence and the confession, Trainum proceeded until the suspect's ironclad alibi proved she couldn't have committed the murder. Years after the case was dismissed, Trainum reviewed the interrogation tapes and realized that he had "fallen into a classic trap. We ignored evidence that our suspect might not have been guilty, and during the interrogation we inadvertently fed her details of the crime that she repeated back to us in her confession." The real perpetrator of the crime was never identified, partly because the investigation was derailed when the detectives focused on an innocent person. Today, Trainum is a strong advocate of videotaping interrogations. Currently, he is still a detective and instructs interrogation methods courses across the nation.

In an attempt to reduce wrongful convictions linked to capital punishment (see Chapter 9 for more details) and confessions, the State of Illinois acted into law Public Act 93-0517, Mandatory Recording of Homicide Confessions, or the Recorded Statements Act, which creates a presumption that any in-custody statement taken at a place of detention (such as a police station) in connection with a homicide (a violation of Article 9 of the Illinois Criminal Code) investigation is inadmissible at trial as substantive evidence if it is not electronically recorded.[115] Today, this act applies the exclusionary rule to confessions that are not recorded.

Consistent with the preceding findings are the results from a study conducted by the Innocence Project of 283 innocence cases whereby 15 percent (43) were linked to false confessions.[116] False confessions fall into three main categories: voluntary false confessions, coerced-compliant false confessions, and coerced-internalized false confessions.

Voluntary False Confessions

Voluntary confessions are self-incriminating statements made outside of questioning or the influence of police and consist of[117]:

- Problems with police interrogation methods by poorly trained detectives
- A morbid desire for notoriety on the part of the suspect

- Efforts to protect someone the suspect loves or honors, such as his or her child or intimate other
- Desire to screw up an investigation, throw police off guard, or get even with officers who made the arrest, thinking that the trial will show his or her innocence
- Internalized memories in which some suspects come to believe they actually committed a crime, sometimes through interrogation tactics that undermine their confidence in their own memory
- Self-punishment for other unrelated transgressions or accepting a less serious crime (for example, detectives might push aggravated assault, not knowing the suspect had actually committed sexual assault)[118]
- Heavy-handed arrest tactics

The Innocence Project reports that about one in five of the 131 exonerated inmates they assisted through DNA testing made incriminating statements or outright confessions to detectives.[119] It should be noted that an *operating mind* is necessary for a voluntary confession. The person making the confession must be aware of the consequences of his or her actions, otherwise the confession is rendered inadmissible at trial.

Coerced-Compliant False Confessions

The other two types of false confessions, coerced-compliant and coerced-internalized false confessions, are significantly different from voluntary confessions, even though they occur within the context of police interrogations. Coerced-compliant false confessions occur when suspects confess, irrespective of their personal knowledge of their own innocence, in an effort to escape the extreme interrogation methods used by investigators. Many would equate these methods with tortuous, threatening, and brainwashing techniques.[120] Most interrogations are conducted on the presumption that the suspect is deceptive and guilty. Training and experience help interrogators learn about their own biases. Overconfident interrogators can discount information received from the suspect (and the crime scene) that might not coincide with the investigator's own theory, and it becomes a personal issue.[121] Employing professional training can aid an interrogator to interpret verbal and nonverbal clues of deceptive and truthful people and how to obtain legally defensible confessions from guilty suspects.[122]

Coerced-Internalized False Confessions

Whereas a coerced-compliant confession might be made by a person attempting to avoid the high-stress techniques of an interrogator, a coerced-internalized false confession occurs when an innocent but vulnerable person is exposed to high-pressure techniques or even immediately following a traumatic event;[123] the person begins to internalize information from an investigator as truth, including information that makes him or her look guilty.[124]

Additionally, both mentally healthy and mentally unhealthy suspects are susceptible to enhanced risk of coercion under certain interrogational circumstances, which include acute states of sleep deprivation, intense distress, drug use, and other factors.[125] These conditions and factors can enhance the suspect's susceptibility to cognitive processing or self-regulation; for example, impaired self-regulation can decrease the suspect's tolerance for distress and enhance the need to terminate the interrogation by saying anything to end the conflict within the suspect's mind. The suspect has little regard for the consequences of his or her behavior at this point. Understanding the basis of enhanced susceptibility to coercion is complex, requiring acknowledgement of various factors of the diverse coercive processes that are inherent in an interrogation. This might include the way in which a suspect responds to coercion and the processes through which susceptibility to these effects are influenced by both chronic and acute vulnerabilities. It should hardly come as a surprise that the courts have yet to recognize the majority of suspect vulnerabilities as sufficient grounds for suppression of evidence, including confessions.

One researcher compares this type of confession to hypnosis. Depending on the skill of an interrogator, it can produce a trancelike state of heightened suggestibility in the suspect.[126] The stress imposed on a person during police questioning can allow an interrogator to suggest ideas and theories, such as statements supposedly made by other witnesses and/or false evidence that the person being questioned will begin to believe.[127] When an interrogator realizes that a suspect is vulnerable, there is a greater opportunity to obtain a confession, but if the suspect is innocent and confesses, the real violator remains at-large.

Popular television dramas can aid interrogators to develop their techniques. For example, in *Law & Order: Criminal Intent*, Detective Robert Goren (Vincent D'Onofrio) pushes suspects around with a particular vigor and cunning, but he always gets his man or woman in the end. In the television drama *Homicide: Life on the Street*, which aired in the 1990s, one particular episode ("Three Men and Adena") depicts the lead detective of the investigation, Bayliss (Kyle Secor), joined by his partner, Pembleton (Andre Braugher), who together interrogated a suspect in the case who was an Araber, a particular kind of street vendor.[128] The entire televised hour (minus commercials) focused on the interrogation.

The *Homicide* interrogators have a time constraint: 12 hours to crack the suspect. Although there are three men, one set, and one story, the Araber never confesses, unlike most of the dramas since this popular televised drama. What was clarified in "Three Men and Adena" is that neither of the two common characteristics among internalized false confessions (suspect vulnerability and the presentment of false evidence) were present. The presentment of false evidence is a common tactic among investigators who want to elicit a desired response; presenting the suspect with something such as a made-up witness statement, lie detector test, or other false evidence goes a long way (and most often is legal within an interrogation). By telling a suspect that his own friend has turned him in and given a statement regarding his involvement in a crime, the person being questioned would probably internalize the information and believe that it might just be true, depending on the suspect, of course.

Popular television dramas that depict realistic situations do not last long in comparison to *Law & Order* and *CSI* shows. Some say that *Homicide: Life on the Street* was one of the grimmest, most realistic portrayals of the life of a police officer ever put on the air.[129] *Homicide* was cancelled at the end of its seventh season and never enjoyed the popularity of *Law & Order.*

■ Snitches

One tool of policing is the confidential informant (CI), or *snitch*. Police and prosecutors exploit the circumstances of other people, usually criminals, and offer incentives that sacrifice a lesser crime to gather evidence in more high-profile crimes.[130]

Many situations where snitches have committed criminal acts of violence, including aggravated assault, have not consistently resulted in liability for the contact officer or the snitch. Often, snitches are unlikely to be accountable or liable when putting officers, the police department, and the public at-risk, particularly if the snitch acts within the *scope of employment*. Snitches usually favor criminal over noncriminal activities and are more likely to commit another crime of violence against a third person or an innocent person. A Boston officer who handles a snitch says, "In a sense, I'm allowing it [harm] to happen to an innocent person. I tell him [the snitch], if you're work'en for me and the department, you can't hurt other people. This one snitch told me, hell man, if I don't jack 'em up, the dudes I run with think I'm work'en for the man [cops]."[131]

Informant Policy Details

To counter at-risk snitch potential, policy manuals contain provisions for informant (snitch) and management development. Accredited police agencies that adhere to the Commission on Accreditation for Law Enforcement Agencies (CALEA) specifically provide a set of requirements guiding agencies in the security of CI files, criteria for paying CIs, and precautions to be taken. Many agencies add CALEA's CI requirements to their own. For example, the Chicago Police Department mandates that a snitch must be interviewed by a detective's supervisor despite detectives' complaints that an interview between the supervisor and the snitch strains the relationship, even to the point of losing the snitch.

An effective CI policy provides a comprehensive plan from initial recruitment to termination of the relationship. A good snitch policy should include conduct for officers in handling informants, including prohibited conduct such as socializing or partying with snitches or a snitch's family members or friends, becoming romantically or sexually involved with snitches, and not trading healthcare (insurance, prescriptions, or medical, psychological, or dental practitioners) providers and other lifestyle amenities with snitches. When the realities of life merge into a snitch–police relationship, it is usually the public that forfeits safety and tax dollars that are used to protect rogue snitches and snitch–officer relationships. Many officers secure the identity of their snitches, and the behavior of reckless officers can produce an opportunity for corruption and snitch manipulation of the officers.[132]

Snitches don't merely lie; criminal activity is their lifestyle choice, but they have to testify in many cases, which can be risky business. Snitches can lie in exchange for leniency in their own case or for money.[133] For snitches to benefit from their lies, they must be able to convince investigators and courts to believe those lies. Investigators and courts, in turn, usually do not or simply cannot check out the truthfulness of a snitch's claim because sometimes it is the only evidence available. Snitch testimony, including testimony of apprehended and jailed snitches, has been considered to be the number one cause of wrongful convictions in capital cases. Some examples are as follows:

- The Center on Wrongful Convictions reviewed 51 wrongfully-convicted cases that were later exonerated.[134] In 1985, Verneal Jimerson's murder conviction rested on the testimony of Paula Gray, a supposed accomplice. Gray was no stranger to the snitch system, and her testimony led to the convictions of three others, one of whom was sentenced to death. After Gray's testimony, she was convicted but released from prison. All four defendants were later exonerated by the confessions of the real killers.[135]
- Steven Smith was convicted for the 1985 shooting death of an off-duty Illinois correctional officer (CO). Debra Caraway told police that she witnessed the crime. During Smith's trial, the jury never knew that Caraway's boyfriend was in custody as the primary suspect for the crime, and the jury was not informed that Caraway was a cocaine user and was high when the crime happened. Caraway testified that only Smith and the CO were in the parking lot, but two friends of the CO were present, and neither remembered seeing Smith. The Illinois Supreme Court reversed the conviction 15 years later.
- In 1993, former police officer and FBI snitch Steven Manning was sentenced to death for the murder of his business partner. His conviction was based solely on the testimony of a jailhouse informant who testified that Manning admitted to the murder when they shared a cell. The informant, a career drug dealer who was six years into a 14-year sentence on theft and firearms charges, was immediately released and entered into the federal Witness Security Program. Manning was released in 2000 after the charges were dropped, and he was sent to Missouri on unrelated charges. In 2004, Manning was exonerated on all charges and claimed that he had been set up by the FBI when he refused to continue to cooperate.[136]
- In Texas, David Spence was charged with murdering three teenagers in 1982. He was allegedly hired by a convenience store owner to kill another girl, but

he killed the victims by mistake. The convenience store owner was originally convicted and sentenced to death but then was acquitted at a retrial. The police lieutenant who supervised the investigation of Spence later concluded, "I do not think David Spence committed this crime." Ramon Salinas, the homicide detective who conducted the investigation, said, "My opinion is that David Spence was innocent. Nothing from the investigation ever led us to any evidence that he was involved." No physical evidence connected Spence to the crime. The case against Spence was pursued by an officer who relied on testimony of prison inmates who were granted favors in return for testimony. Spence was convicted in 1984 and executed in 1997.[137]

In California, it is estimated that up to 20 percent of the state's wrongful convictions on all crimes were based on snitch testimony.[138] In Illinois, it was found that many of the state's capital convictions rested solely on the testimony of witnesses who had incentives to lie. Judge Paul J. Kelly of the US Supreme Court of Appeals, 10th Circuit once observed, "If justice is perverted when a criminal defendant seeks to buy testimony from a witness, it is no less perverted when the government does so. The judicial process is tainted and justice is cheapened when factual testimony is purchased, whether with leniency or money."[139] In a *Frontline* interview regarding federal efforts to fight the drug wars, the US attorney for the Southern District of Alabama said:

And if they don't cooperate, which is what happens a lot of times, then they wind up going to trial and most of the time they get convicted, and then they get a longer sentence than they would if they had cooperated with us. . . . But a lot of times they don't think they're going to get convicted, or there may be other reasons that they just don't want to talk, and they won't do it. And then they get convicted.[140]

Jailed snitches have much to gain from their cooperation, as previously discussed. Snitches inside or outside prison receive special treatment or better facilities, reduced sentences or release, and deals in exchange for their testimony.[141] Of 111 men, 51 were exonerated of crimes involving the death penalty; they were originally convicted, based in whole or in part, on the testimony of in-custody snitches.[142]

Control Snitches

To better control the unreliability of snitches and to reduce the consequences suffered by the wrongfully accused, the Center on Wrongful Convictions suggests documenting the evidence of snitches through recordings and other electronic methods, but the truth is that chronic violent offenders tend to lie about everything, all the time, argue criminologists.[143–146] Lying about anything and everything is a typical strategy of most chronic criminal violators (and drunks) in an attempt to bring their goals closer. Think of it this way: criminals lie to manipulate or exploit others in an attempt to provide or orchestrate an opportunity to commit crime.[147] For example, Eric Leberg explains that a child molester smooth talks judges, parole officers, and young women with children to get closer to kids. Snitches do not generate wrongful convictions merely because they lie; it's how and why they lie and "how the government [prosecutor] depends on lying informants that makes snitching a troubling distortion of the truth-seeking process," explains Alexandra Natapoff.[148] Nonetheless, consistent with these findings is a study of 283 cases identified by the Innocence Project; in 9 percent (25) of those exoneration cases, snitches were responsible for the original conviction.[149]

■ Police Misconduct

In Los Angeles, California, a police officer handcuffed, shot, and planted illegal drugs on a suspect and conducted an arrest for drug possession. This officer's actions led to over 100 convicted persons being released from jail. The area prosecutor estimated that over 3,000 additional cases would be affected.[150]

Among those cases were two Hispanics whose confessions were prepared by police in English and signed by the two suspects, who spoke only Spanish.[151] Four people were wrongfully convicted and sentenced, one to life and the others to 92 years in prison, collectively.

In July 2007, the US government was ordered to pay $102 million to two men and to the families of two other wrongfully convicted defendants who had spent 30 years in prison as the result of FBI misconduct, including perjury.[152] The judge cited the FBI as the sole cause of the wrongful conviction.[153]

There are several inherent problems with the facts linked to police perjury. In many cases, it is the word of a police officer against the word of an alleged felon. Most police officer testimony is accurate and true; however, the only way for a judge to discredit an officer's testimony is to, in essence, brand the officer as a liar. Police officers are aware of the judge's situation, and those officers who turn to criminal activity, such as violating civil rights to get convictions, depend on the judge's biases to ensure their own credibility.[154] It is hard to imagine a police officer as a criminal, but police officers have an awareness of right and wrong and make conscious decisions for their actions, similar to criminals who make conscious decisions to commit a criminal act.[155]

Police Perjury

Police perjury is not only accepted by judges and prosecutors but also by police command. Administrators know of the biases of judges and jurors and are aware that their testimony is more likely to be believed than the accused. Therefore, few officers take measures to cover their tracks when they lie. Even on appeals, the appellate courts cannot question the trial courts' credibility judgment of witnesses unless new, compelling evidence is discovered that directly questions the credibility of a police officer's testimony.[156] Misconduct or incompetence by prosecutors is a required ingredient of police corruption; in jurisdictions where prosecutors conduct the responsibilities of their office in a competent and judicial manner, police corruption is less likely to occur. To clarify this perspective, a former state's attorney in Chicago says, "I would have cops walking up to me as I was preparing a case and I would say, officer, tell me what happened? And they would say, well, how do you want it to have happened?"[157] Think of it this way: in the movie *Righteous Kill* (2008), starring Robert De Niro and Al Pacino, the plot is about a police officer serial killer, and the victims were criminally violent individuals. In the motion picture's promotional ads, De Niro says "there's nothing wrong with a little shooting as long as the right people get shot." Glorifying murder or Dirty Harry (Clint Eastwood) behavior among police officers is depicted on motion picture screens and popular television dramas as appropriate.

On the other hand, police perjury, if accepted, puts the US Constitution on notice that it can be violated without liability.[158] Prosecutors can place the Constitution at-risk more often than police officers because the few prosecutors who misbehave, it appears, have few incentives not to.[159]

■ Prosecutor Misconduct

Three assumptions made about prosecutors are that each prosecutor is competent, each has expertise in forensic protocols, and each is energetic, suggesting that none of them are lazy.[160,161] All of the previous information—from eyewitnesses to interrogations to confessions to snitches—is the end result of many factors. However, eyewitnesses who intentionally or unintentionally distort reality don't necessarily generate wrongful convictions; overzealous interrogators don't generate wrongful convictions; human error in forensic science doesn't by itself produce wrongful convictions; confessions produced by factors other than the truth aren't completely responsible for wrongful convictions; and finally, snitches don't generate wrongful convictions simply because they lie.[162] In each case, a prosecutor has the final say on each of these variables during the case. For example, Marcia Clark, the prosecutor in the 1995 O. J. Simpson case, claims that one reason Simpson was acquitted had to do with the forensic scientist's testimony, which Clark had control over, she admits.

Prosecutorial misconduct, reveals Peter A. Joy, is one of the leading causes or contributing factors of wrongful convictions and is less likely a result of isolated instances of unprincipled choices or the failure of character on the part of some prosecutors.[163] No single theory about prosecutor misconduct can explain the variety of complex forms of abusive behavior that are exhibited by the few prosecutors whose behavior chronically characterizes misconduct.[164] Wrongful convictions are a product of overzealous prosecutors who ignore or fail to disclose (intentionally or unintentionally, i.e., laziness) exculpatory (applied to evidence which may justify or excuse an accused defendant's actions) evidence that would justify the defendant's action (i.e., self defense) or clarify the intent of the defendant (the burden to show that criminal intent existed "mens rea" at the time of the "crime" is upon the prosecution).[165–167] For example, police evidence may show that a defendant's gun was inoperable

(*US ex rel. Smith v. Fairman*, 769 F.2d 386, 7thCir., 1985). Additionally, a prosecutor has an incentive to win convictions because his or her success is determined by those wins, which would impact political ambitions, future elections, and financial and funding benefits.[168] However, Peter A. Joy argues that prosecutorial misconduct is largely the result of three institutional conditions:[169]

- Vague ethics rules that provide ambiguous guidance to prosecutors
- Vast discretionary authority with little or no transparency
- Inadequate remedies for prosecutor misconduct

Occupational Theory

The previous three conditions create perverse incentives for some prosecutors to engage in, rather than refrain from, prosecutorial misconduct. One study suggests that a theory about prosecutorial misconduct can be built from the characterization of prosecutors as agents of trust and prosecutorial misconduct as a violation of the norms of trust.[170] Utilizing a theory from occupational crime can help explain how the structure of the trust relationship creates motivation and opportunity for misconduct. For example, Gary S. Green argues that occupational crime is "any act punishable by law that is committed through opportunity created in the course of an occupation that is legal."[171] Occupational crime can consist of four subtypes:

- Organizational: Law-violating behavior promoted by a corporation or an organization
- Professional: Law-violating behavior committed as a result of being employed in a profession that offers the opportunity for crime
- State authority: Law-violating behavior by government personnel
- Individual: Law-violating behavior committed by personnel employed in a company or organization, but the behavior was committed for an individual's own personal or financial gain

Organizational occupational crime, reports Curt R. Bartol and Anne M. Bartol, can represent a legal entity, such as a company, corporation, firm, or foundation that profits from the law-violating behavior.[172] For example, a pharmaceutical company might ignore quality control standards (and costs) and continue to produce an unsafe, cost-efficient product. Professional occupational crime includes illegal behavior by persons, such as lawyers, physicians, psychologists, and teachers, that is committed through their profession; for example, a defense lawyer might persuade his client to commit perjury. State-authority occupational crime encompasses a wide range of law violations by personnel who are provided with legal authority, such as a prosecutor or a police officer. Finally, individual occupational crime covers all violations not included by one of the previously described categories. For example, an employee might personally utilize an employer's property illegally, or someone might cheat on his or her federal tax return. Green makes the point that none of these violations can be easily explained through the popular concept of white-collar crime, a perspective originally developed by Edwin H. Sutherland almost 60 years ago.[173] For example, Bartol and Bartol provide examples of a therapist who sexually assaults a patient and a correctional officer who utilizes unnecessary force against a prisoner. They both committed violent occupational crimes—the therapist in the professional category and the correctional officer in the state authority category. Neither crime could be adequately explained by white-collar crime categories. Then, too, not every wrongful conviction case linked to prosecutors can be explained through occupational theory either.

Prosecutor Discretion and the Media

Philosophers who influenced the development of the US Constitution, such as John Locke and Baron de Montesquieu, argued that law must limit governmental power because too much power in the hands of a few can lead to serious consequences (also see the section "Separation of Powers Doctrine" in Chapter 3 and the section "The Job of a Prosecutor" in Chapter 7). As John Locke put it, "Wherever law ends, tyranny begins. . ... And whosoever in authority exceeds the power given him by the law . . . may be opposed."[174] In the 21st century, prosecutors hold a free reign to manipulate the judicial process at their discretion and for their own benefits, if that is their intent, the evidence implies.[175] Tactics that prosecutors employ to obtain convictions have led commentators to call them modern versions of "medieval torturers and lawless gunmen."[176,177]

Prosecutor discretion can be described as behavior choices without liability. This thought is consistent with the Center for Public Integrity's reports that since 1970, individual judges and appellate court panels cited prosecutorial misconduct as a "factor when dismissing charges, reversing convictions, or reducing sentences in more than 2,000 cases."[178] In thousands more cases, judges labeled prosecutorial behavior inappropriate but upheld convictions using a doctrine called harmless error. For example, it is little wonder that prosecutors can accumulate the experience necessary to acquire the dubious honor of being recognized as "master framers."[179]

Popular Television Dramas Justify Prosecutorial Discretion

In *Law & Order*, Episode 356, "House of Cards," Detectives Joe Fontana (Dennis Farina) and Ed Green (Jesse L. Martin) investigate the murder of a young mother who had successfully completed drug rehabilitation and whose five-day-old infant son (Nicholas) was missing. The detectives tracked down Arlene Tarrington (Wendy Moniz) and determined that the infant Tarrington claimed as her child is really baby Nicholas, but after Tarrington's defense council claims postpartum psychosis, another man comes forward claiming to be the child's father. Assistant ADAs McCoy and Borgia could not decide which of the two they would rather prosecute for the murder.

Other examples include the presentations seen by millions of viewers who witness prosecutors challenging the soul of democracy: equality. For example, at the end of *Law & Order*, Episode 357, "New York Minute," District Attorney Arthur Branch (Fred Dalton Thompson) gave ADA Alexandra Borgia (Annie Parisse) a speech about how they should stay out of the government's business concerning the deportation of Mrs. Alvarez, an illegal immigrant whom they used as a witness. Ironically, Branch is then approached by a Latino busboy who characterizes himself as an illegal immigrant. As another example, in the *Law & Order*, Season 6, Episode 17, "Rage," ADA Jack McCoy (Sam Waterston) and his assistant, Claire Kincaid (Jill Hennessy), prosecuted an African American stockbroker who killed his boss because he was angry at the way he and other white people treated African Americans in the past, a mental condition referred to as "Black Rage." That episode had an ironic ending similar to the episode "New York Minute." McCoy and Kincaid left the courthouse after winning the case, and McCoy hailed a cab that actually should have stopped for a black man who was standing a block up from them. After Kincaid pointed it out, the cabbie said something like, "Are you getting in or not?" Maybe the defense was not as unjustifiable as the prosecution believed.[180]

Other Reasons for Prosecutor Misconduct

Wrongful convictions associated with prosecutor misconduct can also be explained by the many prosecutors who have been slow to learn and apply modern principles of management and measures of accountability that seem warranted by their position of public power and responsibility.[181] For example, many prosecutors have been unsuccessful in developing efficient office management structures and allocating responsibilities to subordinates.

Some prosecutors are reluctant to accept their role as community leaders and have yet to address the concentration of crime in neighborhoods through community relation programs that engage problem-solving approaches and partnerships with residents and other public and private agencies, similar to other public agencies, such as police departments and their efforts at community policing initiatives.[182] (See Chapter 11 for more details on recommendations to reform prosecutors.)

Above all, many prosecutors lack proficiency in workplace technologies and other scientific advances primarily because it takes time, funds, and training to learn about modern devices and systems. In a sense, technology almost outpaces itself. When a system is mastered, a superior system is developed that incorporates variations in techniques. This can be frustrating, particularly if a prosecutor is confronting a huge case load, limited funds, and inadequate opportunities to prepare for both training and performance.[183]

In the 1970s and 1980s, prosecutors implemented computerized case tracking and management systems in their offices, but few have used these capabilities to compile systematic information about case outcomes or management issues.

Then, too, most prosecutors lack appropriate supervision and monitoring, providing an opportunity for indulgence or a chance to be lazy. For example, prosecutors withhold evidence and knowingly accept what they know is inaccurate testimony of eyewitnesses to win their own argument. This perspective is exemplified in both practice and in the popular media.

For example, the Georgia Supreme Court upheld a murder conviction of a former Riverdale, Georgia undercover narcotics officer who currently is serving a life sentence for the 1997 murder of Beverley Watson, his wife.[184] The state supreme court said that the trial judge "properly" allowed 30 hearsay statements against the defendant, and the prosecutor discredited the testimony of both of Watson's children, who challenged the eyewitnesses. However, "We are very gratified," Fulton County District Attorney Paul Howard says. "Hopefully, people will see there is no question . . . that jurors made the right decision." The remains of Beverley Watson were found in March 1999 in a wooded area near Fairburn, about 20 miles from the couple's home. The bottom line, according to reports, is that there was no tangible evidence or forensic analysis that linked Jim Watson to Beverley Watson's murder. The local medical examiner reported that Watson's cause of death was undetermined.

Another example of prosecutor misconduct including the deliberate withholding of exculpatory evidence from the defendant was a trial conducted by the federal prosecutor in US District Court in Massachusetts during the spring of 2009.[185] Suzanne Sullivan, assistant US attorney, told Judge Mark L. Wolf in a dramatic hearing in Boston that lasted more than two hours about her willful neglect in withholding exculpatory evidence and admitted her guilt. "It is my mistake. . ... It rests on my shoulders." Wolf was appalled by Sullivan's misconduct and by what Wolf characterized as a pattern of prosecutors in the US attorney's office. The consequences of Sullivan's behavior included a fine or additional training linked to prosecutor's constitutional duties. On the other hand, the defendant faced a minimum mandatory sentence of 15 years in prison. The judge commented that the Boston office has a "dismal history of intentional and inadvertent violations." Judge Wolf clarified that he had made similar entreaties to Sullivan's predecessors and achieved little.

Examples of prosecutor misconduct from the popular media include the following:

- *Law & Order*, Episode 379, "Release": After Hudson Moore is found bludgeoned in the back of the Babes Being Bad bus, suspicion initially turns to the company's creator, Chris Drake (Tim Pepper), until video footage leads detectives to a young woman who was with Moore the night he died. After concentrating their investigation on the young woman, the reasons behind Moore's murder soon become apparent, and ADAs Jack McCoy (Sam Waterston) and Connie Rubirosa (Alana De La Garza) struggle to prosecute a man who, although not directly responsible for the murder, could have been responsible for the incidents that led up to the murder.[186]

- *Law & Order*, Episode 285, "Asterisk": ADA Jack McCoy (Sam Waterston) easily pursued Doctor Peter Bosford (Joe Passaro) to testify as to the motive (steroids) for the murder of a famous baseball player's limousine driver. The defense attorney convinced the presiding judge that McCoy discovered a blackmail scheme (the baseball player was a homosexual) through an e-mail sent in error to McCoy by an unknown clerk in the defense lawyer's office. Therefore, McCoy called the doctor to establish the motive of blackmail for steroids, which was in violation of legal ethics because McCoy knew that blackmail for steroids was not the motive. The judge's decision to disallow the doctor's testimony provided the defense attorney with a double standard. McCoy should have argued that he knew about the homosexual blackmail only because the defense attorney made a mistake. If the e-mail had not been delivered to the ADA's office, the authorities would have pursued their original theory that the blackmail was for steroids and probably would have called the doctor to testify. Without knowledge to the contrary, McCoy's action would have been legitimate. It would therefore have been up to the defense to either accept the doctor's testimony when they knew it was not true or dispute the revelation that the ballplayer was gay. McCoy could have pointed this out and persuaded the judge to present a choice to the defense: either let the doctor testify or let the prosecution use homosexuality as a motive. Clearly, the defense sent the memo purposely to alert the ADA of the homosexual lover, knowing they could have it thrown out later and cut off any effort to present an alternate motive because the ADA knew the truth. Yet everyone seemed to accept that this happened simply because of an incompetent legal clerk rather than a purposeful tactic.

Justification and Neutralization of Misconduct

A question that arises from the previous examples is, Can prosecutors who view popular media crime performances easily conjure or justify their own self-interests in similar situations? As of May 2008, there were 18 seasons consisting of 411 episodes of *Law & Order*, and as of August 2008 there were nine seasons consisting of 233 episodes of *Law & Order: Special Victims Unit*; additionally, there are an incredible number of reruns. Both of these dramas and *Law & Order: Criminal Intent*, which is in its ninth season, are featured on television in back-to-back marathons so much that it is likely that a *Law & Order* performance is televised on one television network or another seven days per week during prime time or otherwise.[187] A concern about dramas that can repeatedly influence conduct is that they can help prosecutors (and others) justify misconduct. For example, Bartol and Bartol suggest that people use strategies to neutralize misconduct and separate their inappropriate behavior from their personal codes.[188] More specifically, "what is culpable is made honorable through moral justifications and euphemistic jargon." A reprehensible act becomes personally and socially acceptable when the act is associated with a beneficial or moral end.

Some prosecutors often win cases or obtain guilty pleas with little regard for client welfare, and they see the judiciary process as a game at which they must succeed. For prosecutors, their conviction success rate could determine their future and create or close opportunities for their career advancement.[189] Not surprisingly, the evidence in one study clearly connects wrongful death penalty convictions and prosecutorial misconduct (see Chapter 9 for more details).[190]

It is apparent that any garden-variety prosecutor could spot errors, including suspect eyewitnesses, suspect confessions, inadequate or improper evidence, and fictitious accounts of events or evidence and, for that matter could withhold exculpatory evidence at will. Similarly, experienced university professors know when a student falsifies an essay or cuts and pastes information from the Internet and passes it off as the student's own work. Granted, it is easier to look the other way if you're not a tenured professor. Passing a student who cheats, compared to indicting and convicting a defendant, is a different matter.

> It could be argued that a common denominator in every wrongful conviction case is that a prosecutor brought action upon a defendant.

Sometimes the popular media gets it right. The way it is supposed to work for prosecutors can be characterized in *Law & Order*, Episode 374, "Home Sweet Home." When an eight-year-old child died as a result of a building explosion, Detectives Ed Green (Jesse L. Martin) and Nina Cassady (Milena Govich) followed the trail of evidence to Rosalie Schaffner (Nora Dunn), the owner's ex-wife.[191] ADAs Jack McCoy (Sam Waterston) and Connie Rubirosa (Alana De La Garza) pursued Rosalie Schaffner with concrete evidence that implicated her, but the case took a turn when Rubirosa discovered a small piece of evidence that pointed elsewhere. Without hesitation, the ADA's office discontinued the investigation of Schaffner and directed the detectives to pursue the new leads.

■ How Popular Television Dramas Treat Exonerations

How do popular television dramas depict wrongful convictions? In *Law & Order: Special Victims Unit*, Season 3, Episode 2, "Wrath," a convicted rapist was exonerated after serving several years in prison because new DNA technology had not supported the original evidence that led to his conviction. After his release, he allegedly stalked Detective Olivia Benson because she had testified at his trial. At the end of the episode, Benson shot and killed him, and it came out that he was, indeed, a serial rapist. An obvious question relates to the latest DNA evaluation. Was it an error, or was the bad guy who was exonerated really a bad guy who falsified the latest DNA test? In the story, a reasonable explanation is mentioned, but which test was flawed? "Did the lab guys lie to us then or are they lying to us now?" as ADA Jack McCoy would ask in *Law & Order* (as heard in Season 7, Episode 18, "Mad Dog").[192]

■ What Prosecutors Think About Exoneration

In the great majority of exonerated cases there was, at the end of the day, little dispute about the innocence of some defendants. However, what also exists is a reluctance by prosecutors to react positively to the reverse judgments or to even reconsider closed cases. When they do—and it is rare—it is usually because of compelling evidence that shows errors or parents, friends, or loved ones of incarcerated individuals who demand justice. Some prosecutors continue to express doubts about the innocence of exonerated defendants, sometimes in the face of extraordinary evidence. Three brief examples support this perspective:

- When Charles Fain was exonerated by DNA evidence in Idaho in 2001, after 18 years on death row for rape and murder, the original prosecutor in the case said, "It doesn't really change my opinion that much that Fain's guilty."[193]
- On December 8, 1995, at the request of the prosecution, the DuPage County (Illinois) Circuit Court dismissed all charges against Alejandro Hernandez, who had spent 11.5 years in prison for an abduction, rape, and murder in which he had no role. DNA tests and a confession had established that the real criminal was an imprisoned serial rapist and murderer by the name of Brian Dugan; a police officer who provided crucial evidence had admitted to perjury; and Hernandez's codefendant, Rolando Cruz, was acquitted by a judge who was harshly critical of the investigation and prosecution of the case. Nonetheless, when Hernandez was released, the prosecutor in the case said, "The action I have taken today is neither a vindication nor an acquittal of the exonerated defendants."[194]
- Kirk Bloodsworth was exonerated in Maryland for the strangulation, rape, and beating with a rock of a nine-year-old child.[195] An anonymous call was received by police that Bloodsworth had been seen with the victim; five eyewitnesses testified that Bloodsworth was the person they had seen with the child before her murder. Bloodsworth's conviction was overturned in the appeal process, but when he was retried, he was found guilty again and sentenced to two life terms. When he was returned to prison, DNA evidence excluded him as a suspect, and he was released from prison after serving a total of eight years. The chief prosecutor told the police that she still believed Bloodsworth committed the crime and that she was "not sure."[196]

These are only a few examples of prosecutors who took a hard position about a defendant they once prosecuted, even those sent to death row[197] (see Chapter 9 for details on capital punishment). On the other hand, most prosecutors realize the pitfalls of forensic science as typified in this statement: "If forensic evidence is not objectively tested, analyzed, and interpreted by adequately trained scientists, the search for truth will potentially be compromised, if not defeated," argues Betty Layne DesPortes, Defense Lawyer and Chairwoman of Jurisprudence Section of the American Academy of Forensic Sciences.[198] Yet, it could be wondered in what way it matters if a prosecutor knew that, indeed, a forensic scientist was truthful or not regardless of the scientist's training. Isn't it true that we tend to believe the messenger more often than the message as advanced by the forensic examiner in Chicago, Pamela Fish among others, who totally lied about her findings (detailed earlier in this chapter)? Isn't it also true that other messengers (the popular media through the CSI Effect) distort reality from news reports to commercials to performances without regard for the consequences of their action? When an unscrupulous prosecutor utilizes the tools of the "false profit" (the popular media) to convict an innocent group of individuals, does it matter?

■ Summary

A US Supreme Court justice explains that the error in the felony conviction rate is 0.027 percent, which suggests that 27 factually wrong felony convictions occur in every 100,000 felony convictions. It is hard to tell what the rate is because of the 195,000 felony convictions in 2005, 9 of every 10 were obtained through a guilty plea. One researcher says that the overall percentage is 9 percent, but others put the overall wrongful conviction rate at 1 to 2 percent. One gauge shows that for every 200 defendants who are convicted of a felony through a plea bargain or trial, one or two of those defendants could be innocent, including those who are sentenced to death. Another study advises that of 724 defendant participants who pleaded guilty, 26 were influenced by a judge, 116 were influenced by a prosecutor, 411 were influenced by their own defense counsel, 120 were influenced by their spouse, and 86 said they were conned, but 395 participants reported that they either wanted to get it over with or they pleaded guilty as a matter of convenience.

Wrongful conviction and exoneration are terms that synonymously describe cases in which a defendant is convicted of a crime and later restored to the status of legal innocence. Actual innocence is a claim made in an appeal of a criminal conviction when the convicted defendant presents additional significant or exculpatory evidence that was not available at the trial. The least likely reason defendants are acquitted is innocence. The rapid increase in reported exonerations reflects the combined effects of three interrelated trends, which include a growing availability and sophistication of DNA identification technology, a DNA revolution, and more resources devoted to wrongful convictions.

The role of the public defender is in keeping with constitutional guarantees whereby indigent defendants are provided a public defender or a court-appointed attorney. The traditional defender's office is lawyer driven and case oriented, yet many public defenders and court-appointed lawyers rarely have enough funds to provide an adequate defense. Most often felony defendants are represented by publicly-financed lawyers, but paid and public defender representation in both state and federal cases does not show a significant difference in conviction rates.

The causes of wrongful convictions relate to eyewitness testimony, scientific fraud and incompetence in crime labs, an investigator or interview effect, false confessions, snitches, police misconduct, and prosecutor misconduct. Prosecutorial misconduct is largely the result of vague ethics rules, which provide ambiguous guidance, vast discretionary authority with little transparency, and inadequate remedies. One study suggests that prosecutorial misconduct can be built from the characterization of prosecutors as agents of trust and prosecutorial misconduct as a violation of the norms of trust. The framers of the US Constitution argued that law must limit governmental power because too much power in the hands of a few can lead to serious consequences.

■ References

1. Bell, J. G., Clow, K. A., & Ricciardelli, R. (2008). Causes of wrongful conviction: Looking at student knowledge. *Journal of Criminal Justice Education, 19*(1), 75–95.

2. Gross, S., Jacoby, K., Matheson, D. J., Montgomery, N., & Patil, S. (2004). Exonerations in the United States 1989–2003. *The Journal of Criminal Law & Criminology, 95*(2), 523–560. Retrieved June 30, 2009, from http://www-mickunas.cs.uiuc.edu/pub/Law/crimlaw%20 mcadams/exonerations-in-us.pdf

3. Zhang, L., Welte, J. W., & Wieczorek, W. F. (2001). Deviant lifestyles and crime victimization. *Journal of Criminal Justice, 29*(2), 133–143.

4. Miller, W. I. (2000). Clint Eastwood and equity: The virtues of revenge and the shortcomings of law in popular culture. In A. Sarat & T. Kearns (Eds.), *Law and the domains of culture.* Ann Arbor: University of Michigan Press.

5. Ivkovic, S. K. (2003). To serve and collect: Measuring police corruption. *Journal of Criminal Law and Criminology, 93*, 593–650.

6. Grounds, A. (2004). Psychological consequences of wrongful conviction and imprisonment. *Canadian Journal of Criminology and Criminal Justice, 46*(2). Retrieved June 29, 2009, from http://findarticles.com/p/articles/mi_hb3204/is_2_46/ai_n29066934/

7. Sourcebook of Criminal Justice Statistics Online. (2008). Section 1: Characteristics of the Criminal Justice Systems. Retrieved August 29, 2009, from http://www.albany.edu/sourcebook/tost_1. html#1_u. Also see, USCourts.Gov. (n.d.). *Cost of incarceration and supervised release.* Retrieved November 20, 2008, from http://www.uscourts.gov/newsroom/2008/costs.cfm.

8. Santos, F., & Roberts, J. (2007, December 2). Putting a price on a wrongful conviction. *The New York Times*, p. 3.

9. Lopez, A. (2002). $10 and a denim jacket? A model statute for compensating the wrongly convicted. *Georgia Law Review, 36*(3), 665–722.

10. At year end 2006, 1.6 percent of male inmates and 2.4 percent of female inmates in state and federal prisons were known to be HIV positive or to have confirmed AIDS. Bureau of

Justice Statistics. (2006). *HIV in prisons.* Washington, DC: US Department of Justice. Retrieved November 20, 2008, from http://www.ojp.usdoj.gov/bjs/pub/html/hivp/2006/hivp06.htm#cases

11. The Mid-Atlantic Innocence Project reports that 21 states, the federal government, and the District of Columbia have passed laws to compensate people who have been exonerated. Awards under these statutes vary greatly. For example, several exonerees detail their struggle to win just compensation for their time spent in prison. Kevin Byrd received a woeful $30,190 from the state of Texas for spending 12 years in prison for rape. His summary recounts how the money was divided up. "About half went to his lawyers. He gave $8,000 to a lifelong friend who had spent years trying to vindicate him, and $2,500 to a brother to pay back taxes on the family home. Mr. Byrd put $4,500 down on a used truck. The rest went to rent an apartment. His compensation was gone." Ronald Cotton received $110,000 for 11 years in prison. Others have received as much as $1,000,000 per year in prison. Mid-Atlantic Innocence Project. (2008). *Exonerate.org; facts.* Retrieved June 28, 2009, from http://www.exonerate.org/facts/

12. Risinger, M. D. (2007). Convicting the innocent: An empirically justified wrongful conviction rate. *Journal of Criminal Law and Criminology, 97*(3). Retrieved June 27, 2009, from http://papers.ssrn.com/sol3/papers.cfm?abstract_id=931454#

13. Marquis, J. (2008). *The justice system politics, the media.* Retrieved November 21, 2008, from http://www.coastda.com/

14. Gross, S. R. (2008). *Convicting the innocent: Public law and legal theory working paper series* (Working Paper No. 103). Ann Arbor: University of Michigan Law School. Retrieved November 21, 2008, from nhttp://graphics8.nytimes.com/packages/pdf/national/20080325_bar_doc.pdf

15. Bureau of Justice Statistics. (2007). *State court sentencing of convicted felons, 2004. Table 1.1.* Washington, DC: US Department of Justice. Retrieved June 28, 2009, from http://www.ojp.usdoj.gov/bjs/pub/html/scscf04/tables/scs04101tab.htm

16. Feige, D. (2008, March 27). *With math skills like these, it's no wonder Scalia is a lawyer.* June 27, 2009, from http://www.slate.com/blogs/blogs/convictions/archive/tags/innocence/default.aspx

17. Bureau of Justice Statistics, *State Court Sentencing.*

18. Sourcebook of Criminal Justice Statistics Online. (2006). *Adjudication of felony defendants in 75 largest counties, 2004.* Albany, NY: US Department of Justice. Retrieved November 21, 2008, from http://www.albany.edu/sourcebook/pdf/t5572004.pdf

19. Bureau of Justice Statistics. (2007). *Felony defendants in large urban counties, 2004.* Washington, DC: US Department of Justice. Retrieved June 28, 2009, from http://www.ojp.usdoj.gov/bjs/pub/pdf/fdluc04.pdf

20. Mid-Atlantic Innocence Project. (n.d.). *MAIP news.* Retrieved November 20, 2008, from http://www.exonerate.org/category/maip-news/

21. Risinger, "Convicting the Innocent."

22. Poveda, T. G. (2001). Estimating wrongful convictions. *Justice Quarterly, 18*(3), 689–708.

23. Risinger, "Convicting the Innocent."

24. Marquis, K. H., & Ebener, P. A. (1981). *Quality of prisoner self-reports: Arrest and conviction response errors.* Santa Monica, CA: RAND. Those of us who have experience in departments

of corrections would take issue with RAND's findings. My own experience suggests that it's the other way around. That is, 85 percent of the inmates surveyed would say they are innocent.

25. Bernhard, A. (1999). When justice fails: Indemnification for unjust conviction. University of Chicago Law School, *Roundtable 73.*

26. Denov, M. S., & Campbell, K. M. (2005). Criminal injustice: Understanding the causes, effects, and responses to wrongful conviction in Canada. *Journal of Contemporary Criminal Justice, 21*(3), 224–249.

27. Liptak, A. (2008, March 25). Consensus on counting the innocent: We can't [Sidebar]. *The New York Times.* Retrieved November 21, 2008, from www.nytimes.com

28. JournalStar.com. Death penalty distorted Beatrice case. (2008, November 12). *Journal Star.* Retrieved August 29, 2009, from http://www.journalstar.com/news/opinion/editorial/article_a246917f-9201-54d8-b21c-80cb866ca327.html

29. Gershman, B. L. (2008). *Prosecutorial misconduct* (2nd ed.). Eagan, MN: West.

30. Hornoff, J. S., & Zaitzow, B. H. (2005, November 5). *Life after life: Wrongly convicted but never truly free.* Paper presented at the annual meeting of the American Society of Criminology, Royal York, Toronto.

31. Smith, A. (2001, Winter). Can you be a good person and a good prosecutor? *The Georgetown Journal of Legal Ethics.* Retrieved November 21, 2008, from http://findarticles.com/p/articles/mi_qa3975/is_200101/ai_n8933516

32. Blumberg, A. S. (2000). The practice of law as a con. In B. W. Hancock & P. M. Sharp (Eds.), *Criminal justice in America* (2nd ed.). Upper Saddle River, NJ: Prentice Hall.

33. Illinois Criminal Justice Information Authority. (2002). *The needs of the wrongfully convicted: A report on a panel discussion.* Retrieved June 29, 2009, from http://www.idoc.state.il.us/ccp/ccp/reports/techinical_appendix/reasearch_report.html

34. Cornell University Law School. (n.d.). *Actual innocence.* Retrieved October 28, 2007, from http://www.law.cornell.edu/wex/index.php/Actual_Innocence

35. Death Penalty Information Center. (n.d.). *DPIC innocence critique.* Retrieved September 23, 2008, from http://www.prodeathpenalty.com/DPIC.htm

36. Schwartz, L. B. (1989). Innocence: A dialogue with Professor Sundby. *Hastings Law Journal, 41,* 153–155.

37. Schwartz, "Innocence."

38. Smith v. Balkcom, 660 F.2d 573, 580 (5th Cir. 1981).

39. Gregg v. Georgia, 428 U.S. 153, 225 (1976).

40. Dowling v. United States, 493 U.S. 342, 249 (1990).

41. Legal Dictionary Civil Proceeding. Retrieved September 23, 2008, from http://www.legal-dictionary.org/

42. Radelet, M. L., & Bedau, H. A. (1998). *The execution of the innocent: Law and contemporary problems.* Durham, NC: Duke University.

43. Geimer, W. S., & Amsterdam, J. (1988). Why jurors vote life or death: Operative factors in ten Florida death penalty cases. *American Journal of Criminal Law, 15,* 1–28.

44. Warden, R. (2007). *Executive director of the Center on Wrongful Convictions.* Retrieved June 28, 2009, from http://www.law.northwestern.edu/wrongfulconvictions/aboutus/staff/WardenR.html

45. Gross, et al., "Exonerations in the United States."

46. Gross, et al., "Exonerations in the United States."

47. Gross, et al., "Exonerations in the United States."

48. Gross, et al., "Exonerations in the United States."

49. Governor Mark R. Warner of Virginia exonerated two inmates in December 2005. One of the defendants served 20 years in prison for a rape in Alexandria that a test showed he did not commit. The other man was released in 1992 after serving 11 years for an assault in Norfolk. The governor did not reveal the names of the exonerated men because they had requested privacy. Shear, M. D., & Stockwell, J. (2005, December 14). DNA tests exonerated two former prisoners: Governor orders board review. *Washington Post.* Retrieved October 7, 2008, from http://www.washingtonpost.com/wp-dyn/content/article/2005/12/14/AR2005121401643.html

50. Cardozo, B. N. (2008). *Lessons not learned.* Retrieved September 1, 2008, from http://www.innocenceproject.org/docs/NY_innocence_report.pdf

51. Cardozo, *Lessons Not Learned.*

52. Criminal Court of the City of New York. (2007). *Annual report, 2007.* Retrieved November 21, 2008, from http://www.nycourts.gov/courts/nyc/criminal/NYCCC%20Annual%20Report%20Final%20072508.pdf

53. Heymann, P., & Petrie, C. (2001). *What's changing in prosecution? Report of a workshop.* Washington, DC: National Research Council.

54. The Sixth Amendment to the US Constitution, part of the Bill of Rights, provides that "In all criminal prosecutions, the accused shall . . . have the Assistance of Counsel for his defence."

55. Steinberg, R., & Feige, D. (2002). *Cultural revolution: Transforming the public defender's office.* Cambridge, MA: Harvard University. Retrieved September 8, 2008, from http://www.ncjrs.gov/pdffiles1/bja/193773.pdf

56. Stevenson, B. A. (2005). Testimony of Bryan Stevenson, Esq., executive director of Equal Justice Initiative of Alabama. *Statement before the United States Senate Judiciary Committee.* Retrieved June 30, 2009, from http://judiciary.senate.gov/hearings/testimony.cfm?id=1569&wit_id=4458

57. Bernhard, A. (2003). Exonerations change judicial views of ineffective assistance of counsel. *Criminal Justice, 18,* 37.

58. Bibas, S. (2004). The psychology of hindsight and after-the-fact review of ineffective assistance of counsel. *Utah Law Review, 1.* Retrieved June 30, 2009, from http://www.law.utah.edu/_webfiles/ULRarticles/131/131.pdf

59. Effectively ineffective: The failure of courts to address underfunded indigent defense systems. (2005). *Harvard Law Review, 118*(5), 1731–1752. Retrieved June 30, 2009, from http://www.harvardlawreview.org/issues/118/March05/Notes/Effectively_IneffectiveFTX.pdf

60. Bright, S. B. (1997). Neither equal nor just: The rationing and denial of legal services to the poor when life and liberty are at stake. *Annual Survey of American Law, 783,* 794. Quoting Ira P. Robbins, American Bar Association, "Toward a More Just and Effective System of Review in State Death Penalty Cases," 40 AM. U. L. REV. 1, 76 (1990). Quoting letter from Raymond E.

Lape, presiding judge, First Division, 16th Judicial Circuit, Kenton Circuit Court, Covington, Kentucky, to members of the Northern Kentucky Bar (May 17, 1988).

61. Bureau of Justice Statistics. (2000). *Defense counsel in criminal cases.* Washington, DC: US Department of Justice. Retrieved September 7, 2008, from http://www.ojp.usdoj.gov/bjs/pub/pdf/dccc.pdf

62. Bureau of Justice Statistics, *Defense Counsel in Criminal Cases.*

63. Bell, et al., "Causes of Wrongful Conviction."

64. Miller, W. I. (2005). *Eye for an eye.* New York: Cambridge University Press.

65. Improving forensic science to prevent injustice. (2008, August 25). *The Justice Project Newsletter, 19,* 48. Retrieved August 28, 2009, from www.thejusticeproject.org/wp-content/uploads/forensics-fin.pdf

66. Loftus, E., & Ketcham, K. (1991). *Witness for the defense: The accused, the witness, and the expert who puts memory on trial.* New York: St. Martin's Press. Retrieved September 12, 2008, from http://www.pbs.org/wgbh/pages/frontline/shows/dna/photos/eye/text_06.html

67. Reiner, R. (Director). (1992). *A few good men* [Motion picture]. Culver City, CA: Columbia Pictures.

68. Warden, R. (2001). *How mistaken and perjured eyewitness identification testimony put 46 innocent Americans on death row.* Chicago: Northwestern University School of Law.

69. Warden, *Mistaken and Perjured Eyewitness.*

70. Bell, et al., "Causes of Wrongful Conviction."

71. Stevens, D. J. (2009). *Introduction to American policing.* Sudbury, MA: Jones and Bartlett.

72. Garry, M., Manning, C. G., & Loftus, E. F. (1996). Imagination inflation: Imagining a childhood event inflates confidence that it occurred. *Psychonomic Bulletin & Review, 3*(2), 208–214.

73. Pezdek, K., & Eddy, R. M. (2001). Imagination inflation: A statistical artifact of regression toward the mean. *Memory & Cognition, 29*(5), 707–718.

74. Willing, R. (2004, August 5). CSI effect has juries wanting more evidence. *USA Today.* Retrieved September 12, 2008, from http://www.usatoday.com/news/nation/2004-08-05-csi-effect_x.htm

75. Warden, *Mistaken and Perjured Eyewitness.*

76. Ebbesen, E. B., & Konecni, V. J. (1989). *Probative v. prejudicial value.* San Diego: University of California. Retrieved June 30, 2009, from http://psy.ucsd.edu/~eebbesen/prejvprob.html

77. Ebbesen & Konecni. *Probative v. Prejudicial Value.*

78. Hobbs, P. (2005). Unreasonable doubt: Manipulating jurors' perceptions in a closing argument at trial. *Studies in Law, Politics, and Society, 35*(1), 107–142.

79. Surette, R. (2007). *Media, crime, and criminal justice: Images, realities, and policies* (3rd ed.). Belmont, CA: Thompson Higher Education.

80. Loftus, E. F., & Davis, D. (2006). Recovered memories. *Annual Review of Clinical Psychology, 2,* 469–498.

81. Davis, D., & Follette, W. C. (2004). Jurors can be selected: Non information, misinformation and their strategic use for jury selection. In W. T. O'Donohue & E. Levensky (Eds.), Handbook of forensic psychology (782–805). New York, Elsevier Academic Press.

82. Thomas, W. I. (1923). *The unadjusted girl.* Boston: Little, Brown, and Co.

83. Blumer, H. (1986). *Symbolic interactionism: Perspective and method.* Berkeley: University of California Press.

84. Merton, R. (1949). *Social theory and social structure.* New York: Free Press.

85. Hobbs, "Unreasonable Doubt."

86. Ebbesen & Konecni. *Probative v. Prejudicial Value.*

87. Bowers, W. J., & Foglia, W. D. (2003). Still singularly agonizing: Law's failure to purge arbitrariness from capital sentencing. *Criminal Law Bulletin, 39,* 51–61.

88. Bureau of Justice Statistics. (n.d.). *Civil and jury trials in state courts, 2005.* Washington, DC: US Department of Justice. Retrieved October 28, 2008, from http://www.ojp.usdoj.gov:80/bjs/abstract/cbjtsc05.htm

89. Seager, P., & Wiseman, R. (1999). Fooling all of the people half of the time? The psychology of lying and lie-detecting. *Science Spectra,* 15, 32–37

90. Warden, R. (2004). *The snitch system.* Chicago: Center on Wrongful Convictions. Retrieved June 30, 2009, from http://www.law.northwestern.edu/wrongfulconvictions/issues/causesandremedies/snitches/SnitchSystemBooklet.pdf

91. Collins, J., & Jarvis, J. (2008). *The wrongful conviction of forensic science.* Batavia, IL: Crime Lab Report. Retrieved August 22, 2008, from http://www.crimelabreport.com/library/pdf/wrongful_conviction.pdf

92. Faulty eyewitnesses doomed Dallas county suspects. (2008, October 11). *Associated Press.* Retrieved June 30, 2009, from http://www.usatoday.com/news/nation/2008-10-11-946345956_x.htm

93. Collins & Jarvis, *Wrongful Conviction of Forensic Science.*

94. Thompson, W. (2008). *New study exonerates forensics.* Batavia, IL: Crime Lab Report. Retrieved August 22, 2008, from http://www.crimelabreport.com/library/pdf/7-08.pdf

95. Possley, M., Mills, S., & McRoberts, F. (2004, October 21). Scandal touches even elite labs. *Chicago Tribune,* p. 1.

96. Luscombe, B. (2001). When the evidence lies. *Time.com.* Retrieved September 12, 2008, from http://www.time.com/time/nation/article/0,8599,109568,00.html

97. Sarat, A. (2003, January 15). *Governor Ryan's decision to empty Illinois' death row: A clear sign of America's new abolitionism with respect to the death penalty.* Retrieved September 12, 2008, from http://writ.news.findlaw.com/commentary/20030115_sarat.html

98. Innocence Project. (n.d.). *Omar Saunders.* Retrieved March 20, 2009, from http://www.innocenceproject.org/Content/257.php

99. Smalley, S., & Ranalli, R. (2006, January 22). Police unit to unveil CSI-style unit. *Boston Globe,* p. B1.

100. Smalley & Ranalli, "Police Unit to Unveil."

101. Strange Justice. (2005, June 30). Retrieved June 30, 2009, from http://stju.blogspot.com/2005_06_01_archive.html

102. Lueck, T. (2007, December 4). Sloppy police law work leads to retesting. The New York Times. Retrieved June 30, 2009, from http://www.nytimes.com/2007/12/04/nyregion/04lab.html?_r=3&hp=&oref=slogin&pagewanted=print&oref=slogin

103. Possley, et al., "Scandal Touches Even Elite Labs."

104. Rossmo, D. K. (2006). Criminal investigative failures. Avoiding the pitfalls, part two. *FBI Law Enforcement Bulletin, 75*(10). Retrieved November 20, 2008, from http://www.fbi.gov/publications/leb/2006/october2006/october2006leb.htm

105. Rossmo, "Criminal Investigative Failures."

106. Conti, R. P. (1999). The psychology of false confessions. *The Journal of Credibility Assessment and Witness Psychology, 2*(1), 14–36.

107. Stevens, *Introduction to American Policing.*

108. Costanzo, M., Gerrity, E., & Lykes, M. B. (2006). *The use of torture and other cruel, inhumane, or degrading treatment as interrogation devices.* American Psychological Association resolution. Moratorium on psychologist involvement in interrogations at US detention centers for foreign detainees.

109. Chicago: Former top cop arrested. (2008, November 3). *Time,* p. 39.

110. Costanzo, et al., "Use of Torture."

111. Conti, "Psychology of False Confessions."

112. Schultz, J. (2002, November 10). True crime is nothing like TV. *Santa Cruz Sentinel.* Retrieved October 25, 2007, from http://www.santacruzsentinel.com/archive/2002/November/10/local/stories/01local.htm

113. Schultz, "True Crime."

114. Trainum, J. (2008, October 24). The case for videotaping interrogations: A suspect's false confession to a murder opened an officer's eyes. *Los Angeles Times.* Retrieved November 2, 2008, from http://www.latimes.com/news/opinion/commentary/la-oe-trainum24-2008-oct24,0,7918545.story

115. Cullerton, J., Dillard, K., & Baroni, P. G. (2004). Capital punishment reform in Illinois. *Journal of DuPage County Bar Association.* Retrieved October 3, 2008, from http://www.dcba.org/brief/aprissue/2004/art10404.htm

116. Collins & Jarvis, *Wrongful Conviction of Forensic Science.*

117. Kassin, S. (2007). Internalized false confessions. In E. Borgida & S. T. Fiske (Eds.), *Beyond common sense: Psychological science in the courtroom.* Hoboken, NJ: Wiley Blackwell.

118. Tyler, T. (2003, August 10). Why they lie and confess. *Sunday Star.* Retrieved September 7, 2008, from http://www.williams.edu/Psychology/Faculty/Kassin/files/Toronto_Star_8_03.pdf

119. Conti, "Psychology of False Confessions."

120. Conti, "Psychology of False Confessions."

121. Costanzo, et al., "Use of Torture."

122. Inbau, F. E., Reid, J. E., Buckley, J. P., & Jayne, B. C. (2009). *Essentials of the Reid technique: Criminal interrogation and confessions.* Sudbury, MA: Jones and Bartlett.

123. Kassin, "Internalized False Confessions."

124. Inbau, et al., *Essentials of the Reid Technique.*

125. Follette, W. C., Davis, D., & Leo, R. A. (2007). Mental health status and vulnerability to police interrogation tactics. *Criminal Justice, 22*(3). Retrieved June 30, 2009, from http://www.abanet.org/crimjust/cjmag/22-3/mentalhealthstatus.pdf

126. Gangi, W. (1993). Supreme Court and coerced confessions: Arizona v. Fulminante: In perspective. *Harvard Journal of Law and Public Policy, 16*(2), 493.

127. Kassin, "Internalized False Confessions."

128. South Dakota Dark. (2006, February 2). *Perfect episodes: Three Men and Adena*. Retrieved June 30, 2009, from http://southdakotadark.blogspot.com/2006/02/perfect-episodes-three-men-and-adena.html

129. South Dakota Dark, *Perfect Episodes.*

130. Natapoff, A. (2006). *Beyond unreliable: How snitches contribute to wrongful convictions*. Los Angeles: Loyola Law School.

131. Stevens, *Introduction to American Policing.*

132. Dorschner, J. (2000). The dark side of the force. In B. W. Hancock & P. M. Sharp (Eds.), *Criminal justice in America* (2nd ed.). Upper Saddle River, NJ: Prentice Hall.

133. Natapoff, *Beyond Unreliable.*

134. Warden, *Snitch System.*

135. Warden, *Snitch System.*

136. Warden, *Snitch System.*

137. Death Penalty Information Center. (n.d.). *The innocent executed*. Retrieved October 27, 2008, from http://www.deathpenaltyinfo.org/node/1935

138. Natapoff, *Beyond Unreliable.*

139. Warden, *Snitch System.*

140. Frontline. (n.d.). *Snitch*. Retrieved August 28, 2009, from http://www.pbs.org/wgbh/pages/frontline/shows/snitch/cases/foster.html

141. Huff, R. C. (2002). Wrongful conviction and public policy: The American Society of Criminology 2001 presidential address. *Criminology, An Interdisciplinary Journal, 40*(1), 1–18.

142. Warden, *Snitch System.*

143. Gottfredson, M. R., & Hirschi, T. (1990). *A general theory of crime*. Stanford, CA: Stanford University Press.

144. Paternoster, R., Brame, R., & Bacon, S. (2007). *America's experience with capital punishment*. Los Angeles: Oxford University Press.

145. Samenow, S. E. (2004). *Inside the criminal mind*. New York: Crown Books.

146. Yochelson, S. (1995). *The criminal personality: A profile for change*. New York: Jason Aronson.

147. Leberg, E. (1997). *Understanding child molesters: Taking charge*. Thousand Oaks, CA: Sage.

148. Natapoff, *Beyond Unreliable.*

149. Collins & Jarvis, *Wrongful Conviction of Forensic Science.*

150. Walker, S. (2001). *Police accountability. The role of citizen oversight*. Belmont, CA: Wadsworth/Thomson Learning.

151. Biesk, J. (2002, December 18). *Feds: 2 prisoners will be freed after charges against drug ring*. Retrieved March 20, 2008, from http://www.truthinjustice.org/Bogus_Confession.htm

152. Associated Press. (2007, July 26). Government fined $101 million over convictions. (2007, July 26). *MSNBC*. Retrieved August 28, 2009, from http://www.msnbc.msn.com/id/15012096/print/1/disploymode/1098

153. Associated Press, Government fined $101 million over convictions.

154. Dripps, D. A. (1996). Police, plus perjury, equals polygraphy. *The Journal of Criminal Law & Criminology, 86*(3), 693–716.

155. Samenow, *Inside the Criminal Mind*.

156. Dripps, "Police, Plus Perjury."

157. McIntyre, L. J. (2004). But how do you sleep at night? In S. Stojkovic, J. Klofas, & D. Kalinich (Eds.), *The administration and management of criminal justice organizations: A book of readings* (3rd ed.). Long Grove, IL: Waveland Press.

158. Schoenfeld, H. (2005). Violated trust: Conceptualizing prosecutorial misconduct. *Journal of Contemporary Criminal Justice, 21*(3), 250–271.

159. Innocence Project. (2008). NJ Judge to Order Evidence Search. Retrieved August 28, 2009, http://www.innocenceproject.org/Content/2131.php

160. Possley, M., & Mills, S. (2001, November 14). DNA test rules out 4 inmates. *Chicago Tribune*. Retrieved September 7, 2008, from http://www.truthinjustice.org/chicago-dna.htm

161. National Clearinghouse for Science, Technology and the Law. (2006, August 18). *Forensic science literature and resources: Lessons to be learned*. Retrieved March 20, 2009, from http://www.ncstl.org/education/Blah

162. Natapoff, *Beyond Unreliable*.

163. Joy, P. A. (2006). The relationship between prosecutorial misconduct and wrongful convictions: Shaping remedies for a broken system. *Wisconsin Law Review*, 2006, 399.

164. Bell, et al., "Causes of Wrongful Conviction."

165. TheFreeDictionary. "Exculpatory evidence." Retrieved August 28, 2009, from http://legal-dictionary.thefreedictionary.com/Exculpatory+evidence

166. Green, M. (2005). Crown culture and wrongful convictions: A beginning. *Criminal Reports, 29*, 1–8.

167. Gershman, B. L. (2009). Why prosecutors misbehave. In G. L. Mays & P. R. Gregware (Eds.), *Courts and justice* (4th ed.). Mt Prospect, IL: Waveland Press.

168. Schoenfeld, "Violated Trust."

169. Joy, "Relationship Between Prosecutorial Misconduct."

170. Schoenfeld, "Violated Trust."

171. Green, G. S. (1996). *Occupational crime* (2nd ed.). Belmont, CA: Wadsworth.

172. Bartol, C. R., & Bartol, A. M. (2008). *Criminal behavior: A psychosocial approach*. Upper Saddle River, NJ: Pearson.

173. Sutherland, E. H. (1949). *White collar crime*. New York: Holt, Rinehart, & Winston.

174. Locke, J. (1959). Two treatises of civil government. In C. Morris (Ed.), *The great legal philosophers: Selected readings in jurisprudence*. Philadelphia: University of Pennsylvania Press.

175. Sherrer, H. (2000). *Prosecutors are master framers*. Retrieved October 14, 2007, from http://www.justicedenied.org/master.htm

176. For a comparison of prosecutors to highwaymen who get what they want by holding people at gunpoint, see Kipnis, K. (1976). Criminal justice and the negotiated plea. *Ethics, 86*(2) 93–106.

177. For a comparison of prosecutors to medieval torturers, see Langbein, J. H. (1980). Torture and plea bargaining. *The Public Interest, 58*, 43–61.

178. Center for Public Integrity. (2003). *Harmful error: Investigating America's local prosecutors.* Washington, DC: Author.

179. Gershman, B. L. (1998). *Prosecutorial misconduct.* New York: West Publishing.

180. *Law & Order* on NBC. (2007). *TV Guide.* Retrieved October 19, 2007, from http://www.tvguide.com/tvshows/law-order/100255

181. Heymann & Petrie, *What's Changing in Prosecution?*

182. Coles, C. M. (2000). *Community prosecution, problem solving, and public accountability: The evolving strategy of the American prosecutor.* Cambridge, MA: Harvard University. Retrieved September 3, 2008, from http://www.hks.harvard.edu/criminaljustice/publications/community_prosecution.pdf

183. Russell, S., & Norvig, P. (2003). *Artificial intelligence: A modern approach* (2nd ed.). Upper Saddle River, NJ: Pearson. The authors show that new concepts and methods of artificial intelligence (AI) reached higher technological advancement levels in shorter periods of time from its early inception in 1943 to 2003. As science advances, new devices and techniques are developed. The problem of keeping pace with science is not limited to prosecutors but applies to the entire criminal justice community.

184. FindCarrieCulberson.com. (n.d.). *Topic: Beverley Watson, Georgia.* Retrieved September 7, 2008, from http://findcarrie.conforums.com/index.cgi?board=murder1&action=display&num=1096026278

185. Saltzman, J. (2009, May 13). US prosecutor admits error, hopes for 2d chance. *Boston Globe,* Retrieved June 29, 2009, from http://www.boston.com/news/local/massachusetts/articles/2009/05/13/us_prosecutor_admits_error_hopes_for_2d_chance/

186. TV.Com. (n.d.). *Law & Order.* Retrieved September 6, 2008, from http://www.tv.com/law-and-order/show/180/episode_guide.html?season=17&tag=season_dropdown;dropdown;16

187. TV Guide. Retrieved August 28, 2009, from http://www.tvguide.com/listings/

188. Bartol & Bartol, *Criminal Behavior.*

189. Person, C. E. (1998). *Why prosecutorial misconduct and abuses are taking place so brazenly.* Retrieved October 26, 2007, from http://www.lawmall.com/abuse/abwhy.html

190. Scheck, B., Neufeld, P., & Dwyer, J. (2000). *Actual innocence.* New York: Doubleday.

191. TV.Com, *Law & Order.*

192. TV.Com, Law & Order.

193. Bonner, R. (2001, August 24). Death row inmate is freed after DNA test clears him. *The New York Times*, p. A11.

194. Bils, J., & Gregory, T. (1995, December 9). I just want to go home: A nightmare ends, one continues in Nicarico case. *Chicago Tribune*, p. 1.

195. The Innocence Project. (n.d.). *Know the cases: Kirk Bloodsworth.* Retrieved November 20, 2008, from http://www.innocenceproject.org/Content/54.php

196. Montgomery, L. (2002, May 20). Eliminating questions of life or death: Prosecutor's policy raises questions in Md. *Washington Post*, p. B1.

197. Death Penalty Information Center. (n.d.). *DNA testing and the use of forensic science.* Retrieved September 18, 2008, from http://www.deathpenaltyinfo.org/news-and-developments-studies .

198. Improving forensic science to prevent injustice. *The Justice Project.*

The Death Penalty

If we believe that murder is wrong and not admissible in our society, then it has to be wrong for everyone, not just individuals but governments as well.

Sister Helen Prejean, *Dead Man Walking*

▶ ▶ CHAPTER OBJECTIVES

- Clearly articulate the relationship between the rule of law and *lex talionis* or (law of retaliation)
- Explain in what way fear and criminal justice corruption promotes capital punishment
- Clarify the history and official policy linked to capital punishment
- Offer the issues of death penalty advocates and opponents
- Detail the role of state and federal prosecutors and death penalty indictments
- Provide an understanding of costs and racial discrimination linked to capital punishment

■ Introduction

This chapter highlights the helpful and harmful attributes of capital punishment and characterizes the contributions of the *CSI Effect* on the death penalty as a plausible sanction. America is embroiled in a debate about criminally violent offenders and what to do about them. It's unlikely that a perfect solution exists or that an equitable compromise can be reached because many acknowledge that there are few, if any, precise methods of measuring the universe of criminal behavior, and therefore qualifying measures of control might also remain tentative.[1] For that reason, among others, this chapter will argue that capital punishment is out of step with 21st century democracy and riddled with so many judicial process errors that it should be eliminated from state sanctions. It is hoped that the information in this chapter will help provide a clearer understanding of the issues surrounding the death penalty, but it should be acknowledged that the popular media continues to reinforce capital punishment as the best alternative to dealing with criminally violent offenders (whom the popular media is more than anxious to describe). One source reports that President Obama supports capital punishment in cases in which "the community is justified in expressing the full measure of its outrage."[2] Yet, despite the president's popularity, this wasn't an isolated inattentive remark, recall the Cambridge police officer and the Harvard professor's incident. Nonetheless, there are no finite answers that will satisfy everyone, yet these thoughts might prove helpful: "Thou shalt not be a victim. Thou shalt not be a perpetrator. Above all, thou shalt not be a bystander." These words are engraved at the US Holocaust Memorial Museum in Washington, DC and inspire many readers.

Just as a thought, the dedication of this book might provide a better understanding of the above ideas. In the event some of you skipped the Dedication and plunged into the first chapter, its repetition can prove resourceful: This book is dedicated to Primo Levi, a writer, a chemist, and an Auschwitz survivor; a person whom this author has never met; yet his presence through his words, hastened the conclusion of this book: "Monsters exist, but they are too few in number to be truly dangerous. More dangerous are the common man, the functionaries ready to believe and to act without asking questions." Violence of any kind enables more violence.[3]

■ The Rule of Law Versus *Lex Talionis*

One answer to capital punishment might be in response to what measures more effectively ensure justice through the rule of law (i.e., US Constitution) and the security of the American people. Similar to a two-sided coin, one set of issues relates to democracy centered in abstract rights conferred by an impersonal state that are weaved into equality and due process; the other side includes the ancient calculation of corpse for corpse, flesh for flesh, or *lex talionis*, which amounts to a primal calculus of retaliation and vengeance[4] as strongly endorsed through the *CSI Effect*, which promotes aggressive justice strategies, vigilantism, and fictitious accounts of crime and its process (and clarified through the wars on crime, junkies, sex offenders, poverty, and immigrants, as described in Chapters 3–5).

Immanuel Kant

Some 200 years ago, Immanuel Kant, an influential philosopher, clarified that[5]:

The penal law is a categorical imperative; and woe to him who creeps through the serpent-windings of Utilitarianism [the ethical doctrine that the greatest happiness of the greatest number of people should be the criterion of the virtue of action][6] to discover some advantage that may discharge him from the Justice of Punishment or even from the Pharisaic [self-righteously obsessed with rules[6]] maxim: "It is better that one man should die, than that the whole people should perish." For if justice and righteousness perish, human life would no longer have any value in the world. . .. Hence it may be said, if you slander another, you slander yourself; if you steal from another, you steal from yourself; if you strike another, you strike yourself; if you kill another, you kill yourself. . ... Whoever commits murder must die.

Kant's thoughts are consistent with a perspective offered by an anonymous historian who suggests that:

> In every previous civilization, when the welfare of its criminals took precedence over common good and morality, those societies eventually perished.

■ Fear Can Promote Capital Punishment

It is easy to see how the fear of crime (see Chapter 1), which is repetitively performed on popular television dramas and in motion pictures, has influenced America's fear of victimization and helped shape legal sanctions that led to the following executions:

- Jack Trawick was executed in Alabama in June 11, 2009 for killing Stephanie Alexis Gach in 1992. The 21-year-old community college student was kidnapped, driven to a remote spot, choked, hit on the head with a hammer, and stabbed over and over again. Trawick's history of violence against women dated back to age 10, when he forced a neighbor girl to take off her clothes. Before he received the death penalty for Gach's murder, he had already killed four other young women. He blamed the criminal justice system, which had released him three times from prison. Trawick had been diagnosed, while an inmate in 1970, as a paranoid schizophrenic with homicidal impulses.[7]
- Derrick J. Sonnier was executed in Texas in July 2008. After stalking Melody Flowers for months and having his sexual advances rejected, Sonnier raped her at her apartment. He then stabbed, strangled, and beat her to death. Sonnier turned on her two-year-old son, stabbing him to death and dumping his body in the bathtub with his mother.[8]
- Tony Roach was executed in Texas in September 2007. Roach fatally strangled a 29-year-old white female after burglarizing her residence. Roach knocked on the victim's apartment door, and when he did not receive an answer, he pried open a window and gained entry. He placed a belt around the victim's neck and strangled her. When the victim was dead, Roach sexually assaulted the body and set fire to the residence.[9]
- Douglas Thomas was executed in Virginia in January 2000. Thomas was 17 years old at the time of the crime. He had been dating 14-year-old Jessica Wiseman, the daughter of his victims. Their relationship was serious, and her parents did not approve. Jessica was unwilling to break up with Thomas and became angry with her parents. She helped him in through a window after hours; Thomas entered her parents' bedroom and shot them as they slept. Thomas said Mrs. Wiseman did not die from the first shooting, and Jessica

implored him to shoot her again. He did. Jessica was tried as a juvenile and was released when she was 21 years of age.[10]

- Newton Slawson was executed in Florida in May 2003. Slawson murdered Gerald and Peggy Wood, who was 8.5 months pregnant, and their two young children, Glendon and Jennifer, who were both younger than four years of age. Slawson sliced Peggy Wood's body with a knife and pulled out her fetus, which had two gunshot wounds and multiple cuts.[11]
- Robert Lee Massie was executed in California in March 2001. On January 7, 1965, 23-year-old Massie shot and killed Mildred Weiss during a botched robbery. He pleaded guilty and was sentenced to death. Sixteen hours before his execution in 1967, Governor Ronald Reagan temporarily halted his execution. Later, the *Furman v. Georgia* decision halted executions, and Massie, a model prisoner, was paroled for good behavior in 1978. Massie then killed Boris Naumoff in his liquor store and wounded a clerk in another botched robbery. Massie again pleaded guilty, this time over the objections of his court-appointed lawyer, and Massie was again sentenced to die. As before, Massie welcomed his sentence and, acting on his own novel interpretation of the Sixth Amendment guarantee of self-representation, argued that he had a constitutional right to bypass the appeals process, which is usually automatic in capital cases. Massie's conviction was ultimately overturned in 1985, but he was again convicted and finally executed.[12]

After An Execution, Do Americans Feel Safer?

A former warden at San Quentin, Jeanne Woodford, presided over four executions, including Robert Lee Massie (previously discussed), and in the fall of 2008 she said that Americans do not feel safer after an execution. Currently, Woodford is the director of the California Department of Corrections and Rehabilitation. Director Woodford added, "I came to believe that the death penalty should be replaced with life without the possibility of parole."[13]

Baron de Montesquieu

Baron de Montesquieu, an important contributor to early American ideals, explained that "a man deserves death when he has violated the security of the subject so far as to deprive or attempt to deprive another man of his life. The punishment of death is the remedy, as it were, of a sick society."[14] It might be suitable to define a sick society as an unjust society that sentences an innocent person to prison and both innocent and guilty people to death, but it is difficult to know how many innocent defendants have been executed in the name of justice. Historically, it is easy to recall witches burning in Salem and runaway blacks hung in the South. When inmates are asked if they are innocent, there's a good chance that most say yes.[15] One Internet search for "executed but innocent" produces 2.8 million hits. What methods can be employed to determine innocence? Judge Mark L. Wolf of the

Federal District Court in Boston adds that "in the past decade, substantial evidence has emerged to demonstrate that innocent individuals are sentenced to death, and undoubtedly executed, much more often than previously understood."[16] Yet Judge Wolf declines to rule the death penalty as unconstitutional (see Chapter 8 for Wolf's lack of confidence in federal prosecutors in his courtroom because they continually withhold exculpatory evidence from defendants). The following are a few examples of innocence that can be documented (by sources other than a blog):

- Cameron Todd Willingham was executed in Texas in 2004 for three murders that occurred as a result of a fire in his home. It was one of the first cases that brought forensic misconduct allegations to light. The state fire marshal's office originally ruled that the blaze was an arson started by an accelerant, but a reliable source stated that the fire was not started by arson. The indicators used by investigators to conclude that the fire was arson have since been proven to be scientifically invalid.[17]
- Thomas Arthur had been scheduled to die in Alabama in 2008, but the Alabama Supreme Court voted 5–4 to stay his execution after another inmate confessed to the murder for which Arthur had been sentenced to death. In a sworn statement, Bobby Ray Gilbert confessed to killing Troy Wicker, Jr. more than 26 years ago. Gilbert is serving life in prison for another murder. The stay marked the third time Arthur has been spared on the eve of his execution date.[18]
- Juan Roberto Melendez had been scheduled to die in Florida. He spent nearly 18 years on Florida's death row before being exonerated in 2001. His conviction rested on the testimony of two witnesses; no physical evidence linked him to the crime. New evidence challenged the credibility of the witnesses, and it was discovered that prosecutors withheld a taped confession by the real killer during the original trial.[19]
- Wayne Tompkins, a Florida inmate, faces execution despite new revelations that the state prosecutor prompted a trial witness to lie. Tompkins was to be executed in Florida on October 28, 2008, but was granted a stay of execution to allow time for the state Supreme Court to review his case.[20]

Shoot to Kill Orders and Human Rights

You already know about the numerous defendants who were exonerated from prison and death row and the differences between actual innocence and legal innocence (such as O. J. Simpson), which were detailed in Chapter 8. Included in any discussion of guilt and innocence is *due process error*; on one side of those errors are the number of death sentences imposed on innocent defendants, which can produce many concerns about the comprehensiveness of conventional assessment.[21] Some reports show that 80 death row inmates were exonerated (it is not certain that an assumption can be made that they were all released because they were innocent) from prison in the 1990s, but other reports put the number higher. Also, recall from Chapter 8 that the sentences of 167 death row inmates in Illinois were commuted to life in prison, and four other inmates got shorter sentences because the governor had lost confidence in the criminal justice system in Illinois. There is little question that the irrevocable nature of error in the actual use of the death penalty sets those errors apart from other errors of justice; when an inmate is dead, little can be done to compensate. If error exists in death sentences despite all the precautions and the appeal processes, what about error when an officer shoots to kill?

The popular media continues to promote retaliation, as evidenced by the recent vigilante action films *Gran Torino, Taken, The Wolf Man, Transformers: Revenge of the Fallen*, and *Watchmen,* and the television dramas *Knight Rider* (NBC), *My Own Worst Enemy* (NBC), and *Prison Break* (FOX). The double edge of retaliation, which is often razor sharp, begs an answer to the question, Should the bad guys who are pursued through vigilante or corrupt police action be punished harshly by those who captured them? In the popular television performance *24*, Season 7, Episode 155, "6:00 p.m.–7:00 p.m," the words "Shoot to kill" spilled on the screen by a federal director when he issued directives to his special agents. A US senator in the performance asked the director, "Who issued those orders?" and the director responded, "I did."

By shooting to kill when non-lethal means are feasible, officers bypass the entire legal system and its elaborate protections designed to prevent punishment of the innocent. Instead, it promotes reactive strategies, vigilantism, and fictitious accounts of crime and its process. Officers become judge, jury, and executioner. Little question that police officers in all states are granted authority to use force to accomplish lawful objectives, see *Freeman v. Gore*, 483 F.3d 404 (5th Cir. 2007). But use of force lawsuits are measured by standards established and furthered by the Supreme Court in *Graham v. Connor* (490 U.S., 386, 1989). In *Graham*, reasonableness is measured by: the severity of the crime; the suspect's immediate threat to the safety; and the activity of the suspect resisting arrest. The reasonableness of the use of force can also be measured by what the officer knew at the scene, not by the "20/20 vision of hindsight." An officer may use only that force which is both reasonable and necessary to effect an arrest or detention. Anything more is excessive force, see *Payne v. Pauley*, 337 F.3d 767 (7th Cir. 2003).

Twenty years ago, the Supreme Court abolished the use of deadly force permitted upon a "fleeing felon", see *Tennessee v. Garner* (471 U.S., 1, 1985). A concern that can arise from shoot to kill orders is associated with more than just reasonable standards, but human rights within a democratic framework. In recent years, there have been a number of high-profile pronouncements by officials, not infrequently at the most senior level of government, who have issued orders for the police, federal enforcement agencies (similar to those in the above presentation of *24*), and the military to "shoot to kill," or "shoot on sight," or to use the "utmost force" in response to a particular challenge such as a perceived terrorist threat, but they have also come as a response to widespread looting, to a high incidence of armed robberies, and to an epidemic of drug abuse. There is a temptation for enforcement to seek to escape blame by proclaiming a crackdown on crime, zero tolerance for any individuals suspected of terrorist ambitions, or a policy of unleashing the full fury of the state to root out its offenders. But the rhetoric of shoot-to-kill and its equivalents poses a deep and enduring threat to human rights-based law enforcement approaches.[22] Indeed, human rights law already permits the use of lethal force when doing so is strictly necessary to save human life. The rhetoric of shoot-to-kill serves only to displace clear legal standards with a vaguely defined license to kill, risking confusion among officers, endangering innocent persons, and rationalizing mistakes, while avoiding the genuinely difficult challenges that are posed by the relevant threat.

To do otherwise is tantamount to allowing governments to declare war on crime, junkies, sex offenders, poverty, and immigrants. Under human rights law, the Center for Human Rights and Global Justice argues, enforcement efforts must at once respect and ensure the right to life. Government holds a legal duty to exercise "due diligence" in protecting the lives of individuals from attacks by criminals, including terrorists, armed robbers, looters, and drug dealers. In sum, no derogation is permitted from the right to life, and none is needed. Finally in this regards, the notion that the law of armed conflict is an appropriate frame of reference for a government seeking to deal with law enforcement issues must be soundly rejected for democracy to thrive.

Jean-Jacques Rousseau

Another philosopher who influenced the framers of the US Constitution, Jean-Jacques Rousseau, can guide our thoughts. Rousseau suggested that the death penalty has a purpose: "It is in order that we may not fall victims to an assassin that we consent to die if we ourselves turn assassins. . .. [But] frequent punishments are always a sign of weakness or remissness on the part of the government. . .. [Specifically,] the state [government] has no right to put to death, even for the sake of making an example, any one whom it can leave alive without danger."[23]

Criminals should be punished, but taking the perspective to "kill 'em all and let God sort 'em out" does not advance democracy or social order. It's worth repeating that the most practical prosecutorial method promoted by the media is "try 'em and fry 'em," as typified in the previous chapters regarding the wars on crime, junkies, sex offenders, poverty, and immigrants. As noted at the opening of this chapter, Sister Helen Prejean asks "if we believe that murder is wrong" and we are opposed to violence, how can Americans permit the government to employ capital punishment, including shoot to kill directives, as a legitimate sanction?

In the United States, the popular media provides the description (terrorists) or target (such as immigrants) and strategy (works raids see in Chapter 5) or response which includes aggressive justice (detainment and deportation) initiatives of individuals in targeted groups. In so doing, the popular media glorifies public corruption in the name of justice. Think of it this way: public corruption rarely promotes democracy or social order.

■ Criminal Justice Corruption

Democratic enthusiasts examine the death penalty's opportunities and problems. One problem dominating the thoughts of many enthusiasts relates to corruption, misconduct, and incompetence among criminal justice professionals. Each day, fresh accounts describe the misdirected deeds of police officers, judges, prosecutors, and even high-ranking politicians, such as governors, senators, and some even say America's attorney general. Notions of misconduct and incompetence shade the former US President's (George W. Bush) office suggesting that the president ordered federal enforcement agencies, who were investigating American residents suspected of terrorist activities, to violate those residents' due process rights in the name of justice.[24]

The public wonders, too, about corruption among justice practitioners and celebrities, who are employed to deliver the media's product. When suspects are apprehended by the police, tried, and convicted, the public wonders if prison time and the ultimate sentence (death penalty) can be administered fairly—free from the taint of corruption and racial and socioeconomic bias; free from the disgrace of counsel sleeping through a client's trial; free from the risk of executing an innocent person while heinous offenders roam the streets, sometimes in uniform and other times in stretch limousines. The public wonders about the competence and decisiveness of forensic analyses and criminological accomplishments performed in high-tech laboratories by their favorite actors who conduct extraordinary feats that outsmart Bill Gates or even Einstein and lead to scientific error (see Chapter 8 for detail).

At day's end, despite the eloquence of round-mouthed philosophers, whistle-blowing policy makers, and anxious do-gooders whose words have little affect on the innocent men and women awaiting their fate on death row, some of those souls wonder what happened to their youth, assuming they were competent enough to understand their dilemma (more on this point later in the chapter). The thoughts of the framers of the US Constitution might wonder why justice deserted innocent individuals who now waste away on death row.

Without minimizing America's problem or debate about capital punishment, it should be acknowledged that US wrongful conviction and death penalty errors hardly compare with governments that practice lethal politics or democide (genocide and mass murder). One estimate is that in the 20th century, democide across the globe accounted for over 174 million civilians who were murdered by governments in the name of justice.[25]

■ Death Penalty

The death penalty is legally sanctioned by 35 states (this number varies), the federal government, and the American military. Some jurisdictions abandoned capital punishment sanctions before *Furman v. Georgia* (1972) and include: Alaska, Hawaii, Iowa, Maine, Michigan, Minnesota, Rhode Island, Vermont, West Virginia, and Wisconsin. Prior to *Furman*, every state exercised capital punishment sanctions including the District of Columbia. States without the death penalty (as of March 2009) include:

STATES WITHOUT CAPITAL PUNISHMENT AND YEAR ABOLISHED

Alaska 1957*	New Mexico 2009**
Hawaii 1948	New York 2007
Iowa 1965	North Dakota 1973
Maine 1887	Rhode Island 1984
Massachusetts 1984	Vermont 1964
Michigan 1846	West Virginia 1965
Minnesota 1911	Wisconsin 1853
New Jersey 2007	

Source: Bureau of Justice Statistics. (2008) *Capital punishment statistical tables.* Retrieved July 7, 2009, from http://www.ojp.gov/bjs/pub/html/cp/2007/cp07st.htm
*legislative bills to reintroduce capital punishment
**added

Also, the District of Columbia abolished capital punishment in (1981). Most executions are performed under state authority and many states with capital punishment have not executed individuals in a long time. Many states passed death penalty legislation only for the legislation to be overturned as unconstitutional. As of spring 2008, federal regulations dictate that no jurisdiction can execute a defendant younger than the age of 18 years, but some states, such as South Carolina, have executed offenders as young as 14 years in the past.

Furman v. Georgia

Texas has outperformed other states in the number of executions since the resumption of the death penalty in 1976; prior to that date, Virginia led the nation. Why 1976? Because *Furman v. Georgia* (408 U.S., 238, 1972) put the death sentence in all jurisdictions, including the federal government, on hold.[26] That is not to say that the Supreme Court found capital punishment to be cruel and unusual punishment or unconstitutional. The *Furman* decision found the death penalty to be constitutionally unacceptable because it was thought the penalty was too arbitrary and capricious in its implementation.

Gregg v. Georgia

Gregg v. Georgia's (428 U.S., 153, 1976) decision reported that the death penalty is a legal sanction (depending upon state legislative approval) and is reserved for the worst of the worst criminals (see Post Gregg details later in the chapter). Capital punishment was reinstated in 1976 through *Gregg* and stated "the decision that capital punishment may be the appropriate sanction in extreme cases is an expression of the community's belief that certain crimes are themselves so grievous an affront to humanity that the only adequate response may be the penalty of death."[27]

The Death Penalty Information Center (DPIC) reports 14,371 executions in the states plus 118 in the District of Columbia totaling 14,489 from 1603 to 1972;[28] the Bureau of Justice Statistics reports 1,133 executions in the states from 1976 to 2008[29] and 20 executions from January 1 to March 11, 2009 (see Table 9-1). Texas and Virginia executed no offenders between 1972 to 1982.[30]

Since *Furman*, *Gregg* enabled states to exercise capital punishment, but it took three death penalty provisions in Congress to restore capital punishment to the federal system: the Federal Death Penalty Act in 1994, the Antiterrorism and Effective Death Penalty Act of 1996, and the Foreign Narcotics Kingpin Designation Act in 1999.[31] These acts resulted in three executions.

Death-Eligible Cases

Each of the 35 states (the federal government, and the military) that have death penalty sanctions legislate different capital crime requirements that support a death-eligible case. One estimate is that 10 to 25 percent of all murder and non-negligent manslaughter cases fit their criteria.[32]

> Frequently, the worst crimes are not the ones that result in a death sentence or the other way around.

A serial killer in Louisiana was arrested in the fall of 2008 at a homeless shelter and pleaded guilty to the murder of eight young men[33]; he may have killed as many as 23 men. The Terrebonne Parish district attorney consulted with members of the victims' families and decided against seeking the death penalty. Family members reached a unanimous agreement to accept a plan of back-to-back life sentences for the defendant. One reason for their lack of death sentence support was that they wanted immediate closure, which would not be provided through a death penalty sentence (it takes longer to prepare for a death penalty case, and trying these cases can require as much as two-thirds more time than non-capital-punishment cases).

The following are highlights of some death-eligible criteria legislated by capital punishment states[34]:

- Alabama: 1 of 18 aggravating factors such as Murder by the defendant during a kidnapping in the first degree
- California: First-degree murder with special circumstances; train wrecking; perjury causing execution
- Florida: Capital drug trafficking and sexual assault
- Georgia: Murder, kidnapping for ransom, and aircraft hijacking
- Illinois: First-degree murder with 1 of 21 aggravating factors

TABLE 9-1 EXECUTIONS BY JURISDICTION 1603–1972,* 1976–2008, 2009 (JANUARY 1 TO MARCH 11)

Jurisdiction	1603–1972	1976–2008	January 1 to March 11, 2009	Jurisdiction	1603–1972	1976–2008	January 1 to March 11, 2009
Alabama	708	38	2	Montana	71	3	0
Alaska	12	0	0	Nebraska	34	3	0
Arizona	104	23	0	Nevada	61	12	0
Arkansas	478	27	0	New Hampshire	24	0	0
California	709	13	0	New Jersey	361	0	0
Colorado	101	1	0	New Mexico	73	1	0
Connecticut	126	1	0	New York	1,130	0	0
Delaware	62	14	0	North Carolina	784	43	0
Florida	314	66	1	North Dakota	8	0	0
Georgia	950	44	1	Ohio	438	28	0
Hawaii	49	0	0	Oklahoma	132	88	1
Idaho	26	1	0	Oregon	122	2	0
Illinois	348	12	0	Pennsylvania	1,040	3	0
Indiana	131	19	0	Rhode Island	52	0	0
Iowa	45	0	0	South Carolina	641	39	1
Kansas	57	0	0	South Dakota	15	1	0
Kentucky	424	2	0	Tennessee	335	4	1
Louisiana	632	27	0	Texas	755	423	12
Maine	21	0	0	Utah	43	6	0
Maryland	309	5	0	Vermont	26	0	0
Massachusetts	345	0	0	Virginia	1,277	103	1
Michigan	13	0	0	Washington	105	4	0
Minnesota	66	0	0	West Virginia	155	0	0
Mississippi	351	10	0	Wisconsin	1	0	0
Missouri	285	66	0	Wyoming	22	1	0
				Washington, DC	118	0	0

Source: Developed by the author for this book.
Furman v. Georgia (1972) halted all death penalties from 1972 to 1976.

- Louisiana: Aggravated rape of a victim younger than age 13 years (see the discussion after this list)
- Mississippi: Capital murder and aircraft piracy
- New Jersey: Murder by one's own conduct, by solicitation, committed in furtherance of a narcotics conspiracy, or during commission of a crime of terrorism
- South Carolina: First-degree criminal sexual misconduct with a minor who is younger than 11 years of age; aggravating factor of murder by a sexually violent predator (under South Carolina law)
- Texas: Criminal homicide with 1 of 8 aggravating factors

On June 25, 2008, the US Supreme Court struck down as unconstitutional a Louisiana statute that allowed the death penalty for the rape of a child in which the victim did not die. In *Kennedy v. Louisiana*, the court held that all such laws, in which the crime against an individual involved no murder or intent to murder, were not in keeping with the national consensus restricting the death penalty to the worst offenses. Today, no one is on death row for any offense that does not involve murder.[35]

Death Row Inmates

Typically, more than 100 convicted defendants are sentenced to death each year.[36] At year end 2006, 37 states and the Federal Bureau of Prisons system held 3,228 prisoners under sentence of death (not every death penalty state has inmates on death row).[37] The number of federal death sentences (57) has tripled since 2000, and the number of state death sentences (3,171) declined during the same period.[38] There have also been marked increases in the number of people on federal death row from states that do not have their own death penalty laws. For example, in 2004 a federal jury voted to sentence Dustin Honken to death for the murder of two girls, aged 10 and 6 years, in Iowa who would have testified against him because they witnessed him murder their mother. Honken also received three life sentences for the murder of the girls' mother and two other adults who would have testified against him in a drug case. In 2005, a federal jury recommended a death sentence for codefendant Angela Johnson for aiding Honken in four of the five murders.[39]

Methods of Execution

Death penalty states utilize a prescribed method of administrating death sanctions in keeping with federal legislation. Lethal injection has been used most often, along with electrocution (the electric chair was designed by Thomas Edison), lethal gas, hanging, and firing squad (some states offer the condemned a choice of method).[40]

■ Death Penalty Advocates

Advocates argue that the death penalty is the optimal solution in punishing heinous offenders and that it plays a significant role in specific (individual) and general (at-large) deterrence of crime. Advocates say that capital punishment is not consistent with cruel and unusual punishment nor has the US Constitution or any legislation ever said that it could not be used, and it remains a legal sanction as evidenced by the US Supreme Court's decisions (*Gregg v. Georgia* [1976], *Jurek v. Texas* [1976], *Proffitt v. Florida* [1976], *Dawson v. Delaware* [1992], *Atkins v. Virginia* [2002]).[41]

Paul Rubin

Advocate studies have shown that capital punishment represents a strong deterrent effect, with "each execution deterring between 3 and 18 murders."[42] If Paul Rubin is correct, employing the statistical median (10.5) would suggest a little over 12,000 lives have been saved based on the number of criminals executed since 1976. (Further calculation shows 164,241 saved lives based on 15,642 executions from the year 1603 to March 11, 2009, which appears to be a calculation that might be hard to document, in this author's opinion.)

The argument of Cass R. Sunstein and Adrian Vermeule, law professors at Harvard University, is consistent with Rubin's findings; the professors argue that capital punishment saves lives with each execution.[43] Therefore, they argue that a jurisdiction's refusal to impose the death penalty condemns numerous innocent people to death. They see capital punishment as a life–life trade-off and a serious commitment to the sanctity of human life; therefore, moral jurisdictions are compelled to utilize capital punishment rather than forbid its use because it is an honorable and righteous form of punishment.

Ernest Van den Haag

Ernest Van den Haag explains that capital punishment is America's harshest punishment and that when it is employed, it is irrevocable because it ends the existence of the punished individual instead of temporarily imprisoning the person.[44] If there is an injustice in capital punishment, it does not lay with the nature of the punishment because punishments are imposed on persons, not their race or socioeconomic groups, he adds. Guilt is a personal matter. "Justice requires that as many of the guilty as possible be punished, regardless of whether others have avoided punishment."[45] Capital punishment is an appropriate tool for the government, in Van den Haag's opinion.

Joanna Shepherd

Joanna Shepherd adds that executing more than nine murderers per year in each jurisdiction exhibits greater deterrence than states that execute fewer offenders; she refers to a "threshold effect." That is, nine executions per year is a magic number that can deter criminally violent persons from future capital crimes. In part, Shepherd's conclusion is that capital punishment in the states that executed more than nine convicted criminals every year led to a "net saving of lives."[46]

Advocates, the general public, and the popular media report that because the United States is a violent nation (see Chapters 3 through 5 regarding the wars on crime, junkies, poverty, sex offenders, and immigrants), the death penalty is an appropriate sanction with which to control violence (even though violent crime rates are down from their historic highs of the 1980s and 1990s).[47] Also, the threat of capital punishment enables some prosecutors to negotiate with suspects, especially toward a plea bargain. Without the capital punishment threat, some prosecutors claim, violators would receive less punishment than they actually deserve. This thought is consistent with many prosecutors who were involved in this study for this book in the states with capital punishment as a sanction.

Gallup Poll

A Gallup Poll shows that 69 percent of their participants in 2007 felt that the death penalty is appropriate for persons who are convicted of murder, and although this percentage has declined from a high of 84 percent in 1994, capital punishment continues to be popular.[48] Of the number polled, 59 percent of the black participants had a different opinion; they said they do not favor capital punishment.[49] Additionally, another study shows that when voters elect judges, they do so based on a judge's perspective about capital punishment. An example is as follows:

> The analysis presented [in the study] considers public opinion's influence on the composition of courts . . . and its influence on judge votes in capital punishment cases. In elective state supreme courts, public support for capital punishment influences the ideological composition of those courts and judge willingness to uphold death sentences. On the highly salient issue of the death penalty, mass opinion and the institution of electing judges systematically influence court composition and judge behavior.[50]

This idea is consistent with the previous finding that capital punishment is a local matter, assuming state law provides for it. Through public opinion and state supreme court rulings, many jurisdictions accept that sufficient consequences must be available to effectively deal with their most dangerous of criminals; therefore, many states have continued to incorporate the use of the death penalty as an option.

Advocates also add that heinous offenders enjoy living on the edge and enjoy the forbidden and the exciting, regardless of criminal justice sanctions handed down by the courts.[51] Chronic offenders have no conscience about life or death, continue to commit violent crimes after they are incarcerated, and seek out every opportunity to destroy other prisoners, personnel, and volunteers.[52] Many advocates feel that criminals who have taken another life have forfeited their own life, regardless of the public expense of capital punishment. The public says it does not look favorably upon life in prison without parole options for heinous killers and sexual violators of young children.[53] For example, one prison practitioner offers the following observation for your consideration[54]:

There is something unsettling about advice found among many popular writers, fear peddling entrepreneurs, and bleeding heart liberals who proclaim rehabilitation is a breath away from every serial murderer, pedophile, and spouse basher. It is unlikely that chronic violent predators can be treated in or out of prison with any degree of success towards lower recidivism rates.

■ Pro-Death Penalty Web Site

Statistics available at the Pro-Death Penalty Web site (http://www.prodeath-penalty.com/) suggest that of 635 killers who were executed between 1998 and 2005, they had murdered at least 1,315 people, or an average of 2.1 victims each.[55] Pro-death penalty advocates show specifically:

- 2005 scheduled executions: 60 killers who were executed in 2005 murdered 116 people
- 2004 scheduled executions: 59 killers who were executed in 2004 murdered 88 people
- 2003 scheduled executions: 65 killers who were executed in 2003 murdered 129 people
- 2002 scheduled executions: 71 killers who were executed in 2002 murdered 120 people
- 2001 scheduled executions: 66 killers who were executed in 2001 murdered 267 people
- 2000 scheduled executions: 85 killers who were executed in 2000 murdered 156 people

■ American Death Penalty History

The earliest recorded death penalty case in America was against Captain George Kendall in 1608, who was hung for the capital crime of treason in Jamestown, a colony in Virginia. Historically, 10,598 executions, or 33 per year, were conducted between 1608 and 1929 in America. Most often, the death penalty in early American history was conducted under local legal authority (sheriff) and often included religious leaders, especially if it was a witch trial; in any event, they were highly public and symbol-laden events that gained the attention of most residents and travelers, similar to the social events that surrounded executions in merry Old England.

Early death penalty laws and statutes were created after the Revolutionary War and were adapted from English common law, which included mandatory statutes. That is, death was an automatic sanction if a defendant was convicted of a specific crime. The courts had little or no discretion in sentencing, and juries couldn't easily circumvent what they perceived to be the harshness of mandatory death. During colonial times, hanging was mandatory for murder; rape; heresy; treason; housebreaking–burglary; horse stealing; forgery; counterfeiting; piracy; slave revolt;

sodomy, buggery, and bestiality; and concealing a birth. In New England the list included idolatry; blasphemy; adultery; man stealing; offenses against God and morality; and witchcraft. In the South, the list included embezzling tobacco; stealing hogs; theft; aiding slaves; aiding runaway slaves; and property crimes.[56]

Historically, judicial hanging was utilized often in early America and included five techniques: the short drop, upright jerker, suspension hanging, the standard drop, and the long drop. A cord was wrapped around the neck of a condemned offender. In the drop method, the condemned was dropped through a trapdoor; however, in the upright jerker method, the condemned would be violently jerked into the air by means of a system of weights and pulleys. The objective of the upright jerker was to provide a swift death by breaking the condemned's neck, which didn't happen that often. The upright jerker, in particular, was utilized in several American states, including early Connecticut, where Gerald Chapman, a murderer and gang member, and others were put to death. The upright jerker was withdrawn from use in the United States by the 1930s.[57]

One of the primary differences between the early American capital punishment process and the modern process is that it was formerly a local matter linked to early communities, their local laws and customs, and the demands of the residents. Today, depending upon state laws, the death penalty continues to be a local matter, and it is guided by federal laws and regulations and local prosecutor discretion, making the prosecutor one of the most important and powerful representatives of government (see Chapter 7 for more details).

As the United States became civilized, capital crimes during the premodern period (1930 to 1967) changed, too, and included murder, rape, armed robbery, kidnapping, burglary, and aggravated assault; espionage and treason constituted a capital crime at the federal level. From 1930 to 1967 there were 3,891 executions recorded, or 102 per year. Discretionary statutes were linked to convictions, and there were few rational or meaningful bases to determine who received death and who didn't. However, in capital punishment cases, there is continual scrutiny from legal and other sources, more so than among noncapital punishment cases, to prevent arbitration; appeal is automatic and mandated in all capital cases. Furthermore, Georgia and other states provided new death penalty statutes that would prevent arbitrariness and discrimination.[58]

■ At the Core of the Capital Punishment Debate

Civilized people believe they live in a just and fair world where wrongdoers should be appropriately treated, deprived or punished, and rehabilitated.[59] Yet these actions must be fair and reasonable; people want to legitimately be able to intrude in the lives of violators and alter their behavior.[60] A civilized society requires justification of legal intrusion; nonetheless, some of those civilized people believe that punishment is justified because it achieves some societal goal: deterrence, social solidarity, moral education, incapacitation, and so on.[61] Others think that only offenders deserve to be punished and then only in an amount that is proportionate to the harm associated with the offense.[62] In a sense, a moral evil of different crimes exists.[63] Those civilized folks who accept legalized death as just punishment rely on the notion of retribution or just deserts (wrongdoers are getting what they deserve). Their thoughts can be summed up this way: "People that favor the death penalty agree that capital punishment is a relic of barbarism, but as murder itself is barbaric, they contend that death is a fitting punishment for it."[64] These retributionists accept that there are circumstances in which the infliction of suffering is both an obligation of government and a positive response, versus utilitarianists (the greatest happiness of the greatest number) who believe that punishment must be justified by the value of consequences, and therein lays its morality. "The view that punishment is justified by the value of its consequences is compatible with any ethical theory which allows meaning to be attached to moral judgments."[65]

At the end of the day, a consensus emerges on both sides that some amount of misery and accountability for an offender is linked to a specific crime. For example, when a guilty defendant receives a number of years to serve in prison, that sentence somehow rates higher on an alleged moral yardstick than the death sentence of a murderer who hacked a young family of five to death at the beach. Opponents of capital punishment do not see death as justifiable punishment, or even moral punishment, for the worst of the worst offenders.

■ Opposition to Capital Punishment

Opposition to the death penalty can be found in the beliefs that capital punishment is morally inappropriate (as previously discussed), a weak criminal deterrent of capital crimes, discriminatory against certain socioeconomic classes and persons of color, and too expensive. Equally important, killing someone does not address the root cause of crime, and wrongful convictions have led to the death (and imprisonment) of innocent persons.

The argument continues that capital punishment furthers violent crime because violence-prone individuals identify with the executor rather than the offender, or what is referred to as the *brutalization effect*.[66] The more violence shown by authority or government, the more likely those governed will respond in kind. Early America is one example. The more the English Crown favored violence as a method of control over the colonies, the more resistance there was among the population.[67] Offering a highly debatable perspective, in the fall of 2008, violence in Iraq (after many years of American military occupation) dropped to a four-year low, the *American Forces Press Service* says. Contributing to this reduced violence is the finding that "many Iraqis are now settling their differences through debate and the political process, rather than open conflict."[68] Violence begets violence; as a guide, one study examined the strict enforcement protocol linked to prison custody and compliance among its prisoners.[69] The study compared the enforcement methods between two similar high-risk penitentiaries: Attica in western New York and Stateville near Chicago. Both prisons have similar security level prisoners; in fact, the prisoners in one facility could have easily been prisoners in the other. The results showed that the prison that enforced the rules more often experienced more disciplinary behavior among its inmates (thinking goes that prisoners are rule violators; therefore, harsh enforcement is necessary to control them). The implication is that violent enforcement can lead to an increase in violence among those governed or managed. (A similar experience was had by the framers of the US Constitution in their struggle for freedom from an overzealous English government enforcing English rules and sanctions upon unwilling subjects.) This results in the brutalization effect, which amounts to identifying with the death penalty executioner, in a sense. Many public policy makers advocate (and civil litigation enforces) finding a fair and just balance between control and compliance, regardless of an agency's role and mission, from police departments to jails.[70]

Thus, statistics show that capital punishment appears to enhance crimes of violence,[71] and this book argues that in response to increased violence in the popular media, through the *CSI Effect*, violent persons and the criminal justice community become more aggressive and violent, vigilantism is glorified, and fictitious accounts of crime, criminals, and what to do about them are pervasive. In one study, it was observed that rather than capital punishment decreasing the incidence of criminal homicide, executions in Oklahoma actually served to increase the level of postexecution homicides.[72] Bowers and Pierce also argue that on average, one or more executions in a given month increases the number of homicides by two in the next month. One assumption is that executions stimulate criminal homicides through the process of devaluation of human life and a disrespect of others.

Most Southern states have the death penalty on their books.[73] According to a September 2008 FBI report, the South is the one region that reported a rise in its murder rate in 2007.[74] FBI statistics showed that the murder rate in the country actually declined from 5.7 murders per 100,000 people in 2006 to 5.6 in 2007. The rate declined in the Northeast, the Midwest, and the West. In the South, which includes Texas (even though it's really in the West), the murder rate increased from 6.8 in 2006 to 7.0 in 2007, the highest rate among the four regions. The South consistently has had the highest murder rate among the four regions. That is, the murder rate declines in every region except the South, where executions are most prevalent, explains the Death Penalty Information Center. This isn't news! Earlier evidence was available in the late 1950s. Thorsten Sellin's research involved systematic homicide comparisons among states with and without capital punishment.[75] Those states with capital punishment did not have lower rates of homicide than presumably similar states in the same geographic region. Other researchers in the late 1980s reported that over a 12-year period, the actual homicide rate in death penalty states (8.5 homicides per 100,000 population) was actually a little higher than the rate in states without the death penalty (7.6 homicides per 100,000 population).[76]

Capital punishment advocates, such as Shepherd, Sunstein, and Vermeule (previously discussed), encourage the government to execute more death row inmates, rather than fewer, because in effect it would reduce capital crimes through the threshold effect (nine is the magic number of inmates, at a minimum, that should be executed for best results in each jurisdiction).[77] It could be wondered if the annual 400 or so justifiable homicides performed by the police should be increased, too, in an effort to deter criminal activity;[78] another ill conceived approach that would reduce the democratic spirit and increase violence is through an escalation of the use of force or shoot to kill orders and to freeze the US Constitution. A problem with the death penalty advocates' perspective about the use of violence is that research conducted in a high-custody penitentiary near Chicago showed that of 325 inmates surveyed, the majority of the criminally violent offenders reported that it made little difference if they knew they'd be indicted with a capital crime—they still would have committed the capital offense regardless of the outcome.[79] This finding is consistent with experts who argue that offenders rarely consider the consequences of their criminal behavior; rather, they tend to consider the benefits of their crimes.[80]

Statistics apparently influenced Dallas County District Attorney Craig Watkins, who announced in the fall of 2008 that his office will reexamine nearly 40 death penalty convictions in Dallas County.[81] Watkins says he will start with the oldest cases first because they are most likely to be scheduled sooner. However, Watkins clarifies: "I'm not saying I'm putting a moratorium on the death penalty." Evidently Watkins and other prosecutors might accept the idea that violence begets violence and have had an opportunity to review crime and capital punishment in the United States and historically in England.

Death Row Inmates Exonerated by State: May, 2009

The Death Penalty Information Center shows that 133 exonerations from death row occurred from 1973 to May, 2009, in 26 states. The most exonerations came from Florida (22), Illinois (19), Louisiana (9), and Texas (8), and seven states each had one exoneration during that period. (Check DPIC's website for updates at http://www.deathpenaltyinfo.org/innocence-and-death-penalty) For instance, DPIC reports that Nathson Fields, 55, became the 131st person to be exonerated from death row after a retrial of his case in Illinois resulted in an acquittal on April 8, 2009. Fields and a co-defendant were sentenced to death for murder. The original trial was marred by corruption because Circuit Judge Thomas Maloney had accepted a $10,000 bribe during the trial. Maloney was ultimately convicted and spent 13 years in prison for fixing murder trials before his death in 2003.[82]

England and Capital Punishment

Historically, England (and most of Western Europe) was a very violent nation. For example, the number of homicides from the 13th to the 20th centuries suggests that 20 homicides were committed for every 100,000 inhabitants. That number declined until the 20th century to about five per 100,000. Ironically, capital punishment in England declined, as had capital crimes. For example, there were 3,780 executions from 1509 to 1547, an average of 140 annually.[83] From 1548 to 1553 there were 3,360 executions, an average of 560 per year. As capital punishment declined in England, the estimated number of executions dropped to 90 per year from 1625 to 1649, or a total of 2,160 executions. From 1650 to 1658, 990 executions were reported, and there were over 200 offensible crimes that led to execution in the 17th century. Today, the United Kingdom reports 19 victims for every one million citizens, with a clearance rate of almost 95 percent.[84] Turning the idea of capital punishment upside down can suggest that a less violent punitive governmental response produces fewer capital crimes by the population it governs as demonstrated by these statistics.[85] A study of 100 modern nations confirms that autocratic nations (those that have rulers with absolute authority, thus less democracy[86]) tend to utilize harsh punitive sanctions more often than nonautocratic nations.[87]

Death Penalty Discrimination

Two percent of death sentences in America are based on false convictions, and black males are more likely to be falsely convicted than white males.[88] In 96 percent of the states where there have been reviews of race and the death penalty, a pattern of either race-of-victim or race-of-defendant discrimination, or both, emerged.[89] In a Connecticut study, researchers found that seeking the death penalty often correlates with the race of the victim and the defendant, not necessarily with the severity of the crimes, as the law requires.[90] "There was basically no rational system to explain who got the death penalty," the researcher commented, and he added that seeking the death penalty seemed random, with some exceptions. For example, after a review of 207 murder cases dating back to the early 1970s that were eligible for the death penalty, the following data emerged:

- Black defendants received death sentences at three times the rate of white defendants in cases where the victims were white.
- Killers of white victims were treated more severely than people who killed minorities, when it came time to decide the charges.
- Minorities who killed whites received death sentences at higher rates than minorities who killed minorities.

The previous study is used in litigation that is initiated by death row inmates who challenge the constitutionality of the way the death penalty is applied. The State of Connecticut contested the findings, suggesting that research errors (problems with methodology) were apparent in the study. Nonetheless, other researchers have stood by their recent findings that the process of the death penalty is highly discriminatory, particularly among defendants of color, males, and certain socioeconomic classes, which contradicts the arguments of Ernest Van den Haag and others.[91]

A nationally known expert on the death penalty argues that US Department of Justice reports miss the point on the issue of race and the federal death penalty.[92] Concern was not whether there was "blatant racism against minorities but rather, whether defendants with similar levels of criminal culpability and deathworthiness are treated comparably or differently because of their race or the race of their victims."[93,94]

In 2007, 42 male offenders were executed, of which 28 were white and 14 were black.[95] In 2008, through November 20 of that year, 35 offenders were executed, of which 23 were white, 9 were black, 2 were Asian, and 1 was Latino. Additionally, of the 3,228 inmates on state and federal death rows in 2006, 1,802 were white, 1,352 were black, 28 were American Indian, 35 were Asian, and 11 were of unknown race.

Pre-Death Penalty Costs

Before appeal or a prison's expense of executing a defendant, there are pre-death penalty costs that are more expensive at each stage of the judicial process than similar non-death penalty cases. Everything that is needed for an ordinary trial is also needed for a death penalty case, plus more[96]:

- Pretrial time will be needed to prepare; cases typically take a year to come to trial.
- Pretrial motions will be filed and answered.
- Experts will be hired.
- Twice as many attorneys will be appointed for the defense, and there will be a comparable team for the prosecution.
- Defense and state attorneys spent over 600 hours, and the governor spent close to 60 hours, on a single clemency proceeding.[97]
- Jury selection in capital cases takes 5.3 times longer than in noncapital cases.[98]
- Jurors are more likely to be sequestered (put in isolation).
- Two trials instead of one will be conducted: one for guilt and one for punishment.
- The trial is three to five times longer than typical murder trials.
- All capital cases are automatically appealed, during which defendants are held in high-security custody.

Through all of this, consider the surveyors and witnesses who must testify numerous times and the changes in their lifestyles that are required to meet the expectations of the pre-death penalty judicial process.

Estimated Costs of the Death Penalty

Much of the following data is available from the Death Penalty Information Center (DPIC)[99]:

- New York: It was estimated that in 1995, capital punishment cost $160 million, or approximately $23 million for each person who was sentenced to death, even though there are no executions likely for many years.[100,101]

- New Jersey: A Policy Perspectives report concluded that the state's death penalty has cost taxpayers $253 million since 1983, a figure that is greater than the costs that would have been incurred had the state utilized a sentence of life without parole instead of death. The study examined the costs of death penalty cases to prosecutors' offices, public defenders' offices, courts, and correctional facilities. Since 1982, there have been 197 capital trials in New Jersey and 60 death sentences, of which 50 were reversed. There have been no executions, and 10 men are housed on the state's death row.[102]

- North Carolina: Researchers reported that in 1993, an estimated $2.16 million was incurred per execution over the costs of a non-death penalty system that imposes a maximum sentence of imprisonment for life.[103]

- California: Annually, the state justice system spends $90 million more than ordinary costs on capital cases, reports the DPIC. Of that figure, $78 million is incurred at the trial level. Appeals and habeas corpus proceedings add tens of thousands more. In all, it costs $125 million a year more to prosecute and defend death penalty cases and to keep inmates on death row than it would simply to put all those people in prison for life without parole.[104] In January 2003, despite a budget deficit, California Governor Gray Davis proposed building a new $220 million state-of-the-art death row.[105]

- Tennessee: Death penalty trials cost an average of 48 percent more than the average cost of trials in which prosecutors seek life imprisonment.[106]

- Washington: At the trial level, death penalty cases are estimated to generate roughly $470,000 in additional costs to the prosecution and defense over the cost of trying the same case as an aggravated murder without the death penalty, explains the DPIC. These cases cost an extra $47,000 to $70,000 for court personnel, and the estimated cost of appellate defense averages $100,000 more than in non-death penalty murder cases. Personal restraint petitions filed in death penalty cases, on average, cost an additional $137,000 in public defense costs.

- Kansas: Capital cases are 70 percent more expensive than comparable non-death penalty cases, with median costs at an estimated $1.26 million each from prosecution to execution, advises the DPIC. The costs of non-death penalty cases were calculated through the end of incarceration and were found to have a median cost of $740,000. For death penalty cases, the pre-trial- and trial-level expenses were the most expensive part: 49 percent of the total cost. The costs of appeals were 29 percent of the total expense, and the incarceration and execution costs accounted for the remaining 22 percent.

- Florida: The state could save $51 million each year by punishing all first-degree murderers with life in prison without parole, one source estimates. Based on the 44 executions Florida has carried out since 1976, each cost an estimated $24 million.[107]

Counties manage these high costs by decreasing funding for highways and police and by increasing taxes. Between 1982 and 1997, the extra cost of capital trials was $1.6 billion.

■ Prosecutors and Capital Punishment Indictments

Prosecutors are not equal. Yet, it could be assumed that prosecutors in every county, parish (Louisiana), and district (Connecticut) in every death penalty state have the same opportunity to indict a defendant on capital charges when the defendant is indicted for a capital crime. In similar jurisdictions, each prosecutor has what appears to be his or her professional agenda as evidenced by the following example: in capital punishment states where execution eligibility among defendants is similar, some prosecutors argue for the death penalty and some do not (this decision is not centered in the substantial evidence gathered by the police but rather by a prosecutor's discretion). However, because of such factors as the quality of evidence, time, and financial limitations (among other factors), local prosecutors must pick and choose among which death-eligible cases they will seek a death sentence.[108]

Post-*Gregg*,[109] local prosecutors investigate cases and decide whether a case is death eligible. Discretion among prosecutors is a sober reality, revealing that indeed they are probably the most powerful government officials in the country.[110] In Georgia, the likelihood of a death sentence is about 1.5 times higher in rural areas than in urban areas.[111] In north-central Georgia, the death penalty is almost four times higher than in northern Georgia and 2.5 times more likely than in Fulton County (Atlanta). Murder defendants in Mercer County, New Jersey were almost 50 times more likely to go to trial than comparable defendants in Camden County, New Jersey. One implication of this finding is that prosecutors in Camden County made different decisions about pursuing capital punishment than prosecutors in Mercer County. In some New Jersey counties, two-thirds or more of all death-eligible defendants were sentenced to death, and in other counties less than one-third were sentenced to death.

Researchers report that in the largest county in Washington, King County, prosecutors historically sought a death sentence in 25 percent of the death-eligible crimes.[112] The rate of death sentences sought in the second largest county, Pierce County, is approximately double at 52 percent. Also, in Texas's Harris County (Houston), one-third of the prosecutors sent more people to death row than all of Virginia's prosecutors combined (see "State Death Penalty Convictions Overturned" below for interesting details linked to this finding).[113] Similar statistics can be found across America, implying that local prosecutors decide which defendants will face the death penalty.

Another observer reveals that the high percentage of arrests that do not result in convictions is an issue linked to a prosecutor's decision whether or not to charge a suspect.[114] For example, cases can be dropped out of the system after an arrest in three ways:

- A police supervisor may tell an arresting officer that no evidence exists to make the case. In California, Joan Petersilia found that about 11 percent of all arrests were dropped because supervisors thought there was insufficient evidence for prosecution.

- Prosecutors reject a case because they typically conclude that there is not sufficient evidence to prosecute the suspect.
- Some cases are dismissed later by the prosecutor, a judge, or even a grand jury.

Samuel Walker provides several reasons for prosecutor rejections.[115] For example, in New York City, insufficient evidence or lack of evidence accounted for an estimated 61 percent of the rejected cases. In San Diego, it was 51 percent. Witness problems are the second most important reason, accounting for 18 percent of dropped cases in New York City and 19 percent in San Diego. For most crimes against persons (robbery, rape, and assault), the testimony of the victim or a witness is the primary evidence and accounts for 70 to 80 percent of most rejections. As for dismissals, witness competence accounts for 33 percent of those dismissals in New York City and 20 percent in San Diego. In other words, through the eyes of the prosecutor, witness credibility can determine whether a sexual assault case goes forward in the courts or is simply dropped. Two points require attention[116]

- A prosecutor can divert or merge cases, which accounts for almost one-half of the dismissed cases (as opposed to the dropped cases before trial).
- Many cases are dismissed in the interest of justice, which requires little explanation or documentation on the part of the prosecutor.

Also, decisions to reject sexual assault charges could be traced to the sexual assault victim's failure to appear for a profile interview, refusal to cooperate in the prosecution of the case, or admission that the charges were fabricated.[117] Also, prosecutors can reject sexual assault cases because of case and victim characteristics, including victims and suspects who are acquainted, related, or intimate partners, rather than cases that involve a victim and a suspect who were strangers. The findings from the 444 prosecutors who were surveyed for this book further support this perspective, as discussed in Chapter 10. That is, unethical prosecutors accept only cases they can win, and they can only win if their witness or victim is credible, authentic, and compelling.

Success rates varied significantly across the country from jurisdiction to jurisdiction, and it could be suggested that some prosecutors hold a greater expertise than others. For example, government statistics report that of all offenses in 2000, adjudication outcomes for 64 percent of felony defendants in the 75 largest counties ended in a conviction.[118] Fifty-six percent of violent crimes, 66 percent of property offenses, 65 percent of drug offenses, and 72 percent of public disorder offenses ended in convictions. Of the total conviction rate (56 percent) for crimes of violence, 38 percent were plea bargained, 4 percent went to trial, 37 percent were dismissed, 2 percent were acquitted, and the remainder were changed to misdemeanors or other outcomes.

There is another side of the death penalty linked to this discussion that is worth acknowledging. Outsiders have little knowledge of the process prior to indicting a suspect, especially in regards to capital punishment, or the difficulties of proving guilt in a criminal trial when the death penalty is on table. "The truth is that most prosecutors must work very hard for long hours before trial so that a case will look relatively easy when it is presented and so that the ultimate conclusion will appear inescapable," says a former prosecutor.[119] The amount of office and colleague debate arises over the courtroom merits of a specific case. At home, family members have input into the daily affairs of the case, particularly if the media is involved. Prosecutors know that in a capital punishment case, they will have to meet the highest burden of proof in the American system for all 12 jurors. Nonetheless, how can the following examples appropriately be explained?

- About one-fourth of Ohio's death row inmates come from Hamilton County (Cincinnati), but only 9 percent of the state's murders occur there.[120]
- The city of Baltimore had only one person on Maryland's death row, but suburban Baltimore County, with one-tenth as many murders as the city, had nine times the number of inmates on death row.[121]
- An investigation by seven Indiana newspapers in 2001 found that the death penalty depended on factors such as the views of individual prosecutors and the financial resources of the county. Two Indiana counties have produced almost as many death sentences as all of the other Indiana counties combined.[122]
- In New York, although upstate counties experience 19 percent of the state's homicides, they nonetheless account for 61 percent of all capital prosecutions. Three counties (out of 62 in the state) accounted for over one-third of all cases in which a death notice was filed.[123]

During the course of capital case trials, all close evidentiary rulings are likely to favor the defense because "they can appeal and the prosecution cannot."[124] Prosecutors clearly understand that every point they make will be disputed by the defense and reviewed by the judge, who is usually impartial. Overall, "the courts carefully nurture the defendant'[s] rights while cavalierly ignoring the rights of the people."[125] This last point is played out in most trials, regardless if capital punishment is the sanction requested by the prosecutor.

■ Mental Retardation and Capital Punishment

In *Penry v. Lynaugh* (1989), the US Supreme Court held that "cruel and unusual punishment" under the Eighth Amendment does not forbid executing the mentally retarded, but the court said that a Texas jury was required to consider the defendant's alleged mental retardation as a mitigating factor that led to the crime.[126] Penry was retried for capital murder. Penry again received the death sentence in Texas. Once again, the court ruled in *Penry v. Lynaugh* that the jury was not adequately able to consider Penry's mental retardation in the sentencing phase of the trial. Penry was spared the death penalty. The Supreme Court did not directly rule out the execution of the mentally retarded based on the Eighth Amendment.

In 2002, in the case of *Atkins v. Virginia*, the US Supreme Court ruled 6–3 that executing the mentally retarded is cruel and unusual punishment and therefore violates the Eighth Amendment.[127] The US Supreme Court has held that mentally incompetent inmates may not be executed. Consequently, the Pennsylvania Supreme Court ruled that the State could force two Pennsylvania death row inmates to take antipsychotic medication so they would be mentally competent enough to proceed with their appeals and be executed.[128] The two inmates were sentenced to death but were found to be incompetent to participate in the appeals that were filed on their behalf.

Exactly what mental retardation means and how it is established differs from state to state. For instance:[129]

- Arizona: A condition based on a mental deficit that has resulted in significantly subaverage general intellectual functioning existing concurrently with significant limitations in adaptive functioning, where the onset of the forgoing conditions occurred before the defendant reached the age of 18.
- Florida: Significantly subaverage general intellectual functioning existing concurrently with deficits in adaptive behavior and manifested during the period from conception to age 18.
- Nebraska: Mental retardation means significantly subaverage general intellectual functioning existing concurrently with deficits in adaptive behavior. An IQ of 70 or below on a reliably administered IQ test shall be presumptive evidence of mental retardation.
- Washington: The individual has (1) significantly subaverage general intellectual functioning; (2) existing concurrently with deficits in adaptive behavior; and (3) both significantly subaverage general intellectual functioning and deficits in adaptive behavior were manifested during the developmental period. The age of onset is 18 years of age. The required IQ level is 70 or below.

The American Association on Intellectual and Developmental Disabilities explains that "intellectual disability is a disability characterized by significant limitations both in intellectual functioning and in adaptive behavior as expressed in conceptual, social, and practical adaptive skills. This disability originates before the age of 18."[130] That is, intellectual disability, or what had been called mental retardation, is a lifelong condition of impairment and is characterized by three criteria: significantly subaverage intellectual functioning (low IQ scores); concurrent and related limitations in two or more adaptive skill areas; and manifestation before age 18 years.[131] Some states, such as Illinois, have legislated that a defendant bears the burden of establishing his or her mental retardation status by a preponderance of the evidence at either a pretrial hearing or at the aggravation and mitigation stage.[132] If a court determines that a capital defendant is mentally retarded, the case shall no longer be considered a capital case.

As a matter of interest, in criminal justice university classrooms across the nation, the call for a hold on constitutional guarantees and swift executions makes even the most experienced professor wonder about the future. Although criminal justice students can relate to the causes of wrongful convictions a little better than other students, they are not necessarily more knowledgeable about the behavior of police officers and lawyers, which can include inappropriate and corrupt behavior.[133]

Yet, in the final analysis, no democratic federal or state government should possess the *supreme right to life* (capital punishment) verdict within their legal arsenal because most often their ability to manage basic core institutions, such as education, is so far removed from reality that, as a great philosopher advocated long ago, government is more concerned with the bureaucratic structure than the services and products it is supposed to provide.[134] Civilized nations have discarded the notion that justice should be structured by personal obligation, payback, and revenge; instead, nations should practice a modern regime of democracy. Despite strong public support for capital punishment, federal, state, and local officials must continually ensure that its implementation rigorously upholds constitutional protections, such as due process and equal protection. However, the criminal justice process should not be abused to prevent the lawful imposition of the death penalty in appropriate capital cases. The State of Virginia indicates on its Web site that it will "execute the mentally retarded, the severely brain damaged and the mentally ill"[135] and that seven such mentally handicapped prisoners have been executed in Virginia post-*Furman*. Other states make similar statements on their Web sites.

To provide a better understanding of the death penalty, the California Commission on the Fair Administration of Justice issued the following report on June 30, 2008[136]:

- As of May 1, 2008, California had the largest death row in the nation, with 670 inmates awaiting execution.
- Thirty inmates have been on California's death row for more than 25 years; 119 inmates have been on death row for more than 20 years; and 240 inmates have been on death row for more than 15 years.
- The families of murder victims are cruelly deluded into believing that justice will be delivered with finality during their lifetimes.

With a dysfunctional death penalty law, the reality is that most California death sentences are actually sentences of lifetime incarceration. The defendant will die in prison before he or she is executed. The same result can be achieved at a savings of well over $100 million by sentencing the defendant to lifetime incarceration without possibility of parole.

Finally, in regards to state jurisdiction, how prosecutors feel about capital punishment depends on certain variables. One former state prosecutor, Judge Andrew

L. Sonner, says, "I left the state's attorney's office more than ten years ago, but I still remember the agony of attempting to make the fundamental decision of whether to ask a jury or judge to condemn someone to death. Our system invests an individual prosecutor with unfettered discretion to make that decision. I now believe that to do so rationally and fairly is beyond human capabilities."[137]

State Death Penalty Convictions Overturned

Another perspective worth reviewing is that in 2006 more than two-thirds of state death penalty convictions across the country were eventually overturned, mainly on procedural grounds of incompetent legal counsel, police or prosecutors who suppressed evidence, and judges who gave jurors the wrong instructions.[138] A study at Columbia University School of Law reports that in 68 percent of the capital cases reviewed between 1973 and 1995, state and federal courts found errors that were sufficiently serious to require retrial or resentencing. Seven percent of those whose sentences were overturned between 1973 and 1995 had been acquitted. Ten percent were retried and resentenced to death.[139] Overall, the American Bar Association, along with other organizations, does not support capital punishment and links its perspective to the morals and ethics of a civilized society.

In an examination of 200 DNA and death row exoneration cases, more than a quarter involved faulty crime lab work or testimony. Recent evaluations of crime lab outputs show evidence of negligence to outright deception in 17 states (see Chapter 6 for more details on forensic analysis failures). For example, two inmates from Harris County (Houston), Texas were executed, and Chief Harold Hurtt announced the discovery of 280 hidden boxes of evidence from at least 8,000 Houston cases spanning 25 years. The boxes contained clothing, weapons, and a fetus. There have been revelations of incompetent analysts in the police lab's DNA section, which forced Houston authorities to shudder. Questions arose about everything from firearm identification to blood typing in a jurisdiction that had sent 75 defendants to the death chamber.[140]

In a typical example of the 130 death row inmates in Texas who have been exonerated, consider that the Collin County court in Texas dismissed capital murder charges against Michael Blair in the fall of 2008. Blair had been on death row for the 1993 murder of Ashley Estell. After more than a decade of legal appeals and requests for DNA testing, the hair evidence that had been used to convict Blair was shown to be mistaken. The Texas Court of Criminal Appeals found that no reasonable jury would convict Blair based on the existing evidence.[141]

Actual Innocence Is Not a Constitutional Claim

Herrera v. Collins (506 U.S., 390, 404, 1993, Rehnquist, C.J.) established that "a claim of actual innocence is not in itself a constitutional claim." Under *Herrera* and the cases that followed, a federal court can reject a defendant's petition for financial relief even if it is based on proof of innocence that includes DNA evidence. Of course, not every claim of innocence is justified, and not every high court's decision to ignore a defendant's evidence is inappropriate or ignored, especially by state jurisdictions.

■ Federal Prosecutors and the Death Penalty

In January 1995, the death penalty protocol was revised to require federal prosecutors to submit for an attorney general's (AG) review all cases in which capital charges could be pursued. This process was to be followed regardless of the federal prosecutor's wish to pursue capital punishment. To facilitate this process, the Attorney General's Review Committee on Capital Cases (AGRCCC) was established.[142] The AG makes the final decision on whether or not to seek the death penalty against the accused. Federal prosecutors recommended the death penalty less than one-fourth of the time in death-eligible cases.[143] Some findings about capital punishment and federal prosecutors include the following:

- The South (includes Texas) accounted for about one-half of all the death penalty recommendations.[144]
- A study of 652 defendants found that federal decisions to seek the death penalty were driven by the heinousness of the crime rather than the defendant's age, gender, or race.[145]
- From 1995 to 2000, 40 of the federal cases submitted to the AG for review came from just 5 of the 94 federal districts.[146]

Some of the crimes for which federal defendants have been tried in capital punishment cases include fatal shooting of a bank guard during a bank robbery, death resulting from aircraft hijacking, carjacking murder, federal prison guard murder, kidnapping, sexual assault and murder of a child, murder of witnesses, murder of a federal employee (postal worker), and murder of rival narcotics traffickers.[147] Former police officers were federally sentenced to death, too. For example, former officer Len Davis was called "Robocop" by the residents in New Orleans's Section 8 housing. Davis ordered the murder of 32-year-old Kim Groves, a mother of three, after she filed a brutality complaint against Davis.[148] Federal agents had Davis and other officers under surveillance for drug dealing prior to the killing. Community activists reported that most potential witnesses or victims against Davis were fearful to testify against him.

Davis was sentenced to death in federal court. Along with Davis, six other former New Orleans police officers were convicted on drug trafficking charges.

■ Estimated Costs of Federal Capital Punishment Cases

In the federal system, from 1990 to 1997, the average cost for representation in which the defendant was charged with an offense punishable by death but the prosecution had not sought the death penalty totaled $55,772, compared to $218,112 per case when the prosecution had sought the death penalty.[149] In the same period, the average cost of prosecuting a death penalty case totaled $365,000. This estimate does not include pre-death penalty case expenses as previously discussed.

■ Be Careful What You Ask For: Tentative Death Penalty Conclusions

Borrowing from an article that examined New York's reinstatement and abandonment of the death penalty post-*Gregg*, a public debate addressed the question, is it right? with a focus on retribution, morality, and religion. A second set of questions asked, is it useful? is it cost-effective? is it necessary? versus a focus on costs and alternatives, such as life in prison without parole. The final question discussed was, is it fair? If capital punishment were to be reinstated in New York post-*Gregg*, there were serious reservations about issues such as innocence, race discrimination, arbitrariness, quality of representation, and the makeup of capital juries in an already financially-strapped and overburdened justice system. Based on an extensive evaluation, James Acker concluded that after 1995, when New York enacted a death penalty statute after not having one for more than a generation, the "New York Court of Appeals invalidated the law on state constitutional grounds, New Yorkers invested millions of dollars and an incalculable amount of time and effort in an enterprise that vexed many and ultimately benefited no one."[150] Equally important, during that period, the rate of violent crime across New York declined. Thus, it appears to be an elementary conclusion that capital punishment and violent crime control are not necessarily related variables. Other jurisdictions followed the New York model, such as the Maryland Commission on Capital Punishment, which voted in November 2008 to abolish the death penalty in the state.[151] In a closer look at Table 9-1, it is apparent that many states are hesitant to execute sentenced offenders.

■ Summary

The debate on capital punishment relates to one set of issues centered on democracy and abstract rights versus the ancient calculation as reinforced by the popular media of an eye for an eye, or *lex talionis*, better known as retaliation and vengeance. Democratic enthusiasts examine the death penalty's opportunities and problems; one problem that dominates the thoughts of many enthusiasts relates to corruption, misconduct, and incompetence among criminal justice professionals. Each day, fresh accounts describe the misdirected deeds of police officers, judges, prosecutors, and even high-ranking politicians, such as governors and senators.

The death penalty is legally sanctioned by 35 states, the federal government, and the military. In 1972, *Furman v. Georgia* (408 U.S., 238, 1972) put capital punishment on hold. In *Furman*, the Supreme Court found the practice of the death penalty to be constitutionally unacceptable because the penalty was too arbitrary and capricious in its use. In *Gregg v. Georgia* (428 U.S., 153, 1976), the Supreme Court reported that the death penalty was a legal sanction reserved for the worst of the worst and reinstated it. Frequently since *Gregg*, the worst crimes are not the ones that result in a death sentence or the other way around. Each year, more than 100 convicted defendants are sentenced to death.

Advocates argue that the death penalty is the optimal solution in punishing heinous offenders and that it plays a significant role in specific and general deterrence of crime. Capital punishment as a deterrent saves lives, and one count shows that almost 12,000 lives have been saved based on the number of criminals executed since 1976. These advocates see capital punishment as a life–life trade-off, a serious commitment to the sanctity of human life, and morally correct.

Historically in America, 33 executions per year were conducted between 1608 and 1929. They were conducted under local legal authority and often included religious leaders. The executions were highly public and symbol-laden events that gained the attention of residents and travelers.

Opponents of the death penalty believe that capital punishment is morally inappropriate, a weak criminal deterrent of capital crimes, discriminatory against certain socioeconomic classes and persons of color, and too expensive. Equally important, killing someone does not address the root cause of crime, and innocent persons have been executed. Two percent of death sentences in America are based on false convictions, and innocent black males are more likely to be falsely convicted than innocent white males. Also, 130 exonerations from death row occurred from 1973 to August 26, 2008, in 26 states.

Statistics show that capital punishment appears to enhance crimes of violence, and this book argues that in response to increased violence in the popular media, through the *CSI Effect*, violent persons and the criminal justice community become more aggressive and violent, vigilantism is glorified, and fictitious accounts of crime, criminals, and what to do about them are pervasive.

Before appeal or a prison's expense of executing a defendant, there are pre-death penalty costs that are more expensive at each stage of the judicial process than similar non-death penalty cases. Among other things, these expenses are related to pretrial time, motions that need to be filed and answered, jury selection and sequestering, and automatic appeals. Counties manage these high costs by decreasing funding for highways and police and by increasing taxes. One report estimates that between 1982 and 1997 the extra cost of capital trials was $1.6 billion, and the State of New York estimated that it cost $23 million for each person who was sentenced to death.

■ References

1. Huff, C. R., Rattner, A., & Sagarin, E. (2000). Guilty until proved innocent: Wrongful conviction and public policy. In B. W. Hancock & P. M. Sharp (Eds.), *Criminal justice in America* (2nd ed.). Upper Saddle River, NJ: Prentice Hall.

2. The Pew Forum on Religion & Public Life. (n.d.). *The candidates on the death penalty*. Retrieved November 21, 2008, from http://pewforum.org/religion08/compare.php?Issue=Death_Penalty

3. Stevens, D. J. (1992). Research note: The death sentence and inmate attitudes. *Crime & Delinquency, 38*(2), 272–280.

4. Miller, W. I. (2005). *Eye for an eye*. New York: Cambridge University Press.

5. Kant, I. (1959). Kant's philosophy of law: An exposition of the fundamental principles of jurisprudence as the science of right. In C. Morris (Ed.), *The great legal philosophers: Selected readings in jurisprudence* (2nd ed.). College Park: University of Pennsylvania. (Original work published in 1798)

6. Encarta Online Dictionary. (n.d.) *Pharisaic* Retrieved July 5, 2009, from http://uk.encarta.msn.com/encnet/refpages/search.aspx?q=

7. For an up-to-date list on executions in the US, including that of Jack Trawick, go to Death Penalty Information Center (2009). *Executions in the United States in 2009*. Retrieved July 4, 2009, from http://deathpenaltyinfo.org/executions-united-states-2009

8. Texas Department of Criminal Justice. (n.d.). *Executed offenders*. Retrieved September 12, 2008, from http://www.tdcj.state.tx.us/stat/executedoffenders.htm

9. Texas Department of Criminal Justice, *Executed Offenders*.

10. Pro-Death Penalty.com. (n.d.). *Case summaries for inmates executed in Virginia between 2000–2006*. Retrieved September 12, 2008, from http://www.prodeathpenalty.com/virginia/tables4.html

11. Lethal Injection. (2007, February 14). *A list of 59 inmates executed since Florida resumed executions in 1979*. Retrieved July 5, 2009, from http://lethal-injection-florida.blogspot.com/2007/02/list-of-59-inmates-executed-since.html

12. Owock, S. (2008, March 27). *2001: Robert Lee Massie, who spent a lifetime dying*. Retrieved October 5, 2008, from http://www.executedtoday.com/2008/03/27/2001-robert-lee-massie/

13. Woodford, J. (2008, October 2). Death row realism: Do executions make us safer? San Quentin's former warden says no. *Los Angeles Times*. Retrieved October 7, 2008, from http://www.latimes.com/news/opinion/la-oe-woodford2-2008oct02,0,4155306.story

14. de Montesquieu, C. (1959). The spirit of law. In C. Morris (Ed.), *The great legal philosophers: Selected readings in jurisprudence* (2nd ed.). College Park: University of Pennsylvania. (Original work published in 1752)

15. Personal experiences of the author in prison environments as a teacher and group leader.

16. Liptak, A. (2003, August 12). Signs grow of innocent people being executed, judge says. *The New York Times*. Retrieved September 17, 2008, from http://www.nytimes.com/2003/08/12/national/12DEAT.html?ex=1376020800&en=68a074149c394948&ei=5007&partner=USERLAND

17. National Coalition to Abolish the Death Penalty, (ND). Todd Willingham executed for an accidental fire. (n.d.). Retrieved July 5, 2009, from http://www.democracyinaction.org/dia/organizationsORG/ncadp/content.jsp?content_KEY=2493&t=Innocent%20And%20Executed%20Section.dwt

18. Death Penalty Information Center. (n.d.). *Hours before scheduled execution, doubts about guilt persisted in Alabama case*. Retrieved September 15, 2008, from http://www.deathpenaltyinfo.org/hours-scheduled-execution-doubts-about-guilt-persisted-alabama-case

19. Floridians for Alternatives to the Death Penalty. (2008). *What should we do about Florida's death penalty?* Retrieved July 7, 2009, from http://www.fadp.org/FL_factsheet.pdf

20. Death Penalty Information Center. (n.d.). *Wayne Tompkins*. Retrieved July 5, 2009, from http://www.deathpenaltyinfo.org/search/node/Wayne%20Tompkins

21. Forst, B. (2003). *Errors of justice: Nature, sources and remedies.* New York: Cambridge University Press.

22. Center for Human Rights and Global Justice. (2006, March 8). *Project on extrajudicial executions.* NY: New York University School of Law. Retrieved July 4, 2009, from http://www.extrajudicialexecutions.org/law/shoottokill2006.html

23. Rousseau, J. J. (1959). The social contract: Chapter V: The right of life and death. In C. Morris (Ed.), *The great legal philosophers: Selected readings in jurisprudence* (2nd ed.). College Park: University of Pennsylvania. (Original work published in 1792)

24. Dean, J. W. (2006). *An update on President Bush's NSA program: The historical context, Specter's recent bill, and Feingold's censure motion.* Retrieved September 25, 2008, from http://writ.news.findlaw.com/dean/20060324.html

25. Scully, G. W. (1997) *Murder by the state.* National Center for Policy Analysis. Retrieved July 5, 2009, from http://www.ncpa.org/pdfs/st211.pdf

26. FindLaw.com. (n.d.). *Furman v. Georgia (408 U.S., 238, 1972).* Retrieved October 2, 2008, from http://caselaw.lp.findlaw.com/scripts/getcase.pl?court=us&vol=408&invol=238. *Furman v. Georgia* (408 U.S., 238, 1972) was a US Supreme Court decision that ruled on the requirement for a degree of consistency in the application of the death penalty. The court consolidated *Jackson v. Georgia* and *Branch v. Texas* with the *Furman* decision and invalidated capital punishment for the crime of rape. The arbitrary and inconsistent imposition of the death penalty violates the 8th and 14th Amendments and constitutes cruel and unusual punishment.

27. FindLaw.com. (n.d.). *Gregg v. Georgia (428 U.S., 153, 1976).* Retrieved October 2, 2008, from http://caselaw.lp.findlaw.com/scripts/getcase.pl?court=US&vol=428&invol=153

28. Death Penalty Information Center. (n.d.). *Executions in the United States, 1608–1976, by state.* Retrieved July 5, 2009, from http://www.deathpenaltyinfo.org/executions-united-states-1608-1976-state

29. Bureau of Justice Statistics. (2009). *Number of persons executed in the United States, 1930–2008.* Washington, DC: US Department of Justice. Retrieved July 5, 2009, from http://www.ojp.usdoj.gov/bjs/glance/tables/exetab.htm

30. Texas Department of Criminal Justice. (2009, June 3). *Executions December 7, 1982 through June 2, 2009.* Retrieved July 5, 2009, from http://www.tdcj.state.tx.us/stat/annual.htm. Also see Virginians for Alternatives to the Death Penalty. (n.d.). *Virginia death penalty information.* Retrieved November 22, 2008, from http://www.vadp.org/info.htm

31. United States Code (nd). *Popular name tool.* Retrieved July 5, 2009, from http://uscode.house.gov/popularnames/popularnames.htm#letterF

32. Baldus, D. C., Woodworth, G. G., & Pulaski, Jr., C. A. (1991). Equal justice and the death penalty: A legal and empirical analysis. *Contemporary Sociology, 20*(4), 598–599.

33. Foster, M. (2008, September 23). Families seek closure as LA killer pleads guilty. *Associated Press.* Retrieved July 5, 2009, from http://abcnews.go.com/US/wireStory?id=5870110

34. Bureau of Justice Statistics. (2008). *Capital offenses by state, 2007.* Washington, DC: US Department of Justice. Retrieved July 5, 2009, from http://www.ojp.usdoj.gov/bjs/pub/html/cp/2007/tables/cp07st01.htm

35. Death Penalty Information Center. (2008). *Death penalty for offenses other than murder.* Retrieved July 5, 2009, from http://www.deathpenaltyinfo.org/death-penalty-offenses-other-murder

36. Bureau of Justice Statistics. (2007). *Felony sentences in state courts in 2004* (NCJ 215646). Washington, DC: US Department of Justice.

37. Bureau of Justice Statistics. (2007). *Capital punishment statistics.* Washington, DC: US Department of Justice. Retrieved November 1, 2008, from http://www.ojp.usdoj.gov/bjs/cp.htm

38. Death Penalty Information Center. (n.d.). *Changes in federal death row inmates.* Retrieved November 1, 2008, from http://www.deathpenaltyinfo.org/changes-federal-death-penalty-statistics

39. Death Penalty Information Center. (n.d.). *Federal death row prisoners.* Retrieved November 21, 2008, from http://www.deathpenaltyinfo.org/federal-death-row-prisoners

40. Paternoster, R., Brame, R., & Bacon, S. (2008). *The death penalty: America's experience with capital punishment.* New York: Oxford University Press.

41. Cases available at FindLaw.com. http://www.findlaw.com

42. Rubin, P. (2008). *An examination of the death penalty in the United States.* Testimony of Dr. Paul Rubin to the US Senate, Committee on the Judiciary. Retrieved July 5, 2009, from http://judiciary.senate.gov/hearings/testimony.cfm?id=1745&wit_id=4991

43. Sunstein, C. R., & Vermeule, A. (2005, March). *Is capital punishment morally required? The relevance of life–life tradeoffs* (Working Paper 239, No. 05–06, University of Chicago Public Law & Legal Theory Research Paper Series). Chicago: University of Chicago.

44. Van den Haag, E. (2003). Justice, deterrence and the death penalty. In M. R. Acker, R. M. Bohm & C. S. Lanier (Eds.), *America's experiment with the death penalty.* Durham, NC: Carolina Academic Press.

45. Van den Haag, E. (1986). The ultimate punishment. *The Harvard Law Review.* Retrieved October 2, 2008, from http://www.pbs.org/wgbh/pages/frontline/angel/procon/haagarticle.html

46. Shepherd, J. M. (2005). Deterrence versus brutalization: Capital punishment's differing impacts among states. *Michigan Law Review, 104,* 203–255.

47. Zuckerman, M. B. (1999). Fighting the war on crime. *US News and World Report, 127,* 76.

48. Sourcebook of Criminal Justice Statistics Online. (2007). *Table 2.51.* Albany, NY: US Department of Justice. Retrieved September 12, 2008, from http://www.albany.edu/sourcebook/pdf/t2512007.pdf

49. Sourcebook of Criminal Justice Statistics Online. (2007). *Table 2.52.* Albany, NY: US Department of Justice. Retrieved September 14, 2008, from http://www.albany.edu/sourcebook/pdf/t2522006.pdf

50. Brace, P., & Boyea, B. D. (2008). State public opinion, the death penalty, and the practice of electing judges. *American Journal of Political Science, 52,* 360–372.

51. Samenow, S. E. (2004). *Inside the criminal mind: Revised and updated edition.* New York: Crown.

52. Gottfredson, M., & Hirschi, T. (1990). *A general theory of crime.* Stanford, CA: Stanford University.

53. Fox, J. A., Levin, J., & Quinet, K. (2008). *The will to kill: Making sense of senseless murders.* Boston: Pearson.

54 Stevens, D. J. (2004, March). *Conviction obstacles of sexual offenders.* Paper presented at the annual conference of the Academy of Criminal Justice Science, Las Vegas, Nevada.

55. Pro-Death Penalty.com. (n.d.). *Scheduled executions.* Retrieved July 6, 2009, from http://www.prodeathpenalty.com/Pending/scheduled_executions.htm

56. Banner, S. (2002). *The death penalty: An American history*. Cambridge, MA: Harvard University Press.

57. Banner, *Death Penalty*.

58. American Bar Association. (2001). *Death without justice*. Washington, DC: Author. Retrieved October 4, 2008, from http://www.abanet.org/irr/finaljune28.pdf

59. Lerner, M. J. (1980). *The belief in a just world: A fundamental delusion*. New York: Plenum.

60. Kinsella, N. S. (1996). Punishment and proportionality: The Estoppel approach. *Journal of Libertarian Studies, 12*(1), 51–73.

61. Van den Haag, E., & Conrad, J. P. (1983). *The death penalty: A debate*. New York: Plenum.

62. Bowers, W. J., Pierce, G. L., & McDevitt, J. F. (1984). *Legal homicide: Death as punishment in America*. Boston: Northeastern University Press.

63. Ezorsky, G. (1972). The ethics of punishment. In G. Ezorsky (Ed.), *Philosophical perspectives on punishment*. Albany: State University of New York Press.

64. Jayewardene, C. H. S. (1977). *The penalty of death*. Boston: Lexington.

65. Quinton, A. M. (1972). On punishment. In G. Ezorsky (Ed.), *Philosophical perspectives on punishment*. Albany: State University of New York Press.

66. Stevens, "Research Note: The death sentence and inmate attitudes." Joanna Shepherd's, previous finding suggests that states that have executed more than approximately nine murderers exhibit deterrence. However, in states that have executed fewer persons, there is either no effect or a brutalization effect, but she seems to suggest something different.

67. History Place. (1998). *American revolution. Prelude to revolution*. Retrieved July 7, 2009, from http://www.historyplace.com/unitedstates/revolution/rev-prel.htm

68. Garamone, J. (2008, September). Violence in Iraq continues to drop, corps commander says. *American Forces Press Service*. Retrieved October 2, 2008, from http://www.defenselink.mil/news/newsarticle.aspx?id=51269

69. Stevens, D. J. (1997). Violence begets violence. *Corrections Compendium: The National Journal for Corrections, 22*(12), 1–3.

70. Walker, J. T. (2002). Laws of the state and the state of law: The relationship between police and law. In J. T. Walker (Ed.), *Policing and the law*. Upper Saddle River, NJ: Prentice Hall.

71. Bureau of Justice Statistics. (2007). *Capital offenses by state. Table 1.2*. Washington, DC: US Department of Justice. Retrieved September 26, 2008, from http://www.ojp.usdoj.gov/bjs/pub/html/cp/2006/cp06st.htm

72. Bowers, W. J., & Pierce, G. L. (1990). Deterrence or brutalization? What are the effects of executions? *Crime and Delinquency, 26*, 453–484.

73. Hicks, W. L. (2006). The system-wide effects of capital punishment on the American criminal justice system: The use of computer modeling in death penalty research. *Justice Policy Journal, 3*(2). Retrieved July 5, 2009, from http://www.cjcj.org/files/the_system.pdf

74. Death Penalty Information Center. (n.d.). *Murder rate declines in every region except the South, where executions are most prevalent*. Retrieved September 22, 2008, from http://www.deathpenaltyinfo.org:80/murder-rate-declines-every-region-except-south-where-executions-are-most-prevalent

75. Sellin, T. (1959). *The death penalty*. Philadelphia: American Law Institute.

76. Peterson, R. D., & Bailey, W. C. (1988). Murder and capital punishment in the evolving context of the post-*Furman* era. *Social Forces, 66*, 774–807.

77. Shepherd, "Deterrence Versus Brutalization."

78. Bureau of Justice Statistics. (2007). *Policing and homicide, 1976–98: Justifiable homicide by police, police officers murdered by felons.* Washington, DC: US Department of Justice. Retrieved November 23, 2008, from http://www.ojp.usdoj.gov/bjs/pub/pdf/ph98.pdf

79. Stevens, "Research Note: The death sentence and inmate attitudes."

80. Gottfredson & Hirschi, *General Theory of Crime.*

81. Death Penalty Information Center. (n.d.). *New voices: Dallas D.A. to re-examine death penalty convictions and possibly halt executions.* Retrieved September 22, 2008, from http://www.deathpenaltyinfo.org/new-voices-dallas-da-re-examine-death-penalty-convictions-and-possibly-halt-executions

82. Death Penalty Information Center. (2009). *131st person exonerated from death row.* Retrieved July 6, 2009, from http://www.deathpenaltyinfo.org/innocence-and-death-penalty

83. Radzinowicz, L. (1948). *A history of English criminal law* (Vol. 1). London: Stevens and Sons.

84. Home Office. (2004). *Violent crime in England and Wales.* Retrieved July 15, 2006, from http://www.homeoffice.gov.uk/rds/pdfs04/rdsolr1804.pdf

85. Allen, W. C. (2002). *History of the United States capitol: A chronicle of design, construction, and politics.* Washington, DC: US Government Printing Office.

86. Encarta Online Dictionary. (n.d.) *Autocractic.* Retrieved July 5, 2009, from http://encarta.msn.com/encnet/features/dictionary/DictionaryResults.aspx?search=autocratic

87. Ruddell, R., & Urbina, M. G. (2007). Weak nations, political repression, and punishment. *International Criminal Justice Review, 17*(2), 84–107. This study examines the influence of political repression on the use of punishment in 100 of the world's richest nations. Consistent with earlier empirical work, high levels of violent crime and population heterogeneity is associated with the use of imprisonment. Five different indicators of political freedoms are included in a series of ordinary least squares (OLS) regression models, including civil liberties and political rights, two indicators of democracy, and censorship of the press. Controlling for crime, population heterogeneity, and development, the authors find that autocratic nations use harsh punishment more often.

88. Gross, S. R. (n.d.). *Convicting the innocent: Public law and legal theory working paper series* (Working Paper No. 103). Ann Arbor: University of Michigan Law School. Retrieved November 21, 2008, from nhttp://graphics8.nytimes.com/packages/pdf/national/20080325_bar_doc.pdf

89. Baldus, D., Woodworth, G., Zukermen, D., Weiner, N. & Broffitt, B. (1998). Racial discrimination and the death penalty in the post-*Furman* era: An empirical and legal overview, with recent findings from Philadelphia. *Cornell Law Review, 83*, 1638.

90. Donohue, J. (2007). *Connecticut study in arbitrariness in death cases.* Retrieved July 5, 2009, from http://www.deathpenaltyinfo.org/node/2245

91. Baker, D. N., Lambert, E. G., & Jenkins, M. (2005). Racial differences in death penalty support and opposition. *Journal of Black Studies, 35*, 201–224.

92. Ruddell, R. (2005). Social disruption, state priorities, and minority threat: A crossnational study of imprisonment. *Punishment and Society, 7*, 7–28.

93. Young, R. (2004). Guilty until proven innocent: Conviction orientation, racial attitudes, and support for capital punishment. *Deviant Behavior, 25*, 151–167.

94. Newton, P. J., Johnson, C. M., & Mulcahy, T. M. (2006). *Investigation and prosecution of homicide cases in the US: The process for federal involvement.* Washington, DC: National Institute of Justice. Retrieved November 22, 2008, from http://www.ncjrs.gov/pdffiles1/nij/grants/214753.pdf

95. Bureau of Justice Statistics, *Capital Punishment Statistics.*

96. Death Penalty Information Center. (n.d.). *Costs of the death penalty and related issues.* Retrieved September 23, 2008, from http://www.deathpenaltyinfo.org/COcosttestimony.pdf

97. Cook, P. J., & Slawson, D. B. (1993). *The costs of prosecuting murder cases in North Carolina.* Raleigh, NC: Duke University.

98. Garey, M. (1985). Comment, the cost of taking a life: Dollars and sense of the death penalty. *UC Davis Law Review, 18*, 1221, 1257.

99. Death Penalty Information Center. (2009). *Costs of the death penalty.* Retrieved July 7, 2009, from http://www.deathpenaltyinfo.org/costs-death-penalty

100. Wise, D. (2002, April 30). Capital punishment proves to be expensive. *New York Law Journal*, 1.

101. Wise, D. (2003, September 22). Costly price of capital punishment—case shows effort expended before the state takes a life. *Albany Times-Union*, p. 1.

102. *Press release: New Jerseyans for alternatives to the death penalty.* (2005, November 21). Retrieved July 5, 2009, from http://www.njadp.org/gdcommentary&what=njvoices

103. Cook & Slawson, *The Costs of Prosecuting Murder Cases in North Carolina.*

104. Death Penalty Information Center. (2008). *New voices: Former California attorney general cites costs in call for end of capital punishment.* Retrieved July 6, 2009, from http://www.deathpenaltyinfo.org/new-voices-former-california-attorney-general-cites-costs-call-end-capital-punishment

105. Murphy, D. (2004, December 18). San Quentin debate: Death row vs. bay views. *The New York Times.* Retrieved July 5, 2009, from http://www.nytimes.com/2004/12/18/national/18row.html

106. Morgan, J.G. (2004, July 12). Tennessee Comptroller of the Treasury. (2004, July 12). Retrieved August 29, 2009, from http://www.comptroller1.state.tn.us/repository/NR/nr071204.pdf

107. The high price of killing killers. (2000, January 4). *Palm Beach Post*, p. 1A.

108. Paternoster, et al., *Death Penalty.*

109. *Gregg v. Georgia* (428 U.S., 153, 1976).

110. Ball, J. D. (2006). Is it a prosecutor's world? Determinants of count bargaining decisions. *Journal of Contemporary Criminal Justice, 22*(3), 241–260.

111. Paternoster, et al., *Death Penalty.*

112. Paternoster, et al., *Death Penalty.*

113. Paternoster, et al., *Death Penalty.*

114. Walker, S. (2001). *Sense and nonsense about crime and drugs.* Belmont, CA: Wadsworth Thomson.

115. Walker, *Sense and Nonsense.*

116. Walker, *Sense and Nonsense.*

117. Spohn, C., Beichner, D., & Davis-Frenzel, E. (2001). Prosecutorial justifications for sexual assault case rejection: Guarding the gateway to justice. *Social Problems, 48*(2), 206–235.

118. Bureau of Justice Statistics. (2006). *State court processing statistics: Felony defendants in large urban counties, 2002.* Washington, DC: US Department of Justice. Retrieved July 6, 2009, from http://www.ojp.usdoj.gov/bjs/pub/ascii/fdluc02.txt

119. Sievert, R. J. (2002). Capital murder: A prosecutor's personal observations of the prosecution of capital cases. In W. R. Palacios, P. F. Cromwell & R. G. Dunham (Eds.), *Crime & justice in America: Present realities and future prospects* (2nd ed.). Upper Saddle River, NJ: Prentice Hall.

120. Willing, R., & Fields, G. (1999, December 20). Geography of the death penalty. *USA Today*, p. 6A.

121. Montgomery, L. (2002, May 12). Questioning local extremes on death penalty. *Washington Post*, p. C01

122. National Coalition to Abolish the Death Penalty. (n.d.). *Geographic unfairness*. Retrieved November 22, 2008, from http://www.ncadp.org/assets/Geographic%20Unfairness.doc.

123. Capital Defender Office. (2003). *Capital punishment in New York State: Statistics from six years of representation*. Retrieved June 24, 2009, from http://www.nycdo.org/8yr.html.

124. Sievert, "Capital Murder."

125. Kamm, D. (1982). Practical aspects of prosecution. Case for the prosecutor. *University of Toledo Law Review, 13*, 311.

126. Gershman, B. L. (2002). Why prosecutors misbehave. In W. R. Palacios, P. F. Cromwell & R. G. Dunham (Eds.), *Crime & justice in America: Present realities and future prospects* (2nd ed.). Upper Saddle River, NJ: Prentice Hall.

127. Amnesty International. (2006). *The execution of mentally ill offenders.* Retrieved July 5, 2009, from http://www.amnesty.org/en/library/info/AMR51/003/2006/

128. American Bar Association. (2004). *Cruel and unusual punishment: The juvenile death penalty evolving standards of decency.* Retrieved October 19, 2007, from http://www.abanet.org/crimjust/juvjus

129. Death Penalty Information Center. (n.d.). State statutes prohibiting the death penalty for people with mental retardation. Retrieved July 6, 2009, from http://www.deathpenaltyinfo.org/state-statutes-prohibiting-death-penalty-people-mental-retardation

130. American Association of Intellectual and Developmental Disabilities. (2009). *Definition of intellectual disability.* Retrieved August 30, 2009, from http://www.aamr.org/content_100.cfm?navID=21

131. Paternoster, et al., *Death Penalty.*

132. Cullerton, J., Dillard, K., & Baroni, P. G. (2004). Capital punishment reform in Illinois. *Journal of DuPage County Bar Association.* Retrieved October 3, 2008, from http://www.dcba.org/brief/aprissue/2004/art10404.htm

133. Bell, J. G., Clow, K. A., & Ricciardelli, R. (2008). Causes of wrongful conviction: Looking at student knowledge. *Journal of Criminal Justice Education, 19*(1), 75–96.

134. Ravitch, D., & Loveless, T. (2000). Broken promises: What the US government can do to improve education. Retrieved September 2, 2008, from http://www.brookings.edu/articles/2000/spring_k12education_loveless.aspx

135. Virginians for Alternatives to the Death Penalty, *Virginia Death Penalty Information.*

136. Death Penalty Information Center. (n.d.). *Maryland commission on capital punishment examines state death penalty.* Retrieved September 18, 2008, from http://www.deathpenaltyinfo. org/news-and-developments-studies

137. Death Penalty Information Center, *Maryland Commission on Capital Punishment.*

138. Graves, T.H. (2008). CLE: Adjudication of capital cases in Delaware. State Court Adjudication Issues. State of Delaware. Retrieved August 30, 2009, from courts.delaware.gov/Courts/ Supreme%20Court/pdf/?ACC-DE4.pdf

139. Coyle, M. (2000, June 9). 68 percent error rate found in death case study: Author calls serious problems epidemic. *The National Law Review.* Retrieved July 6, 2009, from http://truthinjustice.org/68percent.htm

140. Strange Justice. (2005, June 30). *A review of appalling "scientific" evidence from government laboratories.* Retrieved July 6, 2009, from http://stju.blogspot.com/2005_06_01_archive.html

141. Death Penalty Information Center. (2009). *Texas death row inmate may be exonerated as prosecution recommends overtuning conviction.* Retrieved July 6, 2009, from http://www. deathpenaltyinfo.org/node/2392

142. Death Penalty Information Center. (2009). *The Federal death penalty.* Retrieved July 5, 2009, from http://www.deathpenaltyinfo.org/federal-death-penalty

143. Klein, S. P., Berk, R. A., & Hickman, L. J. (2006). *Race and the decision to seek the death penalty in federal cases.* Santa Monica, CA: RAND Corporation. Retrieved July 5, 2009, from http:// www.rand.org/pubs/technical_reports/TR389/

144. Muhlhausen, D. B. (2007, June 27). *The death penalty deters crime and saves lives.* Testimony to the US Senate, Subcommittee on the Constitution, Civil Rights, and Property Rights of the Committee on the Judiciary. Retrieved September 18, 2008, from http://www.heritage. org/research/Crime/tst082807a.cfm

145. Klein, S. P., Berk, R. A., & Hickman, L. J. "*Race and the decision to seek the death penalty in federal cases.*"

146. US Department of Justice. (2000). *The federal death penalty system: A statistical survey (1988–2000).* Washington, DC: Author. Retrieved September 18, 2008, from http://www.usdoj.gov/ dag/pubdoc/dpsurvey.html

147. US Department of Justice. (n.d.). *Federal defendants sentenced to death, 1988–2000.* Retrieved September 18, 2008, from http://www.usdoj.gov/dag/pubdoc/_table_set_v_corrected.pdf

148. US Department of Justice (NA). (1996). "Former New Orleans police officer and local hit man sentenced to death." Retrieved August 30, 2009, from http://www.justice.gov/opa/pr/1996/ May96/202.cr.htm

149. American Civil Liberties Union. (n.d.). *The high costs of the death penalty.* Retrieved September 23, 2008, from http://www.nacdl.org/public.nsf/2cdd02b415ea3a64852566d6000daa79/970 6e0aac59259be85256b740055872c/$FILE/DP_WhitePaper.pdf

150. Acker, J. (2008). Be careful what you ask for: Lessons from New York's recent experience with capital punishment. *Vermont Law Review, 32,* 683.

151. Death Penalty Information Center. (2008). *Maryland commission recommends abolition of death penalty.* Retrieved November 21, 2008, from http://www.deathpenaltyinfo.org/ maryland-commission-recommends-abolition-death-penalty

Methods and Findings

If you wish to be a success in the world, promise everything, deliver nothing.

Napoléon Bonaparte

▶ ▶ CHAPTER OBJECTIVES

- Explain the working theory or hypothesis of this study
- Describe the participant selection process and research design of this study
- Clarify the relationship between juries,' defense lawyers,' and judges' perspectives and the *CSI Effect* from the perception of the prosecutors who were polled
- Articulate the most important elements of a case that shape prosecutor discretion concerning an indictment and a conviction of a defendant
- Better understand why prosecutors might reject a case despite substantial evidence provided by the police
- Provide a clear understanding of the implications of the findings of this study

■ Introduction

Chapter 1 reveals that an earlier study about the relationship among Boston police officers, crime scene investigations, and sexual assault convictions led to a concern about prosecutorial discretion.[1] The lessons learned from that study are that first responders (police officers) are limited to the official descriptions of their duty, which amounts to securing the crime scene and nothing more. What experienced patrol officers thought after an average of 10 years of attending crime scenes was considered to be irrelevant; their written reports about the conditions of the crime scene, witnesses, victims, and other factors were scrutinized by intimidating police supervisors, so the officers produced accounts that matched the expectations of their job description. In the final analysis, some prosecutors would charge or indict

311

a suspect based on criteria other than the evidence or reports gathered by officers and investigators. These findings lend support to the idea advanced by the Center for Public Integrity that police officers are asked to support untruthful scenarios at the request of unethical prosecutors, including those who seek the death penalty.[2]

Additionally, after a review of a monograph that was authored by opponents of capital punishment, it was learned that when the crime and the evidence fits the jurisdiction's death penalty requirements, initially moving the case toward capital punishment sanctions is at the sole discretion of the prosecutor.[3]

With these thoughts in mind, it was an easy decision to develop a study consisting of 444 prosecutors from across the nation. The results were so illuminating when they were linked to the scientific literature and criminal justice practices that it required a book to explain how the popular media, through the *CSI Effect*, contributes to wrongful convictions and provides dignity to capital punishment.

This study now provides the empirical evidence from prosecutors to support what those first responders in Boston and opponents of capital punishment implied: to indict (or release) a suspect with a crime, including a capital crime, regardless of guilt or innocence, depends on prosecutor discretion more than the substantial evidence that was collected and analyzed.

■ Methodology: The Survey

A survey was developed after several prosecutors were interviewed. A series of close-ended questions (which included several answer options) and open-ended questions (or write-in answer formats) were crafted and tested in the graduate classrooms of the University of Southern Mississippi.[4] The results were reviewed by colleagues, graduate students, and prosecutors. After the questionnaire was developed, it was pretested, retooled, tested again, and eventually a final draft was distributed to the sample described below.

In all, the final survey (see Appendix 1) contains 31 questions that produce 32 variables, and the results were placed into four categories (see Table 10-1).[5] Questions 1–6 request 7 personal demographic questions (i.e., age, gender, experience); questions 7–18 and questions 22–24 address performance issues (present performance affects future jobs and undesirable benefits of the job); questions 19–21 ask about the impact of the popular media's crime scene investigation performances on judges, jurors, and defense lawyers; and questions 25–31 ask the opinions of the participants about law school.

TABLE 10-1 CATEGORIES OF QUESTIONS

- 7 personal characteristics (questions 1–6)
- 15 performance issues (questions 7–18, 22–24)
- 3 impact of *CSI Effect* (questions 19–21)
- 7 law school experiences and advice (questions 25–31)

■ The Hypothesis: A Work in Progress

At the core of this study lies the working theory or the hypothesis that the popular media has made huge contributions to the criminal justice community, the American public, and democracy, but the popular media also provides its own version of crime, which heightens the fear of victimization and what to do about those fears. This phenomenon is referred to as the *CSI Effect*, which changes real-world expectations of crime and crime control by affecting the decisions of witnesses, victims, jurors, and justice professionals. A *CSI Effect* is a conceptual consequence of the popular media's skill to (1) encourage aggressive reactive criminal justice strategies; (2) glorify vigilantism among justice practitioners and members of the public; and (3) promote fictitious accounts of crime, crime control, and its processes (detailed in Chapter 1). The data from the surveys support the notion that:

> The more a prosecutor reports that jurors, judges, and defense lawyers accepted the perspectives associated with the conceptual consequences stemming from the *CSI Effect*, the more prosecutors thought that compelling witnesses and victims were necessary to indict and convict a defendant, regardless of the evidence or forensic science analyses of that evidence.

The implications are that witnesses (including forensic personnel and expert witnesses) and victims can and do represent human error (including lies, trickery, and other hidden agendas, such as laziness and retaliation), as revealed in Chapter 8 and Chapter 9, and victims can be prompted and rehearsed for their performances like actors.

> Misguided prosecutors can easily open the door to indict and convict whomever they think could be convicted through theatrics. It comes down to theater.

The Center for Public Integrity reveals that a few prosecutors are legally or morally responsible for most of the misconduct among prosecutors; most prosecutors and other criminal justice practitioners are hard-working patriots who are concerned with preserving American liberty.

■ Selection Process

The sample was selected from lists that were available from state prosecutor Web sites, using Google as a search engine. A random process selection was accomplished after first establishing a desired number of prosecutors from the Web site and then dividing that number by the total membership list—if 50 were desired from a list and there were 200 names on the list, then 200 was divided by 50 which equals 4.

TABLE 10-2 STATES REPRESENTED BY THE SAMPLE, *N* = 18

Arizona	Missouri
California	Nebraska
Georgia	New Hampshire
Idaho	New Jersey
Illinois	New York
Kentucky	Ohio
Maryland	Texas
Massachusetts	Washington (state)
Michigan	West Virginia

Therefore, every fourth name was selected for mailing. Duplicate names were deleted. A return-stamped envelope (the University of Southern Mississippi, Department of Criminal Justice), a questionnaire, and a cover letter were stuffed into addressed envelopes. The cover letter and the questionnaire asked participants to copy the questionnaire for others in their offices. In total, 1,100 envelopes were mailed in late summer of 2006. Kim Cox, a competent graduate assistant, developed the mailing lists, prepared the mailing materials, distributed the questionnaires, and entered the returned data into computer grids.[6]

A total of 455 questionnaires were returned, of which 10 were less than one-half completed and one was illegible; therefore, data from 444 questionnaires were entered into computer grids. The returned surveys also contained 41 letters from prosecutors about themselves, their offices, and their jobs (see Chapters 7 and 11 for some of their comments about the responsibility of a prosecutor). Because this was a confidential survey, prosecutors did not identify themselves, but envelope postmarks implied that respondents represented 18 states, as shown in Table 10-2. Admittedly, participants could have returned their questionnaire while traveling in a state other than where they were employed as a prosecutor. Then, too, of the 18 states represented, only Massachusetts, Michigan, New York, and West Virginia are states that had abolished capital punishment (see Chapter 9 for details) at the time of this survey.

■ The Participants in This Study

The average respondent reported 15 years of service as a prosecutor, with a range of 1 to 32 years (see Table 10-3). Sixty percent (264) worked full time, their average age was 49 years, and most of the participants were white (402) males (298) who worked for a state (197) or a county (209), and 77 percent (341) were elected officials. Forty-three percent (192) litigated all types of cases, and 24 percent (107) litigated only felony cases. Also, most of the respondents reported that the state

TABLE 10-3 CHARACTERISTICS OF SAMPLE, *N* = 444

Characteristics	Number	Percentage or range
Years of service	15 years	1–32 years
Full time	264	60%
Part time	169	38%
Age	49	29–72 years
Male	298	67%
Female	136	31%
White	402	91%
Black	28	6%
Hispanic	3	7%
Asian	6	1%
State	197	44%
County	209	47%
City	31	7%
Elected official	341	77%
Appointed official	99	22%
Cases prosecuted (all categories of crime)	192	43%
Felony: Crimes against persons	107	24%
Crimes against property and weapons	106	23%
Crimes committed by juveniles	32	7%
Required future hours education	12	3–25 hours
Percentage of law school training or education used on job	29%	10–80%
How well law school prepares students	Average	45%
Professionalism and money are motivators in enrolling in law school	384	87%
Enhance admissions: Less reliance on LSAT	161	37%
More criminal courses for future prosecutors	159	36%
Don't accumulate college (i.e., student loans) debt	133	30%

Note: Percentages are rounded; missing cases are not shown.

required them to obtain 12 hours of annual training, although several of the states did not have a mandatory number of hours of prosecutor training, nor did they have a specific administrative agency that conducts legal training.

When the respondents were asked about how much law school training they employed in their role as a prosecutor, the typical response was 29 percent. That is, prosecutors employed a little over one-fourth of what they learned as a student at law school to their present job. Perhaps one reason for this low utilization of law school training relates to the fact that most law schools concentrate on civil law as opposed to criminal law, suggested one prosecutor in her accompanying letter. Forty-five percent (170) gave their law school a C or an average grade in preparing students to become prosecutors, and 87 percent (384) reported that professionalism of the job and money were the two reasons they went to law school. Less reliance on the LSAT entrance examination among law schools is the best way to improve law school admissions, reported 37 percent (161) of the prosecutors (see Chapter 11 for more details on law school recommendations). More criminal courses should be required for students who want to become prosecutors, reported 36 percent (159) of the participants. The best advice offered by 30 percent (133) of the prosecutors to law students is not to accumulate college debt, such as student loans.

■ Findings

In a criminal case when making an indictment decision and a conviction strategy, the prosecutors surveyed put more weight on how often they thought judges, jurors, and defense lawyers were influenced by the *CSI Effect* than the merits of the case which includes the substantial evidence gathered by police. For instance, over 82 percent (359) of the participants reported that judges are always or very often impressed with television or media evidence (see Table 10-4). Over one-half (259) of the prosecutors polled reported that CSI television performances always or very often influence juries; a finding consistent with a study of 1,200 jurors from 14 states revealing that constitutionally-mandated requirements provide less influence (than television) upon jurists than expected.[7] Also, approximately three of every

TABLE 10-4 *CSI EFFECT* UPON JUDGES, JURIES, AND DEFENSE LAWYERS

- Judges are always or very often impressed by the *CSI Effect* (82% or 359).
- Juries are always or very often influenced by the *CSI Effect* (59% or 259).
- Defense lawyers always or very often resorted to *CSI Effect* accounts to make their cases (76% or 331).

Note: Percentages are rounded; minus missing cases, N = 440.

four (331) of the prosecutors reported that defense lawyers portrayed unrealistic forensic analysis to win favor with judges and juries.

Additionally, 64 percent (281) of 437 (7 missing cases) participants reported that grand jury (a grand jury serves a purpose in most jurisdictions and is defined below) determinations can predict judiciary outcomes; and 61 percent (267) of 439 (6 missing cases) participants reported that the *elements of the crime* (defined below) can predict judiciary outcomes. That is, some prosecutors are saying that grand juries and the elements of the crime are of less concern during the litigation process than expected. (It was expected that most of the prosecutors would be influenced by grand jury determinations and the elements of the crime. I interpreted that to mean that more than one-third of the prosecutors surveyed see grand jury determinants and the elements of the crime as unreliable components of the justice system.)

The Duty of a Grand Jury   The American Bar Association explains that the primary function of the grand jury is to review the evidence presented by the prosecutor and determine whether there is probable cause to return an indictment against an individual.[8]

Since the role of the grand jury is only to determine probable cause, there is no need for the jury to hear all the evidence, or even conflicting evidence. It is left to the good faith of the prosecutor to present conflicting evidence.

In the federal system, the courts have ruled that the grand jury has extraordinary investigative powers. However, the power is virtually in complete control of the prosecutor, and is pretty much left to his or her good faith.

The National Center for State Courts advises that most state systems use grand juries to some extent in criminal and civil cases; often some grand juries can investigate alleged crimes in their venues, too.[9]

Elements of a Crime: Legal Definition   The elements of a crime are the component parts of the crime. For example, first-degree murder is defined as[10]:

- In most states (not all states have degrees), first-degree murder is defined as:
  - an unlawful killing that is both
  - willful (intent; *mens rea*)
  - premeditated (planned)

  meaning that the killing was committed after planning or "lying in wait" for the victim.

For example, Victoria comes home to find her husband, Chris, in bed with Maryo. Three days later, Victoria waits in her auto near Maryo's workplace. When Maryo leaves work, Victoria shoots and kills Maryo.

Each of those three (unlawful killing, willful, and premeditated) parts relates to the elements of the crime, and the prosecution must show "beyond and to the exclusion of every reasonable doubt" that the defendant is guilty of the crime charged and that the evidence was legally collected, appropriately evaluated, and that the *chain of custody* has not been compromised (as discussed in Chapter 6). Innocence of a suspect is presumed. This feature is supported by the US Constitution and its Amendments and places the *burden of proof* upon "the people" (government) presented by the prosecutor.

Interestingly, when prosecutors were asked to write in rank-ordered items that they relied on to convict a defendant, results showed that credible witnesses, credible victims, and investigative reports were their top three preferences (see Table 10-5). Investigator reports were prioritized, that is, the participants explained that reports developed by their own investigators took precedence over police investigator reports. Note that DNA evidence is ranked as a nonpriority because only .02 percent (31) of respondents suggested its importance.

When asked to write in rank-ordered factors that aid prosecutor performance, 24 percent (311) of the participants reported that substantial and documented evidence was at the top of the list; thus, 76 percent of the prosecutors felt that substantial and documented evidence was not the most beneficial tool leading to a conviction. Nonetheless, that was followed by 22 percent (293) who said that competent investigative units employed by the prosecutor, as opposed to police units are most important; and credible witnesses and victims were in third place, 21 percent (283) of the attorneys revealed (see Table 10-6).

TABLE 10-5 WRITTEN-IN, RANK-ORDERED CONVICTION PREFERENCES

- Credible witnesses (27% or 359)
- Credible victims (24% or 318)
- Prosecution investigator reports (16% or 205)
- A lot of hard work (13% or 171)
- Jury selection (8% or 108)
- Expert witness (4% or 54)
- DNA evidence (2% or 31)

Note: Participants voted three times each; minus missing cases, $N = 1320$. Percentages are rounded.

TABLE 10-6 WRITTEN-IN, RANK-ORDERED AIDS IN PROSECUTOR PERFORMANCE

- Substantial and documented evidence (24% or 311)
- Competent prosecutor investigative units, as opposed to police units (22% or 293)
- Credible witnesses and victims (21% or 283)
- More time to prepare case (13% or 174)
- Excellent legal support (12% or 163)
- More funds to prepare case (4% or 52)

Note: Participants voted three times each, minus missing cases, $N = 1320$. Percentages are rounded.

It should be acknowledged that supervision for an investigator who is under the authority of the prosecutor is a far reach from what popular police television performances typically depict. For example, in *Law & Order*, Episode 374, "Home Sweet Home," 8-year-old Jenna Wechsler died as a result of a building explosion. NYPD detectives Ed Green (Jessie L. Martin) and Nina Cassady (Milena Govich) follow the trail of evidence to Rosalie Schaffner, the owner's ex-wife. ADAs Jack McCoy (Sam Waterston) and his assistant ADA Connie Rubirosa (Alana De La Garza) pursue Rosalie Schaffner despite a lack of concrete evidence, but the case takes a turn when Rubirosa finds a piece of evidence that points them in a new direction. The data in Table 10-6 suggests that the prosecutors who were polled would prefer that their own investigators uncover the required evidence to make the case rather than relying on police detectives such as Green and Cassady. Most often, prosecutor investigators are sworn-in or commissioned individuals with full police powers. Little of their existence is represented in popular television dramas; for example, in *Law & Order* that role is usually played by Jack McCoy's assistant, ADA Connie Rubirosa, who has never played the role of a sworn-in or even trained law enforcement officer with powers of detainment and use of force.

Perhaps the participants in the current study relied more on witnesses and victims because they could prep or manipulate witnesses and victims, but manipulation of forensic science results produced by lab technicians or substantial evidence secured by investigators is another matter. This thought is consistent with the results from the written-in, rank-ordered answers to the question about undesirable benefits of a prosecutor, as shown in Table 10-7. Seventeen percent (225) of the respondents reported that a lack of personal privacy was their most undesirable benefit as a prosecutor, and 17 percent (209) were disenchanted with the publicity created by the media relations public official. Inadequate support staff was reported by 16 percent (191) of the participants, and 14 percent (182) of the attorneys mentioned public interference as undesirable.

TABLE 10-7 WRITTEN-IN, RANK-ORDERED MOST UNDESIRABLE BENEFITS

- Lack of personal privacy (17% or 225)
- Media publicity (17% or 209)
- Inadequate support staff (16% or 191)
- Public interference (14% or 182)
- Assaulted verbally or physically (9% or 116)
- Lack of professional autonomy (7% or 93)
- Impartial judge (3% or 34)
- Prosecuting former clients or their family members (2% or 20)

Note: Participants voted three times each minus missing cases, $N = 1325$. Percentages are rounded.

The first four undesirable characteristics seem to be consistent with privacy in preparing victims and witnesses for an adjudication process that could include plea bargaining issues or trial. This idea also finds congruence with a perspective revealed in Chapter 7 whereby popular television performances, such as *Law & Order*, guide the skills necessary for prosecutors to be recognized as master framers in the sense of preparing victims, witnesses, and police officers for court.[11]

Of concern, 26 percent (116) of the respondents reported that verbal or physical assault is an undesirable consequence of the job. The data linked to assault against prosecutors and judges is a finding that appears to be overlooked in the literature, and perhaps these occurrences and others should be researched further to determine the scope and extent of this issue.[12-13]

Nonetheless, prosecutors we re asked to write in their rank-ordered reasons why other prosecutors might reject a case despite substantial documented evidence. Twenty-seven percent (363) of the respondents reported that the primary reason prosecutors do not indict or charge a suspect with a crime is an irrational, unconvincing, or unbelievable victim or witness, or what can be called an uncredible victim or witness (see Table 10-8); also, 15 percent (196) of the participants revealed that inconsistent evidence is a reason for rejecting a case, and 14 percent (186) said uncredible arrest officer reports are another reason.

TABLE 10-8 WRITTEN-IN, RANK-ORDERED REASONS TO REJECT A CASE DESPITE SUBSTANTIAL EVIDENCE

- Uncredible victims and witnesses (27% or 363)
- Inconsistent evidence (15% or 196)
- Uncredible arrest officer reports (14% or 186)

Note: Participants voted three times each, minus missing cases, $N = 1324$. Percentages are rounded.

■ Gang Rapist Released Because Witness Was Uncredible

Based on the previously discussed data, credible witnesses include forensic scientists, victims, and individuals who witnessed a crime, but they are credible only if they are believable on the witness stand (regardless of the quality of the information they would offer).

This finding is consistent with a gang rape that was witnessed by police in a Midwestern city during the summer of 2007. The five gang members were released on the grounds that the victim was too frightened to testify. There could be no case without the victim taking the stand. If she did so, the 18-year-old girl would have to admit that she had been involved in allowing fondling by an acquaintance outside her hotel, and when she headed back into the hotel, where she and her family were guests, friends of the acquaintance forced her to cross a street where all five gang members sexually assaulted her. The police arrived during the altercation (the actual crime, that is; the officers witnessed the sexual assault) and took the gang members into custody. However, the victim was unable to state how many times she had been raped or by whom. The prosecutor saw too many deficiencies in her story and thought she would fold under cross-examination, suggesting the victim was an uncredible victim.

This perspective is consistent with a study conducted by researchers at the University of Nebraska at Omaha.[14] The findings clarify that prosecutors can and will reject a sexual assault case when the prosecutor perceives a victim cannot or will not cooperate in the prosecution of the case. One way to interpret these findings is to say that the weight of prosecution is linked to the capability of the victim, as opposed to the seriousness of the crime.

■ Forensic Analysis Unnecessary

Few of the participants in the current study sought forensic analysis (which is becoming used more often in conducting an arrest of a suspect) for an indictment or conviction for the following reasons:

- It does not prove beyond a shadow of doubt the intention of an offender.
- Most prosecutors relied on the plea bargaining process if they were concerned about witnesses, victims, evidence, or their own competence.
- Timing might add to the decision-making process because of forensic lab turnaround time (see Chapter 6).
- A plea bargain can be reached in a short time period with less expense than other procedures.

This next finding is puzzling because 32 percent (141) of the participants reported that rejecting a case can be in the best interests of justice; in part, this finding can reveal that a lack of resources may exist in a jurisdiction or that a case could be too expensive to litigate. One assumption that can be drawn from this finding is that prosecutors lack the necessary resources to process criminal cases to their satisfaction; however, this finding also implies that prosecutors see police investigation and forensic outcomes as flawed. That is, if the cops made a criminal arrest (in the 21st century when the public has become highly litigious especially against false arrest and denial of due process), there must have been some merit (evidence) to the process not to mention some cops and victims being placed at risk during the altercation and arrest. Then, too, recall the perceived unreliable variables of grand juries and the elements of the crime as explained earlier in this chapter (this final thought pertains to an assumption that a case is not dropped after a grand jury indictment).

Furthermore, when the participants had engaged in discretionary prosecutorial matters, 43 percent (189) reported that practical (bureaucratic) rules guided their behavior, but 13 percent (55) said they seldom or never allowed the rules to influence their behavior. I took this to mean that the practical or bureaucratic rules such as those in the

- Federal Rules of Evidence
- Federal Criminal Procedures and jurisdictional rules of evidence and criminal procedures
- American Bar Association's (and local bar associations') ethical standards
- US Constitution and its Amendments

can be ignored by over one-half of the participants. But the rules are totally ignored by 13 percent of the participants during an indictment and conviction process. Also, 12 percent (52) of those surveyed reported that they held a strong personal incentive. That is, 52 prosecutors in this study held a personal agenda of some sort which reveals that these individuals had few professional boundaries—anything was possible including the withholding of exculpatory evidence and indicting and convicting a person a prosecutor knew was innocent. This finding is consistent with the behavior of the assistant US Attorney, Suzanne Sullivan during the spring of 2009 in Boston who willfully withheld exculpatory evidence that could have released the defendant Sullivan had prosecuted (see Chapter 8 for details).

These findings imply that some prosecutors break the rules, and when they do, they can fix their decisions in the rationale that justice must prevail at all costs. (Note: a similar battle cry about the wars on crime, junkies, sex offenders, poverty, and immigrants). At an extreme, this reasoning is consistent with criminals who use excuses (i.e. I snapped, I don't know what came over me; or it wasn't me, man, besides I was wasted) or "scapegoats" to justify or blame for their misconduct in order to avoid the consequences of their behavior. "Excuses are socially approved vocabularies for mitigating or relieving responsibility when conduct is questioned," argue Stanford M. Lyman and Marvin B. Scott.[15] Apparently some prosecutors employ their own brand of justice to further personal agendas in the name of justice—a vigilante prosecutor, of sorts.

This finding is consistent with findings of the Center for Public Integrity whereby researchers found that in many of the 2,341 jurisdictions across the nation, prosecutors have stretched, bent, or broken rules to win convictions since 1970. Also, the Center has found that individual judges and appellate court panels cited prosecutorial misconduct as a factor when dismissing charges, reversing convictions, or reducing sentences in over 2,000 cases. In another 500 cases, appellate judges offered opinions—either dissents or concurrences—in which they found the misconduct warranted a reversal. In thousands more, judges labeled prosecutorial behavior inappropriate, but upheld convictions using a doctrine called "harmless error."[16]

■ Data Analysis

Apparently, few prosecutors behave inappropriately, and those who do commit the most destruction. One analogy relates to the findings from experts who study chronic criminal behavior. They too find that a few criminal violators in a specific geographic locale of a jurisdiction commit the most crime.[17–18] Additional calculations of the survey data show that there is a statistically significant relationship between witnesses and victims as indictment priorities and low utilization of law school education at the respondents' present job. That is, the lower the score, such as 15 percent of their law school education experiences are applied to their current prosecutorial services, the more likely these participants reported that credible witnesses and victims are the primary factors toward indictment and convictions, and the more likely the same group reported that income was the primary motivator to attend law school in the first place. Poor law students make poor prosecutors. One assumption is that law school curriculums play a role in future indictment processes (and professional behavior) of their graduates (see Chapter 11 for law school recommendations).

Relationships among responses can be referred to as a statistical cross-tabulation, which can aid in a further understanding of the findings. For example, the prosecutors, despite the fact that they have been similarly trained in law schools whose curriculums are accredited and guided by the American Bar Association, have responded differently on this survey about their decision-making process concerning indictments and convictions. Perhaps the thought is too far removed, but because the American Bar Association mentors and regulates most American law schools, it seems similar to asking a physician if he or she would or would not treat an injury of a victim of a motor vehicle crash, despite the fact that practices among doctors vary;[19] or if a police officer would or would not provide emergency services to a bleeding victim at a domestic violence service call; or if a jailer would or would not put a reckless, drunk teen on high-monitored watch while awaiting the teen's parents. There are practices that professionals follow in criminal justice that must be centered on their training,[20] regulations,[21] and personal concerns of the people criminal justice professionals encounter on a routine basis, advises the superintendent of police in Boston.[22]

Also, a significant statistical relationship exists between the participants who reported that the most undesirable benefit of being a prosecutor is a lack of personal privacy from public scrutiny; those same lawyers reported that uncredible victims and witnesses are prime reasons to reject a case. This group also reported that police reports are insufficient criteria in their indictment decision-making process. Additional statistical assessments show that grand juries, the elements of crime, and police-secured evidence have little influence upon prosecutors to charge a suspect with a crime. A lack of privacy and unsuitable victims and witnesses were reasons to reject a case, and police reports did not apparently impact their decisions. This finding is consistent with government statistics. For example, an estimated 56,146 felony cases were filed in the state courts of the nation's 75 largest counties, and only an estimated one-fourth of those felony defendants were charged with a violent offense in May 2002.[23] Apparently, some prosecutors have little confidence in police practices.

Relationship Between the *CSI Effect* and Judges, Juries, and Defense Lawyers

One way to make sense of this analysis is to reveal that statistical relationships show a strong connection between prosecutors who say that judges, juries, and defense lawyers are influenced by the *CSI Effect* and their own future careers. That is, the more the respondents believed that judges, juries, and defense lawyers were influenced by the *CSI Effect*, the more they thought their future careers would be affected by how they behaved when a judge is present.

Accepting the *CSI Effect* as Reality

Equally important, the more a prosecutor accepted the *CSI Effect* as a reality, the more a prosecutor relied upon the skill or capability of a victim or a witness to compellingly perform in front of a jury, regardless of the substantial evidence of the case which includes forensic science analysis. That is, when the participants' responses were cross-tabulated, almost three of every four of those polled who believed judges, juries, and defense lawyers were impacted by the *CSI Effect* also believed that credible victims and credible witnesses were the most advantageous vehicles or devices used for winning a conviction. Conversely, few of the polled prosecutors who believed that judges were influenced by the *CSI Effect* accepted evidence gathered by the police as the most advantageous component toward a conviction.

In essence, prosecutors are mindful of what it takes to win, but regretfully the substantial evidence shows that prosecutors are more concerned with credible (or believable) individuals who can compellingly testify. Prosecutors are cognizant of the reliability studies of eyewitness testimony and phony police reports, including false confessions and manipulated evidence, as discussed in Chapter 8. Also, strengthening this thought are the statements found in the 41 letters from the participants in this study. A typical comment was phrased this way: "The buck stops with me as the primary law enforcement officer representing the people in this county." Another prosecutor spelled it out this way: "If a prosecutor doesn't know the difference between trumped-up arrests and bogus evidence, then that prosecutor should find another job." Yet another wrote: "Verifying eye witness, survivor, and victim accounts and verifying the reliability of evidence is the benchmark of a prosecutor's integrity.

To that end, my office and my personnel take seriously their responsibility to represent the people." Another thought of interest emerged in six of the letters and typically read this way: "My office takes great care to confirm crime lab reports and often my office will have tests repeated in another lab." One interpretation emerging from these responses is that prosecutors understand the responsibility of their office, and most conduct themselves in a professional manner.

Also among the responses of the participants, significant correlations existed between their ideas of future careers, such as judgeships, and a number of other variables, such as the length of service of a prosecutor, inconsistent evidence, jury selection, and a lot of hard work.

■ Implications of the Findings

It first needs to be acknowledged that similar to all surveys, the conclusions are indecisive because data are a snapshot of a participant's thoughts at the time he or she completed the survey, nothing more. That said, the evidence in this study supports the implication that at the core of the wrongful conviction phenomenon are prosecutors who alone possess the authority to initially indict a suspect; if they don't act, little, if anything, happens toward justice, a thought consistent with the literature.[24] Additionally, indicators are present that support three conclusions:

- First, prosecutor discretion to indict a suspect is linked to courtroom-savvy scientists, witnesses, and victims who possess the ability to convince others that their observations about the defendant (and only the defendant) and the event of the crime are absolutely reliable.
- Second, individuals who can be prepared to deliver a compelling presentation are strong motivators for a prosecutor to indict a suspect and litigate against a defendant, regardless of the quality of evidence.
- Third, a small number of prosecutors behave recklessly; among those few, they possess an unchallenged potential to destroy the life of an innocent suspect, his or her family members and friends, and to aid the real guilty party's freedom.

The above thoughts are consistent with Samuel Walker and the work of Raymond Paternoster, Robert Brame, and Sarah Bacon, who argue that prosecutors make private decisions centered on personal expectations for a case that can be manipulated by the prosecutor rather than through the employment of the elements of a case.[25–26]

Going behind the scholarly literature and findings of this study, this author can't help but imagine that first responders and police investigators across the country must feel a sense of frustration with the judicial process because of the incredible amount of prosecutor discretion that is apparently shaped by a lack of commitment to the democratic process, incompetence, or pure laziness. When it comes to the police, the data show that no matter the sacrifice street cops make to identify, arrest, secure evidence, and secure the chain of custody, whether a suspect is indicted or not depends on the discretionary powers of a prosecutor.

Some prosecutors apparently lack professional guidance and the personal motivation to represent the people, giving rise to vast human and legal violations of defendants' rights. Also, professional prosecutors who see the indiscretions and misconduct of a few of their colleagues must feel a sense of frustration, too. Wrongful convictions are more likely to occur when prosecutors ignore the constitutional rights of constituents and pursue a hard-line approach to criminal convictions, especially if the jurisdiction supports capital punishment sanctions. Arbitrary government intrusion into the lives of the American population is obviously unsupported by the rule of law, and is therefore illegal. I guess you can say that there are a lot of Jack McCoy wannabes out there. In this regard, there appears to be an urgent need for public policy response to this problem.

■ Summary

Chapter 1 reveals that an earlier study about the relationship between Boston police officers and a review of a monograph by opponents of capital punishment led to a concern about prosecutorial discretion. A survey was developed with input from colleagues, graduate students, and prosecutors. In all, the final survey contains 32 variables and places them into four categories: personal demographics; performance issues; impact of *CSI Effect*, and opinions about law school.

The working theory of this study is that the popular media provides its own version of crime, which heightens the fear of victimization and what to do about those fears as guided by the *CSI Effect*, which changes real-world expectations of crime and crime control by affecting the decisions of witnesses, victims, jurors, and justice professionals. A *CSI Effect* is a conceptual consequence of the popular media's skill to (1) encourage aggressive reactive criminal justice strategies; (2) glorify vigilantism among justice practitioners and members of the public; and (3) promote fictitious accounts of crime, crime control, and its processes. These notions were supported by data from 444 prosecutors in 18 states.

The more prosecutors reported that jurors, judges, and defense lawyers accepted the perspectives associated with the conceptual consequences stemming from the *CSI Effect*, the more prosecutors thought that compelling witnesses and victims were necessary to indict and convict a defendant, regardless of the evidence, including forensic science analysis. The implications are that witnesses (including forensic personnel and victims) can and do represent human error (including lies, trickery, and laziness), and victims, like actors, can be prompted and rehearsed for their performances. Misguided prosecutors can easily open the door to indict and convict whomever they think they can convict through theatrics.

The implications of the findings include the reality that prosecutor discretion to indict a suspect is linked to courtroom-savvy scientists, witnesses, and victims who possess the ability to convince others that their observations about the defendant and the event of the crime are absolutely reliable. A small number of prosecutors behave recklessly; among them, they possess an unchallenged potential to destroy the life of an innocent suspect. When it comes to the police, the data show that no matter the sacrifice street cops make to identify, arrest, secure evidence, and secure the chain of custody, whether a suspect is indicted or not depends upon the discretionary powers of a prosecutor. Some prosecutors apparently lack professional guidance and the personal motivation to represent the people, giving rise to vast human and legal violations of the rights of the defendant.

■ References

1. Stevens, D. J. (2006). Police training and management impact sexual assault conviction rates in Boston. *Police Journal, 79*(2), 125–154.

2. Center for Public Integrity. (2003). *Harmful error: Investigating America's local prosecutors.* Washington, DC: Author.

3. Paternoster, R., Brame, R., & Bacon, S. (2007). *The death penalty: America's experience with capital punishment.* New York: Oxford University Press.

4. Stevens, D. J. (2008). Forensic science, wrongful convictions, and American prosecutor discretion. *Howard Journal of Criminal Justice Science, 47*(1), 31–51.

5. It is expected that everyone will not agree with the categories selected; however, these categories appear to be reasonable communicative units in an attempt to guide those who feel uncomfortable with strict statistical protocols. In fact, during the entire analytical and statistical process the thought of complicating issues dictated removal of those products. The thinking leaned toward clarity as opposed to appeasing those few ivory-tower statisticians who would find fault with Einstein; and because I'm not even close to Einstein's God-given intellect, I'll keep my version of the findings, for the sake of my audience and my own dignity, closer to a qualitative reference as opposed to the quantitative pit of illusion.

6. Kim Cox graduated from the University of Southern Mississippi with honors and a master's degree and is currently at the University of Vienna in Austria, enrolled in a PhD program. Other graduate assistants who contributed to this work are Linda Moss, who edited the earlier chapters of this work; Lacey Cochran Stewart, who researched prosecutors; Sergeant Shane Steel (Biloxi Police Department, Mississippi), who researched the death penalty; Sergeant Luke Thompson (Gulfport Police Department, Mississippi), who researched police officer behavior; and Jennifer Taylor, a PhD candidate at the University of Southern Mississippi and former police officer, Lafayette, Lousiana.

7. Bowers, W. J., & Foglia, W. D. (2003). Still singularly agonizing: Law's failure to purge arbitrariness from capital sentencing. *Criminal Law Bulletin, 39*, 51–86.

8. American Bar Association (2009). *Frequently asked questions about grand jury system.* Retrieved July 9, 2009, from http://www.abanet.org/media/faqjury.html

9. The National Center for State Courts (2009). *Knowledge and information services: Grand juries.* Retrieved July 9, 2009, from http://www.ncsconline.org/wc/courtopics/FAQs. asp?topic=grdjur The Center advises that all states use grand juries in some capacity. Some state grand juries merely exist de jure; Wisconsin, for example, has a grand jury statute but has not convened a grand jury in decades.

Most states (all but Connecticut and Pennsylvania, and the District of Columbia) retain the option of a grand jury indictment. Eighteen states (Alabama, Alaska, Delaware, Georgia, Kentucky, Maine, Massachusetts, Mississippi, New Hampshire, New Jersey, New York, North Carolina, Ohio, South Carolina, Tennessee, Texas, Virginia, and West Virginia) require an indictment to begin felony prosecutions; four (Florida, Louisiana, Minnesota, and Rhode Island) require an indictment to begin prosecutions that could result in life imprisonment or a death sentence. The Fifth Amendment of the US Constitution requires that felony defendants in federal courts be indicted by a grand jury.

Arizona, Florida, Louisiana, Minnesota, Missouri, Montana, and North Carolina limit the scope of the investigatory grand jury to criminal activity that is brought to their attention by the prosecutor or the court.

Grand juries in Alabama, Alaska, Arkansas, California, Idaho, Indiana, Iowa, Kentucky, Nebraska, Nevada, North Dakota, Ohio, Oklahoma, Oregon, South Dakota, Tennessee, Texas, Virginia, and West Virginia can investigate alleged crimes occurring within their venues (usually the county where the grand jury sits).

10. Findlaw.com. *Murder.* Retrieved July 8, 2009, from www.findlaw.com

11. Gershman, B. L. (1998). *Prosecutorial misconduct.* New York: West.

12. US Marshall Service. (2009). US Marshall's Fact Sheet. Retrieved September 3, 2009, from http://www.usmarshals.gov/duties/factsheets/index.html. Ensures the safe and secure conduct of judicial proceedings and protects more than 2,000 federal judges and approximately 5,250 other court officials at more than 400 court facilities. The only known operational research study on assassinations, which includes assassinations and attacks on federal judges, is the US Secret Service Exceptional Case Study Project (ECSP), a study of all 83 persons in the United States known to have attacked, or approached to attack, a prominent public official or figure between 1949 and 1996. US Secret Service. (2008). *Preventing targeted violence against judicial officials and courts.* Retrieved July 8, 2009, from http://www.secretservice.gov/ntac_aapss.shtml.

One federal study found that most threatening communications or actions against judges, their staff, or their families come from individuals who are angry about a specific court case (see Table 10-10).

TABLE 10-10 THREATS AGAINST JUDGES, THEIR STAFF, OR THEIR FAMILIES

Year reported	Incidents	Unknown sources	Known sources
1998	790	104 (13%)	686 (87%)
1999	814	109 (13%)	705 (87%)
2000	702	109 (16%)	593 (84%)
2001	690	126 (18%)	564 (82%)
2002	565	101 (18%)	464 (82%)
2003	585	105 (18%)	480 (82%)

Source: Vossekuil, B., Borum, R., Fein, R., and Reddy, M. (2009). *Preventing targeted violence against judicial officials and courts.* Washington, DC: United States Secret Service. Retrieved September 2, 2009, from http://www.secretservice.gov/ntac_aapss.shtml.

13. Meeks, B. N. (2005, March 11). Preventing courtroom violence. *MSNBC.com*. Retrieved July 7, 2009, from http://www.msnbc.msn.com/id/7161591

14. Spohn, C., Beichner, D., & Davis-Frenzel, E. (2001). Prosecutorial justifications for sexual assault case rejection: Guarding the gateway to justice. *Social Problems, 48*(2), 206–235.

15. Lyman, S. M., & Scott, M. B. (1989). *A sociology of the absurd* (2nd ed.). Dix Hills, NY: General Hall.

16. Center for Public Integrity. (2003, June 26). *Breaking the rules*. Retrieved July 8, 2009, from http://projects.publicintegrity.org/PM/

17. Sherman, L. (1992). Attacking crime: Police and crime control. *Crime and Justice, 15*, 159–230.

18. McGarrell, E. F., Chermak, S., & Weiss, A. (2002). *Reducing firearms violence through directed police patrol: Final report on the evaluation of the Indianapolis Police Department's Directed Patrol Project*. Rockville, MD: National Criminal Justice Reference Service.

19. Promes, S. B. (2004). Emergency physicians' opioid prescribing practices vary. *Journal Watch Emergency Medicine, 6*, 291–305.

20. Bennett, W. W., & Hess, K. M. (2007). *Management and supervision in law enforcement* (5th ed.). Springfield, IL: Charles C. Thomas.

21. Stevens, D. J. (2006). *Community corrections: An applied approach*. Upper Saddle River, NJ: Prentice Hall.

22. The University of Massachusetts, Boston. *Criminal justice professor unveils community policing attitudes in Dorchester. (2001)*. Retrieved September 2, 2009, from http://www.umb.edu/news/2001news/reporter/1101/dorchester.html. Superintendent Robert Dunford of the Boston Police Department presented this viewpoint during a lecture at the University of Massachusetts–Boston in the spring of 2001 while he was commander of District 11 (Dorchester) in Boston.

23. Bureau of Justice Statistics. (2008). *Criminal case processing statistics*. Washington, DC: US Department of Justice. Retrieved July 8, 2009, from http://www.ojp.usdoj.gov/bjs/cases.htm

24. Krug, P. (2001, Autumn). Prosecutorial discretion and its limits. *The American Journal of Comparative Law, 50*, 643–664.

25. Walker, S. (2001). *Sense and nonsense about crime and drugs*. Belmont, CA: Wadsworth Thomson.

26. Paternoster, Brame, & Bacon. *The death penalty: America's experience with capital punishment*.

Recommendations to Reduce Wrongful Convictions and Eliminate Capital Punishment

CHAPTER

11

> *God grant me the serenity to accept the things I cannot change, the courage to change the things I can, and the wisdom to know the difference.*
>
> Reinhold Niebuhr

▶ ▶ CHAPTER OBJECTIVES

- Describe objectives toward legal and moral accountability of prosecutors
- Characterize recommendations for forensic labs
- Describe admissible evidence and clarify Federal Rules of Evidence potentials
- Identify judicial blindness perspective linked to capital punishment
- Characterize prosecution recommendations such as community prosecution and street-level advocates
- Articulate new law school admission standards and curriculums to aid future prosecutors

■ Introduction

It seems apparent that ancient philosophers and important psychologists agree that human beings have within themselves vast resources for self-directed behavior and resilience (an ability to recover from or adjust easily to misfortune or change).[1] Intrinsic in this notion is that American democracy is revered and cherished, but it is also unpredictable and combative. For example, "nearly every teen in America is on the Internet every day, socializing with friends and strangers alike, creating identities and building a virtual profile of themselves," reports *Frontline*,[2] which adds that parents and children find themselves on opposite sides of a digital divide. Consequently, American youth feel that they possess the personal right to display pictures of themselves online (MySpace and Facebook) and that neither their parents nor the authorities (including school administrators) should interfere with their online conversations, YouTube videos, or suggestive photos of their bodies. Americans defend their personal choices regardless of their age or the vulgarity of their behavior (at an extreme, consider the foul behavior of some celebrities) and expect—more than expect, demand—little if any scrutiny or intrusion into their daily choices by government, neighbors, thugs—foreign born or otherwise, teachers, or parents. Yet wisdom can be linked to making choices (therein lies one task of teachers and parents—help kids make right choices). As noted at the opening of this chapter, Reinhold Niebuhr suggests that we should accept the things we can't change, such as the popular media (and some of our kids' decisions), and that we should be courageous in changing the things we can, such as the role of prosecutors who, according to all narratives, are less accountable than expected (as are our kids) in a democratic society.[3]

Throughout this work it has been said that the criminal justice community goes beyond justice personnel at the local, state, and federal levels and includes awesome professors such as Howard Becker, Travis Hirshci, and Joycelyn M. Pollock and trainers at law academies; association executives and their staff such as the Academy of Criminal Justice Sciences and journal editors and their reviewers such as the Criminal Law Bulletin; accomplished researchers, such as Meda Chesney-Lind, Larry Sherman, and Wesley Skogan; vendors who service prison and police populations; and meticulous authors such as Frank Schmalleger, Larry Siegel, and Samuel Walker. All of these individuals (and the many I haven't mentioned) individually and collectively work hard to protect the essence of freedom through justice and their individual contributions.

Now, because of the number of wrongful convictions and continuation of executions, the adversarial process across the planet is under attack because it is both compelling and chaotic. It is compelling in terms of federal aid (public taxes) paid to American businesses, such as $182 billion to American International Group, Inc. (AIG), and it's chaotic in the sense that AIG reported to have paid $218 million in bonuses to its executives while unemployment rates in the United States continued to rise in the winter of 2009. It is also compelling because everyone, guilty or innocent, is entitled to a fair trial, but it's chaotic because wrongful convictions and capital punishment are ever present. That said, the views of lawyers and nonlawyers diverge, argues Lisa J. McIntyre, a Chicago public defender.[4] She reveals that nonlawyers have the opinion that a fair trial results in convicting guilty defendants and acquitting those who are not guilty. However, Peter L. Berger reminds us (see Chapter 1) that "social reality turns out to have many layers of meaning. The discovery of each new layer, changes the perception of the whole."[5] Unfortunately, things aren't always what they seem! As more is learned about the unlimited power of prosecutors, similar to what has been learned about the unlimited control corporate executives possess over public funds, it becomes apparent that more needs to be accomplished to apply democratic virtues to America's compelling and chaotic circumstances. For example, prosecutors are immune from civil suits for alleged deprivations of the constitutional rights of the accused (see Chapters 7 and 8 for details). Consequently, prosecutors possess unlimited and unparalleled power.[6] Equally important, the harmless error doctrine applies to prosecutors whereby an appellate court can affirm a conviction despite the presence of serious prosecutorial misconduct during trial (see Chapter 9 for details).[7] One result is that the door is wide-open for wrongful convictions and the continuation of the death penalty. So much for the separation of powers doctrine (see Chapter 3)![8]

As all of these inequalities continue to rain down upon the rights and lives of Americans, it could be said that the victories of the haves over the have-nots continue to go unchallenged, in part because of the *CSI Effect*. What has changed in the 21st century is that the opiate of the masses is linked to the new god in town, which has been provided, in part, through the *CSI Effect*. Some say the popular media has the power to change an alleged child molester into a messiah and a ruthless bank robbery into a blessed event. Consider the new threat of personal rights in the "war on sickies" in the winter of 2009. In the name of justice, American officials are talking about involuntary isolation or quarantine of individuals with H1N1 ("Swine") flu virus. What that amounts to is a new battle cry centered in community health which can easily develop into a promising legal method of social control, this author advances.

Furthermore, there are suggestions advanced by some authors that the popular media through the *CSI Effect* has little impact upon justice practitioners, jurors, and wrongful convictions because most researchers (similar to the research design in this book, see Chapter 10) polled prosecutors; therefore, those findings lack empirical evidence directly related to *CSI Effect's* impact upon the justice system.[9] Nonetheless, justice professionals, guilty defendants, and those unfortunately wrongfully convicted recognize that at the core of democracy are law enforcement officers which include prosecutors who are for the most part amazingly gifted, dedicated, and diligent in their efforts to provide incredible contributions to a lifestyle never before experienced by such a robust and diverse population. Yet, empirical evidence is not the only gauge that leads us to conclusions about the impact of the *CSI Effect*, as the hundreds of pages and hundreds of scholars cited on those pages preceding this page demonstrate. It is clear that the gatekeeper of justice is the prosecutor, and that gatekeeper is the most powerful single person in government because if the prosecutor does not act, a judge and a jury are helpless, and police officer reports, sacrifices, and efforts are insignificant in comparison.[10]

> The success of a prosecutor is not necessarily motivated in the guilt or innocence of a suspect but in a prosecutor's ability to transform, beyond a reasonable doubt, circumstances that can demonstrate culpability and conform to what is provided by the popular media.

Other reasons for wrongful convictions and wrongful executions are detailed in Chapters 8 and 9. However, the preceding thought is consistent with the thoughts of the 444 prosecutors who participated in this study (see Chapter 10). More than likely, most prosecutors share a similar interest along with the public, defendants, and justice professionals concerning the integrity of the criminal justice system.[11] The American system has more strengths than faults, and it will resolve the problems of wrongful convictions and capital punishment as it has resolved to some degree of satisfaction larger problems than those such as gender bias, organized crime, and slavery. Therefore, the following explanations and recommendations, including my versions of the future of the prosecutor's office and ideas about prevention of wrongful convictions and crime, can contribute to a dialogue, in some way or another, toward reducing wrongful convictions, ending capital punishment, and revitalizing the democratic spirit as it relates to the rule of law.

■ Problem: Wars on Crime, Junkies, Sex Offenders, Poverty, and Immigrants

Crowded court dockets, bureaucracy, budgetary pressures, and careerism contribute to elevating aspirations above truth and justice and have sprung up largely as a result of the wars on crime, junkies, sex offenders, poverty, and immigrants. Indicting and convicting offenders is not at issue because prosecutors are tasked with winning convictions through litigation which can include plea bargains. The issue is how prosecutors win those trials and plea bargains. "For all the talk prosecutors like to engage in about how their number-one priority is to seek justice, not just win trials, it's numbers—trials completed, trials won, and trials lost—that mean everything," one prosecutor argues.[12] After all in a court room, a reasonable doubt exists when a juror cannot say with moral certainty that a person is guilty. But the emergence of moral causes or ends to justify the means through a series of deceptive wars—such as saving our children from drugs, making sex offenders pay, and protecting our shores from terrorists—contributes to the breakdown of prosecutorial restraint.[13]

I see the emergence of fictitious moral causes as a masquerade of paper faces, ringing jubilantly with justice while drowning a junkie or an immigrant and anyone who looks like one in the sewers below the city.

Robert Merkel, a former US attorney, says that prosecution "is a result-oriented process today, fairness be damned."[14] Apparently, Merkel says that morality takes a hit, too. Another researcher adds the idea that the "rich get richer and the poor get prison" because the justice system is designed to fail the American public—especially targeted defendants through the wars on crime, junkies, sex offenders, poverty, and immigrants—in order to succeed (a Pyrrhic defeat theory).[15] This thought may be useful in understanding some of the history about the criminal justice system, but consider that there are criminally violent offenders, including relentless gang members, congregating in American public spaces such as Main Street in quiet villages, in our families, where we work and play, and where we go to school. It is mandated that the criminal justice community provide public safety to ensure democracy's success. Sometimes I think it comes down to a question I asked a high-profile child sex offender at Attica in New York who talked about his innocence and a corrupt criminal justice system: "Would you rather be tried by your peers or the justice system?" The conversation surprisingly ended with him saying that he did not want to be tried by his peers—"they'd kill me." Nonetheless, consider the following:

- Law enforcement rarely apprehends major criminals and minor drug abusers.[16]
- Clearance rates (crimes known by the police that end in arrests) are on the decline, depending on the crime. For example, less than 4 out of 10 forcible rapists were arrested in 2007, compared to 5 out of 10 in 2002.[17]
- Conviction rates are lower than expected. For example, sex offenders are convicted at the rate of 56 out of 100 arrested, which is actually less than 7 percent of known offenses.[18]
- Prosecutors who provide defendants the benefit of the doubt are regarded as failures.[19]
- A total of 1 in 5 probationers are rearrested for a new crime.[20]
- Correctional systems rarely correct or rehabilitate poor behavior as evidenced by high recidivism rates. After release, an estimated 7 out of 10 former prisoners are rearrested, and one-half are returned to prison.[21]
- A total of 1 in 6 parolees are returned to prison.[22]
- Prior to incarceration, 35 percent of all state prisoners had been on probation or parole.[23]

The wars on crime, junkies, sex offenders, poverty, and immigrants can hardly compare with the wars in the Middle East or any war the American military has fought since this country's formation. For one, the rule of law forbids it, as discussed in Chapter 3. They are not real wars; they are political wars stirred and fueled by the popular media, and they target specific individuals based on status as opposed to behavior that is also forbidden by the rule of law. Yet they're ghetto wars because they target the poor, the underprivileged, and those lacking networks and wealth to buy their way out or get close to federal bailout funds.[24] You could say that rather than paying their way up for comfort's sake, such as described in England's early Newgate Prison system (see Chapter 9 for details), wealthy folks in the United States buy their way out of the justice system but at public expense. While public school teachers raise controversy when telling students "Merry Christmas," prosecutors openly debate targeted groups and detail what their army of cops and garrisons of jailers will do to those people they call misfits, screwups, and scumbags with the encouragement and reinforcement of the popular media through the *CSI Effect*.

Federal Prosecutors

Federal personnel, too, accept ghetto wars that take precedence, rather than going to the root of the problem. For example, one researcher attempted to uncover the factors federal prosecutors employ when deciding whether to pursue or decline a case.[25] Data for the period 1994 to 2000 were compiled from the federal criminal case processing statistics and other sources. Since 1994, as federal criminal justice resources have expanded, declinations have fallen among federal prosecutors. Offenses designated as a national priority, such as the wars on junkies and immigrants, are less likely to be declined than other crimes. Drug cases are aggressively litigated by federal prosecutors in contrast to fraud cases, which are among the most likely to be declined, Michael O'Neill says. Recall from Chapter 8 that federal prosecutors use confidential informants or snitches in their efforts to convict drug traffickers and junkies, and if a snitch doesn't cooperate, those snitches are indicted and convicted, and their sentences are longer than they would have been if they cooperated with federal law enforcement agencies.[26] In federal drug cases, mandatory minimum sentences range from 5 to 20 years, depending on the type and quantity of drugs involved and whether the offender has a prior felony drug conviction. The maximum sentence allowed is life in prison, and in the federal system there is no parole. Too often, the only way out of these draconian sentences is to cooperate and say whatever federal personnel want to hear, one report advises.[27]

However, controlling high-powered executives who prosper from public funds appears to be an issue among federal prosecutors. Nonetheless, the preceding findings suggest that federal attorneys practice law independent of any formal review mechanisms. One implication is that there are few consequences when prosecutors defy what a new president mandates; federal prosecutors will fulfill their agendas with or without the support of the White House (assuming they maintain a low profile). For instance, during the summer of 2009 Suzanne Sullivan (6 months after President Obama's inauguration), an assistant US attorney, told Judge Mark L. Wolf in a dramatic hearing in Boston that she withheld exculpatory evidence in a criminal case (see Chapter 8 for details). Wolf was appalled by Sullivan's misconduct and by what Wolf characterized as a pattern of prosecutors in the US attorney's office. Her penalty? To attend a training program focused on discovery in criminal cases.

Also, many federal prosecutors are subjected to public pressure, and the origins of that public pressure are linked to the popular media.[28] In fact, local TV news is the "public's primary source of public affairs information." Chapter 1 reveals the poor integrity of the news. Also, news reporters embellish characteristics of events and fictionalize events and dramatize conversations they never had. Because crime stories dominate local news programming, the prevalence of this type of reporting has led to a crime narrative or script that includes two core elements: crime is violent, and perpetrators of crime are junkies. We find the popular media in the thick of it, promoting and reinforcing fictitious wars upon targeted groups. An implication arising from Franklin D. Gilliam and Shanto Iyengar's study and the information provided in Chapter 1 is that these wars are interrelated, and the public's pressure to arrest, prosecute, and throw away the key (try'em and fry'em) has become the tool of government and the practice of prosecutors. Due process among targeted groups simply doesn't exist. From this perspective it could be envisioned that an inner-city child who steals 20 bucks and has weed in his tattered jeans can get hard time, but a well-connected executive who accepts a bonus of $51 million of public funds relaxes with high-quality prescription drugs while gazing at the Long Island Sound from a Connecticut shore. How sweet is that?

Recommendations

One recommendation is to apply the law equally; prosecutors (federal and local) should be legally and morally accountable through the rule of law, similar to other local criminal justice practitioners (i.e., Title U.S.C. 42, 1983, but note that federal law enforcement personnel are not subject to Title 42's restraints).[29] Individual prosecutors (federal and state) have absolute immunity from lawsuits seeking to hold them accountable for their trial-related adversarial conduct but not for investigative or administrative actions (discussed later); however, this might change. Other recommendations are to enhance integrity among new graduating attorneys through education (law school curriculum changes are discussed below), allow prosecutors and bar associations to police themselves, and ideally provide public overview with *subpoena power* (legal order demanding evidence) over prosecutors' activities within a specific process.

One major question is that when a defendant is exonerated after decades in prison, why weren't there more safeguards to hold the system accountable along with the individuals who represented the system at the time of the wrongful conviction? A case in progress during the winter of 2008 in the US Supreme Court is associated with that question: maintenance of policy safeguards against systemic prosecutorial misconduct.[30] The idea is that top-level prosecutors must be held accountable for their actions when they set policies that ignore or trample on the constitutional rights of defendants, especially when those actions are responsible for a wrongful conviction, argues Innocence Project researchers. For instance, Thomas Goldstein served 24 years in a California prison for a murder he didn't commit. He has filed a suit against the former Los Angeles district attorney because the district attorney did not have policies in place concerning jailhouse informants who testified for the state and, in this case, resulted in Goldstein's conviction. Because the snitch provided false testimony, the legal brief explains, prosecutors dropped one case against the snitch and reduced the charges in another case. Goldstein's brief says that a prosecutor has a legal obligation to tell the defendant what incentive the snitch received for his testimony. The trial prosecutor, defense, defendant, judge, and jury had no idea about any strong motives for the informant to lie. A federal district court and the US Court of Appeals for the Ninth Circuit ruled that Goldstein's lawsuit could proceed because it involved an officewide administrative policy of the District Attorney's Office rather than a prosecutor's actions in a specific case. A ruling to expand absolute immunity would set a dangerous path for such policies, the brief reported, and would open the door to prosecutors to systemically deprive defendants of their constitutional rights. The Los Angeles District Attorney's Office is the largest prosecuting agency in the United States, with more than 1,000 prosecuting attorneys.

■ Problem: Forensic and Junk Science

It comes as no surprise that most of the errors or incompetence that orchestrated the destruction of innocent people through wrongful convictions and wrongful executions originated with government (county, state, and federal) forensic personnel (see Chapters 6 and 7). The evidence of human error and incompetence is consistent with the experiences of many defendants who have been exonerated and is consistent with those who were wrongfully executed; on the other hand, many innocent convicts have (hopefully) been exonerated through the efforts of public forensic personnel. Nonetheless, the damage is done; shoddy work, poorly operated facilities, and incompetent or corrupt forensic personnel have shaken the criminal justice system like never before, raising doubts about the reputation of unbiased advocates for scientific truth. Was forensic personnel incompetence responsible in the first go-around, or was prosecutor persuasion responsible, but better to ask how can the process be improved?

Improving Forensic Science

The media should be more responsible with their performances, but the media has the right to offer their viewpoint, a position clearly outlined in the First Amendment.[31] Thus, forensic science needs to change; we can't change the media, but forensic science is another matter. Some experts say that because of the failure of forensic science, policymakers usually call for oversight or a governmental body to monitor forensics and forensic personnel.[32] Yet, an oversight initiative of forensic science would not necessarily reduce forensic science shortcomings because forensic science laboratories are largely controlled by police administrations; that is, the police hold a "monopoly" on forensic science agencies.[33]

> Most forensic crime labs are supervised through police command, and as such they fall within the sphere of police budgets and police culture. Forensic science professionals often have to fight "a stubborn police culture" to get the support and independence they need to be "effective and trustworthy."[34]

The controversy that surrounds police control over forensic scientists can cause discomfort to personnel and a disservice to suspects, including their wrongful imprisonment and execution, as clearly emphasized in previous chapters especially Chapters 8 and 9.

Recommendations: Abolish Police Crime Laboratories

Forensic science can be improved by divorcing forensic labs from the traditional command-and-control structure of state and local police departments because traditional departments are "inherently biased and prone to partiality in favor of the prosecution."[35] Most urban jurisdictions have their own crime labs, and some of those labs are shared with other departments.

Hiram K. Evans, a criminalist at the San Bernardino County Sheriff-Coroner Department, asks, under whose authority should crime labs be placed if not the police?[36] Evans recognizes that police crime labs can be described as biased in favor of the prosecution, but if prosecutors provide the administration over forensic crime labs (as many have in California), then those labs would literally be under prosecutors' control. Police crime laboratories should be abolished, Roger Koppl suggests, and all analyses farmed out to private laboratories under "double blind" conditions. Koppl adds, "Forensic scientists should welcome such independence as conducive to greater autonomy for forensic science."[37] In this manner, a check and balance evaluation would exist. Yet think of the expense of Koppl's suggestion.

Forensic Laboratory Reforms

Forensic laboratories are here to stay and can provide the evidence to accomplish the exoneration of the wrongfully convicted and both the release of the innocent and conviction of the guilty. Some experts such as Roger Koppl suggest expensive and complicated changes which include privatization potentials of forensic labs through "rivalrous redundancy recommendations" which in and by themselves are not bad ideas, but through all the twists and turns, these recommendations can lead to a highly competitive profit and loss matrix that gives rise to a stifling of reform rather than helping reform. [38] Another obvious flaw arising from the privatization of all forensic labs is that they would be self-regulating and account-able to a board of directors. The idea of crime lab reform is to simplify forensic science laboratory output centered in practicable and reasonable objectives in an effort to serve the best interests of justice. Therefore, this author feels that forensic science reform should include among other possibilities: autonomy, standardized practices, and community partnerships.

- Autonomy: Coroners and forensic scientists are presently linked to police departments and should become an autonomic organizational structure which could include its own hierarchy; top management would report to city, county, or jurisdictional elected officials or councils, such as a town council or county commissioners' office. That is, none of its managers or personnel are police officers, court employees, or correctional personnel. In this manner, evidence (per se) can be gathered and assessed independent of enforcement bias, and results could be distributed to both prosecutors and defendants. Defendants have equal access to the forensic lab process which includes collection and distribution of results.
- Standardized practices: Methods of analysis should be standardized which would include systematic processes that can be replicated with the potential to produce similar results. This feature would call for hiring, training, and monitoring of personnel protocols, regulations, and ethics established by the managing authority as described above. One goal is to provide reliable results to prosecutors and suspects or defendants.

- Community partnerships: This component suggests that oversight would be vested in the community whereby community members would have input into the decision-making processes of the forensic labs. Because public funds support the enterprise, the public should have representation (but not control) in management (elected officials would do that).[39]

Additionally, labs should be accredited by organizations such as the American Society of Crime Laboratory Directors' Laboratory Accreditation Board or other accrediting agencies and should have routine procedures to measure variables related to quality and a planned system of review to allow those procedures to be updated regularly similar to educational accreditation agencies such as the Southern Association of Colleges and Schools (SACS). That organization is a regional accreditation agency for an 11-state region.

■ Problem: Admissible Evidence

If evidence has not been legally gathered, properly persevered, and controlled, it cannot be used at trial—it is inadmissible or tainted. It has been pointed out that the custody of evidence (see Chapter 6) is relevant to admissible evidence. For example, at the federal level, 30 percent of sexual assault cases are declined by federal prosecutors[40] (see Chapter 4 for details) because of inadmissible evidence, and at the state level three of every four known sex crimes are dropped by station house sergeants, prosecutors, and judges because of a lack of sufficient evidence to prosecute.[41]

Recommendations: Understanding Admissible Evidence

Thomas Payne, a former prosecutor and current university professor, recommends that prosecutors and legal aides assist investigators to better understand what constitutes admissible evidence.[42] Payne advises that materials gathered at a crime scene are not considered to be evidence until those materials individually conform to the rules of evidence, especially rules outlined by the Federal Rules of Evidence, which most states follow as a guideline, and individually fit into the body of the crime.[43]

Payne says the criminal prosecutor is the chief law enforcement officer in his or her district or jurisdiction and must guide field personnel to achieve a common goal of processing materials from the crime scene to the courtroom (this perspective is congruent with street-level advocates, discussed later).

To better understand the relationship between prosecutors and investigators, it is incumbent upon evidence gatherers, regardless of their brilliance as investigators or their laboratory skills, to understand the inequities of the criminal justice system and the endeavors to ensure a fair process. For example, juries are comprised of individuals whose thoughts of wrong and right have been influenced by their own cultural and individual experiences, including popular television dramas as described in Chapter 2, and may be unduly influenced by the efforts of an extremely competent defense lawyer.

One assumption is that inadmissible facts must be carefully shielded from misleading or prejudicial influences that can lead jurors to arrive at an incorrect verdict (it only takes one juror to change an outcome). Therefore, the rules of evidence that govern which set of facts are admitted into evidence are designed to ensure that an objective verdict can be attained.

> "These rules shall be construed to secure fairness in administration, elimination of unjustifiable expense and delay, and promotion of growth and development of the law of evidence to the end that the truth may be ascertained and proceedings justly determined."[44]

To better understand criminal law, consider each violation of criminal law to be a picture. To successfully complete the picture, the government, represented by a prosecutor, must have a piece of information for each element of the particular offense charged. If the prosecutor leaves out one of those pieces (or if one of those pieces of evidence is false or tainted), then the picture is incomplete and the jury will not get an opportunity to decide on what they have seen. In a 2001 episode of *Law & Order: Criminal Intent*, Detective Robert Goren (Vincent D'Onofrio) explained it this way as he held up two fat pickles, one in each hand: "We're very good at connecting the dots," suggesting that the dots represent the elements of a crime (see Chapter 10 for details), which should be clearly provided before a conviction can be rendered. Otherwise, the defense attorney makes a motion for acquittal (release) on the grounds that the people (or prosecutor) have failed to prove all the elements of the offense. If the motion is granted, the defendant is free. However, what we know is that prosecutor misconduct can include efforts to influence a judge and jurors through various sorts of inadmissible evidence and carefully prepared witnesses, victims, and survivors, and some of those witnesses may include the expert testimony of forensic science personnel.[45] Conversely, an unprepared, incompetent, or lazy prosecutor can lose a case, and a guilty offender can be set free.

The Federal Rules of Evidence

The Federal Rules of Evidence (FRE) concerning criminal proceedings have been adopted, almost in their entirety, by most states, yet whether the FRE are followed by those who gather and assess the evidence is another matter. The FRE have been reviewed, and recommendations have been made.[46] One goal of the FRE is to eliminate the confusion caused by conflicting evidence rules in state and federal courts. Therefore, forensic personnel need prosecutor guidance to connect the dots by gathering crime scene materials that would be admissible in court as evidence. Also, findings from a recent study show that confusion continues among federal and state standards, suggesting that policy makers might want to review the rules of evidence and that a more uniform and cooperative system replace the present fragmented relationship between jurisdictions.[47] For example, prosecutors could be made accountable to the FRE, or some other standardized methodology, to turn materials from a crime scene into reliable evidence.

■ Problem: Inappropriate Prosecutor Discretion

In some states prosecutorial charges are reviewed by a court or grand jury before the defendant is indicted. In states where prosecutors review police reports carefully, courts and grand juries approve 90 percent or more of the prosecutorial charges.[48–49] In states where prosecutors uncritically adopt police reports, the approval rate is often lower. Most prosecutors strive to move a case toward truth and justice, but some prosecutors take the position that the factual guilt or innocence is irrelevant compared to morality and adherence to the system—a system that is justified through popular television performances, in particular, a system in which prosecutors perform with more immunity than most criminal justice professionals.[50]

Recommendation

One cure would be if all states mandate that a prosecutor or a committee perform a careful review of all major felony cases before indicting a suspect with a crime. This would result in more work but less chance of wrongful indictments, and the review in some way would enhance the reliability of the evidence through standardized formats, as previously suggested.[51] Also, standardized rules of evidence would clearly aid the system toward fewer wrongful convictions, including wrongful executions. One of those standardized rules of evidence need to include full disclosure from snitches at a defendant's trial. However, no matter the recommendation (or rules or laws or mandates), when judicial blindness exists, little will be accomplished toward reform.

■ Problem: Judicial Blindness

Studies of American courts reveal that a striking contrast exists between official expectations and courtroom practices.[52] Because prosecutors are officers of the court, what has been unearthed about the behavior of the courts describes prosecutors, too. Trial courts are relatively autonomous single work units, entities in themselves that do not report to a single authority figure in a chain of command, argues Edward J. Clynch and David W. Neubauer.[53] Formal rules, which aid in the adversarial process, are "often ignored in favor of shared decision-making among judges, prosecutors and defense lawyers."[54] Trial court actors perform specialized tasks (judges, prosecutors, and defense lawyers), but cooperation produces a blending of roles and a judicial blindness (they see what they want to see) to inappropriate or corrupt behavior, suggests the researchers.

For example, the results of a police study associated with individual searches "paints a disquieting picture, with nearly one-third of searches (115) performed unconstitutionally and almost none visible to the courts."[55] The officers worked in a department that was ranked in the upper 20 percent nationwide, and the observers included an appellate judge, a former federal prosecutor, and a government attorney, explains Jon B. Gould and Stephen D. Mastrofski (for more details see Chapter 3). That is, even while professional observers were present, police officers conducted unprofessional and unconstitutional searches.

The researchers offered the following description about an unconstitutional, egregious search. A black male in his late 20s who was riding a bike was told to pull over by two officers from their patrol cruiser. The biker refused, and the officers called for backup. When another vehicle was seen, the biker stopped, and an officer told him the police received a report that he was selling drugs. The rider denied it several times while one officer searched the rider's knapsack. Another officer patted down the rider's pockets and found nothing. "I bet you are hiding them under your balls. If you have drugs under your balls, I am going to f___ your balls up," one of the officers said. "You sure are nervous. I wonder why you are so nervous," another officer commented, and told the biker to get behind the police car door and pull his pants down to his ankles. The officer put on rubber gloves and felt around the biker's private parts for drugs. Finding nothing, the officer said, "I bet you are holding them in the crack of your ass. You better not have them up your ass." With that, the biker turned, bent over, and spread his cheeks. The officer put his hands in the biker's rectum but found no drugs. As the four officers walked back to their cars, one commented, "I know he had some drugs."[56]

It should be noted that the illegal searches discovered by the researchers were highly concentrated in a few officers (16 percent of the officers in the sample accounted for 24, or 70 percent, of the illegal searches).Furthermore, the officer who single-handedly accounted for the most illegal searches was also one of the most articulate, low-key officers the researchers observed.

A wall of judicial silence justified through judicial blindness is one way to describe the behavior of the prosecutors, legal aides, judges, and other officers who all pretend to be unaware of police brutality.[57] This is consistent with the findings of a study in Brooklyn whereby nearly 40 percent of criminal prosecutions involved drug and gun cases, and the vast majority of those cases were built exclusively on the testimony of police officers.[58,59] This thought is also consistent with the war on poverty, as explained in Chapter 4.

One reason judicial blindness and prosecutor misconduct exists is simply because "it works," argues former prosecutor Bennett L. Gershman.[60] Larry Cunningham adds that *testilying* (lying during testimony) is perjury, and from the prosecutors' perspective, there are other forms of in-court deception by police officers.[61] Judge Irving Younger, in *People v. McMurty*, described the problem of *dropsy* testimony, a prevalent form of testilying in which officers claim that a suspect dropped a substance that was used as the only probable cause to conduct an arrest of the suspect.[62] Why would prosecutors look away? Some might say that prosecutors are either *enablers* of corruption or part of the corruption, or they are lazy or just incompetent. Accountability through subpoena oversight would change the way prosecutors do business.

Another way to accomplish prosecutor accountability would be through the appointment of a special prosecutor with subpoena powers tasked to investigate prosecutors. Some might believe that oversight by lawyers among lawyers is impractical, but a check-and-balance system works well in other areas. Because prosecutors impact the lives of individuals in a free society, it is essential that those who have misbehaved are held accountable for their misconduct.[63]

■ Problem: Wrongful Capital Punishment Convictions

Advocates of capital punishment share a sense of justice and retribution. The thinking might include that the offender did little toward protecting the human rights of his or her victim and now deserves few, if any rights, and should die. Death, those advocates argue, is a responsible reaction from a civilized nation (see Chapter 9 for details). However, ignorance can come in many forms. It could be argued that the same sense of justice and retribution causes individuals to oppose wrongful conviction because wrongfully convicted persons did not commit crimes, as did guilty inmates on death row. The injustice is in the wrongful conviction, not necessarily the penalty. Wrongfully convicted persons who lose their good name, family, and career and suffer a life sentence of prison, rape, and death from AIDS deserve our concern as much as the guilty convicts on death row.[64] One reality about prison, regardless of an inmate's innocence and aside from prison rape, is that more than 3,200 inmates died in state prisons in 2006: 2,700 from illness, 131 from AIDS, 220 by suicide, and 55 by homicide, among other reasons.[65] Additionally, almost 1,100 jail inmates died in custody in the same year, and one-half of them died because of illness. How many of those imprisoned were innocent is a question beyond the scope of this book.

On the other hand, abolishing the death penalty might worsen the problem of wrongful conviction because death penalty cases receive more scrutiny and protection by the courts than other criminal cases. If police and prosecutors cannot identify and convict the guilty party in capital crime cases, what must the rate of wrongful convictions for less-serious crimes be, especially those for which conviction is obtained by plea bargain? Nine of every 10 convictions are obtained through plea bargaining at the federal and state levels. When unscrupulous prosecutors can convince an innocent suspect to accept a guilty plea instead of going on trial in a capital punishment case, what really does it matter what juries think? When suspects accept guilty pleas, they also accept the loss of their right to due process.

Recommendation: End Capital Punishment Sanctions

Nothing can return the life of someone who was executed. Civilized nations cannot afford ignorant governments in this day of terrorism and economic decline. A fair question arises about constituents allowing its government to justifiably execute others, particularly when the government is a defender of equality and human rights. When an offender who is convicted of a capital crime is properly isolated, he or she is no longer an imminent threat. However, be mindful that Donald "Pee Wee" Gaskins and other death row inmates have murdered other inmates and correctional personnel.[66]

Nonetheless, examples of errors in capital punishment trials have been offered in Chapter 9, such as Thomas Arthur who was scheduled to die in Alabama in 2008, but the Alabama Supreme Court voted 5–4 to stay his execution after another inmate confessed to the murder for which Arthur had been sentenced to death, and Juan Roberto Melendez who was scheduled to die in Florida after serving 18 years on Florida's death row before being exonerated in 2001. Also, Montana's Supreme Court narrowly voted to dismiss a petition seeking an independent audit to retest evidence in hundreds of cases handled by a former state crime lab examiner whose erroneous hair-comparison testimony contributed to several wrongful convictions.[67] This kind of professional behavior seems to mirror the ideal of "kill them all, let God sort them out." Just how competent is that god or that government when they deal with someone's corpse?

For whatever it's worth, one study showed that individual capital jury members are not only more likely to harbor racially prejudiced attitudes, but they also are more likely to favor convicting innocent defendants over letting guilty ones go free.[68] A finding among juries in Columbus, Ohio (Franklin County) is consistent with this perspective. The county has experienced a decline in death penalty indictments and death sentences because jurors are increasingly choosing sentences of life in prison without parole; prosecutors are seeking fewer death sentences. In the fall of 2008, a Franklin County judge told a news reporter that it is becoming harder to find jurors who will follow state law and consider capital punishment as a sanction.[69] One juror candidate, a 36-year-old truck driver, explained that although he favors the death penalty, he would have a hard time handing down a death penalty verdict because, "It would haunt me for the rest of my life." Results also reveal punishment orientation to be influenced by a negative view of human nature and a belief in a rigid adherence to law, or what can be called judicial blindness. However, other evidence is telling us that when jurors are repeatedly asked whether they can "follow the law" and impose the death penalty, they begin to believe that the law actually requires them to reach death verdicts, argues Craig Haney.[70]

Repetitious reminders can be an "obedience drill" in which jurors feel they are voluntarily relinquishing the power to deviate an objective outcome. Also, the personal characteristics of many death qualified jurors render them receptive to arguments that they must follow the implicit promise made to the court. Also, John H. Blume in a legal brief about capital punishment juries explained that among typical findings reported was that[71]:

- 30 percent of capital jurors may not be qualified for such service because they would automatically vote for death.

- Many juries in death penalty cases believed that the death penalty was mandatory or presumed for first degree murder cases.
- In interviews with 916 jurors from 257 trials in 11 states it was learned that nearly one-half of those jurors said they had decided what the punishment should be before the sentencing phase had begun.

■ Other Solutions

Wrongful convictions can be controlled by moving to a more humane, controlled, and standardized system of prosecution. In addition, special prosecutors and oversight committees could help. These committees could be comprised of community members, such as teachers, religious leaders, parents, and social service personnel in particular, and some could be appointed by town managers, mayors, or some elected government member.

Other recommendations include the involvement of bar associations around the country that want to accept responsibility for enforcing their own ethical standards and closely scrutinize the ethical misconduct of prosecutors. Typically, bar associations deal ruthlessly with small-time lawyers who are down on their luck but shy away from cases that involve those who are invested with great power. Whatever methods are used to control prosecutors, those who influence policy should become vigilant to prevent witch hunts. Organizations such as the American Prosecutors Research Institute (APRI) conduct studies about state prosecutors in an attempt to explore empirical evidence to support the performance measurement framework identified by APRI's study, *Prosecution in the 21st Century*.[72] Their concern is the fair, impartial, and expeditious pursuit of justice and ensuring public safety. For example, 975 participants were asked numerous questions about a number of topics, including the competence of their local prosecutor's office, if local prosecutors do a good job, if those prosecutors hold people accountable for their crimes, and if the local prosecutor administers justice for crimes such as prostitution, marijuana use, public intoxication, and trespassing. These can be helpful tools toward enhancing the performance of American prosecutors.

■ The Future of Prosecutors: Community Prosecution

Catherine M. Coles reported that a recent transformation, referred to as community prosecution, is a practice pursued by many prosecutors.[73] Key components of this transformation include prosecutors' new concern for crime prevention and low-level crimes, as well as prosecuting violent felonies; the adoption of a problem-solving approach to matters of public safety; close collaboration with other justice and government agencies; and a respectful partnership with community residents, explains Coles. This partnership or collaboration with community members should ultimately shape the activities of prosecutors while creating a new sense of accountability to local neighborhoods.[74] Prosecutors are attempting to emulate community relations efforts, which include community policing initiatives such as collaboration with community members concerning their ideas about problems that lead to crime, their ideas about resolving those problems through problem-solving strategies before crimes happen, and by empowering those community members and community police officers to act on their agreed-upon resolutions. The goal is ultimately to control crime, reduce the fear of crime, and enhance quality-of-life experiences.[75]

■ Historic Account of Community Prosecution

Community prosecution can be traced to the pioneering efforts of Multnomah County District Attorney (DA) Michael Schrunk, who established the Neighborhood DA Unit in Portland, Oregon in 1990 in response to business leaders' concerns that quality-of-life crimes would impede the development of a central business district.[76] In 1991, community-oriented prosecution initiatives in Kings County, New York and Montgomery County, Maryland involved reorganization of the prosecutors' offices along geographic lines and efforts to form new working relationships with their communities. Community prosecution has been adopted by many other jurisdictions since then, and estimates vary as to how many prosecutors' offices have adopted community prosecution strategies, explains John S. Goldkamp, Cheryl Irons-Guynn, and Doris Weiland.[77] The American Prosecutors Research Institute estimates that by the end of 2000, nearly half of all prosecutors' offices may have been engaged in activities that would qualify them as participating in a community prosecution strategy. The interest in community prosecution is strong at all levels of government. In 2000, 62 prosecutor sites received grants to plan or implement new programs or to expand or enhance existing programs, and in late 2001, 75 additional sites received funding to plan, implement, or enhance community prosecution programs.[78]

■ Empowering Communities Toward Community Prosecution

The Office of Justice Programs (OJP), a division of the US Department of Justice, attempts to play a key role in helping communities through comprehensive partnerships to prevent crime and improve their quality-of-life experiences.[79] The OJP uses community policing efforts as a guide in this recent model of prosecution. At the core of the OJP's thinking is the notion that offenders are not generally held accountable to victims or the communities where they committed their crimes. "Restorative or community justice allows victims and the community to participate in the criminal justice process and works to right the wrong and 'restore,' to the extent possible, the victim and community," the OJP's annual report states.[80] Community justice moves the focus away from arrest, prosecution, and adjudication toward solving problems to prevent crime, reduce recidivism, address public safety needs, and provide quality prosecutorial services.

■ Key Dimensions of Community Prosecution

Similar to other criminal justice community relations innovations, community prosecution models vary depending on needs, resources, and expertise of personnel, but they share underlying features, explains John S. Goldkamp, Cheryl Irons-Guynn, and Doris Weiland. Seven key dimensions characterize community prosecution initiatives:

- Target problems: Quality-of-life arrests, such as drug traders and prostitutes
- Geographic target area: Urban or inner city and business districts
- Role of the community: Recipient of prosecutor services, advisory services, and sanctioning panels
- Content of response to community problems: Facilitating community self-help and crime prevention efforts
- Organizational adaptations and emphasis: Field offices staffed by attorneys and special units
- Case processing adaptations: Vertical prosecution (the same prosecutor handles the case at every stage) and horizontal prosecution (community prosecutors do not prosecute cases)
- Interagency collaboration and partnerships: Police, city attorney, housing

The thinking goes that most community prosecution initiatives have been developed in response to crime problems that affect particular neighborhoods or other geographic areas. Participants are assessed for personal, school, family, and employment issues and referred to appropriate agencies for help. They learn leadership skills and engage in positive activities. How community prosecution sites define the community's role and which individuals or groups will represent the community determine the level of community involvement. In some jurisdictions, community activists identify the pressing crime-related problems affecting neighborhoods, but the prosecutor's office develops the strategies, often with the help of community police or other agencies.

Strategies have taken many forms. Depending on the size and resources of the prosecutor's office, a community prosecution program can be represented by one or two prosecutors, lay employees, or an entire unit of community-oriented prosecutors, investigators, community relations specialists, and clerical staff members. Methods of prosecuting cases from targeted neighborhoods differ, but generally prosecutors remain physically located in a central office to handle trial caseloads efficiently, and they meet regularly with residents and hear concerns about crime and quality-of-life issues. The rationale for this approach is that these attorneys will better understand the community context associated with their criminal cases and will develop more productive working relationships with the community and precinct officers. In some community prosecution programs, community prosecutors do not try cases themselves. Instead, community cases are assigned to the trial division for litigation, and community prosecutors act as liaisons between trial attorneys and community residents. This allows community prosecutors to immerse themselves in the community, participate in neighborhood meetings and events, and facilitate problem-solving strategies. In other jurisdictions, community prosecutors carry the same caseloads as other attorneys in the office and add outreach and problem solving to these responsibilities. Some sites have combined community prosecution with community courts. To solve their targeted problems, community prosecutors often join forces with other agencies, combining resources that community members might otherwise access in a piecemeal manner, if at all. In nuisance abatement efforts, community prosecutors have relied on the civil justice system and housing and licensing agencies.

On the other hand, some community prosecution initiatives are purely collaborative, functioning as part of a task force with other agencies. The CLEAR program in Los Angeles, for example, was created in 1996 by an interagency gang task force to address the community's gang problems by targeting specific geographic areas or gangs and using suppression, intervention, and prevention tactics. It is a partnership of police agencies (police, sheriff, district attorney, city attorney, and probation department), public officials, and community residents.

■ Street-Level Advocates

A variation in the evolution of community prosecution models is the street-level advocate (SLA) model, explains Catherine M. Coles. The key components of the SLA model relies less upon collaboration with community members and more upon prosecution–police collaboration. For example, Coles describes the activities of a prosecutor named Jan Lesniak in Indianapolis. Lesniak says that as an increased understanding grew between the prosecutors' office and the police, they shared a greater satisfaction for their work because they quickly saw the results of that collaboration in the form of a drug house being closed, a block cleared of drug dealing, burglaries reduced in an office park, arrests decreasing in a zero-tolerance zone, a massage parlor shut down, a park reclaimed for the community, and successfully prosecuting a neighborhood drug dealer, to the relief of local residents.

Here's How It Works

Street-level advocates operated in every Indianapolis Police Department (IPD) district office and in the Marion County Sheriff's Office, and they continued to operate in those agencies after the two agencies merged (Indianapolis Metropolitan Police Department) in January 2007. The SLAs work closely with police and community committee members to address quality-of-life issues, such as drugs, nuisance abatement, and domestic violence. Their duties include screening and filing all felony cases (except drugs, homicides, and sex crimes), selecting a small number of cases of particular importance to the local community that they will prosecute personally (they follow-up on other cases with prosecutors in the municipal and felony courts), and helping to devise and implement other strategies for reducing crime and improving public safety. Paralegals collect neighborhood impact statements and needed police reports, work with the court watch program, and share other tasks involving contact with citizens and neighborhood associations.

Prosecutor Jan Lesniak described her experiences to Catherine M. Coles, saying that[81]:

> I learned quickly that seeing criminal activity on the street is much different than reading about it in a probable cause affidavit. High drug trafficking area does not mean that once in a while, someone is selling drugs on that corner; it means that the same people come to sell drugs on that corner at the same time every day. From observing first hand, I was able to help the officers better articulate some of their observations so that the facts rose to the level of reasonable, articulable reason to stop, or probable cause to arrest.

The point is that prosecutors who work with police can aid the police with probable cause arrests, and the prosecutors, in turn, learn more about officer practices and offender activities. This produces stronger cases, which ultimately means greater conviction rates. Jan Lesniak thinks that it is easier to perform the arrest according to legal guidelines the first time than to repair damage. Lesniak says:

> I began making training tapes to be played at roll calls and also at detective meetings. The first tape explained felony screening.... This offers great opportunities for providing needed information and fostering a better relationship between law enforcement and our office.... The officers are much more likely to accept my decisions now that I have observed the problems and their responses first-hand.... In turn, I try to communicate my new perspective to the deputy prosecutors downtown.

Lesniak's experiences mirror Thomas Payne's thoughts about educating officers in the rules of evidence.

The National Survey of Prosecutors (NSP) surveyed 749 county governments in 2001 and asked about adoption of community prosecution practices. What was learned is that adoption of community prosecution, regardless of the model, can be predicted by organizational size and structural complexity.[82] One explanation is that traditional organizational structures are unique unto themselves, as are the communities in which they operate. Organizational size and structural complexity are relevant, yet there is something to be said about expertise and the relationship and history among prosecutors, police, and the community.

Similar to community policing, no one model fits all. However, a consensus exists among community prosecution providers revealing that although prosecutorial jurisdictions are different, three integral components of community prosecution can be developed at most jurisdictions[83]: (1) partnerships with a variety of government agencies and community-based groups, (2) use of varied and innovative problem-solving methods to address crime prevention and public safety issues, and (3) community participation and resources. The experts say that community prosecution is not a panacea in solving every prosecution problem, yet considering the alternatives, it is an attractive device for crime control and a reduction in wrongful convictions.[84-85]

■ Does Community Prosecution Work?

Community policing has failed to live up to its expectations because community members avoid meetings and responsibility and because police officials are reluctant to empower officers and community members to fulfill problem-solving strategies, experts say.[86-87] Reasons for community member avoidance can include language and cultural barriers and personal privacy issues.[88] The Chicago Alternative Policing Strategy (CAPS), for example, discovered after lengthy community problem-solving strategies were employed throughout the city (and millions of dollars were spent) that large populations within the city were rarely, if ever, represented at meetings despite efforts to enlist their attendance. One problem facing police was that empowerment "contradicts many of the tenets that dominated police thinking for a generation."[89]

Unlike community policing efforts, quality-of-life (QOL) policing does not include an empowered community partnership associated with its strategy; for that reason, the evolution of community policing has changed to QOL, which resembles the street-level advocate model. There is less collaboration among community members and more partnership with public agencies. Lawrence W. Sherman shares his thoughts about community relations programs, which might well apply to a community prosecution strategy and at the same time enhance a street-level advocate strategy:

> Ironically, a central tenet of community prevention programs has been the empowerment of local community leaders to design and implement their own crime prevention strategies. This philosophy may amount to throwing people overboard and then letting them design their own life preserver. The scientific literature shows that the policies and market forces causing criminogenic community structures and cultures are beyond the control of neighborhood residents, and that "empowerment" does not include the power to change those policies. It is one thing, for example, for tenants to manage the security guards in a public housing project. It is another thing entirely to let tenants design a new public housing policy and determine where in a metropolitan area households with public housing support will live.[90]

■ Advice to Prosecutors from a Prosecutor

When information is in the hands of a prosecutor, and he or she has no reasonable doubt of a defendant's guilt, the prosecutor should appropriately pursue the case vigorously and fairly, says Bennett L. Gershman an experienced prosecutor.[91]

However, when a prosecutor is not sure of the truth and may hold a reasonable doubt, the prosecutor should attempt to resolve the doubt. If the prosecutor is unable to do so and little or no alternative course of action is reasonably available, then the only ethical course of action is to dismiss the case, no matter how difficult that action might be. Insisting on prosecuting the case presents an unacceptable risk that an innocent person will be convicted, but the evidence reveals that many prosecutors apparently are corrupt and unethical (see Chapter 6). I took this to mean that prosecutors should stop paying attention to television shows and pay more attention to the morality and the reality of their job.

■ The Other Side of Prosecutor Misconduct

Joshua Marquis reminds us that when judges make mistakes, appellate courts will reverse or remand those cases, and those cases are referred to as *judicial error*.[92] When defense attorneys fail to represent their clients properly, the conviction of the accused is often set aside because of inadequate assistance of counsel. Yet when prosecutors err, it is called prosecutorial misconduct, a term that implies hiding evidence, lying to a jury, or framing an innocent suspect. First, only a very few corrupt prosecutors have been indicted, tried, and imprisoned. Second, most errors, although few, made by prosecutors are harmless, suggesting that there is no malice and no injustice resulting from their error. For example, Marquis, who was both elected and appointed by the governor to replace an indicted prosecutor in Clatsop County, Oregon, claims that over a 33-year period, appellate courts raised 44 issues associated with prosecutor errors.[93] In only eight of those cases was it found that a prosecutor had been prejudicial. Marquis says that comparing those statistics to the thousands of criminal appeals rendered during the same time period provides a rate of prosecutorial misconduct of less than one-tenth of one percent. Recall that Marquis is the prosecutor who provided flawed statistics about the success of prosecutors and his statistics were used by US Supreme Court Justice Antonin Scalia concurring in *Kansas v. Marsh* (see Chapter 8).

Sometimes prosecutors admit to error. For example, a federal prosecutor in Los Angeles asked a court to set aside the conviction of a man who served 16 months in federal prison for blowing the whistle on an ex-employer's cyber security holes.[94] McDanel, aged 30 years, was convicted in 2002 under the Computer Fraud and Abuse Act for sending 5,600 e-mail messages to customers of his former employer warning about a security hole in the company's service that left private messages vulnerable to unauthorized access. A federal prosecutor said that the government was conceding that point and filed a rare confession of error acknowledging that McDanel was convicted through an incorrect reading of the law. It seems that more prosecutors need to own up, and maybe it's time to talk about prevention.

■ Prevention

Prosecutors rely on the police, which, like all criminal justice entities, are reactive-driven organizations in practice. A crime is committed, police respond (if the crime is reported or observed), and the entire justice system stands ready to perform its tasks. However, what has been well documented in the past few decades is that when agencies develop and practice preventive or proactive strategies in response to public safety, crime is more efficiently controlled, the number of victims is reduced, the professional nature of criminal justice personnel is enhanced, and compliance by the general population to official directives is more likely.[95–98] Therefore, one recommendation is that prosecutors support a similar strategy when attempting to administer justice. Prevention, or at least the reduction, of wrongful conviction proves to be crucial to the health of a democratic nation. Prevention can include recommendations about law schools.

■ Law Schools

Broadening the characteristics associated with integrity and personal accountability might best serve the public and the profession if those issues were addressed in a comprehensive manner when students are in law school. For example, law schools should instruct and require students, through a practicum, how to collaborate with public agency personnel, community members, and other prosecutors. They should be instructed in the fine art of *street-level advocacy*, as previously discussed. Perhaps if community prosecution strategies were classroom topics and were taught in practicums or internships, future lawyers and prosecutors would have a greater chance of avoiding the pitfalls of community relations programs in police investigative units. However, law schools have difficulty with their own agendas, some practitioners say as evidenced by the sample in the study for this work (and the following descriptions). Those weren't glowing reports from the 444 prosecutors in this study about their alma maters. Recall that the prosecutors in the sample employed 29 percent of their education at work, and only 45 percent of the sample revealed that law school prepared students for future jobs (see Chapter 10).

Recall from Chapter 10 that the participants reported they had to enhance their educational standards an average of 12 hours per year. Some states require that their prosecutors spend more time in the classroom, and other states have little, if any, annual educational requirements. Using the medical profession as a guide, technology, which includes surgical equipment, outpaces the skills of personnel. The hospitals that employ physicians and medical staff members mandate continued certification and classroom time or those individuals can lose their jobs. It is clear from the medical community that personnel who do not keep pace with continued education mandates, or what the medical community calls continuing medical education (CME), can jeopardize the health and welfare of the public, become an obstacle in meeting state medical board requirements, and place other physicians and the medical support staffs at risk, which includes malpractice suits.[99-100] There is also an ongoing examination of patient charts by the physician and by medical support staff and colleagues.[101] Physicians tend to collaborate more often with other medical professionals than do prosecutors, and most often physicians continually engage in training or advanced studies to keep pace with their profession. This information does not suggest that physicians and the medical profession are error free, as evidenced by the number of malpractice suits brought against them. However, that is one of the issues: prosecutors are not as accountable as physicians and other professionals.

Nonetheless, a law school dean says that the mission for most law schools is abstract.[102] Jay Conison also questions the admission process, which is consistent with the sample in this study whereby 37 percent of the participants said that the LSAT should be replaced as a law school admission requirement and admission standards should be localized. One measure of law school success relates to its graduates; what they become and what they do are necessarily relevant to the school's success.

Dean Conison says that preparing law students for the profession is the core function of a law school. Do the educational practices of law schools prepare young men and women as competent and ethical criminal prosecutors?

One answer comes from Roy Stuckey at the Clinical Legal Education Association, which identifies best practices specifically for law schools in preparing students for their jobs.[103] Stuckey emphasizes that law schools should "treat the teaching of essential lawyering skills and professional values as part of the core curriculum, and law faculty (should) coordinate what is taught throughout the entire curriculum to ensure that students have sufficient opportunities to acquire and develop the skills and values they will need as 21st century practitioners." These and other efforts to identify necessary skills, competencies, and values have had some impact on curriculums, particularly on skills training, and some impact the ABA's Standards for Accreditation. Dean Jay Conison adds:

> But the [American Bar Association] standards have little changed the approach law schools take toward analyzing and planning their educational work. Law schools still tend not to assay what it means to prepare their graduates to be competent and responsible lawyers; articulate the educational goals of the curriculum or of individual courses or groups of courses; identify intended outcomes; or determine the best means to gauge the attainment of those goals and intended outcomes.

Conison's conclusion is consistent with the 444 prosecutors who were surveyed for this work: the mission of law schools regarding the preparation of their students remains vague, and law schools are left without a sound basis for determining whether their graduates are succeeding in meeting this fundamental educational goal.

Can the public expect prosecutors to practice law with integrity when their educational process is seriously challenged by their own graduates, including the prosecutors who participated in the study for this book? Law schools might consider a move toward a pragmatic or practical curriculum.

Does the media help confuse law school curriculum expectations? In *Law & Order*, Episode 336, "Fixed," the character of Jacob Lowenstein tells Detectives Joe Fontana (Dennis Farina) and Ed Green (Jessie L. Martin) that he earned a jurist doctorate (law degree) while incarcerated for a felony.[104] This is an urban legend that includes other prerogatives. It's a myth that prisoners can earn professional or advanced degrees while in prison, especially law degrees. Convicted felons forfeit several rights, including the right to be bonded, for example, and a felon would be ineligible for the bar exam. Most prison college courses, if available, are courses in humanities or business.

■ The Future of the *CSI Effect*

The future of the *CSI Effect*'s influences is a hard call. Two things are clear: reality shapes the popular media; and the popular media, especially television dramas, shape reality. For example, when a freelance photographer asked Senator Hillary Clinton a question in New Hampshire during the presidential primary campaign in early January 2008, Senator Clinton had tears in her eyes when she replied. Newspapers across the country showed Senator Clinton's tears, and television programs repeated the moving performance very often during newscasts. As expected, Web sites, including YouTube, were dominated by Clinton's unusual tearful response. One newscaster compared Clinton's tears to other female politicians, and the debate continued about the personal weaknesses and strengths of Clinton as a female president. Weeks later, in a *Law & Order: Special Victims Unit* episode, Detective Olivia Benson (Mariska Hargitay) broke down for the first time in more than 200 episodes and cried during the final moments of show. It could be said that popular television programs play off of or emphasize real situations to enhance their presentation. Scripts can be written to match an historic event and a performance can be produced accordingly, or events such as Detective Benson's crying can be edited into an existing show. Cut and pasted *Law & Order* reruns now contain product placements that fulfill the producers' financial dreams.[105]

If popular television dramas influence the future behavior of some viewers, consider the impact that *Criminal Minds*, Season 3, Episode 12, "3rd Life," which aired on January 9, 2008, had on pushing vigilantism into the minds of many. Lindsey (Gina Mantegna), a teenager, was abducted along with her girlfriend and was held in an elementary school washroom. Her girlfriend's disfigured body had been found at a construction site. The hand and face of the girl had been so badly mutilated that an identification was impossible. In the final moments of the episode, Lindsey, who was on the floor in restraints, told her abductor that nothing he could do to her would compare with what her father would do to him. The abductor began to respond when Jack Vaughan (Fredric Lehne) entered and hit the abductor across the face with the stock of a shotgun, knocking him to the floor. Lindsey demanded that her father kill him. Spencer Reid (Matthew Gray Gubler) heard the commotion and flung open the restroom door to see Lindsey now standing in front of Reid and Vaughan, who was pointing the shotgun at the abductor. Reid called for Vaughan to put the weapon down, but Lindsey whispered, "Kill 'em, dad, for what he did to Katie." The abductor begged for his life. Reid kept talking, telling Vaughan that Lindsey's mother wanted him to protect their daughter from all of the violence in his life. He asked him when the violence will end if he kills the abductor right in front of her. "When does it stop?" Reid asked. Vaughan answered, "Tomorrow," and pulled the trigger, shooting the abductor in the head. Vaughan and his daughter walked out of the school and moved to another city. Apparently no indictments were forthcoming. Vaughan was in a federal protection program and was apparently a strong witness on a case. The expectation was that if Vaughan would have put the shotgun down, the abductor would have been arrested. Was this a case of blind justice or vigilantism?

Here's another example from a *Law & Order: Special Victims Unit* story line, Episode 162, "Informed." An FBI agent (Star Morrison, whose alias was Dana Lewis, played by Marcia Gay Harden) had worked with Detective Olivia Benson (Mariska Hargitay) in monitoring a predator who raped, tortured, and killed 23 women. In the closing scenes, Morrison killed the predator. Few wanted to prosecute the federal agent for murdering the predator, including the NYPD or federal commanders. At the end of the day, the agent was about to get away with murder when she committed suicide just as Benson was attempting to get her confession.

A federal judge has ordered that several United States Attorneys be criminally investigated for their conduct in the 2008 prosecution of United States Senator Ted Stevens. What this means is that it is very likely that Senator Stevens was wrongfully convicted of the criminal charges that were brought against him by the government. If prosecutors can bring down a U.S. senator and you're not a US senator imagine how much at risk you are if wrongly accused of a crime. Does the general population understand when and how our legal rights are violated by prosecutors? Current regulatory control over prosecutorial behavior for violating the law or their failure to provide a defendant with all the legal discoveries in which to defend him or herself is not necessarily working in the best interest of constituents.

For instance, by circumstance you happened to be in the wrong place at the wrong time with the wrong story when police engaged you through an aggressive "zero tolerance" road block or a search of your bags, or targeted you during a sweep after a sporting event. The mere innuendo by the cops or a prosecutor that you're a sex offender translates to unemployment, poverty, and public ridicule beyond your wildest comprehension, but, if you're unlucky to be convicted for whatever—good-bye freedom, thin crust pizzas, and boring vacations with extended family members, hello godless cesspools punishing you with rotting teeth, a bleeding rectum, warts on both feet, all the while you wonder about AIDS, and you so want your sanity. Yet these amazing experiences are less important than drawing in the incredibly rank air that validates your own worthlessness and helplessness.

You struggle not to breathe, not to comply, not to respond as a human being despite your innocence—every convict is innocent—but eventually you succumb to behavior that promotes survival because you've learned the most ancient of laws—survival of the fittest.

■ Summary

American democracy is revered and cherished, but it is also unpredictable and combative. For example, the success of a prosecutor is not necessarily motivated in the guilt or innocence of a suspect but in a prosecutor's ability to transform, beyond a reasonable doubt, circumstances that can demonstrate culpability. The popular media, through the *CSI Effect*, contributes to the prosecutor's ability to transform the circumstances by the emergence of moral causes or ends that justify the means through a series of deceptive wars. Consequently, innocent people are convicted and executed. The reality is that law enforcement rarely apprehends major criminals and minor drug abusers; clearance rates are on the decline; conviction rates are lower than expected; prosecutors who provide defendants the benefit of the doubt are regarded as failures; 1 in 5 probationers are rearrested for a new crime; correctional systems rarely correct or rehabilitate poor behavior; 1 in 6 parolees are returned to prison; and 35 percent of all state prisoners had been on probation or parole prior to incarceration. Therefore, it is recommended that the rule of law be applied equally, and prosecutors (federal and local) should become accountable for their performance. In addition, government forensic laboratories and their personnel are another source of error and incompetence; most often labs are supervised through police command. Abolishing police crime laboratories is one answer. Autonomy, standardized methods, and community participation were suggestions to aid labs toward reform.

Prosecutors must also be accountable to the Federal Rules of Evidence or some other standardized method of turning materials from a crime scene into reliable evidence. Also, courts and grand juries must carefully review all major felony cases before indicting a suspect thereby enhancing the reliability of the evidence through standardized formats.

Advocates of capital punishment share a sense of justice and retribution, yet retribution does little to deter violent victimization and plays an unhealthy yet expensive role in a democratic society. A recommendation is to end capital punishment as a criminal justice sanction.

Wrongful convictions can be controlled by moving to a more humane, controlled, and standardized system of prosecution. Bar associations around the country can enforce their own ethical standards and closely scrutinize the ethical misconduct of prosecutors. Other recommendations include community prosecution, street-level advocacy, and changes in law school admission standards and law school curriculums.

■ References

1. Rogers, C. (1980). *A way of being.* Boston: Houghton Mifflin.

2. Growing up online. (2008, January 22). *Frontline.* Retrieved September 3, 2009, from http://www.pbs.org/wgbh/pages/frontline/kidsonline/

3. Center for Public Integrity. (2003). *Harmful error: Investigating America's local prosecutors.* Washington, DC: Center for Public Integrity.

4. McIntyre, L. J. (1999). But how do you sleep at night? In S. Stojkovic, J. Klofas, & D. Kalinich (Eds.), *The administration and management of criminal justice organizations: A book of readings* (3rd ed.). Long Grove, IL: Waveland.

5. Berger, P. L. (1963). *Invitation to sociology: A humanistic perspective.* Garden City, NY: Anchor Books.

6. Davis, K. C. (1969). *Discretionary justice: A preliminary inquiry.* Chicago: University of Illinois Press.

7. Gershman, B. L. (2002). Why prosecutors misbehave. In W. R. Palacios, P. F. Cromwell, & R. G. Dunham (Eds.), *Crime & justice in America: Present realities and future prospects* (2nd ed.). Upper Saddle River, NJ: Prentice Hall. Also see, Stevens, D. J. (2009). CSI Effect: Prosecutors and wrongful convictions. *Criminal Law Bulletin, 45*(4), 921–930.

8. Findlaw.com. (n.d.). *US Constitution: Article 1. Separation of powers and checks and balances.* Retrieved March 21, 2009, from http://caselaw.lp.findlaw.com/data/constitution/article01/01.html

9. Cole, S. A., & Villa-Dioso, R. (2009). Investigating the CSI Effect: Media and litigation crisis in criminal law. *Sanford Law Review, 61*(6), 1335–1374.

10. Marion, N. E., & Oliver, W. M. (2006). *The public police of crime and criminal justice.* NJ: Prentice Hall.

11. Roberts, P. C. (2003). The growing problem of wrongful conviction. *The Independent Review, 7*(4). Retrieved September 3, 2009, from http://vdare.com/roberts/independent_review.htm

12. Delsohn, G. (2003). *Prosecutors: A year in the life of a district attorney's office.* New York: Dutton.

13. Shelden, R. G. (2001). *Controlling the dangerous classes: A critical introduction to the history of criminal justice.* Boston: Allyn Bacon. The overall theme of this book is that the making of laws, their interpretation, and their application throughout the history of the criminal justice system has, historically, been based on social class and gender and has been racially biased. One of the major functions of the criminal justice system has been to control people from the most disadvantaged sectors of the population, that is, the "dangerous classes." This theme is explored using an historic model, tracing the development of criminal law through the development of the police institution, the juvenile justice system, and the prison system.

14. Roberts, "Growing Problem of Wrongful Conviction."

15. Reiman, J. (2007). *The rich get richer and the poor get prison: Ideology, crime, and criminal justice* (8th ed.). Boston: Allyn Bacon.

16. Felson, M. (2006). *Crime and everyday life* (4th ed.). Los Angeles: Sage.

17. Sourcebook of Criminal Justice Statistics Online. (2007). *Percent of offenses cleared by arrests or exception means in 2007.* Albany, NY: US Department of Justice. Retrieved September, 2009, from http://www.albany.edu/sourcebook/pdf/t419.pdf. Also see, Sourcebook of Criminal Justice Statistics Online, (2003). *Percent of offenses cleared by arrests or exceptional means in 2002.* Albany, NY: US Department of Justice. Retrieved September 3, 2009, from http://www. albany.edu/sourcebook/pdf/t4192007.pdf

18. Sourcebook of Criminal Justice Statistics Online. (2007). *Table 5.0. Felony convictions and sentencing per 100 arrests.* Albany, NY: US Department of Justice. Retrieved July 11, 2009, from http://www.albany.edu/sourcebook/pdf/t500022004.pdf

19. Roberts, "Growing Problem of Wrongful Conviction."

20. Bureau of Justice Statistics. (2008). *Probation and parole in the United States, 2006* (NCJ 220218). Washington, DC: US Department of Justice. Retrieved October 12, 2008, from http://www.ojp.usdoj.gov/bjs/pub/pdf/ppus06.pdf

21. Sourcebook of Criminal Justice Statistics Online. (2003). *Table 6.50. Recidivism rates of prisoners released in 1994 from prisons in 15 states.* Albany, NY: US Department of Justice. Retrieved October 12, 2008, from http://www.albany.edu/sourcebook/pdf/t650.pdf

22. Bureau of Justice Statistics, *Probation and Parole in the United States.*

23. Bureau of Justice Statistics. (1995). *Probation and parole violators in state prisons, 1991* (NCJ 149076). Washington, DC: US Department of Justice. Retrieved October 12, 2008, from http://www.ojp.usdoj.gov/bjs/pub/pdf/ppvsp91.pdf

24. Stevens, D. J. (2003). *Applied community policing in the 21st century.* Boston: Allyn Bacon.

25. O'Neill, M. E. (2004). Understanding federal prosecutorial declinations: An empirical analysis of predicative factors. *American Criminal Law Review, 41*(4), 1439–1498.

26. Bikel, O. (1999, January 12). Snitch. *Frontline.* Retrieved September 3, 2009, from http:// www.pbs.org/wgbh/pages/frontline/shows/snitch/etc/script.html

27. Brown, E. (2007). *Snitch: Informants, cooperators, and the corruption of justice.* New York: Public Affairs.

28. Gilliam, Jr., F. D., & Iyengar, S. (2000). Prime suspects: The influence of local television news on the viewing public. *American Journal of Political Science, 44*(3), 560–573.

29. Stevens, D. J. (2002). Civil liabilities and arrest decisions. In J. T. Walker (Ed.), *Policing and the law.* Upper Saddle River, NJ: Prentice Hall.

30. Innocence Project. (2008). *Innocence Project and affiliated organizations urge US Supreme Court to maintain safeguards against systemic prosecutorial misconduct.* Washington, DC: Author. Retrieved July 11, 2009 http://www.innocenceproject.org/Content/1580.php

31. "Congress shall make no law respecting an establishment of religion, or prohibiting the free exercise thereof; or abridging the freedom of speech, or of the press; or the right of the people peaceably to assemble, and to petition the government for a redress of grievances." The Bill of Rights to the US Constitution was ratified on December 15, 1791. Supreme Court Justice Potter Stewart, in his dissenting opinion in *Ginzberg v. United States* (383 U.S., 463, 1966), said, "Censorship reflects a society's lack of confidence in itself. It is a hallmark of an authoritarian regime." Retrieved March 21, 2009, from http://www.ala.org/ala/aboutala/ offices/oif/firstamendment/firstamendment.cfm

32. Koppl, R., & Krane, D. (2008, September). Potentially flawed science deciding many cases. *OnlineAthens*. Retrieved October 8, 2008, from http://www.onlineathens.com/stories/091408/opi_331950086.shtml

33. Koppl, R. (2007). *Breaking up the forensic monopoly: Eight ways to fix a broken system*. Retrieved October 8, 2008, from http://www.reason.com/news/show/122464.html

34. Crime Lab Report. (2008, October). Crime labs under police unresolved issues. *Crime Lab Reports, 2*(10). Retrieved October 20, 2008, from http://www.crimelabreport.com:80/library/monthly_report/10-2008.htm

35. Crime Lab Report, "Crime Labs Under Police."

36. Evans, H. K. (2008, October 8). Letter to the editor. *Crime Lab Report*. Retrieved November 4, 2008, from http://www.crimelabreport.com:80/library/supp_reports/08-11.htm

37. Koppl, R. (2008, October 28). Letter to the editor. *Crime Lab Report*. Retrieved November 4, 2008, from http://www.crimelabreport.com:80/library/supp_reports/08-11.htm

38. Koppl, "Breaking Up the Forensic Monopoly."

39. This notion is similar to community policing initiatives as found in Stevens, D.J. (2010). *Introduction to American policing*. Boston: Jones & Barlett.

40. Bureau of Justice Statistics. (2007). *Federal prosecution of child sex exploitation offenders, 2006* (NCJ 219412). Washington, DC: US Department of Justice. Retrieved October 30, 2008, from http://www.ojp.usdoj.gov/bjs/pub/ascii/fpcseo06.txt

41. Walker, S. (2001). *Sense and nonsense about crime and drugs: A policy guide*. Belmont, CA: Wadsworth.

42. Payne, T. (2007). *The role of the criminal investigator in forensic investigations: Introducing a new paradigm for prosecutors*. Unpublished manuscript, University of Southern Mississippi.

43. Counseller, J. (2008, October 18). So far so good for the restyled Federal Rules of Civil Procedure. *Washington Law Review*. Retrieved July 10, 2009, from http://lawreview.wustl.edu/slip-opinions/so-far-so-good-for-the-restyled-federal-rules-of-civil-procedure/

44. Cornell University Law School. (n.d.). *Federal Rules of Evidence, 102*. Retrieved November 3, 2007, from http://www.law.cornell.edu/rules/fre/. Corpus delicti: It was a general rule not to convict unless the corpus delicti could be established, that is, until the dead body had been found. Instances have occurred of a person being convicted of having killed another, who, after the supposed criminal had been put to death for the supposed offense, made his appearance—alive. The wisdom of the rule is apparent, but to ensure justice, in extreme cases, it may be competent to prove the basis of the corpus delicti by presumptive, but conclusive, evidence.

45. Cornell University Law School, *Federal Rules of Evidence*.

46. Gershman, "Why Prosecutors Misbehave."

47. Counseller, "So Far So Good."

48. Miller, L. L., & Eisenstein, J. (2005). The federal/state criminal prosecution nexus: A case study in cooperation and discretion. *Law & Social Inquiry, 30*(2), 239–268.

49. Feeney, F. (1998). *German and American prosecutors: An approach to statistical comparison* (NCJ 166610). Washington, DC: US Department of Justice. Retrieved October 12, 2008, from http://www.ojp.usdoj.gov/bjs/pub/ascii/gap.txt

50. Gershman, "Why Prosecutors Misbehave."

51. Miller & Eisenstein, "Federal/State Criminal Prosecution Nexus."

52. Clynch, E. J., & Neubauer, D. W. (1999). Trial courts as organizations: A critique and synthesis. In S. Stojkovic, J. Klofas, & D. Kalinich (Eds.), *The administration and management of criminal justice organizations: A book of readings* (3rd ed.). Long Grove, IL: Waveland Press.

53. Clynch & Neubauer, "Trial Courts as Organizations."

54. Clynch & Neubauer, "Trial Courts as Organizations."

55. Gould, J. B., & Mastrofski, S. D. (2004). Suspect searches: Assessing police behavior under the US Constitution. *Criminology & Public Policy, 3*(3), 315–362.

56. Gould & Mastrofski, "Suspect Searches."

57. For more information see Stevens, D. J. (2009). *Introduction to American policing: An applied approach.* Sudbury, MA: Jones and Bartlett.

58. Cunningham, L. (1999). "Taking on testilying: The prosecutor's response to in-court police deception." *Criminal Justice Ethics*, 18, p. 26.

59. Cunningham, L. (2002). Taking on testilying: The prosecutor's response to in-court police deception. In W. R. Palacios, P. F. Cromwell, & R. G. Dunham (Eds.), *Crime & justice in America: Present realities and future prospects* (2nd ed.). Upper Saddle River, NJ: Prentice Hall.

60. Gershman, "Why Prosecutors Misbehave."

61. Cunningham, "Taking on Testilying."

62. 314 N.Y.S. 2d 194, 195 (N.Y.C. Crim. Ct. 1970).

63. Horton, S. (2007, September 8). The federal prosecutor: A calling betrayed. *Harpers.* Retrieved October 12, 2008, from http://www.harpers.org/archive/2007/09/hbc-90001135

64. Roberts, "Growing Problem of Wrongful Conviction."

65. Bureau of Justice Statistics. (2007). *Deaths in custody statistical tables, 2006.* Washington, DC: US Department of Justice. Retrieved March 21, 2009, from http://www.ojp.usdoj.gov/bjs/dcrp/tables/dcst06spt1.htm

66. Montaldo, C. (n.d.). *Donald "Pee Wee" Gaskins.* Retrieved November 27, 2008, from http://crime.about.com/od/serial/p/gaskins.htm

67. Strange Justice. (2005, June 30). *A review of appalling "scientific" evidence from government laboratories.* Retrieved October 12, 2008, from http://stju.blogspot.com/2005_06_01_archive.html

68. Young, R. L. (2004). Guilty until proven innocent: Conviction orientation, racial attitudes, and support for capital punishment. *Deviant Behavior, 25*(2), 155–167.

69. Futty, J. (2008, November 3). Death penalty cases in Franklin County becoming rarer. *Columbus Dispatch.* Retrieved November 9, 2008, from http://www.columbusdispatch.com/

70. Haney, C. (1997). Violence and the capital jury: Mechanisms of moral disengagement and the impulse to condemn to death, *Standard Law Review, 49*, 1447–1482.

71. Blume, J. H. (2004). An overview of significant findings from the capital jury project and other empirical studies of the death penalty relevant to jury selection, presentation of evidence, and jury instructions in capital cases. *Cornell Law School.* Retrieved July 10, 2009, from http://web.knoxnews.com/pdf/112208carjack2.pdf

72. Nugent-Borakove, M. E., Budzilowicz, L. M., & Rainville, G. (2008). *Performance measures in prosecution and their application to community prosecution at two sites in the United States, 2005–2006* (ICPSR20401-v1). Ann Arbor, MI: Inter-University Consortium for Political and Social Research.

73. Coles, C. M. (2002). *Community prosecution: District attorneys, country prosecutors, and attorney general.* Cambridge, MA: Harvard University. Retrieved March 21, 2009, from http://www.ksg.harvard.edu/criminaljustice/publications/da_cp_ag.pdf

74. Coles, C. M., & Kelling, G. L. (1999). Prevention through community prosecution. *The Public Interest, 136,* 69–84.

75. Stevens, *Introduction to American Policing.*

76. Boland, B. (1998). Community prosecution: Portland's experience. In D. R. Karp (Ed.), *Community justice: An emerging field.* Lanham, MD: Rowman and Littlefield.

77. Goldkamp, J. S., Irons-Guynn, C., & Weiland, D. (2002). *Community prosecution strategies: Measuring impact.* Washington, DC: US Department of Justice, Bureau of Justice Assistance. Retrieved March 21, 2009, from http://www.ncjrs.gov/html/bja/commpros/bja1.html

78. Goldkamp, et al., *Community Prosecution Strategies.*

79. Office of Justice Programs. (1996). *Annual report, 1996.* Washington, DC: US Department of Justice. Retrieved March 21, 2009, from http://www.ojp.usdoj.gov/

80. Office of Justice Programs, *Annual Report.*

81. Coles, *Community Prosecution.*

82. Cunningham, W. S., Renauer, B. C., & Khalifa, C. (2006). Sharing the keys to the courthouse: Adoption of community prosecution by state court prosecutors. *Journal of Contemporary Criminal Justice, 22*(3), 202–219.

83. Wolf, R. V., & Worrall, J. L. (Eds.). (2004). *Lessons from the field: Ten community prosecution leadership profiles.* Alexandria, VA: American Prosecutors Research Institute, Center for Court Innovation.

84. Boland, "Community Prosecution."

85. Coles, *Community Prosecution.*

86. Stevens, *Introduction to American Policing.*

87. DuBois, J., & Hartnett, S. M. (2002). Making the community side of community policing work: What needs to be done. In D. J. Stevens (Ed.), *Policing and community partnerships.* Upper Saddle River, NJ: Prentice Hall.

88. Skogan, W. G., & Hartnett, S. M. (1997). *Community police, Chicago style.* New York: Oxford University Press.

89. Kelling, G. L., & Moore, M. H. (1988). *Evolving strategy of police.* Cambridge, MA: National Institute of Justice. Retrieved March 21, 2009, from http://www.ksg.harvard.edu/criminaljustice/publications/pop4.pdf

90. Sherman, L. W. (1998). *Communities and crime prevention.* Retrieved March 21, 2009, from http://www.ncjrs.gov/works/chapter3.htm

91. Gershman, B. L. (2001). Prosecutor's duty to truth. *The Journal of Legal Ethics.* Retrieved October 12, 2008, from http://findarticles.com/p/articles/mi_qa3975/is_200101/ai_n8949921

92. Marquis, J. (2003). A district attorney responds. In Center for Public Integrity (Ed.), *Harmful error: Investigating America's local prosecutors.* Washington, DC: Center for Public Integrity.

93. Marquis, "District Attorney Responds."

94. Poulsen, K. (2003, November 14). Prosecutors admit error in whistleblower conviction. *Security Focus.* Retrieved July 10, 2009, from http://www.securityfocus.com/news/7202

95. Lord, V. (1996). An impact of community policing: Reported stressors, social support, and strain among police officers in a changing police department. *Journal of Criminal Justice, 24,* 503–522.

96. Peak, K. J. (2006). *Policing in America.* Upper Saddle River, NJ: Prentice Hall.

97. Central Florida Police Stress Unit. "Avoiding 10 fatal errors." Retrieved September 3, 2009, from http://policestress.org/ten.htm

98. Stevens, D. J. (2008). *Police officer stress: Sources and solutions.* Upper Saddle River, NJ: Prentice Hall.

99. Larson, R. (1999, March 21). Medical advances can outpace doctors; retraining not enforced, critics say. *The Washington Times.* Retrieved July 10, 2009, from http://www.psychlaws.org/generalResources/article12.htm

100. Office of Continuing Medical Education. (2008). *Medical acupuncture for physicians.* Retrieved July 10, 2009, from http://www.medsch.ucla.edu/public/cme/Courses/acupuncture02/acupuncture2006.asp

101. Croasdale, M. (2006, July 24). Doctors seek more help to get back in practice; researcher programs considered. *AMNews.* Retrieved October 12, 2008, from http://www.ama-assn.org/amednews/site/free/prl20724.htm

102. Conison, J. (2006). Success, status, and the goals of a law school. *University of Toledo Law Review, 37.* Retrieved October 12, 2008, from http://law.utoledo.edu/students/lawreview/volumes/v37n1/Conison.htm

103. Stuckey, R. (2005). "Best practices for legal education." Clinical Legal Education. Retrieved September 3, 2009, from http://www.cleaweb.org/resources/bp.html

104. TV.com. (2004, December 4). *Law & Order, Fixed.* Retrieved October 12, 2008, from http://www.tv.com/law-and-order/fixed/episode/372086/summary.html

105. When *Law & Order* first reran on TNT, new digital technology was used to insert product placements (paid appearances of name-brand products) into the show. The easiest to spot is Coca-Cola; any time you see a Coke can sitting on a desk, it has been added digitally (*Source*: TV.com).

Questionnaire

■ Confidentiality Statement

Please don't sign this survey because it's confidential. After the results are posted, your survey will be discarded. The purpose of this study is to compare experiences of criminal prosecutors in order to advise students at Southern Miss and elsewhere about your profession as a career. Feel free to copy this survey for others in your office. Thank you. Dr. Dennis J. Stevens, Professor of Criminal Justice, University of Southern Mississippi. Please direct questions to Box 5128, Hattiesburg, MS 39406-0001.

1. Approximately how many years have you been a prosecutor? _____

2. As a prosecutor, are you: Full time _____ Part time _____ Temporary _____ It depends _____

3. How old are you? _____ Male _____ Female _____

4. How would you describe your race: White _____ Black _____ Hispanic _____ Asian _____ Other _____

5. As a prosecutor, do you work for (check all that apply): State _____ County _____ City _____ Other _____

6. Do you hold an appointed _____ or an elected _____ prosecutor's job?

7. What types of cases do you prosecute most often? Check up to three.

   A. Felony _____   F. Juvenile delinquency _____

   B. Misdemeanor _____   G. Sex crimes _____

   C. Drug _____   H. Weapons _____

   D. Crimes against persons _____   I. Other _____ Please identify _____

   E. Crimes against property _____

8. How often do prosecutors feel that their present performance might affect their future job opportunities? Always _____ Very Often _____ Sometimes _____ Seldom _____ Never _____

9. What three factors best aid a prosecutor's performance? Rank: 1 = best, 2 = second best, and 3 = third best. Choose three only.

A. More time to prepare a case _____

B. More funds to prepare a case _____

C. An excellent legal support team _____

D. Substantial and documented evidence _____

E. Competent investigative unit _____

F. Credible witnesses/victims _____

G. Other _____ Please identify _____

10. How often do grand jury indictments predict the eventual outcome of a case?
Always _____ Very Often _____ Sometimes _____ Seldom _____ Never _____

11. How often do the elements of a crime predict the eventual outcome of a case?
Always _____ Very Often _____ Sometimes _____ Seldom _____ Never _____

12. How often is it desirable for prosecutors to have their own prosecutorial agenda?
Always _____ Very Often _____ Sometimes _____ Seldom _____ Never _____

13. How often does a prosecutor's performance lead to a judgeship or another job?
Always _____ Very Often _____ Sometimes _____ Seldom _____ Never _____

14. How often do prosecutors hold strong incentives to make department priorities their own?
Always _____ Very Often _____ Sometimes _____ Seldom _____ Never _____

15. How often do prosecutors accept formal bureaucratic controls that regulate their behavior?
Always _____ Very Often _____ Sometimes _____ Seldom _____ Never _____

16. Identify the three best personal benefits provided to prosecutors. Rank: 1 = best benefit, 2 = second best benefit, and 3 = third best benefit provided prosecutors. Choose three only.

A. Getting justice for victims _____

B. Furthering the democratic process _____

C. Potential of future executive careers _____

D. Putting away bad guys _____

E. Contributing to the stability of government _____

F. Prestige _____

G. Other _____ Please identify _____

17. Identify the three most *undesirable* benefits provided to prosecutors. Rank: 1 = worst benefit, 2 = second worst, and 3 = third worst. Choose three only.

A. Media publicity _____

B. Lack of personal privacy _____

    C. Lack of professional autonomy _____

    D. Inadequate support staff _____

    E. Public interference _____

    F. Interference from superiors _____

    G. Assaulted _____ most often is it: verbal _____ physical _____

    H. Other _____ Please identify _____

18. Identify the top three reasons a prosecutor might reject a case even when substantial and documented evidence exists. Rank: 1 = most likely reason to reject, 2 = second most likely reason, and 3 = third most likely reason. (These were write-ins.)

    A. Uncredible victims and uncredible witnesses _____

    B. Uncredible arresting officer reports _____

    C. Notoriety of defendant_____

    D. Lack of expertise to present a solid case _____

    E. Lack of confidence in prevailing judicial system _____

    F. Inconsistent evidence _____

    G. Supervisor's directive _____

    H. Lazy or unmotivated prosecutors _____

    I. Incompetent or untrained prosecutors _____

    J. Other _____ Please identify _____

19. In criminal trials, how often are juries influenced by CSI television programs more than substantial and documented evidence?
Always _____ Very Often _____ Sometimes _____ Seldom _____ Never _____

20. In criminal trials, how often are judges impressed with *unrealistic* CSI television techniques?
Always _____ Very Often _____ Sometimes _____ Seldom _____ Never _____

21. In criminal trials, how often do defense lawyers attempt to portray *unrealistic* CSI television processes as more reliable than the substantial and documented evidence of the case?
Always _____ Very Often _____ Sometimes _____ Seldom _____ Never _____

22. How often do you think some prosecutors *unknowingly* charge an innocent person?
Always _____ Very Often _____ Sometimes _____ Seldom _____ Never _____

23. What does it mean when a prosecutor dismisses a case in the "best interests of justice?"

_____

24. (Write-ins) Rank the top three items prosecutors rely upon to criminally convict a defendant? Choose three only.

   A. DNA evidence _____

   B. Expert witnesses _____

   C. Jury selection _____

   D. Witnesses _____

   E. Credible victims _____

   F. Officer reports _____

   G. A lot of hard work _____

   H. Other _____ Please identify _____

25. How many hours of continuing legal education are required each year in your job? _____

26. What percent of your education from law school do you actually apply to your job? Check one.
   90%–100% ___ 80%–89% ___ 70%–79% ___ 60%–69% ___ 50%–59% ___
   40%–49% ___ 30%–39% ___ 20%–29% ___ 1%–19% ___

27. In law school, how well are students prepared to do the job of a prosecutor? Expertly ___ Very Well ___ Average ___ Below Average ___ Not Sure ___

28. (Write ins) Identify the reasons you originally went to law school. Check all that apply.

   A. Money _____   D. Professionalism of the job _____

   B. Parental influence _____   E. My friends encouraged me _____

   C. Prestige _____   F. Other _____ Please identify _____

29. If you could change anything about law school admissions, what would it be?

   _____

   _____

30. When in law school, in your opinion, what should students do to ensure a chance of becoming a prosecutor?

   _____

   _____

31. What advice can you give students who wish to become a prosecutor?

   _____

Index